*Russell Brunson - ClickFunnels*

## Legal Disclaimer And Terms Of Use

# You Suddenly **LOSE**
# EVERYTHING...

*What Would You Do From*
**Day 1 To Day 30**
*To Save Yourself...*

# CONTENTS

# INTRODUCTION

I'm so excited that this copy of the 30 Days book has reached you and is now in your hands, ready to change your life as you know it. But before you dive into the 30 blueprints I know you've been waiting for, I want to share the story of how this book came to be, because to be honest, I'm still shaking my head in disbelief at exactly how much each member of the Two Comma Club was willing to share.

In fact, I am TOTALLY CONVINCED, that ANYONE, as long as they faithfully apply the tested and proven marketing secrets found in these 30 Day marketing plans, could become the next "Two Comma Club" Success Story. And that includes you.

You may already know that I'm the CEO and co-founder of a company called ClickFunnels. I'm that guy on stage who is handing out the "Two Comma Club" awards to entrepreneurs who have built successful funnels. But what a lot of people don't know, is that every day I see between 750 and 1,000 new people signup to ClickFunnels to build funnels hoping to turn their dreams into a reality.

Many make it, but many more don't. And that fact drives me crazy!

So I asked all my Two Comma Club winners a very personal question to find out EXACTLY what they would do to get back on top if they lost everything:

> You suddenly lose all your money, along with your name and reputation, and only have your marketing know-how left.
>
> You have bills piled high and people harassing you for money over the phone.
>
> Plus, you have a guaranteed roof over your head, a phone line, an internet connection, and a ClickFunnels account for only one month.
>
> You no longer have your big guru name, your following,

*or JV partners. Other than your vast marketing experience, you're an unknown newbie.*

*What would you do, from day 1 to day 30, to save yourself?*

At first I was nervous to send the email but just seconds after I clicked "send" my nerves turned to excitement as I waited to hear back from them.

Over the next few days, the responses started to pour in from members of this exclusive club telling me their stories of when THEY were in that exact spot... no product, no list, no traffic, and no funnel... and then detailing EXACTLY what they did in a simple, step by step daily process!

These were not quick emails they sent back to me, but detailed battle plans! Some made me laugh and others made me cry as I re-lived with them what it was like when they first got started. Some started from homelessness, others had jobs they hated, and others just wanted more. But all of them ended in the same spot... onstage, with a "Two Comma Club" award in their hands!

What you're about to read in the following chapters is different than anything you've ever seen before. As I re-read each 30 day plan, I looked out for "loopholes", like having to spend sums of money in some form or another, using special programs well beyond the reach of the average person, or having to "know" certain people. And as amazing as it might sound, the blueprints were almost flawless. There and then, I knew beyond the shadow of a doubt, that if anyone followed these plans to a T, they were almost GUARANTEED to make money! These plans make failure virtually impossible!

## Meet Your Dream Team

Before I go futher, I want to introduce you to the 30 individuals who were crazy enough to agree to help serve you at their HIGHEST level... for FREE!?!

This is your dream team and the concepts each of their blueprints are based on:

- *Trey Lewellen: The Reactive Startup* - The Proprietary "Reactive

Startup Formula" That Makes Launching Your Product Pain-less...And Virtually Guarantees Your Success!

- *Liz Benny: High Ticket Coaching* - Secrets Of A High-End ($10K+) Coaching Program

- *Garrett J. White: Application Video Funnel* - The "Core 4" For Achieving Success

- *Alison J. Prince: Ecommerce Funnels* - How My School-Age Daughters Built Their Own 6-Figure ECommerce Empire...In Just 9 Months!

- *Dana Derricks: The Dream 100* - The "Dream 100" Method That Helped Generate Millions In Revenue For Myself And My Clients

- *Julie Stoian: Start as a Service Provider* - The 3 "Profitability" Steps You Absolutely Must Accomplish During Your First Week To Establish Credibility, And Attract High-Ticket Customers And Clients

- *Stephen Larsen: Mid-Range Info-Product Launch* - The "Purple Ocean" Approach To Identifying Products That Your Fans Would Body-Check Their Grandmas To Buy!

- *Stacey and Paul Martino: Three Weeks to Webinar Launch* - The 3 Non-Negotiables For Setting Yourself Up For Success (...Before You Even Start Your Funnel)

- *Ed Osburn: Free 7-Day Challenge* - The #1 Factor That's Exponentially More Powerful Than A Testimonial For Getting Your Clients And Customers From A "Maybe" To A "Yes!"

- *Tyler Shaule: Fundraising for Nonprofits* - 4 Simple Steps To Crafting Your Fundraising "Offer"

- *Rachel Pedersen: Service Packages via LinkedIn* - How I Take Entrepreneur Clients From $4,000/Mth To Pulling In Up To $7,000 PER DAY!

- *Jeremy McGilvrey: Sell Funnels on Instagram* - My Foolproof "HCBA" Hack That Pin-Points Profitable, In-Demand Niches In Just MINUTES

- *Peng Joon: Live Events* - How To Attract Attendees To Your $1K-Per-Ticket LIVE Event In Just 45 Minutes...(And FILL Every Seat In The Room!)

- *Myron Golden: Bible Success Blueprint* - The Strategies I Use To Help My Clients Rake In Up To $10 MILLION Per Year Each

- *Jaime Cross: Ecommerce Funnels* - Mastering the "Convergence Quadrant" Method: Optimize Your Offers Before You Ever Start Building Your Funnel!

- *Dan Henry: Pre-sell Courses With Webinars* - The Unusual Approach That Led Me To Build A $3 Million Business In Just ONE Year

- *Joe McCall: Mindmap* - Simple Techniques That Create An Irresistible High-Ticket Coaching Offer

- *Spencer Mecham: Affiliate Marketing* - How To Attract Buyers To Your Affiliate Programs On Autopilot

- *Anissa Holmes: Facebook Live Summit* - How To Leverage FB To Land Clients To Consistently Fill Up Every Slot In Your Schedule

- *Dean Holland: Coaching Packages via JV Webinars* - How To Come Up With A Valid Product Idea And Create A Webinar Strategy That Optimizes Your High-Ticket Sales

- *John Lee Dumas: Teach a Masterclass* - The 2 Most Important Practices I Use EVERY DAY To Stay Focused On My 7-Figure Businesses

- *Rob Kosberg: High-Ticket Sales via Webinars* - My Top-Secret "Embarrassingly Simple" Strategies That Enable Me to Land $25,000 Sales (Day After Day) From A Webinar

- *Natalie Hodson: Ebook Launch* - How To Identify And Approach Your PERFECT Influencers To Promote Your Lead Magnet... (And Get The Most "Yeses" Possible!)

- *Pat Rigsby: Coaching One-on-One and Masterminds* - "I've Repeated The Same EXACT Process Over And Over Again To Create 7 Businesses That Make At Least $1 Million Per Year."

- *Caitlin Pyle: Online Courses via Autowebinars* - How To Build IN-STANT Credibility And Authority In Your Niche (Even If You're "New And Unknown" At The Moment)

- *Akbar Sheikh: Coaching Clients via Facebook* - How To Create An Almost INSTANT Coaching Practice That Attracts Your Perfect Client

- *Rhonda Swan: Three Weeks to Webinar Launch* - How I Traded My All-Day "Hustle" For A Tripwire Funnel That Shot From "Zero" To 6-Figures In Just WEEKS!

- *David Asarnow: Facebook Marketing Services* - The Lost PHI-LOSOPHY That Earned Me An 8-Figure Award...FOUR TIMES!

- *Raoul Plickat: Connect on Instagram* - Tapping Into Your "A.G.P." To Accomplish Any Goal In HALF The Time!

- *James P. Friel: High-Ticket Consulting* - The SINGLE Biggest Mistake That Holds New Business Owners Back...(and keeps them from ever achieving the success they dream of!)

This panel of funnel building experts are about to radically and ruthlessly transform you into an internet marketing expert! Before you begin on this journey, all I ask is a commitment from YOU – a commitment to implement what you're about to read...

You know how the old saying goes: "you can lead a horse to water, but you can't make it drink..."

Well, here is the water, now it's your job to take a drink.

Remember, you're just one funnel away,

Russell Brunson

# Chapter 1

# THE REACTIVE START-UP

*by Trey Lewellen*

# TREY LEWELLEN

## *CEO*

**Physical Product Sales**
*NGOABuyersClub.com*

*Trey's entrepreneurial journey took off in 2012 after working several years at the job he thought he wanted. He quickly shifted from working for someone else to becoming an entrepreneur when he was inspired by a successful business man to create his own wealth. Since then he has hosted a series of trainings on MrOnIt.com, unstoppable cores, vlog, Critique Your Funnel, Funnel Hack Fridays, and Kommerce Kings.The success in Trey's sales career made him passionate about teaching others how to achieve their definition of success, and his own coaching business, the Trey Lewellen Mastermind, was born. He began to share with others the lessons, tips, and tricks he learned from his own experience and research to help them build their own long-term, sustainable online businesses.*

*"I've learned that in order to be happy in life, you need to figure out what your talents and strengths are... then run with them! Don't settle for anything less than what your abilities can get you."*

*- Trey Lewellen*

## The Reactive Start-up: 30-Day Roadmap To An Online Business

What you're about to read is NOT theory, but actually a proven and working strategy!

You'll find the following roadmap to be profound, realistic, doable, and repeatable. You will not have to possess any tricks, tactics, or superpowers, nor will you need to be educated in any field or hold any licenses, training, or diplomas. With that said, I give you my 30-day roadmap to a successful online business I coined "The Reactive Start-up."

Before starting with Day 1, I want to be extremely clear with the knowns: I have no connections, my name is worthless, I have a ClickFunnels account, and most importantly, I have ZERO money! The following would be my exact 30-day roadmap to a successful online business with the above circumstances.

## Day 1: Downsizing

It's time to get to work. And I have a long day ahead of me. I will create a morning routine to follow over the next 30 days so I can be ALERT,

ACTIVE, and REACTIVE. Yes, this means waking up earlier than most of the world and also going to bed before most of the world. The night prior to Day 1, I'll be in bed at 9pm with an alarm set to 4:15am.

My morning routine will be as follows, and will be repeated for every day forward:

4:15am: Wake up, take shower
4:30am: Make coffee and eat a biscotti (chocolate and almond)
4:45am: Listen to Tony Robbins (Personal Power II)
5:30am: Read a motivational book (Crush It! by Gary Vaynerchuk)
6:00am: Elliptical (hitting target heart rate)
6:40am: Priming Exercise with Tony Robbins
7:00am: READY TO START THE DAY!

Today, I'll be calling my bank to let them know I've lost all my credit cards and will need replacements. Doing so will allow any and all recurring monthly transactions (gym membership, magazine subscriptions, Netflix, newspapers, car wash, etc.) to be automatically cancelled.

For the bills that are received via direct mail such as utilities, cell phone, mortgage, and electric, I will be calling to negotiate a lower rate or lower percentage. (Keep in mind: everything is negotiable. And check out the book Secrets of Power Negotiating by Roger Dawson.)

I will be putting my car on Craigslist for sale and purchasing a car with the profit from the sale (no loan).

Day 1 is for downsizing and getting rid of anything unnecessary.

## Day 2: Niche Selection

If I'm going to build a business, I should mold it around what I love. Those who love what they do never have to work another day in their lives. Which brings me to picking out a niche that I absolutely enjoy.

Picking a niche can be difficult at times, so to help me decide, I will think of something that I absolutely love talking about. For some people, this could be their kids, gardening, a sport they used to play, remote-control airplanes, or the latest and greatest beer they just brewed in their basement. These are all niches that can become prof-

4

itable businesses!

To help me pull out my thoughts, I like to use whiteboards and/or 18" x 12" sheets of paper. I typically will purchase packets called Artist Sketch Pads that keep all my ideas on one big notepad. I could go to a park or coffee shop and sit for hours on end just unleashing my brain of all the things I enjoy doing and why. This will help me pull out the niche I am destined to build a business around, but maybe I just didn't realize it until now.

Here are 46 niches that I would consider going into:

- Beer Brewers
- Bicycling
- Bodybuilding
- Bow Hunting
- Cars (specific models)
- Cats (specific breeds)
- Cigars
- Coffee
- Computers
- Cooking
- Crane Operators
- Dads
- Dirt Bikes
- Dogs (specific breeds)
- Doomsday Prepping
- Eighteen Wheelers (truckers)
- Emergency Medical Technicians
- Engineering
- Farmers
- Firefighters
- Fishing
- Fitness
- Fraternities and Sororities
- Gardening
- Grandparents
- Hunting
- Juicing
- Makeup
- Mechanics
- Military
- Moms
- Motorcycles (Harley)
- Musical Instruments (I'm a guitar player)
- NASCAR
- Nursing
- Police
- Quilting
- Self-employment
- Sewing
- Smoking/BBQ
- Spinners (Soul Cycle, etc.)
- Sports (specific teams in a specific sport)
- Tea
- Triathletes
- Weight Loss
- Wine

# Day 3: Barnes & Noble

Now that I have my niche selected, today will be all about the nearest bookstore. I could also visit Amazon under Magazine Subscriptions or Magazines.com.

I will go to a bookstore such as Barnes & Noble and flood myself with magazines. The ones that are displayed to show 100% of the cover are the most popular and sell the best. Then the next most popular magazine will show around 60%, and so forth up the rack.

I will then pull out all the magazines I can find that talk about my niche. So if I chose cigars as my niche, I would go and grab ALL of the magazines regarding cigars. I'll take today to look through the magazines and familiarize myself with the articles—what language they are using to talk to their audience and the common buzzwords.

There should be postcards inside the magazine that allow readers to order that magazine fairly inexpensively. Magazines will be monthly, bimonthly, quarterly, or bi-quarterly. The problem here is that I would have to wait an entire year to see who is advertising inside these magazines. The solution? I can call the number on the cards and ask if I can purchase the back issues for the previous 12 months. Most if not all will say yes, and I might actually get the back issues for FREE if I let them know that in the near future I might be looking to place an ad in their magazine and wanted to make sure it's a good fit!

Next, I'll find all the magazines that work parallel with my selected niche. For instance, since I picked cigars, the parallel magazines could be magazines about whiskey, barbecue, expensive watches, yachts, and so on and so forth. I will also write these magazine phone numbers down for later, once I have my first product underway.

*Cost: $50–$100*

(I'll be able to afford this from all the money I save by canceling all my monthly subscriptions.)

# Day 4: The Foundation

Today's job is to get everything out of the magazines and blow it up on my wall.

What I like to do is cut out each individual ad and glue it to a large sheet of paper, allowing myself to see what ads start to repeat themselves and show up in other magazines. For each magazine, I have a separate large sheet of paper, typically the size will be 3' x 3' to fit all the ads on it.

As I start to receive the back issues, I can cut and paste the ads inside those to the sheet of paper as well. I'll start to notice a lot of overlapping ads, as well as ads that just ran once. I'll take notes on the ads that are running multiple times throughout the prior 12 months.

Here is an example:

## Day 5: The Journey

The objective for the next 25 days is two-fold.

First, I am going to acquire free product(s) and use those products to gain from 10,000 to over 30,000 FREE leads (i.e., email addresses). Part 2 will take place after the email list is created—I will survey them on what t-shirt design they would buy. I will take that design and create a shirt email launch to sell as many of those shirts as possible.

## Days 6–8: Donations

The first thing I'll do is write down all the phone numbers from the collage of product ads that are now pasted to my wall. Those are going to be my first go-to's when it comes to donations. From the ads, I'll know which products they are trying to promote and most likely own inventory for.

What I tend to do when calling the numbers is ask for the marketing department, or if it's a larger company, I'll request to speak with the manager of marketing. Most likely this person will have enough weight in their role that they'll be able to make a decision on the donation.

Here is why they'll want to donate to me. I'm going to explain to them that I will be growing an email list of 10,000 to 30,000, depending on how many other companies I get involved in the project. By their donation, they'll receive the new leads for FREE! At ZERO cost to them, all they need to do is gift the product. (Donations on product(s) are easier to come by than you might think, you just have to show the donator the advantage of doing so.)

The donation retail amount I am looking for will need to be around $300 to $700. I have found this price range leads to the most generated leads. The cost isn't too low nor is it too high to make the leads think the giveaway is a scam or impossible to win.

I give this three days, because more than likely the decision will have to go back and forth with co-owners or someone of higher authority. I also might find that they are out of the office the day I call, or I have to leave a message and follow up the next day. Whichever roadblocks I come into contact with, I will need to overcome them and have donations on their way by the third day of calls.

(If the company is not willing to donate, see DAY 9 for another way I can work with them while they are on the phone with me.)

Lastly, if the company I call doesn't have a product in that price range, I can simply have more than one donation to achieve the $300 to $700 benchmark.

## Call Script

*Hello, <FIRST NAME>, this is <MY NAME> with <COMPANY>. I saw you were advertising in <MAGAZINE_NAME> and wanted to reach out and let you know we are doing a FREE GIVEAWAY in the next two weeks and thought your <PRODUCT> would make a great fit for the giveaway! The best part—when you donate, you'll* *receive all the names and email addresses we collect during the giveaway. Would you like to donate?*

(Note: Of course, for anyone signing up to be added to an email list, they must give permission and be given the opportunity to unsubscribe if desired.)

## Day 9: Joint Venture

From Days 6–8, I will have made some really nice contacts with the advertisers asking for donations. Within those companies, some have really big email lists, but they may not even be emailing often. If they are emailing, it's often about internal offers that they've recently come out with.

When calling them, I make it a point to discuss their email list and the size. However, sometimes bigger doesn't mean better. For instance, a company might have 50,000 emails and get 1,000 clicks, while a newer company might have a 7,000 list and achieve 500 clicks. Both lists are fantastic, although the smaller company has a much more active list.

I will let them know that in the next week I am going to be pushing out a massive $300 to $700 giveaway. There is no cost to enter the giveaway, all I ask is that they email their list about it. The WIN-WIN here will be that when they email to the giveaway, they'll receive in return all the leads generated from all the other companies involved!

This is where it really starts to become fun. Once I have ONE company on board, I can go back to the companies who previously said no and let them know about the other companies who are now participating. As the companies keep stacking on one another, I create leverage as I continue to make phone calls.

The goal here is to get as many companies on board as possible—the bigger the total number of subscribers on the lists, the more FREE leads that'll be generated.

## Day 10: The Opt-in Funnel

Before any leads can be collected, I will need to create a page that collects the lead. The industry term for this is an "opt-in page." I'll want this page to be extremely basic, with just a headline of what they'll be receiving if they win, the value of the giveaway, how to enter, the date on which the giveaway ends, and any terms needed for my state. (I will consult with an attorney for the proper terms that I'll need to use.)

Most opt-in pages will only have a name input field and an email input field. I like to add a phone number field that is optional. I may or may not share the phone numbers with the participating parties. Since the phone number field is optional, I'll receive around 30% of total opt-ins. So for every 100 people who give me their email addresses, about 30 will also give me their phone number.

I strive for an 80% to 90% opt-in ratio, thus for every 100 people who click over to the giveaway, I like to capture 90 email addresses.

## Day 11: Monetize The Thank-You Page

Most thank-you pages I see are a headline and a confirmation of what the client just purchased or became a part of. I like to do things a little differently. On the thank-you page that comes directly after the opt-in, I'll present a congruent affiliate offer.

Affiliate offers are products sold by companies that are willing to give up a big portion of the sale revenue to incentivize other companies to push traffic.

To find affiliate offers, I can do a number of things. I like to search for "<NICHE> affiliate program." For example, if I were in the golf niche, I would google "golf affiliate program" to see what already exists. I'd also check affiliate websites such as ClickBank, A4D, W4, and Tapstone. I can also google "affiliate conferences <CURRENT YEAR>" to see which ones all the broker houses are attending and call the people on that list.

If the clients who are opting in are not taking the offer, then I will try a different one. I'll want around 1,000 clicks before making a decision.

To gauge whether the affiliate offer is congruent, the key performance indicator (KPI) I look for is around $.10/email. For example, if the affiliate offer is paying out $10, and for every 100 emails I receive one sale, I'm on track! ($10/100 emails = $.10/email).

For another example, let's say the affiliate payout is $5. I would need 2 sales for every 100 emails collected.

I'll be keeping all the profit collected, since the deal with the other companies providing the clicks is that I'll be giving them the other leads collected. Using the example of $.10/email, for every 1,000 emails, I am on track to collect $100.

*PROFIT: $.10/email > $1,000 to $3,000+*

## Day 12: In-House Case Study (Payday)

We recently went through this exact process and acquired just over 30,000 email addresses, making $3,000 on the thank-you page and another $12,000 on the 20-day autoresponder. If there is any doubt that this 30-day roadmap won't work, here is undeniable proof...

We sent a giveaway to lists with a cumulative number of subscribers of two million email addresses. The lists drove over 33,431 clicks, and we had a 96% conversion from click to lead.

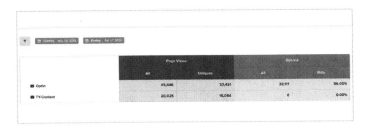

From there, we were able to post a congruent offer on the thank-you page that paid out a $3,000 check, along with some other affiliate offer payouts from other campaigns.

We then followed up with everyone who opted in to the giveaway with 20 emails (see Day 13), one email per day, which generated another $12,000, making the company around $15,000 from a FREE generated list.

The best part is that we are not done. We currently hold a buying audience, and it is our job to keep presenting offers they will absolutely love!

# Day 13: Welcome Campaign

Today, I will want to start putting together an email campaign where I send out a daily email to everyone who opted in to my list. This allows them to get to know who I am and how excited I am about my particular niche.

I'll be able to set up an email sequence within ClickFunnels Actionetics.

*Email 1* The first email I send out will be my welcome email, which will explain who I am and my mission as well as my love for the niche I've selected. It's also a really good idea to ask a question in this email such as "What state are you from?" or "What is your favorite <NICHE> product?" or "Why are you passionate about <NICHE>?" Anything that will get the lead to reply. Doing so will show all the email providers that I am not a spammer but am actually having conversations with everyone on my list.

*Email 2* For Email 2, I like to survey the people who are on my new list. This allows me to better understand them as an avatar: their needs, wants, and fears. I use SurveyMonkey or Google Forms to send out my surveys.

A favorite question I love asking inside the surveys is "If you could wave a magic wand to make the most painful problem disappear, what would that be?" This was given to me by a good friend and mastermind client, Sid Mylavarapu.

Some other questions, from the book 80/20 Sales and Marketing by Perry Marshall, are...

- What have you recently googled regarding <NICHE>?
- How important was it to find an answer to that question: Low/ Medium/High
- Did you find the answer you were looking for? Yes/No

From those questions, I will bring to the surface all the HIGHs and NOs giving me problems that exist with high urgency for the answer.

Lastly, the most important question for this 30-day campaign would be to ask:

*What is your favorite saying/phrase/quote regarding <NICHE>?*
I will use these responses on Day 15.

**Emails 3–6** For Emails 3 through 6, I will want to send out affiliate offers that I found from Day 11. A good affiliate offer will make around $.02/email. For example, for every 1,000 emails I send, I'll be looking to make around $20.

Sending out the next three email messages at 30,000 email addresses per send should generate approximately $1,800.

*PROFIT: $1,000 (10,000 emails at $.10/email) to $12,000 (30,000 emails at $.20/email)*

**Email 7** For Email 7, I am going to ask my leads what their favorite shirt is to get a good feel of the type they are proud to wear. The reason for doing this is to get a grip on what designs they like—the color of the shirt, the size, the brand, and so on. In a few days, I am going to design a shirt that will outdo any in their closet.

Here is the typical message I'll send out for Email 7.

*Subject: Show Me Your Closet*

*Hey, <FIRST NAME>, I'm about to do something really fun and creative and would like to have your help in the process. I'm going to be designing a good-looking t-shirt that shows off the passion that you and I both love, <NICHE>. With that said, I need your help! It would mean the world to me for you to go to your closet and take a picture of your most favorite shirt revolving around <NICHE>— you know the one. The shirt that, no matter how dirty or smelly it is, you'd put it on in a heartbeat! My goal is to receive more than 100 shirt examples, and by doing so find the trends and come up with the most badass <NICHE> shirt anyone has ever seen! So hurry—go to your closet, take a picture of your favorite <NICHE> shirt and reply back to this email! I look forward to seeing it!*

# Day 14: ZERO RISK

I've found that one of the easier products to sell quickly is t-shirts. They sell easily, I don't need to describe them, all the buyer cares about is what design is displayed on the shirt. When I get the design right, I'll have a six-figure shirt ready for sale. Back in April 2018, I was able to sell 5,571 shirts in two weeks with a $21 price point and made over $117,000 using this exact same strategy!

The best part about selling t-shirts is there are no upfront costs. No investment cash needed. Zero risk. There are companies out there that already have a full warehouse of inventory of t-shirts, sweaters, long-sleeve shirts, and much more waiting to be printed on. In fact, I use Printex (which is located in Hannibal, Missouri) to do all of my printing when selling t-shirts. Printex also will drop-ship the shirts, which means I never have to see or touch the product that is sold to the end consumer!

The other main reason I really enjoy using Printex is because of their location—they sit right smack-dab in the middle of the USA. This is a plus because I am only two to three zones away from any mailbox. If I were to ship from California and had an order come in from Florida, I'd be paying double if not triple the price for postage.

# Day 15: The Design

I know what I excel at and what I really fail at. One of those failures would be creating a design that goes on a t-shirt. Luckily, some other entrepreneur knew of my weakness and created 99designs. This is a website that allows people to submit a phrase and have access to 40+ professional designers who will design beautiful artwork for their t-shirts.

I will make sure to put the word "guaranteed" in the project title. Doing so will let the designers know I mean business. Guaranteed means that one of the designers who submits the winning design chosen by me will get paid. This will pull in some of the top designers on 99designs because they have a better chance of winning and getting paid.

I usually just go with the lowest bid amount, which is $199. Following the guidelines above will pull the top designers to build me a really nice shirt design.

## Days 16–19: Designs In Review

Once I submit a request, the campaign will stretch over five days in order for all designers to see the campaign, submit their work, and then have it reviewed by me. While I am waiting on designs to come in, I will remind myself about some tips I've learned along the way.

- *Tip #1: Give stars, but only 4 and below.* If I give someone a 5-star review, the other designers will see this as me choosing the winner before the contest is over. I like to only give 4-star reviews, even if I really like the design.
- *Tip #2: Make the project guaranteed.* This means no matter what, I'll be choosing a winner at the end.
- *Tip #3: Don't freak out.* It never fails—the worst designers always submit their designs on Day 1, while the top designers wait till the last few days to submit their artwork. I must be patient—the best designs come at the end of the campaign cycle.
- *Tip #4: Allow all artists to see the other designs.* This is the power of 99designs. As designers place their work onto my campaign wall, other designers get to watch and learn what I like and don't like, and then will react to building me more of what I love.
- *Tip #5: Give feedback.* When I am placing 4 stars and below, I will make sure I am chatting with the designer and giving them feedback on things I really like and don't like as well as changes I would like to see. They don't know what I'm thinking, so this helps them to improve their design so it fits my needs.

## Day 20: 99designs Is Complete

The day has come! I have my finalist and some really good-looking designs—so good, it's hard to choose. But I won't be making the final decision—my newfound audience will be. One of the biggest lessons I learned early on was that people don't think like me nor do they purchase what I think is cool. So when I found something I thought was a cool product and tried to go and sell it, it would bomb. However, when I asked my client list their opinion on what they would buy, it always sold like deep-fried Oreos at a carnival!

I will need the cumulative power of my audience to now vote on their favorite t-shirt design before I take it to market.

The first step is to choose three designs that came from 99designs. Next step is to ask the designers to place the artwork on a solid-color t-shirt—I usually tell them to use a black shirt. The shirt should also be blank, meaning there is no creative sparkle in the shirt image, not on a person or with any background. The background I want is white.

The reason for this is I want to make it easy and non-deceptive for the audience to choose which shirt they truly do love. When I show the three shirts to my audience, the only thing that will be different in the three images is the design itself, nothing else.

Now that I have the three shirts with their designs, I will put them side by side and create an image of all three together. I'll also place an A, B, and C above the shirts so that my audience can easily tell me which one they would buy.

The last thing to do is ask the list. I'll send an email to my list letting them know I am ONE day away from launching my first t-shirt, but before I do, I want their opinion. I will paste the image into the email with the three shirts and the A, B, C above them, then ask my audience to promptly reply on which shirt they would buy. Using the word buy is crucial. If I use words like love or wear, I'll receive inaccurate data. When I use the word buy, people will put more thought into it, because they are making a transaction, spending money inside their head when giving me their answer.

## Day 21: Build The Shirt Funnel

Before the big launch tomorrow, I need to build out the t-shirt funnel. This will be a two-page funnel. Page one will be the order page, and the second page will be the order confirmation page.

On the order page, I'll want to have a few things in place: a headline talking about the shirt, an image, and a paragraph describing the color and brand, and possibly a size table (to help the person buying the shirt know what size they'll need to purchase to fit them appropriately).

This page will also contain the order form, allowing someone to purchase with a credit card.

## Days 22–28: LAUNCH

T-minus zero! It's time to launch the shirt offer. I am going to launch the offer to my email audience over a seven-day course. Doing so will create an inverted bell curve of sales. I will have a great number of sales come in the first two days, then sales will slow down tremendously the next three days, and then spike the final two. This creates a compounding effect of sales through a seven-day cycle—I love it!

The following would be my email schedule.

- *Day 1: Email twice.*
- *Day 2: Email twice.*
- *Days 3–5: Email once.*
- *Day 6: Email twice.*
- *Day 7: Email three times.*

Days 1 and 2 will be about the launch of the new t-shirt.

Days 3 through 5 will be subtle reminders that the shirt is still for sale.

Day 6 will be a reminder that the shirt offer will be going away the next day at midnight and they must purchase it within the next 48 hours to own one.

Day 7: These are all countdown emails. I like to send one at 10am letting them know they only have 10 hours left to purchase. The next email will go out around 6pm and then another at 10pm for the final closing at MIDNIGHT.

It might sound like a ton of emails going out, but when I break it down into days over a seven-day period, it's very few. The biggest thing I must do is stress the URGENCY to purchase the first two days and then again the last two days. The majority of the population buys on impulse the first two days and then from scarcity of missing out the last two days.

## Day 29

I'll go over everything that happened with the lead generation and the t-shirt offer. What were the conversions on the lead gen from click to lead? Could I change the headline and possibly raise the conversion? Did I make $.10/email or more on the affiliate offer that was placed on the thank-you page?

Reset and repeat Days 6 through 29.

# Day 30: Reactive Growth

Building a database for my company will be the best thing I ever do for it. And now with my 30,000+ new email addresses, I can expand more into profit! Over the next 90 days, I will focus on the following:

**1. *Email them more often.*** I should be emailing my list two to three times per day! Hunting for more offers from affiliates, working with brokers, renting out my list, selling my list, and selling my own internal offers.

For every email I have in my database, I average around $.30/month/email. For easy numbers, a 100,000-email list would generate $360,000 per year (100,000 emails x.30/email x 12 months).

**2. *Call them.*** I will create outbound phone campaigns to my own internal offers or external affiliate offers. From the 30,000 emails I've collected, I will have received around 30% phone numbers, which is around 9,000 phone numbers ready to answer and talk about products in my niche!

And 9,000 phone numbers are worth around $2/number to me. And I like to call them once every three months. If the only thing I did over the next year was collect the 9,000 phone numbers, I would still be able to generate around $72,000 in revenue (9,000 phone numbers x $2/number x 4 times per year).

**3. *Direct mail them.*** By obtaining a client's email address or their phone number, I can do a reverse lookup for their address with a 70% accuracy rate. If I were to collect 30,000 leads and do a reverse lookup, I would have approximately 21,000 mailing addresses.

I like to mail $997, or a three-pay of $397 programs, with a .05% to 1% take rate. When I mail out 21,000 mailers and achieve a 1% take rate, I generate 210 sales at $997, a total revenue of $210,000.

**4. Find congruent joint venture offers to email, call, and mail out to my new audience.** I learned this concept called "relational capital" from Jay Abraham, where your problem is someone else's solution to their problem.

For example, if I were in the garden niche selling t-shirts but I find out my customers are also interested in the best dirt to purchase for their plants, instead of going out and creating a dirt company, I would partner with someone who already has a dirt company in place with manufacturing, customer service, internal/external systems, etc. This will allow me to market what my customer wants without ever having to go through the hassle of building a dirt company while reaping the rewards as if I had!

**5. Create a continuity program to collect monthly paychecks.** As my business grows, I'll want to start offering my clients continuity, where every month they receive something in exchange for their hard-earned dollars. I can do a quick Google search of other continuity programs already in place around my selected niche, figure out which ones I can model, and determine whether I can create something better.

# FINAL THOUGHTS

First off, congratulations on reading this entire chapter. As you can see, from the beginning to now the end, you don't have to possess any tricks, tactics, or superpowers, nor must you be educated in any field or hold any licenses, training, or diplomas to create a business out of thin air. Many entrepreneurs when first getting started think they have to spend money, work long hours, and have an extremely complicated system to make a dime. In fact, I've proven the exact opposite (along with many of my colleagues), that a simple system can be as effective if not more so for making income for yourself. The big key here is to pick one chapter and stick to it, burn the ships as they say. Do it until completion. No other chapter will be easier or have fewer difficulties along the way; they all come with their own challenges. Lastly, no matter what anyone says, money doesn't come easy—if it did, everyone would have it!

# RESOURCES

- 80/20 Sales and Marketing by Perry Marshall
- 99designs (99designs.com)
- A4D (a4d.com)
- Actionetics (clickfunnels.com/actionetics)
- Amazon.com
- Artist Sketch Pads
- Barnes & Noble
- ClickBank (clickbank.com)
- Craigslist (craigslist.org)
- Crush It! by Gary Vaynerchuk
- Google Forms
- Magazines.com
- "Personal Power II" by Tony Robbins
- Printex USA (printexusa.com)
- Secrets of Power Negotiating by Roger Dawson
- SurveyMonkey (surveymonkey.com)
- Tapstone (tapstone.com)
- Tony Robbins' Priming Exercise (tonyrobbins.com/priming-exercise)
- W4 (w4.com)

Chapter 2

# HIGH TICKET COACHING

*by Liz Benny*

# LIZ BENNY

## *The Queen Of Kapow*

Life And Business Transformation
LizBenny.com

*Liz lives and breathes the philosophy of 'playing life full out'. And it's not about doing that in a way that other people say is right or proper; it's about being 100% authentic to herself. That's where Liz believes true happiness happens, and she wants that for everyone! It took Liz a while to find business success, although she earned a Masters with Distinction from her work in Positive Psychology. After this, ironically, Liz found herself stuck in a job that was draining her soul, so she made a decision and set out to create a better life for herself and family – a life she'd always dreamed of.*

*She firmly believes that EVERYONE deserves happiness, and her passion is drawing that out of each and every person she works with.*

*Here's the thing: She knows how to make a ton of money in business, but she also knows that if you're not grounded in what makes you truly happy... then all the money in the world will never be enough! Ever! Liz's main focuses at the moment is sharing her message of how to be authentic; and she does this through her work as a keynote speaker, assisting others to KAPOW with various training programs, and one-on-one business mentoring.*

*People say that she has a magnetic and engaging personality that you literally get swept along with. But deeper than that, Liz has a raw passion to impact the world positively before she dies, and has a goal of helping 1 Billion People live true, real and authentic lives. Crazy goal - Yes. Impossible - No!*

## KAPOW Restart: Coming Back From The Ashes

Hey, and a massive KAPOW! I truly hope this inspires you, to know that if you are ever in this type of situation, you are just a short time away from getting yourself out of whatever horrible situation you're in...JUST a short time. My friend and mentor Russell Brunson says, "You're only ONE funnel away." I know this having experienced it. HOWEVER, if you're not there, you need to TRUST that you can have the success you desire. I promise!

For the purposes of this chapter, I am going to put myself in the hypothetical situation of being a version of Liz Benny who has nothing but bills piling up, a sick wife, kids who hate school, a mother-in-law with cancer, no clients, and no systems or products set up to create income to pay the bills, let alone feed the family.

This is an ironic story to write for you all because recently I quite literally lost more than seven years of business documents in a freak Apple encryption situation when I changed my computer password. I tried everything to get the information back. After a 47-minute conversation with Mr. Apple Support, the following happened:

"The next step, Elizabeth, is to wipe your hard drive," he said.

"Okay, I'll just restore it from the backup," I said, saddened because I knew my last backup had been four months prior and I would lose an entire unreleased webinar.

Then Mr. Apple Support said something that created an ever-expanding empty pit in my stomach, which then filled slowly with the most extreme sense of guilt.

"No, Elizabeth. The backup won't work. It's encrypted, too. You have lost it all."

*You have lost it all.*

Those words reverberated in my ears faster and faster as I mentally scrambled for another solution in my foggy brain. But my mind was blank, and the harder I thought, the foggier things became. I'm not sure how long I sat there, silently moving my lips, hoping maybe THAT would conjure up the exact right words to say in order to remedy the situation.

In my mind I know only a few seconds passed, but in the moment I would have sworn I sat there silently with Mr. Apple Support on the other end of the line for 15 minutes. And yet, all I could say in reply was...

"I don't want to have this conversation anymore. Thank you. Goodbye."

I'm still unsure why I thanked him. Probably because I was in shock.

I suppose it doesn't really matter, because the point is this: I was literally, in that moment, FULL of guilt for having lost my wife's and children's photos and memories. They were gone. POOF! Just like that.

But at the same time, I was grateful in a way that I'd never expected.

I realized that although I'd lost all original files—Photoshop files, logos, templates, checklists, webinars...everything I'd built my business on...

- *I knew enough to rebuild.*
- *I knew I WOULD rebuild.*
- *I was confident in my ability to scale my business and produce income.*
- *I knew I had the knowledge, resources, and tenacity to create any business I wanted...FROM SCRATCH.*

Because, in that moment, it's what I had to do.

I gave myself a few weeks off from my business. No building. I wasn't under pressure. And that allowed me the space to work out that Mr. Apple had actually been wrong. My backup wasn't encrypted...and I was able to reclaim ALL my files. (Well, nearly all of them. No silver lining is completely perfect.)

This is, however, a SUPER FUN exercise for me to do for you...knowing that it's easy to create a business you love. Below, I'll map out exactly what I'd do in the first 30 days to build my business from the ground up.

## Day 1: Decision Day

It's decision day, first and foremost. No BS. Today is the day I'm working out exactly what I'm going to do to pull myself out of this hole. I need to know where I'm going, so Day 1 is all about gathering up my internal resources and then mapping out a plan. Time to roll...

*Looking After Myself* It is of paramount importance that I'm making powerful decisions from Day 1.

There are people I owe money to who will likely come at me if I don't communicate. Fair enough! With that said, I can make the money more easily if I'm in flow. So as a first priority, I need to call them really quickly to let them know I intend to pay them, that I'm in a squeeze financially, and that I need a little grace period so I can pay them.

Right, now that's done, I also need to have an honest talk with myself and make sure that I'm solid internally (belief-wise) for the steps I'm about to take. I've seen so many fail already with half-hearted efforts, so I'll take myself into my KAPOW CAVE to create the time and space to emotionally get ready for this 30-day sprint. I turn on some inspirational music, close the curtains in my office, and turn on one light. Blocking out all distractions is important right now, more than ever before!

During this KAPOW CAVE time of solitude, I focus on "armoring up," staying the course, focusing on where I expect to be at the end of the 30 days. While I don't have a detailed plan yet, I know that if I'm not solid emotionally and ready for the journey, I'll just end up burned out and drained of all my money and confidence like everyone else who tried and failed. Fortitude is key. Resilience is key. I'm going to hear NO. I'm going to have naysayers. So armoring up allows me to shut them out so I can focus on the game at hand.

A final stage of preparing myself internally for this rebuild is forming an accountability relationship with someone. When I say I'm going to do something, I do it. The best way to ensure I stay focused is to tell someone I respect what I'm doing and then ask them to hold me accountable, especially for the next 30 days.

After calling my friend and asking them to hold me accountable, I take a pen and paper and draw a 30-day calendar to secure my focus for the next 30 days.

Once I've buttressed my internal resources, I step into the external phase of the process. NOW I'm ready to shift to the specific steps of what I'm going to do to dig myself out of this. I have until the end of the day to get the external phase done. It's time to...

*Take Care Of Business* Right! I'm SOLID, ready to go, and NOW it's time to get clear on HOW I'm going to rebuild. There are many business models from which I can choose. I know the webinar game so well I could do it in my sleep. The same is true with the consulting/coaching game...and funnels and social media and so on. There are a lot of right paths I could take, but I'm not interested in that. I'm interested in pursuing the BEST path.

I know from experience that starting with understanding WHY I want to build a business is going to serve everyone better in the long run. I don't want to build a business for the sake of making money, but I know that I need to make money in the short term, too. So strategically, the first thing I need to focus on is how to create an income stream in the short term that I'll want to build for the long term.

Note: I'm ONLY giving myself to the end of the day to make the decision of what the business model is going to look like. Tomorrow is action day, and I'm not about playing around being indecisive. I am, however, going to be strategic and ensure that the business I'm creating is right for my customers, for me, and for the world.

Based on those criteria, I will have worked out the game plan based on my background and marketing knowledge, my drive to help others shine, and my tenacity and energy.

Strategically, I want to find the fastest path to profits. In my case, it would be to start coaching heart-centered entrepreneurs who have a message they want to get out into the world. The plan is to get them results quickly and then sell a scalable online program to other heart-centered entrepreneurs, including recordings from the consulting I did with the initial clients.

BUT before I even start to go too far down the rabbit hole of what my offer is going to be, I simply MUST search online to find at least three people who are doing what it is that I'm looking to do. Why? Well, I have a very short space of time...and I'm not about to mess around being innovative with my approach. I need to ensure that the market I'm entering is a HOT market, that there are BUYERS, and that the people who are doing what I'm wanting to do are SUCCESSFUL.

Also, as I have no name, no guru status, I need to ensure that I lean on my strengths—I have knowledge and belief. These are MUSTS to step forward with, or else imposter syndrome will significantly reduce my likelihood of success.

One final but incredibly important thing I must do before moving forward is to work out from where I'm going to attract my target market. What traffic source am I going to use to get eyeballs on my offer? I decide that, given my experience, the best thing to do is use Facebook Ads, Facebook Lives, organic posts, and an email series (after a free offer) to attract applicants to my consulting offer. I'll work the specifics out tomorrow...but I know that Facebook is the main area for me to use right now.

*What Movement Can I Take A Stand For?* I get specific about what the vision is for the movement I'm about to start. Even though I'm beginning with consulting clients, I have to be clear that this is a movement. I'm more likely to be successful if I'm taking a stand for something I believe in, rather than just plodding along.

*My Origin Story* I work out what my origin story is. I have to work out why I'm doing this and what makes me want to help my prospective clients/customers. What happened in my life that led me to believe I MUST help my specific customers?

*Ask Campaign* I create an Ask Campaign to share on social media to get direct feedback from the market about what their pain points are and what it would feel like if these pain points were alleviated. I post this in FB Groups on my personal page and send messages on FB to people who are in my target market, respectfully asking them to assist me in better understanding what I can do to help them.

*What's My Offer?* I work out what the first offer is going to look like by first asking myself what my prospective clients need to do to get the success they desire. The first offer is a one-on-one or group coaching offer (which will be sold as a high-end beta program). I'll be able to serve these first clients at a very high level. This is important because for the first lot of clients through, I literally want to do anything and everything to ensure they get results, have an amazing experience, and are raving fans.
My offer would include the following:

· Course curriculum

- Six weeks of group coaching calls
- One-on-one quick-start call
- Bonuses (templates, spreadsheets, etc.)
- All recorded content
- Access to future course content (I may reshoot footage later.)

***What Are My Bonuses?*** I'll also work out what bonuses I could offer the high-end clients. These bonuses could also easily become part of a future course. The more I focus on ensuring the offer is solid AND there are buyers for it, the better success I will have. With that said, I am also wanting to focus on what my competition offers. I'll get an understanding of their price points, their pitch, their branding, and the specifics of their offers. I want to make sure that my offer is better and more solid and has a point of difference that will ensure that it's a no-brainer to work with me.

***Why Wouldn't Someone Buy My Offer?*** Then I'll move on to ask myself why people would say NO to my offer. Like, for real. Why would they say NO if my offer is so insanely amazing? What fears do they have? What internal objections do they have? I'm an unknown—will that be an objection? If so, how will I overcome it? For each objection I can think of, I'll create an honest reply. Ideally, I will have thought of all the reasons, so that I'm prepped and ready if objections arise during the sales calls!

***Stories That Will Sell My Offer*** Next, I take a break. It's been intense so far, and now it's time to take a walk with my phone. During this walk, I'm going to use Voxer to send myself voice messages of 10 stories I can tell that will help my target market believe in me—believe that I'm authentic, that I have what it takes to get them success, that I understand their pain, and that I get where they are wanting to go.

For example, "I remember when I was a little kid down on the farm, and I knew that I was meant to make a difference in the world. I just knew it. I would daydream about being on stage. I would practice my speeches in the mirror and would have conversations with the nonexistent audience as I stood there alone in my bedroom..."

**Why Me?** After this, it's time to consider how I'm unique in the marketplace. Effectively, there are thousands of people who could do what I'm proposing to do for my target market, but I must work out what makes me different. If I'm like everyone else, I'll fail. I don't stop on this question until I work out exactly what my point of difference is. To derive this, I'll focus on my experience, my passion for being real and raw, my magnetic personality, and genuine solutions.

**Target Market Research** Next, I move on to the intricacies of my target market. I want to understand, to a VERY DEEP degree, what their pains are, what they desire, and what male and female versions of my target market would look like.

**Social Proof/Testimonials** Finally, I want to make sure that I have evidence that I'm the person who can assist my target market in getting results. I start thinking about what outcomes I have created in order to help my target market feel that I can assist them with what they desire. Personal success stories are fine here, but my ideal is to find the success stories that I've helped create for others.

Right! This has been a FUN and intense day. This is always my most fun day of any business creation. And this has probably taken me about seven hours of solid, focused time. Now it's SUPER important to have a break and be with my family. I know tonight I'm not going to be able to sleep, because I'm riding on the energy of excitement now, so it's important that I hang out with my family before they go to sleep.

I'm also going to take this time to communicate with them about what I'm going to do over the next 29 days. I know from experience that I can't work as easily, as productively, or as ruthlessly (which is sometimes needed) if I don't have the support of my family, specifi-cally Kristi, my wife. More to the point, I know if Kristi sees me work-ing endless hours, shut off from her and the kids during these next 29 days and she's not aware of the plan, purpose, or where the light at the end of the tunnel is, then there may be some undue turbulence in the "home department" that makes the "business department" harder than it needs to be.

After dinner and hanging out, I spend the time from 9pm till midnight working on creating a brand (name of business, logo, colors, and of course domain name). I use WorkFlowy to brainstorm ideas. After finding a domain I love, I quickly check if it's available onhttp:// godaddy.com/ GoDaddy. This process will normally take around 20–30 minutes, to find a domain that I love that represents a movement I can and will stand for and will make sense to my target market. When I find the domain that "sings" to me, I buy it straight away and move on. I'm not here to mess around and take four weeks on this decision. It's do or die, so I must DO.

After the domain is purchased, I head over to Envato and search the logo section. I want to find a logo that is bold, that will speak to the hearts of my target market, and that is easy to use in horizontal and vertical form. I'm giving myself 30 minutes maximum to find the logo I'm going to use. Once I find it, I buy it and then proceed to find a designer onhttp://fiverr.com/ Fiverr who can modify the logo to my requirements. I move quickly here, giving specific directions and clear instructions—including making sure that my logo is changed to colors that will attract my target market. I want the logo back tomorrow so I can use it to start marketing.

I know in my heart that most people would want to move more slowly than I have today, but I know that the power of momentum will drive me through this time to get my debts paid and have a solid business income coming in to support my family. So going slow is not an option, and furthermore, it's harder to restart than to ride the momentum.

And after all the activity of Day 1, I have a tremendous amount of momentum.

## Day 2: First Day Of Action

*Looking After Myself* Quite honestly, I probably ended up staying up till 2–3am last night working on the project, so today it's SUPER important to look after myself and rebalance my body/internals before jumping into action. I go for a brisk walk with Kristi to connect with her. I ensure that I've had a ton of water, as I will continue to do each day, and I also ensure that I've watched a motivational video on YouTube before starting work. I do this because I know being in the right state of mind is going to enable me to be more productive.

*Taking Care Of Business* The list of things to do in my business today is mainly about ensuring that there's nothing in my way that will stop me from being able to market my business from tomorrow onward. I do the following by lunchtime:

- Ask Kristi to be my photographer and take 10 photos of me—some with a blank, solid-color background—because I want to be able to "clear cut" myself out, so I can paste my photo into a variety of backgrounds to use in my marketing images.
- Open an account with Clipping Magic to remove the background from some of my photos, so when I create marketing material, I can put a cool background behind me.
- Open an account with Stencil so I can create email banners, Facebook Ads, and the like there.
- Map out my funnel on a piece of paper. I'm going to create a short FREE giveaway that my target market will want, so my first funnel will look like this:

  - Step One: FREE OFFER upon opt-in
  - Step Two: Video thank-you and message about opportunity to work with me personally. This page will have a Book a Call section on it and will include real scarcity and urgency. The opt-in will trigger an email series where I'll use story-based messages to inspire people to put in an application to work with me.
  - Step Three: Thank-you page with phone number to call

- Create a Facebook page for my business and brand it accordingly.
- Do a Facebook Live video (with 10/10 energy, excitement, and conviction) on my new Facebook page about my new venture and

**32**

the new opportunity to work with me. I share this video to my personal Facebook page. Behind the scenes, I ask my friends to share my message on their Facebook pages IF they have friends who fit the target market I'm looking to serve.

- Create a Facebook Group for the clients I'm about to bring in and then create a first welcome video message for members of that group.
- Open an account with Zoom to deliver content.

The afternoon is spent working on my FREE offer, building the funnel for it, and working on a content calendar for social media. I know it's super important to get regular content out over the next month, so my customers know I'm serious about what I'm doing. I want to ensure that my content is relevant to my market and that I'm authentic, vulnerable, and real.

## Day 3: Committed Action

*Looking After Myself* Today is SUPER important to look after my spirit because I know I could start to get a little wobbly now. I drink water, I connect with Kristi, and I make sure that I've exercised and watched something inspirational before working.

*Taking Care Of Business* Today I continue my Facebook Lives and ensure that I'm sending people to my free offer funnel. In the background, I'm also going to start working on my coaching funnel, which could otherwise be called a Getting Beta Clients For My Online Course Funnel.

In this funnel, I make certain that I'm 100% transparent about looking to personally mentor a small number of people to get incredible results and that I'll be looking to leverage their results for future marketing purposes. I use this as a sales approach because I want to show people that their results are what I'm hungry for. I also say, with integrity, that I'll be offering my coaching services for $25,000 in the future; however, I'm looking to ask for their help in refining what my online program is like, so I'm looking to help 15 people at just $1,497 for a six-week coaching period. The offer will be stacked so high that it's a no-brainer but will look to repel non-ideal (headache/pain-in-the-butt) clients.

Oh, and I need to set up an order page that only I will see, because I'm going to mostly be doing phone sales for the first round of clients. I will, however, make sure that the post-purchase emails are all automated and ready to go, so I don't have to tell 15 people the same message over and over. The instructions on when the group coaching is going to start and particulars are all in that email.

NOW more than ever, I need to bring the energy and conviction into my messaging, so that I make sure the tone of every video I do is energetic, excited, and confident. Without confidence—in myself and in my ability to get results for others—I'm not going to be successful.

## Days 4–6: Consistency

*Looking After Myself* These days, I continue to ensure I'm looking after my mindset, my body, and my relationship. Without these pillars, the wheels will very likely come off.

*Taking Care Of Business* During these days, I...

- Stay consistent with my Facebook Lives.
- Create a Facebook video ad campaign to give away my free offer.
- Create a retargeting ad campaign to my coaching funnel.
- Close calls with applicants who have applied.
- Send a FREE gift to all applicants who have paid already.

Based on the information I've gathered from the Ask Campaign, client applications, and Facebook Likes and Comments, I prepare for the delivery of my group coaching to my clients. I've set the start date of the program at a week from now. I'll create my slides in Keynote and ensure that they are branded and look professional. They also MUST be structured in a logical way so that the information is easily understood by my clients.

# Day 7: Rest And Regroup

*Looking After Myself* Re-center, take time off, meditate, speak to my woo-woo friends to see if I'm in balance, and have time in nature. Nature always makes me feel at peace.

*Taking Care Of Business* Tonight, I plan out my next week and see if there are any looming barriers that I need to be aware of. My aim is to keep this process simple, so if I feel like things are too complicated, I'll "cut the fat."

I will also spend some time putting together a one-page video funnel that is aimed at getting referrals for clients from my Facebook contacts. I speak from my heart to my fans and to my friends about what I'm aiming to do. I ask humbly for help in tagging someone they know who needs my services. I remind them that I'm raw and real (a key differentiator from my competition). I know that between my Facebook friends and their friends, there are people who need my help.

Oh yeah, and I've also found that it helps to sweeten the deal by saying I will pay a referral fee for any successful referrals.

# Days 8–13: Marketing Strong

*Looking After Myself* Each day, I'm working on my mindset. I know if I start to freak out or get worried or annoyed, then I'll have a difficult time in the results department. Belief in myself is KEY, so I keep looking after myself and my mindset all week.

*Taking Care Of Business* This week is pretty much full of marketing my program like my life depended on it. My main areas of focus are to...

- Stay consistent with my Facebook Lives.
- Tweak my Facebook Ads to my free offer.
- Share my free offer in Facebook Groups where my target market hangs out.
- Tweak retargeting ads to my coaching funnel.
- Close calls with applicants who have applied.
- Send a FREE gift to all applicants who have paid already.

And I also ensure that I'm building community spirit with my new clients in a Facebook Group. I don't want anyone to feel left behind or unsupported during this time. It's SUPER important to focus on the early adopters and ensure that they are communicated with and feeling like a part of where we are going. I have to be solid here, even if I'm feeling wobbly inside. I have to stay confident and on top of my game.

This week, I'm also finalizing content and closing last-minute sales.

## Day 14: Rest And Regroup

*Looking After Myself* Re-center, take time off, meditate, speak to my woo-woo friends to see if I'm in balance, and have time in nature.

*Taking Care Of Business* Again, just as I did last week, tonight I plan out my next week and see if there are any looming barriers to success that I need to be aware of.

I'm nearly halfway there. So today I rest a bit. I'm simply making sure that I'm on course, that I've anticipated any future obstacles, and then gearing up for the rest of this 30-day journey.

## Days 15–20: Delivery

*Looking After Myself* Consistency in looking after myself is key. I make a point of having magic moments with Kristi and the girls so we all feel connected as a family. I'm building up steam now and getting really excited about how things are panning out, so I'm sharing success with my family so they can feel like the loss of time with me is worth it.

*Taking Care Of Business* It's time to deliver content to my clients! I also want to make sure I keep my leads coming in. With that said, I'm going to be focusing this week on...

- Staying consistent with my Facebook Lives where I'm delivering VALUE.
- Staying consistent with my community development in my group.
- Tweaking my Facebook Ads to my free offer.
- Sharing my free offer in Facebook Groups where my target mar-

ket hangs out.

- Tweaking retargeting ads to my coaching funnel. I'm keeping my Facebook Ads running during this time to pick up a few more clients. I only want ideal clients, though. Bad-egg clients will shatter this whole push.
- Delivering course content in a structured manner.
- Delivering group coaching content in a mastermind manner.
- Uploading all content to a members area in ClickFunnels.

Furthermore, I have to listen to my clients' concerns, needs, and desires. They will say things during this time that may change the marketing for the full launch of my course.

At this point, I am most likely in a position to pay back some of the folks I owe money to, so I make sure that I do so. I make a solid point of thanking them for giving me some leeway with their payment terms.

## Day 21: Rest And Regroup

*Looking After Myself* Re-center, take time off, meditate, speak to my woo-woo friends to see if I'm in balance, and have time in nature. (Are you noticing a pattern? Make sure that you know what helps you stay centered and balanced, and then build that into your day as well.)

*Taking Care Of Business* Again, I will plan my next week and see if there are any looming barriers to success that I need to be aware of. My aim is to keep this process simple, so if I feel like things are too complicated, I'll "cut the fat."

## Days 22–27: Delivery And Webinar

*Looking After Myself* Exercise is one thing that may have slipped during these last few weeks, so I make a concerted effort to work out (properly) at least five out of seven days this week. I tell my accountability partner this also. As with the other weeks, I'm continuing to drink a TON of water and communicate with Kristi about where I'm at business-wise, and I also ensure I have special Lizzy Time with the girls so they know that they're more important than work.

*Taking Care Of Business* This week, I will continue delivering content to my clients and making sure leads are coming in. I'll gather testimonials about the process I've taken my clients through so far and any wins they've had as a result of last week's training.

I'm also going to start working on a webinar to sell the scalable course I intend to make, because I have spent a ton of time working with my clients now, and I understand what they need and want. I've also refined my offer even more so it make sense to my target market.

During this week, I'm laser focused on overdelivering to my clients. I want them to have success. I do, however, maintain a healthy boundary so I am able to "turn down the volume" of how hands-on I will be in the future.

## Day 28: Rest And Recover

*Looking After Myself* Re-center, take time off, meditate, speak to my woo-woo friends to see if I'm in balance, and have time in nature. And I make sure I have huge family time.

*Taking Care Of Business* Again, just as I did last week, tonight I plan out my next week and see if there are any looming barriers to a successful week that I need to be aware of. My aim is to keep this process simple, so if I feel like things are too complicated, I'll "cut the fat."

## Days 29–30: Start Of Phase Two

*Looking After Myself* This week is going to be big. As with the other weeks, I'm continuing to drink a TON of water and communicate with Kristi about where I'm at business-wise, and I also ensure I have special Lizzy Time with the girls so they know that they're more important than work.

*Taking Care Of Business* As well as servicing my clients as I have done so far, I am going to focus on finishing and launching my webinar live this week, with paid traffic. It's a tall ask, but it doesn't have to be perfect...in fact, imperfect action always beats perfect inaction (and overthinking), so I'm going to go for it!

# FINAL THOUGHTS

If you sell digital products and coaching and ever find yourself in a similar position, I'm confident that the structure I've laid out in this 30-day plan will get you back on your feet and moving forward... building momentum as you go.

And if you follow what I've laid out above, then you'll avoid two of the biggest pitfalls of most business owners who are either launching a new business, scaling an existing one, or reviving a dead one.

1. Lack of confidence, discipline, and inner peace
2. Lack of a clear plan and well-defined outcomes

So wherever you are in your business, you can do it. I've helped so many people from so many different backgrounds and life circumstances that I'm convinced anyone can be successful. You have EVERYTHING you need inside of yourself right now to make it happen. Because when you control your mindset, discipline, and focus while channeling your energy and strengths, you're able to create win-win solutions. A win for you...and a win for the people you're helping!

In closing, I want nothing more than for you to be successful, so in one final attempt to ensure the following point sticks...

Please do not waste time trying to be perfect!

Take massive action and...

Go get it done.

KAPOW!!!

Liz

# RESOURCES

- Clipping Magic (clippingmagic.com)
- Envato Market (graphicriver.net)
- Facebook Ads
- Facebook Lives
- Fiverr (fiverr.com)
- GoDaddy (godaddy.com)
- Keynote
- Stencil (getstencil.com)
- Voxer (voxer.com)
- WorkFlowy (workflowy.com)
- Zoom (zoom.us)

# Chapter 3

# APPLICATION VIDEO FUNNEL

*by Garrett J. White*

# GARRETT J. WHITE

## *Founder, Wake Up Warrior*

Consulting
*WarriorBook.com*

*Garrett J White is the founder of the Wake Up Warrior Movement and author of bestselling books "Warrior Book" and "Be The Man". He is creator of Warrior Week and host of the number one podcasts Warrior On Fire, Warrior Wealth and Date Your Wife.*

*What started as a desire to set himself free from the bondage of his own failing life after the banking crisis of 2008, soon transformed into the launch of a movement in late 2012 that is quickly changing the business world we have known for decades using an*

> unconventional method known as the Warriors Way.
>
> Garrett also co-owns DKW Styling Salon and BMS Training systems in the hair industry. He lives in Laguna Beach, California with his three children Parker, Bailee and Ruby.

## Day 1: The Reality Check

Regardless of my reality with my money, I will still invest in my children daily and drive them to school every day.

I must know where I am before I can determine where I can go.

I will...

- Investigate all of the chaos in my finances.
- Assess the reality of what I owe, who I owe, and why, and create a simple "Here is the reality of my money" checklist.
- Inform anyone I owe money to that I will need 90 days, and that from there I will catch everything up and everyone will be made whole.
- Create a "PIT" DOLLAR FIGURE. This is the amount of money I am in the hole.
- Create my "PEAK" MONEY target. This is the amount of money I am committed to producing to dig myself out and put myself back on top of the game in less than 90 days.
- Assess all areas of my CORE 4 (body, being, balance, business) and create my DAILY (every single day for the next 30 days) WAR MAPS (see details below) with the Clear Daily Actions.

I will also establish my DAILY WAR.

These are the things I will be doing every single day by noon to keep me in power and keep the game moving forward for my offer in the next couple of weeks and beyond.

I will start with CORE 4 today, but will start with the DAILY 8 on Day 6 of this 30-day sprint.

## The Daily War

CORE 4 (A Daily Game Of Power As Taught By Wake Up Warrior)
- Body (Fitness and Fuel)
  - I will work out every morning.
  - I will drink a green smoothie every morning.
- Being (Meditation and Memoirs)
  - I will meditate for 20 minutes twice a day.
  - I will write in my journal about my feelings and thoughts 20 minutes daily.
- Balance (Partner and Posterity)
  - I will send a text of love to my wife every morning, appreciating and honoring her.
  - I will send a video text of love to each of my children.
- Business (Discover and Declare)
  - I will study Expert Secrets by Russell Brunson for 20 minutes every morning.
  - I will share what I am learning in my own language every day online.

## Daily 8

- VIDEO: Live Stream (10 mins.)
  - I will teach and train on this video every day (marketing).
- PHOTO: IG Picture (x3)
- AUDIO: Daily Fuel Podcast (10 mins.)
- TEXT: FB blog (300 words)
- Join one new network per day on Facebook until I am at a MAX of 10 groups.
- Spend 60 minutes per day per group adding value.
- Build prospect list daily by 10 and engage each of them via chat.
- Add 25 new personal friends on FB from groups.

**44**

# Day 2: What Do I Want?

- *OUTCOME: Establish the reality of where I am committed to go.*
- *Start With Daily War Core 4 only.*

I will lock in the target of what I truly want.

If I have gotten myself into this situation, I will ensure that I will never go back to this place again and things will be different when I produce this time.

I must learn from the mistakes that got me here, for they are the access points to my new level of production.

Today is not a waste of time. I am going to allow everything I create today in my head to hit my heart, because it is the fuel that will allow me to keep going weeks from now.

The first 30-day target will be to set up the systems to set me free again and to make money.

As part of my daily routine, I will do a MIDDAY MEDITATION for 20 minutes and WALK for 20 minutes.

It is not okay to spend the month just planning and building—I must start getting paid also.

This is a MUST, not negotiable.

In this case my target is $100K (received).

I will also put myself on track to do another $100K a month for the rest of the year with the systems that I will build and the game I am going to play.

This is a target then of both money and strategy.

*What do I want economically?*
Answer: $100K in 30 days.
*What do I want my lifestyle to look like?*
I will be a solo backpack entrepreneur for the next six months without a team.

Since I f**ked up badly enough to lose everything, I obviously need some time alone to just manage myself and the game I am creating, so I will leverage only my own skills the next six months.

# Day 3: Why Do I Want it?

- *OUTCOME: Establish the reality of my why and what is driving me to create.*
- *Start With Daily War Core 4 only.*

***The why?*** This is going to be crucial.

I will surf today for an extra hour and also go for a very long walk (10+ miles) and contemplate my why while taking notes on my cell phone as I go, documenting ideas as they come.

Once I return from the walk?

I will write out the why on my boards.

I will also find a picture of my family.

I will get a picture made of the financial target I am hunting down.

I will take the photo of my family and the money target and hang them in my home office alongside of my why statements.

These I will look at 50+ times a day as I am working in my office.

They will be the first things I see in the morning and the last things I see in the evening before bed.

I will ensure that one room of the house is mine 14–16 hours a day.

I will have the sit-down conversation with my wife about where I am—the financial PIT I have put our family in—and then I will paint the vision for where we are going in the next 60 days.

I will ask for her support and will let her know that I will likely be on edge for the next 30 days but that I am still 100% committed to living the Warrior's Way and will be taking her on a date every week over the next four weeks.

# Day 4: What Happens If I Don't Get What I Want?

- *OUTCOME: Establish the reality of the clear consequences for failure.*
- *Start With Daily War Core 4 only.*

Today, I will identify all the obstacles inside myself and the game I am about to play again solo.

How can I f**k this up?

What could I do or have I done in the past to mess up the game for myself?

Understanding my weakness and the reality of failure allows me to build the paths necessary for the success of what I am creating.

This is not saying I am going to fail, but being willing to live by the TRUTH the way I see it such that I am able to clearly see where I may stumble and why.

I will take the entire day to outline the challenges I am going to face and the solutions in my mind where I stand in that moment to be able to handle them.

I will go on another 10-mile hike and document my answers on my phone. When I return from my hike, I will do the following:

- I will narrow them down to the top 10 risks or obstacles and my current solutions and write them on the whiteboards inside my home office.
- I will also write down the strategies I am going to leverage to overcome these obstacles.
- I will spend a good hour before bed reviewing everything I have done so far the first four days.

## Day 5: What Happens If I Do Get What I Want?

- *OUTCOME: Establish the reality of the clear consequences for success.*
- *Start With Daily War Core 4 only.*

I will put myself into massive pain today.

I will spend several hours in the ocean surfing and sitting on the beach.

As I do, I will envision two things.

First, I will look at the painful consequence of me failing on my mission.

Yes, you read that right—of me failing.

I need to get some leverage for myself, and that means I need to see the clear reality in me, my family, and my future if I fail.

This will create massive pressure that, armed with the rest of the work, will give me the ability to launch into an intensity necessary to sell.

I will write out the impact on...

- Me
- My marriage
- My children
- My life

I will tattoo the s\*\*t out of this pain all over my soul and then hang that failure reality in plain view next to the WHY photo of my wife and children along with the dollar amount.

I will then write a statement on my forearm in marker:

*"Failure Is Not An Option, Go Motherf\*\*ker"*

This will be written on my arm every single day until the target is hit.

This is no BULLS\*\*T. I want a visual reminder for me and everyone who sees me about what I am committed to!

And I will spend an hour writing this on my arm and reviewing everything I have done in the first five days.

**Weekly Date Night With My Queen** Tonight and every week, I will coordinate a babysitter and take my wife out.

We will not have any money, so it will be something for FREE.

That night, I am going to make love to my wife and confirm to her the status of the rebirths of myself and the business.

Yes, SEX and connection with my wife will matter.

# Day 6: What Problem Will I Solve?

- *Saturday Date Morning With Kids*
- *Today, I start the full Daily War (CORE 4 + DAILY 8).*

Today, I will determine the domain and the problem that I am going to solve.

I am very clear that my path is in consulting.

This is my X FACTOR—working directly with producers on the issues of power, production, and profit. And although I got my a$$ kicked and lost everything again, my skills are still there.

The domain will be BUSINESS.

I will brainstorm the problems that I know with 100% certainty I can solve for businessmen or women inside this domain.

Specifically, I will focus my energy on...

- Advertising
- High-Level Fulfillment
- Leadership of Teams
- Marketing Strategy
- Sales Systems

Today, I will choose the top five problems.

1. Lack of qualified leads
2. Underperforming sales teams and systems
3. Underwhelming fulfillment of products and services
4. Overwhelm and failure to lead teams
5. Dysfunction of home life while experiencing the first four problems

I will post these problems on the WALL.

Today, I will also start my Daily General's Tent, which is 30 minutes for me to review right before bed what I did each day and what I am committed to doing the next day.

This will be the formal debrief from the day that I have been doing informally for Days 1–6.

The focus on this is clearly laid out below.

This will involve four phases.

1. Return and report on what I did for the day.
2. Lessons Learned: I will assess what I learned today from what worked and what didn't work out for me.

3. Course Correct: I will adjust strategy for the next day based on what did not work today.
4. New Targets: I will set my numbers and targets for tomorrow's game.

Everything in the daily debrief will be money- and marketing-driven.

## Day 7: What Pain Will I Resolve?

- *OUTCOME: Clarify the painful consequence of the problem in my prospects' lives.*
- *Sunday Family Date Morning*

Regardless of my reality with my money, I will still invest in my family outing weekly.

Each day, I will START WITH THE DAILY WAR then REVIEW GENERAL'S TENT from the previous night.

I will spend today outlining the matrix of painful consequences that a prospect would be facing because of failure to solve each of the problems above.

Each one of these painful consequences will be one of the angles I will take with my marketing messages that I am sharing with my Daily War.

At this point, my Daily War has been going for seven days, and I will already have located my first two to five clients and started the seduction process with each of them.

I will study them. Study their social media presence and start testing the waters with the painful consequence that they are seeing and facing inside their worlds to see if what I am finding is accurate.

This is the magic sauce that will set up my marketing efforts in a few days.

I will walk through each of the problems and link the painful consequence of the problem on each of the four domains of life.

When I experience <PROBLEM>, the unintended consequence on my...

- BODY is...

- BEING is...
- BALANCE (marriage and kids) is...
- BUSINESS (money and lifestyle) is...

By the end of today, I will have the PAIN WEB built, and I will be starting to express this during my DAILY WAR to the marketplace and inside the groups I am sharing in.

This PAIN WEB is what I will reference every time I write sales copy.

I will post these as sticky notes and stick them on the wall next to the problems so that I can see, then stand back and review them.

- *Complete Daily General's Tent*

# Day 8: Who Are The People I Will Serve?

- *OUTCOME: Clarify the specific target I am going to serve with this promotion.*

Today, I will narrow in on a specific target of the man and woman I am after.

I will identify how the problem and the painful consequences will impact them individually.

I will research specifics about their lives overall and choose the location of those prospects inside of the United States and other English-speaking countries. I will consider these demographics:

- Age
- Belief Systems
- Economics
- Family
- Religion
- And everything else I can find

At the end of the day, I will print off a picture of the MAN and WOMAN who will operate as my avatars, and I will post those pictures right next to the rest of the problem and pain statements on the wall.

I will arrange them so the pictures are right there in the center of all the research.

I will name the man Bob.

I will name the woman Mary.

If I have a clear idea of who I want to be my first four or five clients, I will print their pictures off from social media and have them on my board also.

When I write copy, create videos, and produce any other marketing assets, I will leverage all of this in the space of these prospects so that I am speaking directly to a person and not a vague concept of a person.

- *Complete Daily General's Tent*

During tonight's General's Tent, I will begin building the PROSPECT LIST from my Daily War and start specifically with the Daily Seduction to the offer coming in two weeks.

## Day 9: What Product Will I Provide?

- *OUTCOME: Create the product or service I am going to offer.*

I will spend the day today researching offers to my target.

I will find the top 10 offers on the web of coaches, consultant programs, and events that are speaking to my prospect.

I will identify where they are dominating.

I will study their marketing copy, sales systems, and FRAME they are selling from.

And I'll find the weakness and solidify in my mind why I am the f**king choice above them all.

I will identify where they are weak and determine where I can dominate inside the weakness I see or how I can position myself against the competition.

I am really looking to see what is already selling and why.

I am also cross-checking the types of clients they are getting results for, what that might mean for me as a producer and consultant, and how my offer will be different.

At the end, I will be offering a coaching and consulting package angled at the target of MONEY and lifestyle as a businessman or woman.

Just because I have lost my empire two times now (the first time for real and the second for the purpose of this book) does not mean I don't know how to build sh*t and get paid.

My ability to guide my students to get the money is not damaged by my inability to keep my own money.

My program will focus on the skill of getting money, not on the skill of keeping money.

That way, my integrity is SOLID as F**K, and I can own the frame in selling.

- *Complete Daily General's Tent*

Every day, I will continue list cultivation and start building files for each prospect, tracking their moves on social media and looking for leverage points when it comes time to offer.

## Day 10: What Package Will I Provide It In?

- *OUTCOME: Finalize the packaging of the product.*

I will spend today creating my consulting package. This means I will outline the specific structure of the game.

The program will be six months.

I will determine...

- How many training calls we will have
- Focus of the calls
- Form and technology used to deploy our training together
- Blueprints I am going to deploy with them to leverage in their own businesses to get paid
- Outcomes they can expect

I'll come forward with "WHAT I EXPECT from your results as a client of mine," knowing that until I truly know the whole picture of a client's story, it will be difficult to actually know what results are truly possible, so I will go off of past results.

I will create the assessments that I will use to measure the results they are going to get.

I will also create the FRAME inside of which they will be able to operate.

But the time I am done today, I will have the entire program framed up and ready to go.

- *Complete Daily General's Tent*

# Day 11: What Positioning Will I Frame?

- *OUTCOME: Specify the positioning of WHY ME against the other options in the market.*

**Why Am I The Solution?** Today, I will...

- Outline all of my past case studies, including the specific results they got and the process I took them through.
- Narrow it down by the end of the day to the TOP 10.
- Tell all their stories and share the results they have gotten.
- Create specific before-and-after charts that show the clear hero's journey of each client, starting with the painful problems they were facing when I met them and what their results look like today.
- Ensure that I have six men's and four women's stories and that I have a variety of backgrounds—economic, social, and racial—so that I have the stories I need to connect with the prospect when I need to.

And I will be clarifying the game with them on my boards.

- Who they were

- Whey they mattered
- What results they got
- How we worked together in the past

By the end of the day, I will have the master list of case studies.

Also, I will have the frames I need to create the 10 five-minute case-study videos, where I will draw out the story of each student and the journey they took to get results on my whiteboards.

- *Complete Daily General's Tent*

## Day 12: What Pitch Will I Make?

- *OUTCOME: Simplify my pitch, pricing, and promotion.*

Today, I will finalize my financial target.

The target is simple: 10 clients for 6 months of consulting each.

*Tuition is $10K.*
*Again, the target is $100K.*
*This will allow me to hit my target.*

I will be doing this through sales calls and interviews with prospects over the phone and will be collecting credit card information for the initial commitment of $10K. (It will be $10K regardless.)

I will start testing this pricing in pre-sales content inside of my Daily War and with my growing prospect list through private messages.

I must start the pre-frame game in a way that allows the price to start being known but without it being a shock.

Easier to warm up to the number over two weeks than be hit right in the face with it.

I will also spend tons of time embedding the results and case studies of my students.

For anyone with a payment plan need, I will push to the second 60 days and simply take a $2K deposit to add them to the next group, which I will launch 60 days from then.

The first round will be $10K, period.

I will also shoot the first five case-study videos today and shoot the next five tomorrow, so that I have assets to start sharing with my prospect list privately via chat with links to individual pages with the videos on them.

No attempt to sell yet. Just starting the seduction game.

- *Complete Daily General's Tent*

Continue list cultivation and start building prospect files for each prospect tracking their moves on social media, looking for leverage points when it comes time to offer.

- *Weekly Date Night With My Queen*

# Day 13: Create The Funnel Content Framework

- *OUTCOME: Frame out the entire FUNNEL I will be building.*
- *Saturday Date Morning With Kids*

Today, I draw out the funnel on my whiteboards.

This is my sales funnel in ClickFunnels.

It will have...

- Landing Page
- Content 1 Page: I AM A MARKETER
  - The man who can make it rain controls the game.
- Content 2 Page: I AM A CLOSER
  - The land of maybe is a lie—it is either yes or no.
- Content 3 Page: I AM A LEADER, NOT A SAVIOR
  - I can show you the way, but I won't carry you there.
- Content 4 Page: POWER, PRODUCTION, AND PROFIT
  - The art and science to having it all
- Content 5 Page: ARE YOU READY TO HAVE IT ALL?

- Application Page: WHY SHOULD I ACCEPT YOU?
- Schedule Page: THE PRODUCER CHECKUP

The pages will be simple. They will have a black background with simply my signature logo, Garrett J. White. No sexy graphics. Just functional and automated.

I will be loading my autoresponders later.

Once I have the whiteboard drawn out and done, I will grab some coffee, and I will not go to sleep until the funnel is built and only waiting on the Actionetics email copy and the videos I will be shooting tomorrow.

Daily Seduction to my growing lists from my DAILY WAR.

- *Complete Daily General's Tent*

# Day 14: Deploy The Early-Bird List
- *OUTCOME: Start building the EMAIL list for pre-launch.*
- *Sunday Family Date Morning*

Today, I will create a temporary landing page for the new funnel.

I will shoot a three- to five-minute video that I will put on the page with an opt-in and one autoresponder that will tell them "Thank you for getting on the early-bird list."

I will do a live Q&A webinar for only the early birds the last 7 days of my 30-day run.

This will give them incentive to opt in.

On the other side of the page, I will be speaking to the four-part video training series I am going to be taking them on.

I will have specific release dates for each of the videos, so that they can see that there is some really cool s**t coming.

I will also create the frameworks for all five of my content videos that I will be recording tomorrow.

TODAY, I will begin to start promoting individually to my list of prospects from my DAILY WAR to get them registered for the training series.

- *Complete Daily General's Tent*
- *Weekly Date Night With My Queen*

## Day 15: Shoot The Five Content Videos

- *OUTCOME: Complete five RAW core videos for the funnel.*

Today is my video day.

I no longer have my teams to run my studios. So I will be on my own with this.

But this is how I started, so it's no problem.

I will be shooting from my iPhone, using my hand as the microphone and my arm as the tripod.

I will shoot in my home office and also on the beach down below my home.

I will draw in the sand on the beach videos and will be drawing on and using whiteboards to teach the content of each video.

- *Complete Daily General's Tent*

## Day 16: Shoot "The Application" And "The Opt-In" And Create Application

- *OUTCOME: Complete the application and opt-in videos and finalize the application.*

Today, I will watch all of my videos I shot yesterday two or three times.

I will take notes on key ideas and statements I said.

Then I will shoot the application video.

Once I have shot the application video, I will shoot the thank-you video for the post-application.

The final VIDEO I will shoot at the beach.

This is the opt-in video, the most important video of all.

It is the HOOK.

I will make sure I am rested, have meditated, and am ready to go when I shoot that last video.

I will also clarify and create my application that I will be using for the call to action in the series I am about to publish.

- *Complete Daily General's Tent*

## Day 17: Edit All Videos In iMovie

- *OUTCOME: Edit all videos and export then load to Vimeo.*

Today, I will load all my videos in the series into iMovie, and then it is time to "step into the matrix."

I will create simple intros and transitions inside of each video.

Since I don't have my team to help make this magical, I am going to choose to keep things simple and focus on the content.

I will add text in certain spots and will also load some B-roll photos over the edits every couple of minutes just to keep the viewers engaged.

Because I was shooting and writing on my whiteboards in my office for most of my videos, I won't need a ton of B-roll, but I will use some photos from the past of me as a trainer teaching others.

I will not go to bed until all of the videos are exporting and being saved as MP4s on my desktop.

This is going to be a long day, but I am going to lock myself in a room and ensure that this gets done.

- *Complete Daily General's Tent*

## Day 18: Build Sales Funnel

- *OUTCOME: Funnel built, tested, and ready to deploy*

Okay—today, I have to start gluing everything together.

This means that I am going to have to build the actual pages for the entire funnel.

I am going to have to add the videos, images, and application.

Then I am going to test all of the links, pages, and buttons.

I will review the COPY on all the pages once the funnel is built and up.

I will not be relying heavily on the copy for this funnel but will be leaning heavily on the video assets.

With that said, I will ensure that my headlines, sub-headlines, and body copy above and below the videos are on point and ready to go.

- *Complete Daily General's Tent*

# Day 19: Write #1–6 Autoresponders And Add To ClickFunnels

- *OUTCOME: First six emails written and loaded into ClickFunnels*

Today, I am going to write all the email copy.

My focus will be Emails 1–6.

They will be written and then activated inside of the funnel, leveraging Actionetics.

Once someone opts in, these emails will go out every single day for 10 days.

Each of the emails will spoon-feed content to the reader that they would have seen inside the videos.

- Emails 1 and 2 go to Video #1 "Power, Production, Profit"
- Emails 3 and 4 go to Video #2 "I'm a Marketer"
- Emails 5 and 6 go to Video #3 "I'm a Closer"

Each of the emails will be compelling by itself as stand-alone content and will be written as a mini sales letter more so than like a regular email.

Within each email, I will teach content that they will see in the corresponding video.

I will also start testing this COPY inside of the GROUPS I am part of—not just inside of my autoresponder—so I can see how they are received.

I will write them like BLOG POSTS.

Start building engagement inside the groups and keep adding to my list of prospects as they engage with the content.

- *Weekly Date Night With My Queen*
- *Complete Daily General's Tent*

## Day 20: Write #7–12 Autoresponders And Add To ClickFunnels.

- OUTCOME: *Second six emails written and loaded into ClickFunnels*

Today, I am going to continue cranking out my email copy.

Once it is complete, I will load into Actionetics, and we are good to go.

- Emails 7 and 8 go to Video #4 "I'm a Leader, Not a Savior"
- Emails 9 and 10 go to Video #5 "Are You Ready to Have it All?"
- Emails 11 and 12 go to the application page

All of these emails are now complete, and I will load them all up in sexy formatting into ClickFunnels so they are ready to go.

These emails are not for a one-time use, as I will be using these same autoresponders as part of my ongoing campaign with this funnel.

I am not creating this funnel and business just to be profitable for a month—it is going to be my new game for a year or more.

I will keep testing this COPY inside of the GROUPS I am part of—not just inside of my autoresponder—so I can see how they are received.

I will write them like BLOG POSTS.

Keep building engagement inside the groups and keep adding to my list of prospects as they engage with the content.

- *Complete Daily General's Tent*

# Day 21: Test And Deploy The FUNNEL To My Lists

- *OUTCOME: Start driving traffic to my funnel.*
- Sunday Family Date Morning

I will...

- Spend the first five or six hours of my day testing my funnel.
- Do everything I can to break it.
- Test for mobile, desktop, and a variety of browsers.

Once I feel it is as solid as I can get it, I will begin to deploy it to the lists.

This is my chat list I have built, as well as my personal pages on social media.

I will write a SOLID frame for WHY, which I will send to each person I have engaged with from my Daily War efforts.

Each of the messages will be customized and well thought out.

At this point, I should have 100+ individuals who sit on my chat prospect list who I have been chatting with and adding value to the past two or more weeks.

I will also go LIVE on Instagram and Facebook, start sharing the new series that I have available online, and begin the actual hard promotion of it.

I will not start promoting in the groups yet and will retain my promotion to just the one-on-one game with each of the individuals, only growing my chat list of prospects.

I will keep posting some content from the emails inside the groups and start the beginning phase of prepping them for the launch of the funnel the next day.

I will keep testing this COPY inside of the GROUPS I am part of as before, writing them like BLOG POSTS to continue building engagement.

- *Complete Daily General's Tent*

# Day 22: Promote My A$$ Off

- *OUTCOME: Gather first applications.*

Today, I will be tracking everything and promoting everywhere.

I will start to promote in the 10 groups I am part of.

I will have added enough value at this point to not get slammed.

This means I will start sharing the FREE training in the funnel that I have already been sharing via chat and in FREE LIVE streams in the groups I am part of.

I will also go to my personal page with an offer for people to message me directly to learn more about the limited 10-student acceleration program I am creating.

My personal page will be for direct promotion to chat.

It is time to cash in on the goodwill and value I have produced in the previous weeks.

I started with my DAILY WAR almost two weeks ago, to connect with and build relationships with whoever is running the group, so we are totally on the same page.

By this time, I should have several of the group leaders ready to run a webinar with me, or at minimum to authorize me to GO LIVE with them inside the group and promote my new funnel.

At the end of the day, this is a FULL-ON BLITZ, all day long in the groups and also in chat.

I will be closing individuals via chat as well as via the funnel to application.

Everything will end at the application.

But I will not wait for my HOT PROSPECTS, who I have been chatting with one-on-one for weeks, to go through the entire funnel.

I will have already built relationships with and been on the phone with many of them, so it will be time to get the first couple on board and ready to roll.

- *Complete Daily General's Tent*

# Day 23: Promote and Pitch (1)

- *OUTCOME: Collect 10K in tuitions today!*

Now my days are going to get very simple.

I am going to be involved in two games, promoting hard all day inside the groups, chat, and my growing email list of opt-ins.

I am going to balance the game between launching a business and the push to get to $100K, so I am going to stick with the HOT prospects and have patience with those who are not ready yet.

I am building a business again, not a Hail-Mary income solution for 30 days only.

I am not building a funnel.

I am building a business.

Scheduling one-on-one calls for interviews for the 10 spots.

I will do them always that day or the day after.

I will text them as the applications come in and will get them on the phone as soon as I can after I get the application, even if that means I call them right after it comes in.

Knowing how lethal I will have been in seducing the prospects the past two weeks, I am confident I will have my first three or four interviews today and take my first YES CLIENT into the game.

$10K target today.

I will not get off the phones until I have collected $10K.

I will have already hand-selected the three or four prospects who I feel are a perfect fit weeks ago and will have been working on it, so this is going to happen.

- *Complete Daily General's Tent*

# Day 24: Promote and Pitch (2)

- *OUTCOME: Collect another 10K in tuitions today!*

I have some cash now.

I will...

- Start cultivating new clients by giving them assignments.
- Launch my new Ads Manager and start getting ads approved today for the funnel.
- Start spending $2K–$4K a day as soon as I can, but it is going to be a new account, so I'll have to scale to this with $100 a day and get some ads approved first.
- Get two or three ads up and running today to test the click, image, and copy.
- Start getting more intense with my list now.
- Send specific private messages to those I believe are a fit for this program with me.
- Send custom VIDEO and AUDIO messages to them once they have confirmed they are part of the funnel.
- Leverage the notes I have taken for weeks on each of them, which will allow me to align the offer with the needs and desires they have.
- Have my first one or two $10K tuitions collected by now.

This is giving me momentum.

Tomorrow, I will start adding scarcity to the lists.

Today, once I have collected tuitions, I will begin building my ad sets on FB to deploy ads.

- *Complete Daily General's Tent*

# Day 25: Promote and Pitch (3)

- *OUTCOME: Collect another 10K in tuitions today!*

Today, I will have two or three interviews, and my target is to get to three or four closes by the end of the day.

But if things are going as planned, I should be in the mix on this: $30K–$40K collected.

I will also be deploying two or three more ads and spending $200/day per ad.

I will start getting traffic and my first applications from them.

Having $30K–$40K is going to create the breathing room I need to keep pushing the game.

This means putting the squeeze on the prospects.

I will have six seats left.

I will update my copy to reflect this.

- *Complete Daily General's Tent*

# Day 26: Promote and Pitch (4)

- *OUTCOME: Collect another 10K in tuitions today!*

Today, I will have two or three more interviews.

These interviews are going to be one or two hours each.

They are just as important for me to figure out my prospects as they are for the sales process.

By the end of the day, I will be at 50% sold out at 5 for $10K.

Total $40K–$50K collected.

I will add my five students to a private FB Group and begin giving them assignments to get each of them ready for our one-on-one journey that will begin in less than a week.

The assignments I will give them will be about having them get clear on where they are today.

Today, I will deploy $300/day to each of my ads to the funnel.

I am averaging roughly $10/email.

That is 300 new emails a day and averaging three or four applications.

It is working perfectly.

I will also ship a welcome gift to all the new students, so they feel validated for their efforts and investment.

- *Complete Daily General's Tent*

**66**

- *Weekly Date Night With My Queen*

## Day 27: Promote and Pitch (5)

- *OUTCOME: Collect another 10K in tuitions today!*
- *Saturday Date Morning With Kids*

Today, I will do another two or three interviews.

The target is to add one person per day for the next five days, to have it sold out by the thirtieth day.

I will also start something new today.

I am going to schedule a Referral Strategy Call with all of my current clients, meaning the first five who have signed up.

I will do those calls tomorrow.

The focus of those calls will be to get them on point, but also to ask for one referral from each of them of a person like them who they feel would be a perfect fit for the program.

I will close another $10K today.

That will take me to $60K and 6 clients.

Today, I will deploy $500 in ads to my funnel.

- *Complete Daily General's Tent*

## Day 28: Promote and Pitch (6)

- *OUTCOME: Collect another 10K in tuitions today!*
- *Sunday Family Date Morning*

Today is going to be a hustle.

I will have 50+ in the mix and only 4 spots left.

I will likely have to lean on some people today.

I will have my six client calls and ask for referrals.

I am not expecting them to close as part of this group.

I want the referrals for the next round I am going to be selling.

Today, I will close one more client at $10K.

And I will deploy $650 in ads to my funnel.

- *Complete Daily General's Tent*

# Day 29: Promote and Pitch (7)

- *OUTCOME: Collect another 10K in tuitions today!*

Today is another day of hustle.

But I am close to my target.

I will have another two to four interviews today.

My target is to close at minimum one person at $10K to take me to 8 clients and only 2 seats left to hit my target.

During today's game, I will schedule a "surprise" webinar for all of the opt-ins to the funnel and the applicants who I have not gotten hold of yet.

I will announce it in the morning and then invite them to attend a Live tomorrow at noon.

This will be in addition to the video series.

The focus will be HOT SEATING prospects during a webinar.

Today, I will end with 8 total clients and deploy $750/a day per ad in ads to my funnel.

At $10 a lead, that is 75 emails today and several more applications.

- *Complete Daily General's Tent*

# Day 30: Promote and Pitch (8)

- *OUTCOME: Collect another 20K in tuitions today!*

Today, I will close it out.

I will push everyone to the webinar at noon.

The focus of the webinar will be to customize the content of the videos and close hard LIVE on the final seats.

Interviews will all be scheduled this afternoon and evening.

I will not go to sleep until the final two seats are sold.

Once they are sold, I will lock down the group of 10 clients and then roll out the program individually and add some small-group BONUS events with them virtually.

I will lay my head down tonight and sleep well, knowing I did not just make money.

Tonight, I will also lock my ad spend at $1K a day, assuming that I have been able to naturally get the increase by FB, with no issues the past week.

I will not take the ad spend less than $1K a day for the rest of the year.

This use of ad spend from profits will allow me to repeat this and the DAILY WAR every single day, as well as repeat what I just did every 30 days until I decide not to anymore.

Pay for my annual membership of ClickFunnels.

Celebration date night with my wife and children!

# RESOURCES

- Actionetics (clickfunnels.com/actionetics)
- Expert Secrets by Russell Brunson
- Facebook Live
- iMovie (imoviewindows.com)
- Vimeo (vimeo.com)
- Wake Up Warrior

## Chapter 4

# ECOMMERCE FUNNELS

*by Alison J. Prince*

# ALISON J. PRINCE

## *2 Comma Momma*

**Ecommerce**
**0-100k.com**

*Alison built multiple million dollar online brands and decided it was time to teach her 10 and 13 year old daughters how to sell products online. Within 9 months, these girls (who were in junior high and elementry) made their first 6 figures selling scarves.*

*She is now teaching over 2,000 others how they can build their profitable ecommerce business and living a #becauseican Clan life.*

Starting an e-commerce site from scratch isn't new to me; I've done it before multiple times, and I know I can do it again. In fact, the idea kind of excites me a little bit because it's my chance to kick fear in the teeth again, grab life by the proverbial horns, and feel that energy that comes from building and growing something new.

Because this isn't my first time attacking a new business, I know there are two commodities when starting a business: time and money.

Well, I don't have any money, so I need to leverage the time I do have and turn it into money FAST—all while balancing my primary role of wife and mom. I don't have time to shoot the breeze when I work. I'm here to get it done, bless lives, make money, and get home, because each day includes getting my four busy kids out the door to school and chauffeuring them to activities after school and on weekends. I plan out my "power hours" and get things done.

## Day 1

*Big Goal: Plot out my 30-day process (by weeks).*

To start out each day, I get up at least one hour before my family to get the day's game plan in place. I know my long-term goal: start my own e-commerce business. It can get me cash in the door fast with the added bonus of working at home in my pj's.

Selling products online is an easy way to build trust with people quickly. It's something tangible; they can touch and feel and incorporate it into their lives. But the best thing about selling products online is that choosing them doesn't need to be complicated. If Chia Pets have grown an empire on clay and seed, that's proof enough that it's not the product, it's the process.

I need to set up the high-level process today to maximize my results when I launch my profitable e-commerce site. Here's what the layout of the next 30 days looks like:

1. Find parties.
2. Find products for the parties.
3. Throw my own parties.
4. Throw my own party (again).

Parties? Yes! Parties make it fun when you're selling online, and I know they can make my business profitable on Day 1.

If there is any time left on Day 1, I will start searching for trending products—in other words, what's selling online. If I sell what people are buying, it will make this game a lot easier.

## Day 2

*Big Goal: Find the right parties.*

Here is the real issue I'm facing when starting an online business selling products: *I need traffic.* If no one comes, no one buys. That's why today is all about getting everything ready so that everything moves the moment I turn my ClickFunnels site live.

On Friends when Ross and Rachel threw parties, it always seemed to be that the camera panned to Ross sitting on the couch all alone at his, but the ones Rachel threw in her apartment were buzzing with excitement galore.

Here's the reality: both of these types of "parties" are happening online every single day. What I need to do is make sure I find those Rachel parties and weed out the Ross ones.

I'll imagine the ever-popular Rachel using my product at her party. She would tell EVERYONE there where she got it, so of course everybody else would want it, too! Getting my products in the hands of others will be so much easier if the Rachels of the world are showcasing my product than if I attend Ross's party or merely wander down the hall, knocking on doors, seeing if someone wants to buy it.

These online Rachel parties are hosted on social media 24/7. The parties never stop. And that's a good thing when selling products online. Partygoers (or in this case, social media followers) are constantly engaging with the party throwers (influencers) and this is the perfect setup for me.

But how am I going to actually FIND the people throwing these Rachel parties? How am I going to find the influencers who know how to get an engaging audience? *I'm going to Instagram!* With this handy little app full of influencers, we are (sometimes literally) sitting on the direct lines of communication with all the Rachels of the world. I just need to look for them.

Instagram's hashtag search provides my first shot at getting an invitation. With it, I can see where people are gathering at parties like Rachel's—parties that will complement my future business. There are also some Ross parties out there, and I move right on by those along with any party that could get the cops called for bad behavior. I only want to attend where my products will sell and, quite honestly, where I feel comfortable.

As I scroll down the list in Instagram, here are some of the basic requirements I look for in my perfect online parties:

- They have good engagement on Instagram.
- They are micro-influencers; in other words, they have fewer than 100,000 followers on Instagram. Rachel threw a great party in her apartment; I don't want a big party (over 100K followers) where an amphitheater would have to hold everyone. Things can get expensive. In this case, a smaller following is definitely better.
- They currently sell other products and have good interaction on those posts.

As I find the parties I want to attend, I'm making a list using Google Docs (also FREE). The more, the merrier.

Doing this pre-work today will save me hundreds of hours in growing a strong, solid customer base and will allow me to be profitable on the day I launch.

# Day 3

*Big Goal: Find trending products.*

Yesterday, I searched for the trending parties (influencers). I was able to see what products were getting engagement and what resonated with people.

Today will be my day to research and find trending products. My goal is to make a list of what products are selling. I check on the influencers' feeds and other sites like Amazon to see what people

**74**

are buying.

This is not to steal ideas.

Because I can't order unique items from China, I need to look at something I can get quickly (two or three shipping days), and that's usually more of a commodity-type item. Later, I'll be "un-commodifying" it.

*Note: I've been known to sell blocks of wood I found behind my shed and turn those sales into $9K within 24 hours. My girls sold scarves and made six figures. I won't overthink and make this process complicated!*

## Days 4–5

*Big Goal: Find out where to get the trending products.*

Days 4 and 5 are focused on researching where to source the commodity-type products I've identified locally. I have to be able to get these products in two to three days.

Normally, I get samples to test the products. I ask the vendor if I can get a sample, but if they don't do that, I'll have to take an educated risk. I'll ask for testimonials from other clients and research vendor Facebook pages, Instagram feeds, etc. to make sure they are high-quality products. I don't want to sell junk. No way.

To save time, I will also ask the vendors if I can use their pictures on my site to resell the products. (Of course, I would never use them without asking!)

## Day 6

*Big Goal: Choose a logo, colors, and a name.*

I have to make today short because I have soccer games and a piano recital to attend. Those take priority, because my kids will never be this age again.

For a logo, I'll head to Canva. I've got a 14-day free trial, so I'll use one of their pre-designed logos or whip up a simple one of my own. I'll use the free color-dropper Chrome extension, then search "color palettes" on Pinterest to find the color scheme I want to use. I don't have a lot of time to spend, so I just choose and go. I'll eventually use these on ClickFunnels to personalize the template I select.

Oh, and as for the name of my business? I'll let my kids choose.

## Day 7

*Big Goal: Rest.*

This is my rest day, a day to spend time with family and enjoy a respite from business building. It's an important "reset" for me personally, and ultimately will be beneficial for my company. I take time to worship, take a nap, go out for walks, visit with friends and my 95-year-old grandpa and just be very present in the moment.

## Day 8

*Big Goal: Un-commodify.*

Monday starts out early because I just can't sleep. This is getting way too exciting!

Today's focus is on "un-commodifying" the main product I'm about to sell by building an offer. I know that I'm selling a product that another seller could get elsewhere, as I purchased from a vendor instead of a manufacturer. That means I need to make my offer something they can't refuse.

This doesn't mean I need to sell it for pennies. My goal is to make money, and underpricing is exactly the WRONG way to achieve it. Instead, my offer will deliver greater value than anyone else's. I've done this before. I know this strategy will work.

Here's an example: cake stands.

There are a billion and a half out there.

BUT what if my cake stand is the most valuable because of an offer that looks like this:

*Purchase A Cake Stand And Receive...*
*A FREE Downloadable Recipe Book Filled With*
*50 Five-Minute (Cup)Cake Recipes Perfect for*
*Last-Minute Bake Sales and Parties*
*A Free Set of Beautiful Cupcake Liners*
*AND Free Shipping*

WOW! Now THAT's an offer!

For just pennies, I've set myself apart from my competition—and didn't sacrifice my profit margins!

I'll also add in a faster shipping option as my order bump, then set up Offer #2: my upsell.

Hmmm...what else will they need to make beautiful cup-cakes quickly?

How about a piping set—the things that make pretty swirls on top? I can find them super cheap on eBay (I know, I looked this morning) and I'll actually sell them for FREE!

Yes, FREE...if they sign up for a monthly cake-celebration package. The front offer is now built out. Done!

# Day 9

*Big Goal: Set up ClickFunnels.*

It's time to start setting up my first funnel. I use the Daily Deal template and customize it with my colors, logo, and business name. Then comes adding in the product. Thank heavens ClickFunnels has these templates all built out! Talk about a time (and cost) saver!

I'll also add in ClickFunnels' Pro Tools Freebies found at CFPro-Tools.com:

- CF USA ONLY Shipping
- CF Customer Info
- CF Best Seller Highlight
- CF Rearrange Highlight

I'll then focus on additional pages and customizations, which include:

- Creating a pop-up offering 10% off if a customer attempts to leave without buying
- Setting up email automation to send an email to any customer who does not purchase, again offering a 10% off coupon
- Adding my upsell

- Creating an About Us/Contact page
- Adding in customer information on Thank-You page

## Day 10

*Big Goal: Get an invite to the party.*

Now that I've got my list of online parties I really want to attend (that is, the influencers I'd like to work with), today's big question is figuring out how to get INTO the party to sell my products.

I don't know them.

They don't know me.

I can't offer them money to promote me. (My wallet's empty, after all!)

I need to create a three-way win: a win for the influencer, a win for their customer, and a win for me.

This is the day I'll reach out to the Rachels, the influencers, and get them to notice me. It's my job to convince them why they want to work with me. Influencers want to make money from me just like they do when they sell other people's products. I just need to show them how easy I will make it for them.

I'll talk about the revenue they can make, explain the quality of the product, and review how simple it will be for customers to convert with my value-added offer.

*(Here's a tip: When you approach an influencer, talk to them like they are a person. You'd think that was obvious, but I'll just throw that out there. Use their name, talk about their product, and make the interaction personal to them. Another tip: throw in a little non-spammy time-sensitive message so they'll take action quicker.)*

I know some won't answer, but that's okay because I'm planning on sending these out to multiple "parties" from the list that I built clear back on Day 2.

*(Hint: Dana Derricks' Dream 100 Book is a must-read when it comes to spoiling influencers and creating long-term relationships with them.)*

# Day 11

*Big Goal: Set up the 3x undercover funnel.*

The 3x undercover funnel is my focus for today as I wait for influencers to respond. I love how "3x undercover" sounds James Bondish...because it totally is.

When I get a customer, I want to woo their socks off. I want to sell to them again and again...and again. AND I plan to sell to them two additional times before their original order ships. So that's three orders in one—meaning additional income for me without having to pay a dime in advertising fees.

What?? Yup.

It all starts with the thank-you email.

On the thank-you email (which gets seriously high open rates), I'll tell them to watch out for an email the next day offering them a gift. I underscore that it's one they DEFINITELY don't want to miss out on. (How much do you love the e-comm-style soap opera email sequence Russell talks about that I'm building out?)

They were just thinking about how they got a good deal from me on their first purchase and now I'm offering even more! This trains customers to open future emails from me.

In that second email, I'll present another offer: free sprinkles so sparkly that they could win first prize at the county fair with their cupcakes!

I'll give them a gift certificate (or a code) to buy that one additional product—they'll just have to pay shipping and handling. Or they can buy two or three and I will waive all shipping and handling charges. One caveat: this offer expires in just 24 hours.

Here's what's awesome: their first order still hasn't gone out, so I can combine their orders and my margins will be a lot higher.

On the third day after their original purchase, they're getting another email from me, this time offering them a serving knife for free if they pay shipping and handling, and again they can get free shipping if they just order two or three.

The fourth day after the sale, with my margins now sky-high, I'll combine all the orders and ship THREE ORDERS IN ONE.

Happy customers because they feel like they just got a fantastic deal. Happy business because the bottom line just grew.

## Day 12

*Big Goal: Create content.*

I should at this point either have samples or know that I'm not getting any. Either way, I need to create a video for Facebook today. Fortunately, I have a video camera in my pocket—my phone.

No sample? No worries. There are plenty of ways to make a video with the still pictures I got permission from the vendor to use. A quick Google search provides tons of ideas.

What else is happening today?

I'm going to...

- Build out an affiliate program on my shop's site.
- Set up a Facebook page and add at least 9–12 pieces of content.
- Set up an Instagram page and add at least 9–12 pieces of content.

## Day 13

*Big Goal: Get date commitments.*

I start hearing back from influencers, which gives me the chance to share more about my offer and their commissions. I also want to get them to commit to the date on which they'll promote my product—preferably between Days 15 and 20. If they agree to do it during that time, I'll give them a bonus commission. Once confirmed, I send videos and product pictures.

## Day 14

*Big Goal: Rest.*

After a very busy week, getting to wind down and have some family time makes me pretty dang happy.

## Day 15

*Big Goal: Test and tweak.*

Today, I'm testing and tweaking my funnel by doing trial runs with my sister (or brother or mom—whoever will pick up the phone) to

# 80

make sure all emails are firing correctly. I set up ShipStation using a free trial offer. I know that sometimes they offer a free 60-day trial, so I'll definitely be on the hunt for that.

## Day 16

*Big Goal: Get my ducks in a row.*

I don't have any cash in my pocket yet, so I unsubscribe from Canva. I make changes and minor tweaks to my emails and call my vendors to get an updated inventory count. I don't want to oversell!

Okay, my ducks are now officially in a row. Here we go.

## Day 17

*Big Goal: Launch influencer #1.*

I kiss my kids as they head out the door, say a quick prayer (probably the third or fourth of the morning), and officially launch my ClickFunnels shop.

Influencer #1 launches. I bite my nails as I watch the back end. I have a free Hotjar account hooked up so I can see when and where customers get stuck or have issues.

I've left my day 100% open to address any issues that arise during the launch.

Now that I have orders coming in, I use the funds received to order the products. I also order shipping bags and boxes from Amazon so I can get orders out as soon as possible.

## Day 18

*Big Goal: Launch influencer #2.*

Place orders for the primary products and for the 3x undercover email funnel.

## Day 19

*Big Goal: Launch influencers 3+.*

Flood the day with the rest of the influencers who've agreed to promote my products.

Place orders.

## Day 20

*Big Goal: Eat ice cream.*

What have I planned for today? Celebrating with my family! Turning off everything and playing! No checking my phone or my computer. No researching, no tweaking funnels, no planning for the future. Today, my entire plan is to laugh as much as I possibly can and make a lot of memories with the most important people in my life. Ice cream may be involved. It's a very good day.

## Day 21

*Big Goal: Rest.*

I may see if there's any ice cream left in the freezer.

## Day 22

*Big Goal: Wait by the mailbox.*

Check the mailbox every 15 minutes until my products arrive. I snap a selfie (or six) in front of the post office as I begin shipping products out to my new customers. I've included a small surprise and call to action in each package to make them want to shop with me again.

## Day 23

*Big Goal: Build influencer list.*

Today's game plan? Ship out more products and prepare to contact even more influencers. I'm building out my list to keep things going strong AND rescheduling the first influencers.

## Day 24

*Big Goal: Think about funnel #2.*

Line up more influencers and start building Funnel #2. I'm keeping buyers HOT!

## Day 25

*Big Goal: Show some love.*

Today, I'm sending out an email to my customers, asking them to follow me on social media. More importantly, however, I'm going to spoil my influencers—the Rachels who have helped me get my business off the ground. I'm shipping them a thank-you gift I know they'll appreciate because I want to spoil them and work on developing terrific long-term relationships.

This gift doesn't have to be big. For influencers who've had babies, I've sent out paper plates, plastic forks, and paper towels with a note that says I'm doing their dishes for a week. When an influencer's husband was out of town and she was too tired to make dinner for her kids, I sent them a meal. Find a pain point, relieve it, and I'll have a fan for life. It's just how humans work. We like to feel spoiled and loved.

## Day 26

*Big Goal: Ship and hire.*

From here on out, I'll keep shipping out products as orders roll in and post even more on social media. By now, I may need to hire my first employee (or maybe my daughters) to ship products, and I definitely want to get that off my plate as fast as possible.

## Day 27

*Big Goal: Work on the books.*

Today, I'll start looking at additional trending products to sell and start building out additional offers. I'll schedule funnel #2 to launch in two weeks.

## Day 28

*Big Goal: Rest.*

I'm really happy today's a rest day. I need it!

## Day 29

*Big Goal: Offer giveaways.*

With the end of my first 30 days nearly in sight, I'll begin a giveaway sequence getting customers to share my social pages. It's important that I begin growing those platforms so I can use them to launch my next (and future) funnels.

## Day 30

*Big Goal: Keep it going.*

In one month, I've put the pieces in place to build a thriving online business. I continue to do what I've been doing: growing, spoiling, profiting, and smiling. Talk about a party!

I high-five my kids as they walk through the door and give my husband a hug. I have a smile on my face, and I'm ready to get started on the next 30 days—or 30 years—ahead.

# RESOURCES

- Amazon.com
- Canva (canva.com)
- Dream 100 Book by Dana Derricks
- Google Docs
- Hotjar (hotjar.com)
- Pinterest (pinterest.com)
- ShipStation (shipstation.com)

## Chapter 5

# FIND YOUR DREAM 100

## by Dana Derricks

# DANA DERRICKS

## Goat Farmer

Non-Broke Entrepreneurs
*Dream100Book.com*

*Dana, hailing as the premier expert on the Dream
100 and author of 8 books, featured on Forbes, Inc.,
ABC, and more... has personally worked with over
1,000 entrepreneurs in his career and has directly
been responsible for hundreds of millions of dollars
in revenue, while impacting millions of lives. He also
is a world famous goat farmer.*

# Day 1

## *What I WILL Have Done*

- Understood that my life isn't over, it's just beginning
- Set myself up to successfully document the ENTIRE journey (which I'll later sell)
- Gotten into the habit of recording and documenting everything I do (creating assets)

## *What I Will NOT Have Done*

- Spent ONE second feeling sorry for myself or dwelling on anything negative that's led me to this point
- Skipped ahead or not taken the few minutes to get myself set up to document the journey (I'd regret that like crazy later on)

## *Action Steps*

- I will think about the WORST thing that's ever happened to me in my life. Then I'd compare that against what I'm dealing with now. I've instantly crushed any power this situation had against me.
- I'll grab a free screencast recording program that records my screen and webcam.
- I'll set up my ClickFunnels Membership Funnel area to upload and save all my videos into for safekeeping (because I will eventually sell access to them).
- I'll go feed my goats and remember that I always have a fallback plan if this stuff doesn't work. (The price of goat milk has been steadily rising.)

# Day 2

## *What I WILL Have Done*

- Spent EVERY single second actively focused on the solution to get where I need to be
- Given myself permission to NOT be pushed around or harassed by my debtors
- Completed my "Holy crap, the world isn't actually ending" list of saleable skills

- Brainstormed and selected something I can dangle as a carrot that I'll purchase once I've successfully gotten myself out of this mess

### What I Will NOT Have Done
- Fallen into the false thinking that any amount of reading, watching videos, browsing social media, or going through courses will get me out of my situation...the ONLY way out is for me to take action like crazy
- Spoken to the people harassing me for money or anybody else that's 1) not paying my bills for me and 2) not directly going to help me get out of this situation

### Action Steps
- List out ALL the skills and knowledge I have obtained over the years that is genuinely valuable and that I could sell.
- Prioritize my list of skills and knowledge in order of most to least valuable, with prices attached to each (finding values will require basic research).
- Set up my phone, emails, and social media to NOT allow incoming messages from debtors or anybody else who may cause pressure and noise.
- Write down all the things I wish I could purchase or have if my finances were in order (e.g., house, car, vacation, something for family, etc.).
- Narrow in and select ONE item I WILL purchase once my finances are in order and put a picture of that in front of me at my workplace (e.g., specific service like creating done-for-you amazing logos, or weekly done-with-you coaching to show how to create amazing logos).

# Day 3
### What I WILL Have Done
- Selected ONE of my skills to start selling to get me some breathing room

**88**

- Built my list of "the crap that'll make me riches is my list of niches" I could be selling my skills/knowledge to
- Made a final selection on the niche market I'll be in

## What I Will NOT Have Done

- Thought I can operate my business without a cash register by NOT putting full efforts into sales and marketing
- Wasted any time or energy getting distracted by anything that's not going to put immediate money in my pocket

## Action Steps

- Create a list of 15+ niche markets that desperately need the skill/knowledge I've chosen.
- Choose ONE niche that I'll absolutely dominate.
- Plant my flag in the ground and become THE go-to expert on <SKILL I'M SELLING> for that specific niche.

# Day 4

## What I WILL Have Done

- Figured out and descriptively defined WHO my ideal, perfect avatar (customer/client) is
- Figured out and descriptively defined WHO my ideal, perfect avatar (customer/client) is NOT
- Defined my "why" and the bigger mission/purpose I'm serving
- Gotten my "free marketing is the best marketing" Attractive Character nailed down

## What I Will NOT Have Done

- Gotten lazy with or haphazardly breezed through building out my avatar, why, and Attractive Character
- Put ALL of my focus on making money or on anything material, which goes against the real reason I'm doing this

## Action Steps

- Define who my ideal, perfect avatar is (e.g., wealthy, 30–45 years old, female, married, etc.).

- Define who my ideal, perfect avatar is NOT (e.g., broke, < 30 or > 45 years old, male, not married, etc.).
- Finish the following sentence: I am helping <QUANTITY> <TITLE OF AVATAR> to <BENEFITS> by <WHAT I DO>. Here's a sample of one that's filled out: *I am helping 500 pediatric dentists to improve their patient retention, satisfaction, and overall experience by providing immensely valuable and necessary training for their staff.*
- Put that on my wall right next to my workplace.
- Brainstorm all the different parts of me that I could attach myself to that help express who I am, make me different, and allow me to stand out, and that could be used as my Attractive Character (e.g., racing, sports, goats, colors, music).
- Nail down my selection and absolutely OWN one of the options and use that as my Attractive Character. (My Attractive Character will be "everybody's favorite goat farmer.")

# Day 5

## *What I WILL Have Done*

- Perfected a script to send to past customers/clients to build a database of testimonials
- Reached out to all my past customers/clients

## *What I Will NOT Have Done*

- Forgotten to feed my goats
- Underestimated the value of social proof and testimonials, and how much easier this will make everything else we do

## *Action Steps*

- Write out a list of ALL the people I've worked with in the past and gotten results for or helped out.
- Craft a script that I'll send to all of them to get a testimonial that I'll use in my marketing moving forward.
- Deploy this script to every single person on my Dream 100 list:

*"Hey, <NAME>!*

*It's Dana. I have a small favor to ask...but it's RE-ALLY important...*

*I'm in the process of preparing to launch something super exciting and am in need of just a handful of success stories/reviews to highlight what some of my clients are experiencing.*

*You were one of the first that came to mind.*

*The testimonial doesn't have to be anything crazy, just a video shot right on your phone is perfect!*

*Just mention the following in your video:*

- *Your backstory before you met me*
- *A problem you encountered and how it made you feel, both externally and internally*
- *The epiphany you had (ideally from me or some of my materials)*
- *What you tried before that didn't work*
- *The new action(s) you took or plan to take*
- *The end results you've seen or plan to see*

*Would you do that for me?? It'd seriously brighten up my day!!*

*Thanks a million."*

# Day 6

## What I WILL Have Done

- Built my funnel (SINGULAR) that sells the service I'm offering

## What I Will NOT Have Done

- Explored 700 different types of funnels and different opportunities I could pursue
- Built three-fourths of a funnel 600 times, so I have 0 total funnels completely built and ready to launch

## Action Steps

- Log in to my ClickFunnels account > build funnel > Funnel Cookbook > model an existing funnel that fits the service I'm providing > fill in the blanks > launch it!

# Day 7
## *What I WILL Have Done*

- Built my Dream 100 list of clients I will target with my service (at LEAST 50 entries)
- Gotten as much of the data as I possibly could for each entry on my Dream 100

## *What I Will NOT Have Done*

- Built my list to fewer than 50 clients
- Gotten lazy or listened to the voice in my head saying, "They'll never work with me."

## *Action Steps*

- Brainstorm a list of all the products or services (complementary to mine) that my perfect avatar would buy either before or after my service and start searching for those products or services online. Enter them into my Dream 100 list.
- Search for LISTS of my ideal customer/client avatar on social media, Google, any association websites, memberships they're involved in, associations, certifications, etc. Enter them into my Dream 100 list.
- Fill in as much data as possible on every single entry of my Dream 100 list (e.g., phone number, mailing address, Facebook, or LinkedIn).
- Opt in to ALL their lists, get into their groups, buy their stuff (if possible), and follow them as closely as possible.

# Day 8
## *What I WILL Have Done*

- Deployed my outreach campaign for my Dream 100 list of clients who I will target with my service

### What I Will NOT Have Done

- Given up or gotten dejected if I don't hear back right away or am told no

### Action Steps

- Craft a script that I'll send to ALL my Dream 100 that I will target with my service.
- Deploy this script to my Dream 100 list. (I know based on experience that being humble doesn't work—I've tested it.)

> *"Hi, <NAME>,*
>
> *I absolutely LOVED your <SOMETHING THEY SAID OR DID>!!!*
>
> *Also, I read a little of your story and <SOMETHING PERSONAL>.*
>
> *Keep reading.*
>
> *My name is Dana, and I've <AMAZING ACHIEVEMENT #1>.*
>
> *I'm the #1 <SERVICE> in <NICHE>.*
>
> *I also <AMAZING ACHIEVEMENT #2>.*
>
> *Anyway, I'd like to open up the possibility of sharing my service (which complements and adds value to you, it most certainly does not compete directly) to your audience to make us both more money while, most importantly, adding significant value to your customers/followers by helping them <BENEFITS>.*
>
> *I hand-picked you and am typing this message from scratch directly to you because I have something that can be VERY valuable to your followers.*
>
> *I've created an incredible <OFFER> to <BENEFITS>, and am certain that this would fit perfectly with your <THEIR PRODUCT/SERVICE> and will even make it BETTER for your customers!!*
>
> *Cool, right?*
>
> *You just send some of your tribe over to me. I'll take*

*good care of them AND write you the check for the referral!*

*We change more lives together.*

*My <OFFER> sells for one payment of <AMOUNT>, and I'd be happy to share a portion of that with you. You'll walk away with nearly <PROFITS> on EACH sale, withOUT lifting a finger.*

*Last thing, I'd love to send over a complimentary <OFFER> for your review so you can see it's the real deal.*

*I am limiting the number of partnerships, though, so please don't read this and not reply immediately.*

*Got it? Awesome!!*

*Please feel free to reply directly, or you can also reach me on <CHANNEL>.*

*Thanks so much for partnering with me! So excited!"*

# Day 9

## What I WILL Have Done

- Reached back out to as many of those who I messaged yesterday as possible with a sample of my actual service, customized for them

## What I Will NOT Have Done

- Skimped out on what I deliver to them, leading them to believe my actual service is anything but world-class
- Gotten tired (I can sleep when I'm dead) or distracted (my attack goat will go crazy on me)

## Action Steps

- Create a sample of the service that I decided to sell to every single person I sent a message to yesterday on my Dream 100 list. (For example, If I'm selling email copywriting, I'll revise/rewrite some of their emails and send them the sample.)
- Send the customized sample to every person on the list with

**94**

this script:

> "<NAME>,
> It's Dana again. I'm sorry, I seriously couldn't contain my excitement in working with you (and showing you just how powerful my <SERVICE> is), so I made this <SAMPLE> just for you—see the attachment!
> Cool, huh?
> Take a peek and please shoot me a reply ASAP. I've got others I'm going to offer this to, but I will keep your spot safe for a few more days.
> Thanks for replying!"

# Day 10

## What I WILL Have Done

- Closed EVERY single lead that has replied to me so far to work with me (get my $$ situation right)
- Followed up with all the leads that didn't reply to me

## What I Will NOT Have Done

- Gotten scared to sell or close deals, because this is about cashing checks and snapping necks, not about my feelings
- Thought my follow-up was too extreme or aggressive. (I remember how obnoxiously aggressive the government was in their follow-up with me when I forgot to pay my tax bill on time or an employee filed unemployment on me.)

## Action Steps

- Send this follow-up to every single person on the list with this script:

> "Hey, <NAME>.
> It's Dana. Sorry I didn't follow up with you.
> My inbox absolutely exploded with replies to the few I sent a message to yesterday (the same exact one

*I sent to you).*

*I'm already working with three others, but still have that one spot reserved for you...*

*Can you please give me a quick reply to let me know you're seeing these messages as well as confirm you received the sample <SAMPLE> I sent over, on me?*

*I know you're busy and your time is valuable, that's why I hand-selected YOU to work with.*

*Can't wait to work with you, but I need to hear back please!*

*Thanks again."*

# Day 11

## What I WILL Have Done

- Closed EVERY single lead
- Reached back out to all those I requested a testimonial from to get them to send it to me

## What I Will NOT Have Done

- Felt like I was bothering people or that this "wasn't working" because I didn't get a 100% response rate

## Action Steps

- Reach back out to every single person on the list that I requested a testimonial from with this script:

  *<NAME>,*

  *It's Dana again. I'm sorry I didn't follow up with you, I was sifting through the testimonials I received and noticed you were one of the only names that hadn't sent me your testimonial!*

  *Please send that over—it means the world to me for you to take a few seconds to do that. (See instructions in the last email, reply if you don't see them.)*

  *I sincerely appreciate your help. I hope that this re-*

*minder is the last one I have to send in order for you to*
*send that over to me.*

*Thanks for replying with your testimonial!"*

# Day 12

## *What I WILL Have Done*

- Closed EVERY single lead
- Followed up with all the leads that didn't reply to me

## *What I Will NOT Have Done*

- Taken my foot off the gas for one second or stopped doing what was working just because it became boring or no longer "sexy"
- Allowed anybody or anything else to distract me, including shiny objects, people, debtors, the fact that my neighbor's van is on fire outside, etc.

## *Action Steps*

- Send this follow-up to every single person on the list with this script:

  *<NAME>,*

  *Sorry, I meant to follow up with you sooner...I've been swamped with leads wanting to work with me...*

  *Here's what <NAME> just said about my <SERVICE>:*
  *<TESTIMONIAL>*
  *...and here's what <NAME> said about it:*
  *<TESTIMONIAL>*
  *...and <NAME> said:*
  *<TESTIMONIAL>*

  *By now, you can probably see it's actually more costly to NOT work with me than it is to reply with a quick "Yes."*

  *Shoot me a reply with a "Yes" if you're in.*

  *I've got one spot left and it's yours, but ONLY if you're serious and reply ASAP.*

*Best-case scenario? Everything I said is true and you benefit immensely.*

*Worst-case scenario? Everything I said is false and you ask for your money back, and I give it to you AND let you keep the <SERVICE> that I give you.*

*The only way you can lose is to not respond.*

*I know you're a winner, though.*

*Can't wait for your reply and to knock this out for you!"*

# Day 13

## What I WILL Have Done

- Closed EVERY single lead
- Followed up with every single new customer/client to get more work and/or get referrals from them

## What I Will NOT Have Done

- Been afraid to go back to my customers/clients thinking they hate me, my work sucked, or that they'll demand their money back (one of the most costly mistakes any entrepreneur makes)

## Action Steps

- Send this follow-up to every single person who has worked with me:

> *"Hey, <NAME>!*
>
> *It's Dana.*
>
> *I just wanted to take a minute to first tell you how grateful I am to work with you!*
>
> *That's something I do not take for granted, trust me.*
>
> *With that being said, is there anything else you're looking for? Got another project in mind?*
>
> *If not, who do you know that could use <RESULT>?*
>
> *I'll give you $250 cash for each person you send my way that uses my service.*

*Yep, that's ME paying YOU just for sending folks my way.*

*Just simply reply with some names and emails, and I'll take it from there.*

*Thanks again for the reply! You're the best."*

# Day 14

## *What I WILL Have Done*

- Closed EVERY single lead

## *What I Will NOT Have Done*

- Taken my foot off the gas

## *Action Steps*

- Repeat steps from Days 8–13 until I've won a ClickFunnels 2 Comma Club award.
- Looking forward, get prepared to transition out of done-for-you and into more of a coaching/teaching role to get back my time. (Now I'm $$ rich, but time poor...I need to be $$ AND time rich.)

# Day 15

## *What I WILL Have Done*

- Transitioned my business from trading time for dollars into selling scalable products
- Understood that I'll always make more $$ showing people how to successfully do the thing, as opposed to actually doing the thing for them

## *What I Will NOT Have Done*

- Fully abandoned what's paying the bills or stopped/reduced the quality of fulfilling on existing customers/clients

## *Action Steps*

- Gather all the recordings of everything I've documented to this point, including building out my Dream 100 list, soliciting tes-

timonials, building my funnel, drafting outreach and follow-up scripts, etc.
- Put everything into the ClickFunnels membership site area (to be sold).

# Day 16
## What I WILL Have Done
- Built out the assets to sell my course/program

## What I Will NOT Have Done
- Gotten distracted or actively added more customers/clients into my done-for-you service, or I'll never be able to leave it

## Action Steps
- Build a sales page in ClickFunnels (using Russell's proven template) where I'll sell access to my course/program.
- Shoot a video pitching my course/program > toss it onto my sales page.
- Get payment processing and everything taken care of inside ClickFunnels account to start taking in passive $$.

# Day 17
## What I WILL Have Done
- Created the best asset for selling that my business will ever have
- Understood that selling the thing itself is hard, selling the thing that sells the thing is easy, so I'm going to create my "thing that sells the thing" (TST)

## What I Will NOT Have Done
- Anything but spent full time and attention on building this asset
- Built more than one of the items below...ONLY BUILD ONE, then test

## Action Steps
- Build out one of the following, depending on how my audience

**100**

consumes information (my TST).
- Audio book
- Book (using Dana's template)
- Mini webinar
- Perfect Webinar (using Russell's template)
- Video series

# Day 18

## *What I WILL Have Done*

- Gotten my "thing that sells the thing" into the hands of every single human being possible

## *What I Will NOT Have Done*

- Been shy about who can see and consume my TST

## *Action Steps*

- Hit up every single human being in my network who is a potential lead (including existing customers/clients) to invite them to consume my TST.

> *"Hey, <NAME>!*
>
> *It's Dana.*
>
> *I'm SUPERRRRRRRRRRRR excited to share something with you...*
>
> *I've been working on a top-secret project and I JUST finished it.*
>
> *YOU are the first person that came to mind to get a sneak peek at it...*
>
> *Can I send you one of the first copies of my <TST>, on me??*
>
> *You're seriously one of the only people in the world to get your hands on it...*
>
> *Just simply reply with a yes and I'll zip it over to you...but please do NOT share this, k?*
>
> *You're going to absolutely LOOOOVE this!"*

# Day 19

## *What I WILL Have Done*

- Figured out and descriptively defined WHO my ideal, perfect avatar (customer/client) is for my NEW course/program
- Figured out and descriptively defined WHO my ideal, perfect avatar (customer/client) is NOT for my NEW course/program
- Defined my "why" and the bigger mission/purpose I'm serving

## *What I Will NOT Have Done*

- Gotten lazy with or haphazardly breezed through building out my avatar, why, and Attractive Character
- Failed to trust the same exact process that put $$ in our pocket to do it again

# Day 20

## *What I WILL Have Done*

- Built my Dream 100 list of potential affiliates I will target to promote my NEW course/program (at LEAST 100 entries)
- Gotten as much of the data as I possibly could for each entry on my Dream 100

## *What I Will NOT Have Done*

- Built my list to fewer than 100
- Gotten lazy or listened to the voice in my head saying that "They'll never promote my stuff."

## *Action Steps*

- Brainstorm a list of all the products or services (complementary to mine) that my perfect avatar would buy either before or after my course/program...and start searching for those products or services online. Enter them into my Dream 100 list.
- Search for LISTS of my ideal customer/client avatar on social media, Google, any association websites, memberships, associations, certifications, etc. Enter them into my Dream 100 list.
- Fill in as much data as possible on every single entry of my

Dream 100 list (e.g., phone number, mailing address, Facebook or LinkedIn links, etc.)

- Opt in to ALL their lists, get into their groups, buy their stuff (if possible), and follow them as closely as possible.

# Day 21

## What I WILL Have Done

- Continued to deploy my outreach campaign for my Dream 100 list of clients
- Fully understood that I need to stick with this and it'll pay major, major dividends...but won't be the most enjoyable task I've ever done

## What I Will NOT Have Done

- Given up or gotten dejected

## Action Steps

- Craft a script that I'll send to ALL my Dream 100 who I will target with my service.
- Set up my affiliate program in just minutes in Backpack (part of ClickFunnels full suite).
- Deploy this script to my Dream 100 list.

> *"Hi, <NAME>,*
> *I absolutely LOVED your <SOMETHING THEY SAID OR DID>!!!*
> *Also, I read a little of your story and <SOMETHING PERSONABLE>.*
> *Keep reading.*
> *My name is Dana and I've <AMAZING ACHIEVEMENT #1>.*
> *I'm the #1 <SERVICE> in <NICHE>.*
> *I also <AMAZING ACHIEVEMENT #2>.*
> *Anyway, I'd like to open up the possibility of sharing my course/program (which complements and*

*adds value to you, it most certainly does not compete directly) to your audience to make us both more money while, most importantly, adding significant value to your customers/followers by helping them <BENEFITS>.*

*I hand-picked you and am typing this message from scratch directly to you because I have something that can be VERY valuable to your followers.*

*I've created an incredible <OFFER> to <BENEFITS> and am certain that this would fit perfectly with your <THEIR PRODUCT/SERVICE> and will even make it BETTER for your customers!!*

*Cool, right?*

*You just send some of your tribe over to me, I'll take good care of them AND write you the check for the referral!*

*We change more lives together.*

*My <OFFER> sells for one payment of $<AMOUNT>, and I'd be happy to share a portion of that with you. You'll walk away with nearly $<AMOUNT> on EACH sale, WITHOUT lifting a finger.*

*Last thing, I'd love to send over a complimentary <OFFER> for your review so you can see it's the real deal.*

*I am limiting the number of partnerships, though, so please don't read this and not reply immediately.*

*Got it? Awesome!!*

*Please feel free to reply directly, or you can also reach me on <CHANNEL>.*

*Thanks so much for partnering with me! So excited!"*

# Day 22
## What I WILL Have Done
- Closed EVERY single lead

### What I Will NOT Have Done

- Gotten scared to sell the promotion or close deals because they're people just like me, so no need to be nervous

### Action Steps

- Send this follow-up to every single person on the list with this script:

> "Hey, <NAME>...
> It's Dana. Sorry I didn't follow up with you.
> My inbox went crazy with replies to the few who I sent a message to yesterday (the same exact one I sent to you).
> I'm already working with three others, but still have that one spot reserved for you to get this in the hand of your audience...so they can <BENEFITS>, too!
> Can you please give me a quick reply to let me know you're seeing these messages as well as confirm you received the offer of having a copy of <COURSE/PROGRAM> I sent over, on me?
> I know you're busy and your time is valuable, that's why I hand-selected YOU to work with.
> Can't wait to work with you and get this in your audience's hands, but I need to hear back please!
> Thanks again."

## Day 23

### What I WILL Have Done

- Closed EVERY single lead

### What I Will NOT Have Done

- Allowed anybody or anything else to distract me, including the fact that what I'm doing is ACTUALLY WORKING and it feels kind of weird

## Action Steps
- Send this follow-up to every single person on the list with the testimonial script I used before.

# Day 24
### What I WILL Have Done
- Closed EVERY single lead
- Created my course/program to deliver to those who purchased it (Yep, I sold it before I made it...like the gangster I am.)

### What I Will NOT Have Done
- Gotten caught up in analysis paralysis or any other BS that stops me from getting this done, because done is the new perfect

### Action Steps
- Organize every single recording I've created to this point that helped me successfully run my service into the ClickFunnels membership program area.
- Add in every single asset I used to build my service, including the scripts, Dream 100 build-out, tutorial videos, etc. (I won't short-change this, but give them EVERYTHING they need to be successful.)
- Go through the entire course/program and jot down notes where somebody might get stuck or have questions, and then stop and answer those questions and give them anything else they may be missing.
- Stop and ask myself if I'm proud of what I've just created...AND tell myself I have full conviction that this will give my buyers results. If I can't say 100% yes to both, I will go back in and make it better.
- Launch and deliver my course/program to my buyers!

# Day 25
### What I WILL Have Done
- Closed EVERY single lead

### What I Will NOT Have Done
- Taken my foot off the gas (Yep, it's worth repeating one last time.)

### Action Steps
- Repeat steps from Days 21, 22, and 23.
- Looking forward, prepare to transition out of working "in" my business (and being such a critical piece for its operation) to working "on" my business to get back my time and allow for maximum growth (and get one of those nice ClickFunnels 8 Figure Club awards).

## Day 26
### What I WILL Have Done
- Given myself permission to NOT have to do every single thing in my business and been okay with delegating tasks to my team members; even if they don't get them done quite as well as I do, it's getting done
- Added the most critical member of my team to immediately help me offload
- Recognized which tasks I should and should not be doing on a daily basis
- Visualized what working ON my business will enable me to do as opposed to working IN my business

### What I Will NOT Have Done
- Gotten caught up in anything that's distracting; I am laser-focused on growth

### Action Steps
- Write out a list of ALL the tasks I'm doing in my business, and then segment the list in order of priority (1's being absolutely critical for my business to continue to operate, 2's being medium importance, 3's being less important).
- Throw up ads for an assistant to delegate tasks to.
- Interview and go with the candidate who fits the personality pro-

file of a rockstar assistant.

- Allow assistant to start taking noncritical tasks (3's and 2's) off my plate and provide them with support to do their job very well.

## Day 27
### What I WILL Have Done
- Added the next most critical member of my team to immediately help with revenue growth

### What I Will NOT Have Done
- Thought or expected that a salesperson could/will outperform me, because they're not me

### Action Steps
- Put ALL the templates I've used and recordings of me actually selling and closing deals into a nice neat place where my salesperson can access them for training.
- Throw up ads for a commission-only salesperson to continue revenue growth.
- Interview and go with the candidate who fits the personality profile of a rockstar salesperson.
- Allow salesperson to start going after leads and closing deals and provide them with support to do their job very well.

## Day 28
### What I WILL Have Done
- Added the next most critical member of my team to immediately help with revenue growth

### What I Will NOT Have Done
- Thought or expected that an affiliate manager could/will outperform me, because they're not me

### Action Steps
- Put ALL the templates I've used and recordings of me actually

closing Dream 100 joint ventures in a nice neat place where my affiliate manager can access them for training.

- Throw up ads for a base-plus-commission affiliate manager to explode revenue growth.
- Interview and go with the candidate who fits the personality profile of a rockstar affiliate manager.
- Allow affiliate manager to start going after leads and closing deals and provide them with support to do their job very well.

# Day 29

## What I WILL Have Done

- Added the next most critical member of my team to immediately help with business growth and sustainability

## What I Will NOT Have Done

- Thought or expected that an operator could/will outperform me, because they're not me

## Action Steps

- Put ALL the systems and recordings of me actually running my business in a nice neat place where my operator can access them for training.
- Throw up ads for an operator to ensure business growth and sustainability.
- Interview and go with the candidate who fits the personality profile of a rockstar operator.
- Allow operator to start taking care of the day-to-day tasks of the business and overseeing employees and provide them with support to do their job very well.

# Day 30

## What I WILL Have Done

- Reflected and shown gratitude for where I am, where I came from, and where I'm going.

### What I Will NOT Have Done
- Gotten complacent or taken my foot off the gas. This day is to be used as motivation to KEEP moving forward and accomplishing the mission I set out on Day 4.

### Action Steps
- Reflect on the journey that led me to the beginning of this, the past 30 days, and what the future will hold for me.
- Show gratitude to these people:
  - Every single customer/client who helped me get out of the hole that I found myself in
  - Every single member of my team who has taken me beyond where I imagined possible
  - Russell, for creating one of the most powerful software platforms in history, which inspires millions to achieve their dreams every single day

# FINAL THOUGHTS

You've got the roadmap, now use it.

You CAN and WILL succeed, as long as you buckle down and do every single thing I told you to. Success is the ONLY result.

Enjoy.

# RESOURCES

- ClickFunnels

Chapter 6

# START AS A SERVICE PROVIDER

*by Julie Stoian*

# JULIE STOIAN

## 2CCX Coach, Funnel Builder, and Digital Marketing Strategist

Internet Marketing
*TheDigitalGangsta.com*

*Julie Stoian is a digital marketing consultant and marketing coach, making her mark on the internet through her popular brand Create Your Laptop Life™. Julie has inspired and equipped thousands of up and coming business owners with the skills and strategies they need to create, build, and grow profitable online businesses.*

*Julie started her journey to entrepreneurship as a blogger and writer, garnering the attention of me-*

*dia outlets like The New York Times and Washington Post with her no-holds-barred approach to social media. After a rocky divorce and unexpected pregnancy in 2014 that left her needing to build a profitable business quickly, Julie transformed her passion and love for internet marketing into the 7-figure business she has today.*

*In addition to her business, she is also a head coach and funnel builder working with Russell Brunson and ClickFunnels.*

*Julie has been featured on media outlets like Anderson LIVE, BBC World Have Your Say, and Rachel Ray, as well as numerous business and marketing podcasts and blogs such as Content Academy, Boss Moms, GoDaddy Garage Blog, and Funnelhacker Radio.*

## Day 1

Day 1 of my internet business apocalypse would certainly be a nerve-wracking day.

With just a ClickFunnels account and no following, friends, clients, or other social proof, I know that the FASTEST way to getting back on my feet is to find the right customer who will advertise for me (through word-of-mouth referrals). I also know that in the online space, the fastest route to cash is through a tangible deliverable. Since I'm not an e-commerce expert and the margins are slimmer (not to mention I need money for inventory), I will go my favorite route—offering done-for-you services.

On Day 1, I only have one goal: figure out who I will serve and what result I will get them. For me, the result is easy. I will build them a marketing funnel to help them get leads and sales. The question that takes me a bit longer to answer is "Who will I serve?"

I sit down with a sheet of paper and write down all the dream clients I would love to work with and look for the common themes among them. Are they coaches, course creators, influencers, men, women, entrepreneurs, start-ups, established? Once I have that list sorted, I have my who and my result.

Everything builds off of there.

## Day 2

Today is a fun day. It's the day I get to figure out my business assets. I'm going to keep it super simple and "Oprah-fy" my business by simply using my name. I decide on Julie Stoian Media, LLC, and I set up my business entity, buy the domain (inside of ClickFunnels), and then use Photoshop to create a quick logo and brand board.

## Day 3

On Day 3, my main objective is to get a basic website up. I know I will be using funnels mainly for my business, but since people still think of a website as a sign of online legitimacy, I use ClickFunnels to create a basic site.

I set up a home page, about page, contact page, and services page. The services page will double as the entry point into my funnel.

I write up some copy and use my logo and brand board to create a simple, clean design.

Since photos are important as well, I ask my husband to take a few photos with my phone at dusk, and I spruce them up in Photoshop and use them in my design, so I appear as personable and approachable as possible.

## Day 4

When it comes to social media and a service-based business, the platform I will focus on for leads is Facebook. But I will also secure social channel usernames for Twitter, YouTube, LinkedIn, Instagram,

**114**

and Pinterest.

Once I have those, I will get to work adding my details, branding, and photos to them all.

Lastly, I will set up a simple G Suite account to create a professional email address (julie@juliestoian.com) so I can send marketing emails when the time comes.

## Day 5

Even though LinkedIn isn't my primary real estate online, as an agency looking for businesses to hire me, I will need a properly optimized LinkedIn profile. When people look to see if you're "legit," one of the key searches they do is for a LinkedIn profile. I want to be ready!

So on this day, I spend time filling out my work history, finding and requesting connections, and publishing one or two long-form cornerstone pieces of content that show off my funnel knowledge on the native LinkedIn platform.

## Day 6

Today is a big day, since I will be setting up my first funnel. It's a business-intensive funnel, and it will be the primary way I create custom proposals for my clients.

The funnel starts on the services page. I write a long-form services page that is a hybrid of direct-response copy as well as a bit of bragging about what I can do. The whole goal is to get them to click the Book Strategy Call button.

That goes directly to my scheduler (I use Acuity) where I'll ask a few questions before allowing them to book a call.

Next, I'll set up the back end of the funnel. I know that I will be selling $1,000 business intensives on these calls, so I create an order form and order confirmation form that I can use to collect payment.

On the order confirmation form, I set up another schedule type with Acuity, which is the place to book the two-hour intensive call. I create a much longer and more in-depth questionnaire so I can do research on the potential client before the call.

Lastly, I go into my email and set up some custom email replies specifically for after the discovery call (if they don't book in the intensive). I save them as canned responses, so I can send them quickly when people aren't sure if they want to sign up for the intensive with me.

## Day 7

With my social, web, and funnel presence all set up exactly one week after I start, I will be ready for my first free traffic activity. Using Facebook, I will deploy an "attraction" marketing strategy that has me entering Facebook Groups full of my ideal clients and responding to questions in a way that is so helpful or controversial that they can't help but reach out to me on Facebook.

I set up a spreadsheet to monitor the groups, to capture the comments I make, and to follow up with leads who reach out via private message (PM).

By the end of the day, I expect to have two or three discovery calls booked in for the next day.

## Day 8

Today is the day I get money for the first time since I started! I aim to close at least one of the three discovery calls I have, and that means $1,000 in hand for a business intensive.

It's important to get money in hand as fast as possible, not just for the sake of income, but also because of the mental pressure it relieves. This is why I recommend people start service-based businesses at first, because that money comes so quickly. Imagine how many books or low-cost physical products you'd have to sell to get $1,000 in profit?

Now that I have an intensive, the rest of the day is spent repeating what I did yesterday (prospecting in groups) and monitoring my key performance indicators so I have more discovery calls booked.

I'm also going to buy DotComSecrets and Expert Secrets and study up on my funnel skills before the upcoming intensive.

## Day 9

Phase two of my plan begins next. The business intensive is only the first part of my service offering. Once I complete the two-hour intensive, I will be sending a report to the customer along with a high-ticket, done-for-you (DFY) custom proposal.

I know that these can take time, so today I will set up my report templates. That way, I have the hard work done. This means creating a pricing sheet and a "How I Work" document, plus a slide template to build out the funnel while we're on the call.

From this day forward (and every day), I will repeat what I did on Day 7 so there is always a steady supply of new leads and discovery calls. It takes me about one and a half hours a day, but until I have enough money for ads (or enough client referrals), I will consider this activity my #1 priority...always.

## Day 10

By this day, I should have completed my first intensive and hopefully have my first high-ticket proposal out to bid. I might even have more intensives based on my discovery calls (booked by prospecting in FB Groups). Depending on how much time I spend on the phone or in groups, I may have another two or three intensives booked (another $2K–$3K).

And if I've had at least one intensive and high-ticket proposal sent out (for $10,000 or more), I might even have a deposit and contract in hand for $2,500 or more.

With a steady influx of cash, I'm ready to set up my first visibility campaign with Facebook Live and Facebook Ads.

I sit down and map out at least 10 topics I can talk about for 5 minutes. I focus on curiosity and value.

Then I go on my business page and do my very first Facebook Live.

After it's over, I log in to the Ads Manager and run a $20 boost to interests that have my ideal client.

## Day 11

As an agency, I need as much passive income as I can get, since a lot of my work is so time-heavy. I want to get affiliate commission on the software services I recommend. Today's task is simply to set up myself on as many affiliate programs as I can, so when I start working with clients, I get the recurring residual revenue. ClickFunnels has one of the most lucrative affiliate programs out there, so I begin there.

I might also sign up for additional affiliate programs like these:

- Active Campaign
- Acuity
- AWeber
- ConvertKit
- Host providers
- Teachable

# Day 12

Since I am a funnel-builder mini-agency, as I'm nearing the two-week mark, I know that I have an increasingly full schedule. I am actively managing...

- Attraction marketing on Facebook (5–7 hours a week)
- Discovery calls to close intensives (2–3 hours a week)
- Intensive meetings (2–6 hours a week)
- Fulfillment on DFY client work (15 hours a week)
- Business building for myself (8–9 hours a week)

This means I have a full-time schedule—and I'm on Day 12. Tell me, what other business model can you do this with?

Today's task is really about getting organized. I need to time block my calendar so I'm getting all of these things done throughout the week, because they are all important ingredients to make the machine run.

My plan is to save Fridays for business building. I do nothing else but focus on the processes I need to grow.

Monday through Thursday, I allot my mornings for intensives and done-for-you work, and I use the afternoons for prospecting and discovery calls. I do this so I'm sure to save my best brain power for the hardest work first.

# Day 13

On Day 13, I'm ready to start some more varied marketing. I go to ManyChat and set up my first Messenger bot. I am going to attach the bot to my first Facebook Live, as well as all Lives going forward. (My plan is to do one at least three times a week from my idea sheet I did on Day 10.)

I plan to create a simple bot sequence that gives the viewers who comment something that's valuable and free. In order to do this, I need to create that "something free," so I will look at all the possible pain points I can solve and create a tool, report, or download to offer.

Now that I have my something free, I'm going to go into ClickFunnels and create a simple lead-generation funnel to advertise that freebie. I'll set up an opt-in page with a headline and email fields, and then a thank-you page with a video that invites them to check out my services.

With that funnel built, I'll put the link in ManyChat, and now my bot is ready for my first aggressive paid campaign.

# Day 14

Today, I take my best three Facebook Lives and turn them into a Facebook Ad campaign. I use the objective engagement, so that I can get people to comment on the Lives and receive the bot notification with the freebie.

Once I've finished setting it up for the first time, I will screen-record myself setting it all up as well as write the directions in a Google Doc. This way when it's time to hire my first VA, I have the standard operating procedure all done, and all I have to do is go live with the topics. Then everything else is taken care of.

# Day 15

For the next two weeks, I am only going to add a few new things to my plate, since the system I've set up is going to require most of my time.

However, I do realize that not all clients are created equal. I can do the same amount of work for two clients, but the return on investment on one is infinitely better if they have a large network or a lot of influence, or if they work with a lot of my ideal clients. So I will go back to that list of people I created on Day 1 and begin a strategic infiltration of their world through Russell's Dream 100 strategy.

It requires me to join their groups, buy their products, and send snail mail to them in hopes that I can develop a relationship.

I'll find the top 10 on that list and sign up to their lists and all their free (and maybe paid) products as well.

## Day 16

Continuing on yesterday's task, there's a lot involved with getting on someone's radar. Part of this includes tracking down their shipping info to send them a gift. I don't want it to look like a bribe, but I do want it to get their attention (and not be just a letter). One of the ways to find something they like is to see what they pin on Pinterest or whether they have any public and searchable Amazon wish lists.

Once I have some ideas, I'll package up the gifts and send them out.

## Day 17

In anticipation of some happy clients, today I will set up the way I get feedback, testimonials, and case studies. The goal is to make it as easy as possible for a client to give positive feedback. Rather than just asking for a testimonial, I'll set up an email or a form with a few pointed questions that can be compiled into a testimonial.

Another way to get feedback is by asking them if they are up for an interview. Since I don't have a podcast, I will do the interview via Facebook Live and be sure to promote their business during the interview. It'll serve as a great case study later.

## Day 18

If I've been keeping up with all my activities, one of the things that should be happening is I should be collecting leads from my bots/Lives. I might also be getting people going to my website and filling out the form for the discovery call. It's probably time to start emailing them!

Today, I'll set up a nurture email sequence of five emails where I give my origin story, explain my expertise, showcase any proof or testimonials, and then invite them to a call with a strong call to action.

I'll set it up right in Actionetics on ClickFunnels, so that anyone who opts in automatically gets this sequence.

## Day 19

Today, I'm going to set up Trello for my client projects. Nearly three weeks in, I should have some client work now, which means I need an onboarding process. As I build out my agency, how will I track tasks? Due dates? Other people?

I'm going to follow James P. Friel's Trello system and set up a board for each of my clients. Inside the board will be lists with the following titles:

- Not Started
- In Progress
- For Review
- Completed
- On Hold
- Important Info

Each task in the project will be a card. Some of the cards will have microtask checklists. This way, I can keep track of all projects that are rolling in.

## Day 20

One of the easiest ways to get new clients in an agency is with a referral network. There are two primary sources of referrals: colleagues and clients.

In order to incentivize people to drop my name, I first need to give my clients some bonus or perk for referring me. Maybe it's extra services or a finder's fee. For this program, I'm going to create a nicely designed PDF doc then email my existing clients and explain that if they refer me, they will get some sort of bonus or finder's fee.

Next, I will aim to join between 5 and 20 other freelance and agency Facebook Groups, networks, or masterminds. I know if I start to get to know complementary service providers, I can extend the referral network program to them, offer to white-label my services, and more.

## Day 21

I've got one more week officially to turn this into a full-time job that replaces my lost income. As a recap, here are the things I'm doing regularly in my business:

- Attraction marketing on Facebook
- Discovery calls to close intensives
- Intensive meetings
- Fulfilling DFY client work from high-ticket proposals
- Courting my Dream 100
- Regularly asking for testimonials and referrals
- Connecting with other freelancers and agency owners
- Doing regular FB Lives (and boosting them)

At this point, the next two big tasks on my radar are to start hiring a team and to create another lead-generation funnel that I can run ads to. Today, I'll focus on the team building.

My goal is to get as much off my plate as quickly as possible, so I can spend my time building relationships and making sales. So I will draw a "dream" org chart for my agency then figure out where the pain is the worst and hire there first.

I'll write up job descriptions for each role so they are ready to go.

## Day 22

As my visibility grows, I want to make sure I'm known for something. Even if I have a full-service agency, there's usually one primary reason people come to see me. I am going to pick that one thing and design a service-provider webinar or demonstration that I can do live each week to establish myself.

I will show off my Facebook Ad knowledge, because most people

**122**

who want ads also need funnel help.

Today, I'll set up a registration page and thank-you page for my webinar/demo and send an email out to my contact list inviting them to attend. I'll build as much curiosity in the email and the registration page as possible and hint at the fact that for people who attend there will be a special offer that I don't normally sell.

## Day 23

Now that the webinar funnel is up and running, I'll start some Facebook Ads. My goal is to target the people who've been watching my Lives (a custom audience). I'll upload my email list if it's large enough, and I will also do interest targeting based on Facebook pages.

I'll run a video registration ad for the next few days to see how many sign-ups I can get.

## Day 24

To prepare for the webinar, I need to make an incredibly juicy and irresistible offer. Since I do done-for-you services, I have scarcity built right in, because my time is limited. I want to create an offer that's easy enough to do an upsell with (like ads and funnels).

To create the offer, I'll make the stack slide on Google Slides and then push people to a simple Wufoo or Google Form to claim their spot for this special deal. It's in my best interest to get these people on the phone, so I can easily upsell them to more services on the call.

## Day 25

Since there are a few more days till the webinar, I'll go back to the org chart I created on Day 21, go into my network groups, and place a job listing. At this point, I should have enough cash flow from intensives, done-for-you work, and affiliate commissions to easily be making $5K–$10K a month.

Based on my budget, I can afford maybe $2,000 a month in extra help, so I'll look for a virtual assistant or funnel builder who can reduce the tasks I'm doing day-to-day that are below my pay grade.

# Day 26

Since I used to be an SEO (search engine optimization) person, I know that optimizing my business for search engines is still a good idea, even though I'm not a hardcore blogger. On this day, I'll set up a basic WordPress blog on a subdomain and style it so it matches my site.

The goal is to put at least three pieces of long-form SEO-optimized content that will help people find me when they are searching online.

Going forward, I will begin blogging approximately once a week. One of the easiest ways to do this is to simply repurpose my Facebook Lives into keyword-optimized blog posts.

I can also make simple YouTube tutorials and turn those into blog posts as well.

# Day 27

The Dream 100 strategy that began on Day 16 needs some follow-up. Today, I'll follow up with any leads or conversations with my Dream 100 after receiving my packages. If I want to work with an influencer's audience, I'll come up with a special offer that is ONLY for their tribe and give a kickback referral fee to the influencer.

If I want to work with the influencer directly, I'll pitch a sample project idea that doesn't interfere with what they're currently working on. I'll offer to do it for free and show them how I can create a new revenue stream out of thin air without them having to do any of the work.

# Day 28

Today's the day of the service-provider webinar. My plan is to show off just how much I know and to ignite their imagination about what's possible if they work with me. Since I'm not selling knowledge but time, I can be more liberal in my demonstration. At the end of the webinar, I will pitch my special offer and give people 48 hours to reserve a spot through my form.

Once the webinar is finished, I'll send out a replay to my list and non-attendees and remind them of the special offer as well.

# Day 29

I'm nearing the end of my 30 days and feeling quite proud that I've created a full-time income in less than a month. I figure it might make a good story, so I create a pitch and go looking on major media sites and podcasts to see if anyone is interested in it.

The goal is to seed the idea for a course or book down the road on "How To Create A Five-Figure Funnel-Building Agency In The Next 30 Days."

# Day 30

Not gonna lie, this 30-day blueprint is exhausting and grinding. Today, I rest. I look back at all the things I've set in motion—the momentum—and hopefully the fat stacks of cash I have started to accumulate.

From here, I'll continue to grow my agency, leverage the relationships I've built, and work to position myself as an influencer and expert in fast-growing agency models.

# RESOURCES

- Active Campaign (ontraport.com)
- Actionetics (clickfunnels.com/ actionetics)
- Acuity (acuityscheduling.com)
- AWeber (aweber.com)
- ConvertKit (convertkit.com)
- DotComSecrets by Russell Brunson
- Expert Secrets by Russell Brunson
- Facebook Ads Manager
- Facebook Live
- Google Docs
- Google Forms
- Google Slides
- G Suite (gsuite.

google.com)

- ManyChat (manychat.com)
- Messenger bots
- Photoshop (photoshop.com)
- Teachable (teachable.com)
- Trello (trello.com)
- WordPress (wordpress.org)
- Wufoo (wufoo.com)

# Chapter 7

# MID-RANGE INFO-PRODUCT LAUNCH

*by Stephen Larsen*

# STEPHEN LARSEN

## *Funnel Builder*

Funnel Building / MLM
*SteveJLarsen.com*

*For two years, Steve Larsen was the Lead Funnel Builder at ClickFunnels for Russell Brunson, and put over 500 under his belt (but honestly, lost track a year ago). His podcast, Sales Funnel Radio, was created to share best practices, teach the finer points of marketing and "funnelology", and frankly just lets him nerd out as long as others keep listening. Long walks on the beach aren't his thing, but he loves slappin' five.*

# How I'd Restart In 30 Days If I Lost Everything

Because my situation is so dire in this example, it's also extremely followable and talkable. I'm going to use that to my advantage. Rather than keep my current state quiet, I'd get loud about it. Anything I do from this moment on will be documented in detail over a daily podcast, plus Instagram and a new Facebook Group, for others to follow. Each day will have both a business-building aspect and a publishing aspect. I can start one with a free RSS (rich site summary) feed into iTunes at Auphonic.

I'd go directly into selling mid-priced info products to those seeking wealth. I like how simple the pitch is and how it more easily lets me sell to those who have money.

## Day 1

This first day would be a lot of research. Before doing anything else, I'd go look at the top "make money" podcasts and list out the biggest and most frequent publishers. I wanna know what products podcasters have been talking about and promoting recently.

I also wanna see what products these podcasters are using their ad money to promote. I'd type those product names from the podcasters into Google, YouTube, and Facebook, and click on the ads that show up. The keywords "how to make money" are obviously a huge red ocean. I wanna see what others are buying and what communities already exist.

Day 1 is successful when I've found several info products about making money that are also being talked about by influential podcasters, have ad money behind them, and have active internet communities.

Tomorrow, I start podcasting.

## Day 2

Beyond selling a cool product, I need to sell a cool idea.

Today, I'd look for the biggest complaints on the existing info products I found. I wanna find the ideas that sold the product and look for a big one I don't agree with at all, almost on a moral level. This idea will let me throw rocks at the red ocean and not a person. People can rally with that, regardless of the product.

Then, I'd write and create a podcast intro and outro that include my rally for the red ocean to change. My intro would briefly tell everyone my personal intense situation and that they should follow to watch my next moves, and then I take steps away from the red ocean. My outro would invite them to my free Facebook Group.

In Today's Episode: The first four episodes are just the story portion of a webinar but dripped out over four episodes. So today I'd publish my origin story.

## Day 3

My morning would be spent listing the A-, B-, and C-level influencers and podcasters in the red ocean. I'd reach out for video interviews that would be turned into podcasts. I'd try to get at least seven.

In Today's Episode: Before publishing, I'd read forums and Facebook Groups in the red ocean. I wanna find another main belief they have about what it takes to be successful that I don't agree with. I'd use the Epiphany Bridge Script to write, record, and publish a story to break and rebuild that major false belief.

## Day 4

Today, I'd interview three red-ocean experts on video. (It's fine if they're C-level influencers.) The prompts would be: "What are the three biggest pitfalls a new person needs to watch out for in order to get wealth?" and "What's the single greatest thing a new person could do to speed up their success toward wealth?"

These would be combined to use as my podcast freebie download.

In Today's Episode: I'd use the Epiphany Bridge Script to write, record, and publish a story to break and rebuild their second major false belief in the red ocean.

## Day 5

Today I'd reteach, in three videos, what I learned from yesterday's interviews. I'll use these later. I'd make a fourth video as a call to action (CTA) to join me on a free webclass, using the Who, What, Why, How Script. These videos will be used later.

In Today's Episode: I'd use the Epiphany Bridge Script to write, record, and publish a story to break and rebuild their third major false belief.

## Day 6

Today's task is to create a publishing funnel by using one of the free opt-in templates on ClickFunnels. When visitors opt in on the first page, they get the videos of the three expert interviews I did. It'd be called "The Hidden Pitfalls Of Wealth Creation." Now I can start list building.

The next three days, they'll get three more videos from me, reteaching in more depth what I learned from the experts. The fourth video will invite them to my free webclass (but the page isn't built yet).

In Today's Episode: My episode would thank everyone for listening and invite them to get my free course on avoiding hidden pitfalls. I'd be sure to make a specific outro for this to push them to the funnel.

## Day 7

I'd rest and reflect today. Smile. Serve. Meditate. Envision my goal as if it had already happened.

## Day 8

Today is about more data. I'd spend the day asking forums and internet communities what they're struggling with on their journey to wealth. The goal is to just get clearer on where people aren't being served.

I use the last half of the day asking gurus and sellers, "How challenging is it to do what you do? Why?" I doubt many will answer, but the ones who do will give me an idea of where other sellers fail in their fulfillment. I'll use this later in my sales message and offer, and this information will also let me know what testimonials I should find.

In Today's Episode: I'd share several stories of rags to riches, including my own and how I lost it all. The CTA for this episode is all about asking people what they're fed up with in their pursuit of wealth. I'd send them to a Google Form to collect their answers.

## Day 9

Today, I wanna get to know a few more of the aggressive, critical, and more loud-mouthed consumers in the red ocean.

Looking through Facebook Groups and red-ocean-product communities, I wanna find a few people I can get to know and see if I can help them. My aim is to give them value and eventually results—for free, if I have to. I'll ask them to jump on a call with me. If that doesn't work, I'll keep asking more. I only need a few.

In Today's Episode: I'll interview a red-ocean influencer about common pitfalls and ask them to share the interview with their audience.

## Day 10

Today will be all about getting results for consumers in the red ocean. It's highly likely I won't have the expertise they require. I'm looking for something I can latch on to or outsource in order to get results for the red ocean. As I try to help people one-on-one, I'll document the process that helps most. If a pattern appears, it'll become a checklist for the future product.

From this, I know where my new course can be prolific. I'll try to do it with at least 10 people. My goal is to find a "purple ocean" that isn't too blue with risk or red with saturated competition. These one-on-one interview sessions are critical in finding red-ocean voids.

In Today's Episode: I'll publish a few interviews with those who I was successfully able to help.

## Day 11

It's time to start building pressure for the launch. Today, I'll put together a waiting list page for people to opt in for the future product's early-bird access and pricing. The page will list benefits and outcomes, since I only have a rough draft of the actual offer at this point. The page will have testimonials of the people I've been able to help in person, on a forum/community, or other.

In Today's Episode: I'll tell backstories of red-ocean consumers I've met. There will be a new outro pushing people to the waiting list page.

## Day 12

I want to start creating more relationships with existing red-ocean communities and their gurus, for future joint venture (JV) opportunities. Today, I'll Facebook Live into several communities and do nothing but help and teach based on what I've learned. It'll be some of my best stuff. I'll refer those who reach out to me to my podcast freebie to get them indoctrinated.

In Today's Episode: Interview with a red-ocean guru, preferably from the Facebook communities I just added value to.

## Day 13

Revisit my rough draft of the offer and make adjustments to the plan based on red-ocean community needs. Then I'd go back to another community, answer more questions, and do more Facebook Lives, simply teaching. I'm trying to get known as a value adder.

In Today's Episode: Interview with a red-ocean guru, preferably from the Facebook communities I just added value to.

## Day 14

I'd rest and reflect today. Smile. Serve. Meditate. Envision my goal as if it had already happened.

## Day 15

Today, I'd write my headlines and promise for my webinar. Then I'd go back to another community, answer more questions, and do more Facebook Lives, simply teaching. Again, I'm trying to get known as a value adder.

The other thing I want to do today is list out all the most common price points people are used to seeing and paying. Now I can charge just a little more and be seen as a premium course.

In Today's Episode: Interview with a red-ocean guru, preferably from the Facebook communities I just added value to.

# Day 16

Time to start preparing for the webinar itself. I'd build just my webinar registration process today. Because I have no cash in this scenario, I'd just go live on YouTube at the time of the webinar and embed the live feed on a ClickFunnels page that they can watch.

I can use the app tawk.to (or similar) for live chat with those watching. I'll also build a registration page and thank-you page and add people to a list. I'd return to all the places I've been adding value—plus my own list from my podcast opt-ins, Facebook Group, and Instagram—and begin promoting my free webclass.

In Today's Episode: Talk about the exciting new webclass that's coming up and tell people to go register. Plus, they'll get a free ClickFunnels funnel to attract leads for their big wealth-making deals. It's my affiliate link, of course.

# Day 17

It's time to get the webinar script and slides done. Use the Perfect Webinar Script. It's a full-day activity. I'd certainly practice it. Promote the webinar registration page with email, Facebook Live, and Instagram again.

In Today's Episode: Interview with a red-ocean guru (ask them to JV after the interview). Make mention of the new course coming out.

# Day 18

Create the order and confirmation pages. Get video testimonials to put on the order page from a few people who I've helped in the past. Also, I'd build an affiliate program and contest. I need to invite those I've interviewed to do a JV with me for a 50/50 split when I launch. Promote the upcoming webinar to outlets again.

In Today's Episode: Interview with a red-ocean guru. Mention the new course coming out.

# Day 19

The webinar is soon, so today I'll create the members area where the course will be built. I'll look at the previous topics I found the red ocean struggling with and make the top six topics the titles of my six course modules.

It's key that I ask what they're struggling with under each module. A simple Google Form is enough to collect their responses. Now I can customize each module.

It's part of my pitch that the course isn't done. "Can I go over a special offer I made for you? Now, to be clear, the course is not done. Module One is launching in two weeks, which means you get early-bird pricing today..." This lets me prove that the idea works, and I get paid for it without wasting time making something that doesn't sell.

I'd be sure to place the schedule of when each module launches on the first page of the members area.

Promote the registration page like crazy through all channels.

In Today's Episode: Talk about a few of the super prolific product topic ideas. Talk about JVs who've agreed to promote.

## Day 20

IT'S WEBINAR DAY and a busy one! Time to let all that pressure I've built up hit my live broadcast page. It's best to deliver the script while standing up (matters a lot)!

Then I'll create the replay page. Honestly, I'd give someone who has Funnel Scripts my product for free if they let me log in to their account to write the webinar follow-up sequence and cart-close sequence.

It's important to share numbers with potential JVs. I'd use the opportunity to schedule webinars with their audience next week.

In Today's Episode: Publish a few of my numbers on an episode and talk about a few of the people who bought. Invite the listeners to register for the next free webclass opening.

## Day 21

I'd rest and reflect today. Smile. Serve. Meditate. Envision my goal as if it had already happened.

## Day 22

This whole week would be used to create the product as fast as I could with the personal expectation that it's "broken" and I get to continue to improve it.

My offer would include a live group Q&A session each week, so I can start to see what else needs to be created and where the holes in the product are.

I'd pull my phone or computer camera up and use buyer responses to create Module One.

I'd also keep one JV webinar spot open today.

Today, the cart closes at midnight for the people who didn't buy the offer yet.

In Today's Episode: Bring in a very happy student/buyer who visually appears to be sold on the importance of the product and has personally been bitten by the red ocean.

## Day 23

More filming today. I'd pull my phone or computer camera up and use buyer responses to create Module Two.

I'd also keep one JV webinar spot open today for someone I previously interviewed. The film editing would be simple.

In Today's Episode: Bring in a very happy student/buyer who visually appears to be sold on the importance of the product and has personally been bitten by the red ocean.

## Day 24

I'd pull my phone or computer camera up and use buyer responses to create Module Three.

Again, keep one JV webinar spot open today.

Today, I also want to reach out to people who saw the webinar but didn't buy. I want to know their reasoning. It's some of the most valuable info for my script editing.

In Today's Episode: I'll very briefly talk about the last three modules I just filmed and the major red-ocean problems they help to solve. Then, I'll tell everyone to go register for the next webclass because it's opening again soon.

## Day 25

I'd pull my phone or computer camera up and use buyer responses to create Module Four.

I'd go to my attached Facebook Group that came with the offer and find one of the hyper buyers to go through and create bullet-point lists of the modules. I'll have those printed and sent to the future buyers.

I'd use some money from previous sales for red-ocean gurus on Instagram to do some mentions and shout-outs.

In Today's Episode: I'd talk about the affiliate program and the upcoming affiliate contest to win a free ticket to our $5K two-day workshop (coming soon).

## Day 26

I'd pull my phone or computer camera up and use buyer responses to create Module Five.

It's time to make adjustments to the webinar script, headlines, stories, and offer before the next live webclass. I'd look at feedback and rewrite whatever is needed.

In Today's Episode: I'll talk about the adjustments I made, how I'm personally feeling about how everything is going, and where the product will keep helping to SAVE people from the nasty red ocean in the future.

## Day 27

IT'S WEBINAR DAY! STAND AND DELIVER! After the webinar is over, I'd do another live Q&A for all those who didn't buy.

In Today's Episode: Another passionate student/customer interview.

## Day 28

I'd rest and reflect today. Smile. Serve. Meditate. Envision my goal as if it had already happened.

## Day 29

I'd pull my phone or computer camera up and use buyer responses to create Module Six. It's time to reach out to red-ocean relationships again and ask if they'd like to speak at a workshop.

In Today's Episode: Talk about my personal journey in industry. Get vulnerable. Talk about how knowledge and execution are the only things that matter (pre-framing for future workshop).

## Day 30

Download a free event funnel template from ClickFunnels. Email the list, message the Facebook Group, go live wherever appropriate, and sell a limited $5K two-day workshop.

In Today's Episode: Announce the upcoming workshop for those who want even more of a personal experience. I'd make them apply to attend though. It's not open enrollment.

# FINAL THOUGHTS

Funny enough, even in a situation of poverty, a lack of opportunity is never the issue. The issues start when the entrepreneur doesn't learn to say no. I've never met a successful person who didn't go through a period of sickening obsession over ONE idea for a period of time.

I think it's key to give yourself an emotional license to suck at "normal" life things so that you can obsess. Also, my strategy places a heavy emphasis on publishing, because whoever controls content controls ideas and belief. Plus, it lets me build a list and is a kind of barter I can use when talking to other influencers. I don't ever wanna spend time actually creating everything in my offer without knowing how well it sells first. So I test parts of the offer and ideas on my podcast.

Last, I learned from Joe Polish that there's no relationship between being good and getting paid, but there's a huge relationship between being good at marketing and getting paid. With that in mind, there's no higher-leverage skill a marketer can devote time to than that of storytelling. You'll learn how to affect the very blueprint that your customers use to see the world. It's a superpower.

BOOM!

# RESOURCES

- Auphonic (auphonic.com)
- Facebook Live
- Google Forms
- tawk.to

Chapter 8

# 3 WEEKS TO WEBINAR LAUNCH

*by Stacey and Paul Martino*

# STACEY AND PAUL MARTINO

## *Founders of*
## *RelationshipDevelopment.org*

Relationships
*RelationshipBreakthroughSecrets.com*

Stacey and Paul Martino have proven that it only takes ONE partner to transform a relationship... ANY relationship! The Martino's are on a mission to empower people to get the Unshakable Love and Unleashed Passion they want in their relationship... even if their partner REFUSES to change! Stacey and Paul, are the founders of RelationshipDevelopment.

*org and creators of RelationshipU®. Through their revolutionary Relationship Development® methodology, they are changing the way relationship is done!*

*Today, through their strategic coaching, online programs and sold-out live events, Stacey and Paul have helped save thousands of marriages around the world (by working with only one spouse). Trained and certified by Tony Robbins, Stacey is a certified marriage educator, divorce preventionist and strategic interventionist. As a six-time best-selling author, Stacey is a sought-after relationship expert, and is the Relationship Expert for Aspire Magazine.*

My family was staring at me from across the kitchen table.

Maybe Paul and I waited too long before we told them what was really going on.

Their faces were serious. They were concerned, and rightly so.

"How much do you have left?" my sister asked.

"Thirteen hundred in cash," Paul said. "And we have about sixty days before they start foreclosure on this house."

We had lost everything.

With two babies sleeping in their beds upstairs, we sat around the kitchen table with our siblings, cards on the table, and asked for their help in making a good decision about what to do next.

During the recession of 2008, all of our corporate consulting contracts got frozen at once. Those were tough years for many businesses, people, and even governments.

Paul and I had been trying RELENTLESSLY for two years to save our technology businesses and recover our finances. But with no marketing skills and just guessing, our consulting business ended up going under.

We had already had our real estate investment property go into foreclosure—now we were fighting for our home. The only home our two babies had ever known.

Paul and I felt like we were under a dark cloud when it came to money.

After two years of zero progress and zero dollars coming in, our state and our mindset were BROKEN.

Thank God for all our years of personal development. At least we knew enough to REACH OUT to trusted people for counsel on making a good decision about our next step.

That was the day our financial recovery began. Paul and I both took corporate jobs and started to rebuild our financial house.

It took us two long years of saving here and there to try to get even $10,000 in the bank as a safety net.

Here's what I want you to learn from our lesson.

When you are at a panic point in life, who you surround yourself with MATTERS. The mindset, expertise, and experience of the people you CONSULT is going to MASSIVELY impact the results you are going to get.

Back then, Paul and I had ZERO marketing skills.

But our siblings believed in us 1,000%.

That said, notice what decision they helped us to make: get jobs.

Because that was their mindset and that's what they knew.

By the way, thank God for them and their support at that time. There are NO mistakes in life.

If we hadn't taken those jobs or if we had found a way to revive our IT consulting business, then Relationship Development would never have been born.

Back then, Paul and I took the LONG way.

This is why when Russell approached us about this project, Paul and I were a BIG FAT YES.

To write this chapter for you, Paul and I sat down together and answered THIS QUESTION...

*If the Paul and Stacey Martino of today, with all the marketing expertise we know today and ClickFunnels, could go back in time to 2010 and be the ones to sit down at the kitchen table with the Paul and Stacey of that year, what would we coach OURSELVES to do?*

WOW!!! That's wild, isn't it?

Knowing everything we know right now, after saving over 10,000 marriages with our proven solution, doing multiple seven figures in annual revenue by helping people heal their families and create their unshakable love and unleashed passion...

If we were to go back in time and sit down with OURSELVES, with our two beautiful babies sleeping upstairs, this is EXACTLY what we would tell US to do, day by day, week by week, for the first 30 days, to GUARANTEE financial freedom and a life by design!

Although the voice you will hear in the writing of this chapter is mine, please know that Paul and I crafted this entire plan together, to serve you.

What we are laying out on the pages that follow is THE EXACT PATH we would have chosen! Without a doubt, what you are about to read can and will change your life...if you implement it.

Maybe you are already financially safe and simply want a proven system to get you where you want to go. If so, this will serve as a tremendous shortcut on your path.

However, if you are living in your own "kitchen table moment," we hope that we can be the trusted counsel you can turn to. And we deeply hope that sharing our story with you serves you and helps you to truly create your life by design with this powerful proven system.

Let's do this!

# Day 1

*"For every action, there is an equal and opposite reaction."*

— Newton's Third Law of Motion

*"Garbage in, garbage out."*

— Unknown

*"That which you think, in any moment, attracts unto itself other thoughts that are like it."*

— Abraham (Law of Attraction)

However you want to look at it, whether strategic or spiritual, your beliefs and your energy that go into your ACTIONS will determine the results you get from those actions.

If you are in a crap state and you take an action (even the right action), your energy is going into that work. The receivers of your "work" will feel your energy (whether you choose to believe it or not) and will respond in kind.

Magic does not happen from the crap zone.

So Day 1 is all about *getting into state.*

### Step One: Write my List of WHO I Am! I am love, compassion, grace, sunshine, fun, commitment, resourcefulness, intelligence, tenacity, speed, insight, and generosity!

I write this list down on an index card. I'll read it every morning when I wake up and every evening before I sleep.

### Step Two: Crush the False Beliefs. Now it's time to crush those false beliefs! The "drunk monkey brain" fear talk that tries to take over when I am in a tough place.

I gotta crush it, baby.

So I will write down each false belief (the nasty chatter in my head that creates resistance) and then CRUSH it by proving it wrong.

Examples of affirmations that came out of crushing my false beliefs:

- My net worth does NOT equal my self-worth.
- Money is just a VEHICLE to what I want and no more.
- If MONEY can solve my problems, I don't have real problems.
- The ONLY thing that matters in this lifetime is Paul and the kids!

So I will write my affirmations down on the back of that index card and read them morning and night.

**Step Three: Focus on the MOST Important Thing.** When times would get stressful, Paul would say to me, "Remember, Stacey, I don't care if it's just me, you, and the kids in a cardboard box—as long as we are together, I have everything I need."

As we went through our financial crisis, I noticed something unexpected—we were happy.

Every day, Paul and I thanked God that we did the work to create our unshakable love and unleashed passion when we did. Because when this financial crisis found us, we were in fact UNSHAKABLE together.

While other couples were blaming each other and unraveling at the seams, Paul and I were stronger together than ever.

All the work that we had done to become UNSHAKABLE allowed us to face our financial crisis TOGETHER as a rock-solid TEAM!

And with the TWO of us facing a challenge TOGETHER, there wasn't anything we couldn't do!

Every day, while we struggled to pull the money together, we still got to be HAPPY.

We still got to be desperately in LOVE with each other.

We still got to LAUGH with each other.

And we discovered something awesome...SEX IS FREE!

Every day, we FOCUSED on how much we LOVED each other and how we were UNSHAKABLE together. Every day, we FOCUSED on the UNLEASHED PASSION we got to live in.

Every day, we focused on the LOVE that we have for our children and how lucky we were to be their parents. Their smiles, their playfulness, and their snuggles.

A lack of money couldn't take ANY of those things away from us.

Every day, we would FOCUS on our unshakable love and unleashed passion over and over until we were VIBRATING with the energy of gratitude and limitless love.

That's the energy we would bring into our day and our work.

Decide what that is for you.

What is THE MOST important thing in your universe that money cannot ever take from you, that you can focus on and be grateful for until you are VIBRATING with that energy of abundance?

Write it down. Incant it out loud, over and over, until you are vibrating with that energy! Do it every day, before you begin your day and your work!

# Day 2: Celebration: Breaking Through My Panic Point

For the last two decades, Paul and I have studied with the greatest experts in the world in personal development, human behavior, entrepreneurship, success, and fulfillment.

About four years ago, Paul noticed that when people would come to us for help in making the right decision, we kept repeating some of the same principles over and over again.

Then he started to look back at some of our best decisions and recognized that there was a repeatable pattern starting to emerge.

He came to me and said, "What if we could take our ability to make outstanding decisions every time without fail and put it into a repeatable process that anyone could plug in and use for themselves? We could build a tool that people could use to trust themselves to make great decisions in any situation!"

We spent about a YEAR mapping it out and simplifying it into a repeatable tool that anyone could use.

Then we started testing it with our clients, each time revising and simplifying it to get predictable, outstanding results.

After helping a few hundred people through our process, we were ready to teach our 5-Step Decision Making Model. We taught the entire model at our Relationship Breakthrough Retreat (a three-day live immersion event), and people went NUTS for it. We've taught it at that event every year since then!

One of the KEY pieces in that system is...

*"The solution to every problem you currently have is*

*sitting OUTSIDE your current comfort zone, or, by def-*
*inition, it wouldn't be a problem for you right now."*
— Keith J. Cunningham

As I approach the EDGE of my comfort zone, on my way to the so-lution, I will inevitably hit a panic point. This is where everything breaks down and goes to crap.

This is where most people GIVE UP.

What happens next separates the ones who will succeed from the ones who will not.

When I find myself in a panic point, I must remember that the solu-tion I need to BREAK THROUGH is The Mentor and The Tribe.

Unfortunately, most people in a panic point try to figure out what to do themselves. They fail, of course, because what they already know is, by definition, NOT ever going to be the solution to what they need to do next.

When people just do what THEY know, they fail and RETREAT.

What do the ones who break through do differently? They seek out The Mentor and The Tribe solution.

When I am looking at my goal and I know that it is outside my cur-rent comfort zone and I need to break through, I must find a MENTOR who (a) already navigated to that goal successfully for themselves, (b) has a proven process for taking other people to that outcome success-fully, and (c) has many success stories of others they helped to get the SAME goal that I want to achieve.

Bonus criteria: (d) make sure the mentor is seven or eight levels be-yond the next-level goal I have for myself, so that when I achieve that goal and want to go to my next level, my new "problems" won't scare the crap out of them because they already solved those, too.

And now for The Tribe—people who BREAK THROUGH to new lev-els, surround themselves with a tribe of people who are on the same journey, going to the same goal or beyond. These are the people who will catch me when I stumble and celebrate me when I am victorious.

I MUST surround myself with The Mentor who has the solutions and The Tribe that will support me.

With that two-part solution, I can break through a panic point. So what does that mean for Paul and me?

> *Mentor: Our mentor is Russell Brunson.*
> *Tribe: Our tribe is the group of friends in the ClickFunnels community that we have built over the years.*

So I'm going to pull out everything I have from all of Russell's training and dive in. I'm ONLY going to follow his proven process, and I'm going to follow it EXACTLY as he says.

*Tribe:* Instead of going into hiding during my time of struggle or rebuilding, I'm going to bring my tribe CLOSER to me. I'm going to reach out to them EVERY DAY. I'm going to share, serve, and be transparent.

I'm also going to get an accountability buddy who wants to create something BIG within 30 days, so we can hold each other accountable every day.

Every day, we are going to text each other with the three things we commit to do that day to move ourselves forward.

Now we've got a proven strategy (The Mentor) and my peeps (The Tribe). We are ready!

# Day 3: Set Myself Up for Success

> *"If you talk about it, it's a dream, if you envision it, it's possible, but if you schedule it, it's real."*
> — Tony Robbins

After two decades of personal development, we can tell you for sure that people who achieve what they want make a huge impact, live their lives by design, and got where they are by living intentionally.

That includes having systems and processes to set themselves up for success every day.

Not some of the days—every day.

You don't accidentally achieve greatness!

People who set a goal and then HOPE they hit it are going to struggle unnecessarily.

There are two ways to live your life—by default or by design.

A life by design is where you are intentionally designing your days to live on purpose, with a purpose, for a purpose. Living authentically and living the life that is right FOR YOU.

Most people live a life by default. They are living the life they ended up in, living in reaction to everything that's going on around them, trying to do what they think they SHOULD do, and ending up miserable.

Part of living a life by design is strategically designing your DAY to create the results you said you want!

The first and most important part of that is to design and implement your morning routine.

Tony Robbins once asked me, "Of all the tools and strategies you've used to create so much success in every area of your life, what's the ONE tool that you would say is the MOST impactful?"

No question—my answer was, "My morning routine. Getting up and DESIGNING my day, every day. There is NOTHING more important than that. I don't have any days that aren't worth designing."

So what morning routine will I implement and commit to doing every day?

*Morning Routine* For the first five things, I borrow techniques from a video by Tony Robbins on YouTube.

- Priming (breath work)
- Heart meditation
- Gratitude flood
- Visualization of three outcomes
- Raise my vibration
- Prayer
- 10 thank-you statements in my journal
- Walk and consume growth content (Monday–Friday only)

This process takes me about 30 minutes before the walk. I also have a 10-minute version that I can do on days when I need to condense it. But I make sure that I do the full version 90% of the time.

*Beyond the Morning* There are two more strategies I want to implement the rest of my days.

### STRATEGY ONE: DON'T PEE ON THE BREAD!

Imagine for a moment that you were poor, homeless, alone, and had NO food. Can you imagine it? See yourself in dirty clothes, sitting on a bench on the street and feeling hungry. Can you feel it?

Now imagine that a good person came by and gave you a loaf of bread. An entire loaf!

You realize that you haven't eaten in three days.

WOW! You know you could actually make this last at least a few days if you just have a couple of pieces a day.

It feels like a gift from GOD.

Can you feel the RELIEF?

Can you feel the GRACE?

Can you feel how LUCKY and GRATEFUL you feel?

Feel it for a moment.

Feel yourself smile!

Feel your eyes light up!

Feel your soul feel lighter!

Can you feel it?

Let me ask you a question.

Instead of eating it, would you drop your pants and PEE on that bread??

Yes, you read that right.

Would you PEE (urinate) all over that bread?

Yes? No? What's your answer?

Okay, I know. NO, you would not. Correct?

Then why is it that when we are STRESSED and in PAIN over our business, our money, and everything related to work, we tend to bring all our negative energy and emotion to our spouses and our kids?

They are our BREAD when we are hungry.

They are our LOVE, they are our JOY, they are our SOUL, they are our EVERYTHING.

And yet, we PEE ALL OVER the bread when we bring all our money and work stress into our family time!

I will remember in this journey that any negative energy related to money, work, and business must stay at work!

- *Step One: Compartmentalize my time.* Even in this most dire of times, I will only work 10 hours per day and 6 days per week. And when I am not in one of those work hours, I'll compartmentalize my energy, emotion, and focus.

- *Step Two: Transition Ritual.* Before I transition from a "work hour" to a "family hour," I'll create a transition ritual. Something I can do that allows me to leave all my work energy, thoughts, emotions, and actions AT WORK. Close the lid on that box. Shake off the energy of that. And transition to the version of myself that I want to be for my family. They are my BREAD when I'm hungry. I won't waste them by peeing all over them (bringing all that negativity or work into my family time). I will write this ritual down.

## STRATEGY TWO: GIVE.

No matter what is going on in my world, there is always SOMEONE who is suffering more than I am.

I am bankrupt? There is someone who will find out today that their spouse wants a divorce.

I found out my spouse wants a divorce? There's a mother burying her child today.

I am burying my child today? There's a father who can't find his child today.

I will remember there are WORSE problems in the world. Get out of my own pity party about how bad I have it and get into a place of GIVING.

Make a commitment every day to GIVE to someone. A true gift,

**152**

with no strings attached.

I committed to help someone with their love relationship every single day, without any thought of getting paid for it and with no strings attached. I simply committed to make ONE family better every single day as my way of GIVING to life!

There has been a lot already and it's only Day 3. The how-to's are plentiful and the easiest part to implement.

## Day 4: The Who and The What

On this day, we will decide who we will help and what we will do for them.

Who is that person we want to be a hero for? Who is that group of people we are really passionate about?

It's SUPER important to be crystal clear about this and get this RIGHT before we move on.

I've got a lot of friends who have eventually closed down multiple six- and seven-figure businesses because they "hated" their audience.

We must be intentional about who we are going to serve.

Because when times get tough, we are going to break through our challenges FOR THEM. They will be our inspiration to get past the speed bumps and challenges that lie ahead on our journey.

Our WHO is married entrepreneurs with kids. Paul and I wake up every morning to be heroes to the moms and dads who want to have unshakable love and unleashed passion so they can give their kids, spouses, and themselves the lives they deserve.

We'll get as specific as we can about our avatar and write it down.

WHAT result are we going to deliver for them?

What is it that we do for people? What outcome can we help them create? What problem can we solve for them?

We won't underestimate what we can do for others. What seems second nature to us is actually our unique brilliance. We won't fall into that false belief that "Everyone can do what we can do, right?"

WRONG.

We have unique brilliances that are just ours.

If we don't yet know what we can do for these people, we can go on

Facebook and find groups where our people hang out. Start reading their posts and comments. What are they asking for that we KNOW we can solve?

We help real people to (1) save their marriages, (2) bring passion back to passionless relationships, (3) create harmonious co-parenting relationships as they divorce, and (4) find the right relationships for them (5) to divorce-proof great marriages.

That is what we do. Those five things. All day, every day.

# Day 5: Content Day

On Day 5, it's time to start getting some content up on a blog and my Facebook profile.

This will be important soon because as we start driving traffic, people are going to want to check us out and see what we stand for, so we want some pillars of content on our blog for them to find.

We'll create a simple blog and write a few pillar content pieces that we can post there.

A pillar content piece is like us getting on our soapbox and saying what needs to be said for the people we are champions for!

With our avatar, what do they need to hear most? What are they going through that we can vocalize for them? What do they need to know in order to have HOPE again? What can we teach them to start giving them some relief from their problems?

Here is a list of my 5 Pillar Pieces of Content for my blog:

- The Four Steps To Creating A Rock-Solid Alignment With Your Partner, Even If You Guys Can't Agree On Anything!
- How To Reignite The Passion In Your Relationship (No Matter How Long It's Been, How Tired You Are, Or How Busy You Are)
- Five Things You Are Doing Right Now That Are Killing Your Relationship And How To STOP Them
- The Day My Husband Walked Out On Me: How I Single-Handedly Saved My Marriage Even Though My Husband Was NOT Going To Do Anything To Save It
- My Shocking Discovery...It Only Takes ONE Person To Save Any

Relationship (And Why Couples Work Is Actually Destroying Marriages)

On Facebook, as we write these blogs, we'll share them on our Facebook profile page and also share three posts a day. These can be quotes, inspirational messages, or answers to common questions.

Again, there's no one watching us yet. But when we are ready to start bringing traffic back to our page, we will want them to find stuff there.

*Take Action:* Decide what my five pillar blog posts will be about.

# Day 6: Create My Free Offer

On Day 6, it's time to create my free offer to use as a lead magnet. This has to be excellent! Too many people make their free giveaway offer a worthless thing they are willing to just give away.

That's totally the wrong mindset.

I once heard Julie Stoian (a ClickFunnels Coach) describe her process for figuring out the free offer as this:

Figure out EVERYTHING you would give your highest-paying customer to get the result you are promising. Now, pick out the sexiest and most valuable thing from that whole pile. That's going to be your free thing at the front of your funnel.

That's what we are going to make today!

For us, we have two different lead magnets.

- Four-part video program on how to reignite the passion in your relationship, no matter how far gone things seem
- Four-part video program on how to create a rock-solid relationship, even if you and your partner can't agree on anything

With these two lead magnets, we are solving the two biggest challenges that our clients have. One (or both) of these offers will work for almost everyone we serve.

As for the modality, it needs to be digital. This needs to be something we can give away for FREE. We can do video, audio, or PDF.

I happen to have these programs already made on video, so I'm going to use them.

We could also create a Word doc and turn it into a PDF. Last time I checked, the studies still showed that PDF free offers still out-convert audio and video.

Another great tip from Julie Stoian: If you are going to do a PDF, don't do 5 things or 10 things on a list. Do a huge list, like 210 things.

For me, that could be "365 Things You Can Do To Create An Outstanding Relationship In Under 60 Seconds A Day."

*Take Action:* What is a BIG LIST kind of PDF that we can create?

# Day 7: My Day Off

*"On the seventh day, He rested."*

And so shall we. We'll have an amazing day with our family and loved ones today.

# Day 8: Perfect Webinar Week

This week is BIG! It's time to create our Perfect Webinar.

I've heard Russell Brunson say hundreds of times that if he could only use ONE strategy to make the most money the fastest, it would be the Perfect Webinar.

I agree 100%.

Here's a funny story about how I found Russell. Paul and I had grown our business and we were doing well, but we were FAILING miserably online with webinars.

I had bought every webinar program out there and thought I had tried everything. And then, by the grace of God, I found Russell.

When I first started working with Russell, I had ONE need to solve. I needed to be able to convert online (via webinars).

I had been trying for years and failing.

Before working with Russell, our sales conversion rate when we did webinars was one half of 1% (0.5%).

We once had over 18,000 people come to a webinar, and only about 90 people purchased. When I told Russell this, I could see him get visibly ill at the thought.

It was worse than that for me. Yes, it's true, the sales do matter. If we are not profitable, we can't keep doing this business. But it's more than that for me and Paul.

See, when 18,000 people sign up for just ONE of our webinars, they sign up for a reason. There's some kind of pain there. And if I don't do my job and help them get out of fear and take action to join our Quick Start program, then I can't HELP that family.

So when I thought about the 17,910 families that we were NOT helping through our Quick Start program and what might continue to happen in those households and what the kids in that house might be hearing or struggling with...my heart started breaking.

One night, crying in Paul's arms after another failed webinar, we prayed and begged God to send us the answer we needed to help the families that deserve our solution.

And, no joke, God sent Russell Brunson to me in my Facebook feed the next day! (Thank you, John Parkes.)

The very first thing we learned and implemented from Russell was the Perfect Webinar model. We did it EXACTLY the way he teaches it. Exactly!

That's what we are going to implement during Week 2 of this 30-day plan now! Implement it, step-by-step, slide by slide.

And we'll watch as many high-converting Perfect Webinars as we can, so that we can get it into our nervous systems and pick up on all the nuances that go into the process.

Paul and I are very proud to say that when we launched our Perfect Webinar, we converted at 10% live! That had never happened before... ever. We danced and celebrated!

Guess what?! Today, just a few short months later, our Perfect Webinar converts at 20% or more live on the webinar. And we are also doing the same amount of sales in our webinar replay follow-up campaigns as we are doing live on the webinar.

WHOOO HOOOO!

My assignment for Day 8, for every single expert who contributed a chapter to this book, go to their websites, expert pages, etc. and find their Perfect Webinar. Opt in for it. Watch at least four today! And I'll also be sure to opt in to watch Russell's Perfect Webinar, too!

# Day 9: Perfect Webinar Foundation

First, we'll review the Perfect Webinar blueprint from Russell. And we'll grab our DotComSecrets and Expert Secrets books—we are going to need them.

Today, we are going to build the fundamentals for the Perfect Webinar.

- Title
- Big Domino
- Three Secrets

These three pieces of the Perfect Webinar model are so vital to our success. We must get these right before we move on to build the rest of our Perfect Webinar.

We'll dig deep into the programs we have from Russell to figure out our content for these three things.

Once we have what we think is the right answer for us, we'll take it to our tribe! Take it to the ClickFunnels community and ask for feedback.

But we have to be careful here—we don't want every Joe Schmo spouting off their advice when they haven't mastered it themselves!

When we make a request, we'll use a great pre-frame so we filter through what we really want.

We can say something like, "For those of you who are doing the Perfect Webinar and converting at 10% or more LIVE, would any of you be willing to take a look at my three key pieces for my Perfect Webinar and give me some constructive feedback?"

And if someone responds but doesn't indicate that they have achieved the result, we'll say "Hey, thanks. Can I just ask what sales conversion rate you are currently getting on your live Perfect Webinar?"

If they don't respond, we can ignore their feedback.

Those of us who are converting, we know our numbers.

Here are our three pieces of key Perfect Webinar content.

*Title:* How To Get Unshakable Love & Unleashed Passion In Your Relationship...Even If Your Partner REFUSES To Change!

*Big Domino:* It ONLY takes ONE partner to create an unshakable love and unleashed passion in ANY relationship. There is ONE Internal SHIFT that you MUST make to SAVE any relationship! And the ONLY proven solution for making that shift and creating the love you want is the Relationship Development ToolBox.

### 3 Secrets

- Secret #1: The Truth I Uncovered About Why Couples Counseling Is Destroying Marriages!
- Secret #2: After Transforming Over 10,000 Marriages, I Share The Real Reason Why EVERYTHING You Have Tried To Fix Your Relationship Is Keeping You Miserable And Stuck And Has Actually Made Things Worse
- Secret #3: Why This Revolutionary Breakthrough Technique WILL WORK For You NO Matter How Far Gone Your Relationship Is Or How Hopeless Your Unique Circumstances Seem!

*Take Action:* Share it in the ClickFunnels Community for feedback so we can hone in on specifics.

## Days 10–12: Build Our Perfect Webinar

For the rest of Week 2, we'll build our entire Perfect Webinar except our offer. (That will come later).

As we go through our content for the webinar, we'll ask a few trusted friends who also represent our avatar to review it and offer feedback.

I did this by hosting a Zoom meeting and walking through the slides that I had created after I was done with each secret. The feedback that these folks offered was very valuable in helping me switch from using MY vocabulary to using THEIR vocabulary.

Since they were my avatar, hearing them explain their pains or wants in their words was very helpful!

I kept revising my Perfect Webinar to replace some of my words with their words. This way, the content would resonate more with my audience.

We can also find a few key people in the ClickFunnels community who would be willing to watch us practice our Perfect Webinar and give us some feedback. Again, we only want people who are actually doing it and getting great conversions.

*Take Action:* Build my Perfect Webinar and get the right people lined up to give me feedback.

## Day 13: Build My Perfect Webinar Funnel

This is the easiest part of my 30-day plan, thanks to ClickFunnels.

Go into my ClickFunnels account and find a high-converting Perfect Webinar share funnel.

Go through the funnel, page by page, swapping out my copy for the sample copy.

I'm done.

*Take Action:* Build my funnel.

## Day 14: Day Off

What do the flight attendants always tell you during the safety presentation on a flight? Always put YOUR oxygen mask on first, before you put masks on your loved ones.

One day a week, we will rest and rejuvenate, so that we can be of service to others. If we don't care for ourselves (give ourselves oxygen), then we will have nothing to give to anyone else.

## Day 15/Week Three: Traffic Week

This week is all about finding our people and inviting them to our Perfect Webinar.

We'll schedule our Perfect Webinar for next week, on a time and date when our avatar is most likely to be available.

All this week, we will drive FREE traffic to our webinar opt-in.

Here are the strategies we are going to use this week to drive traffic to our Perfect Webinar.

1. Do a daily podcast (with video recording). Put the podcast on our blog, Facebook, and YouTube. Deliver massive value and put it out there every day. At the end of every podcast, invite people to opt in for our webinar and give them the link.

2. On our blog and Facebook, change our banners and calls to action to all go to the Perfect Webinar opt-in page. Everywhere someone can find us, make sure there is only ONE call to action to opt in to our webinar. Change our Facebook profile cover photo to a banner inviting people to our webinar. Change the call to action in our bio to the webinar opt-in. After every blog post, have a call to action for our webinar opt-in.

3. Find the Facebook Groups where our people hang out. Go into those groups every day and just comment on other posts, offering tremendous value and solutions to the people asking for help.

    a. We will NOT share our webinar opt-in in those groups. Just give huge value.
    b. When people click on our profile pictures to check us out, they will see our banner giving them the opportunity to register for our webinar. They will see our Facebook posts and podcasts, all with the call to action for our webinar opt-in.
    c. If we have a blog or podcast that solves what someone is asking about, we can simply answer their question and then say, "Hey, I did a podcast on this very topic. It goes deeper into the solution. If it serves you, here's the link," and then post the link. That's a cool way of sharing.

4. Start our own private Facebook community. On the webinar confirmation page, add a link and invite people to join our free private Facebook Group.

    a. Every day, post value in that group.
    b. Every day, post the webinar opt-in to that group and ASK peo-

ple to comment when they register "I'm IN!"

The key during this week is to BE EVERYWHERE. Be in every conversation and help lots of people.

We will use these free traffic strategies to get as many people as we can into our Perfect Webinar.

But we don't need to be too concerned about our opt-in numbers right now. Many of us have done webinars to only six people before! We still have to deliver as if Oprah is watching...every time!

## Week Four: Create Our Proprietary System And Deliver Our Perfect Webinar

While we are driving the traffic to our webinar, it's time to start building the framework for the course we are going to sell on that webinar!

Yes, we are going to SELL our course before we build it!

This is exactly how I launched my first course! Always (ALWAYS) get PAID to create your content!

The first time we sell this online program, we will sell it first and then build it as we deliver it. The following week, we will do a webinar AGAIN, and we will sell the same course but will already be a week into building it. Eventually, we will be selling the course every week and it will already be created so we won't have to create it again!

The most important thing to remember about creating our course is that it does NOT have to be PERFECT. In fact, I can absolutely guarantee that it won't be.

It's not supposed to be perfect. Any need for perfection that we have is about ourselves.

Perfection is 100% tied to our own needs for certainty and significance.

The only certainty we can rely on as entrepreneurs is the certainty we create. And perfection is the OPPOSITE of creation.

And if our driving force is significance, we are going to run out of steam as entrepreneurs. And if this was all about significance for us, when we hit the BIG roadblocks, challenges, and bumps, we would jump off and find something else easier to do.

The driving force in our business MUST be to SERVE the people who we are here to serve.

Anything less and we can forget creating a massive impact, changing the world, and having any kind of legacy.

When we have a need for perfection, we are suffocating our business.

Have a standard for EXCELLENCE and always bring the BEST we've got and stretch ourselves way beyond our comfort zones...YES! But perfection? NO. Perfection is not for entrepreneurs. Perfection is not for game changers. Perfection is not for people like us.

If we really want to have an impact, if we want to change the world for the better and live our purpose, we have to make it about THEM, the people we serve!

When we do that, we can get through anything.

*Our Proprietary System* So now that our need for perfection is gone, it's time to create our proprietary system.

There are a ton of business models we can use to get our message out there and have an impact on the world, but if we are experts, the foundation of most business models comes back to needing OUR proprietary system in place.

This system is OUR process. How we get the results that we promise. Our methodology. Our X-step system for Y results.

For example, Paul and I developed our 8-Step Relationship Transformation System®. It's our proprietary methodology for empowering ONE partner to transform ANY relationship!

Once we have our proprietary system, it can be used in any business model. It's the modules for our online program, the segments for our live event, the chapters for our book, the episodes in our documentary.

We can do a smaller version of each step in an entry-level program and a deeper dive into each step in our year-long program. Our three-day event can be an immersion into the eight steps and our done-for-you program can be our team implementing them.

This proprietary system is such a foundational piece!

When I first learned about this, I felt overwhelmed wondering how the heck I was going to figure out my proprietary system.

I avoided it for MONTHS because I felt like it was this big monster to overcome.

Well, luckily for me, my mentor at the time, Fabienne, taught me her process for creating a proprietary system in about two hours.

How to create a proprietary system:

1. *Avatar/Muse:* First, you must think of someone you know who would be your IDEAL client and someone you would absolutely LOVE to get paid to create your result for.

2. *State:* Everything starts with your state. You must get into a state of VIBRATING with gratitude for awesomeness to flow through you.

3. *Environment:* Find a spot that you love where you can be for about two straight hours without interruptions. A place that brings out the best creativity and flow state for you.

4. *Modality:* What is your modality? Typing? Writing in a journal? Writing on a legal pad? Talking into your phone? Figure out what your best modality is for capturing everything you are about to capture.

5. *Step One:* In bullet-point format, write down EVERYTHING you would want to teach your avatar to get them that result. Just the topics, not all the details. Examples:

   - How to create alignment with your partner even when you don't agree
   - How to forgive something when you don't feel it was resolved for you
   - How to bring dating back to a busy life

- How to get your partner's support when they aren't happy with how much you give to your business
- How to get over infidelity
- How to understand your partner's energy type
- How to have more sex than you think most people can even have

Keep doing bullet points like this (topics) until you have everything you would need to teach them in order to guarantee them the result you promised. You might have 200+ bullet points. When I did this, I had over 400.

6. *Step Two:* Group like topics together. As you go through your bullet points, you will start to see that some topics naturally go together with others. Start to label them. Put an "A" next to everything that has to do with TOPIC A and so on. For example, there are many topics in my list that have to do with forgiveness. So I made forgiveness Group A and put an A next to each topic that came under the summary topic of "forgiveness." You want to come up with no fewer than 10 groups.

7. *Step Three:* Order. Looking at your groups, if you were to sit down with your avatar, in what order would you want to teach them those topics? There needs to be a logical order to what you would teach first, second, and so on.

CELEBRATE! Now you have your proprietary system! This is YOUR methodology for teaching people how to get the result that you have promised them!

These will be the topics for our online course we are going to teach. We are going to sell this course on our webinar.

However many steps are in our system, that's how many weeks our course will be.

We will NOT teach our students EVERYTHING we know. We will not even teach them everything on the bullet-point list for each step of our system. It would be too much.

When doing an online course, we want to teach two or three real actionable tools or strategies that our students can digest, implement, feel like "I did it," and get a real result!

To figure out what we will teach in our course, we can go into our Facebook Group each day and ask, "What are your biggest questions around X?" X will be the topic of one of our steps.

So if Step One of our system is figuring out our brand, then we would post "What are your biggest questions around figuring out your brand?"

Then we'll let the audience tell US the biggest questions that we need to answer in our course.

*Creating Content* Next, we'll write up an outline and notes for each of our weekly classes. Make a list of questions we are going to answer.

We can package our course to include X number of online audio classes plus Y number of Q&A sessions with us. We can include a private Facebook Group just for course members.

Each week, we will deliver the class via conference call or video live stream and record it. We'll record the Q&A calls, too.

Then we'll package the recordings into our member site in ClickFunnels.

We can always keep adding to it as we grow.

As our students go through our program and get awesome results, we will screenshot their Facebook post celebrations and ask them whether we can use those as testimonials. We will keep gathering testimonials from our students and put them into our weekly webinar, our sales page, and everywhere.

Russell Says: Do your live webinar every week for one year or until it reaches seven figures, whichever comes first!

# FINAL THOUGHTS

What I just described for 30 days took me years to do, because I didn't have this map or ClickFunnels in the beginning of my business.

But now I see people doing this all the time with ClickFunnels!

There's one more thing.

Tony Robbins says, *"Money is a magnifier."* It makes nice people nicer and jerks bigger jerks.

He was right.

Money is awesome, and you can have plenty of it. The sooner you learn that the ENERGY you bring, the love you add, and your intention to serve also matter, the faster you will reach fulfillment.

When Paul and I both worked full-time corporate jobs, we could only help six families a year in our spare time.

The first year we went into business with our solution, we hit $100,000 in revenue and we served 1,000 families! When we hit seven figures with this mission business of ours, we had saved over 10,000 marriages! That's a LOT more positive energy, love, and serving others.

The larger our company gets, the more positive energy we bring, the more LOVE we infuse, and the more families we serve.

And so more come to us. Bigger, faster, stronger.

The truth is, the more people you serve, the more will come through you for them. And the more will come TO you so you can serve them!

Paul and I serve MANY. And we have made a promise to God that as more is given to us, we will serve more people with it! We keep our promise.

We don't lead from ego. We are not driven by significance. We always do the right thing. And we follow our divine guidance.

And to us, much is given!

Regardless of where you are on your journey right now, whether just starting out or at the top of your mountain, please remember it

DOES matter what energy you bring, how much love you infuse, and your intention of service.

Bring more positive energy into this world we live in. Lead with LOVE. YES, even in your business. Hold an intention of serving others. Do the right thing all the time, even when it's hard. Use your influence, power, and money to move the world forward in positivity, love, and light.

For your children, for my children, and for our grandchildren.

Live your purpose. Follow your heart. LOVE others. Make a lot of money. And do amazing things with it...for the greater good!

God bless you!

# RESOURCES

- DotComSecrets by Russell Brunson
- Expert Secrets by Russell Brunson
- Zoom (zoom.us)

# Chapter 9

# FREE 7-DAY CHALLENGE

## by Ed Osburn

# ED OSBURN

## *Laptop Lifestyle Mentor*

Health Professionals - Chiropractors
*TheChiropracticPhilanthropist.com*

*The Chiropractor's Laptop Lifestyle is the brain-child of Dr. Ed Osburn.*

*Out of pure necessity and desire to connect and create an online presence and extremely lucrative business—Ed rocketed to the very TOP of the Chiropractic profession's most notable and distinguished contributors.*

*Honoured in 2015 as an Icon, Maverick and Genius by The Chiropractic Leadership, Ed is determined to bring the light of Chiropractic to the globe by train-*

*ing Doctors to EXPAND outside their four walls and into the online world.*

*First launching the Chiropractic profession's #1 iTunes podcast (The Chiropractic Philanthropist), smashing successful virtual podcast training for Chiropractors, establishing an online training Academy (Laptop Lifestyle Academy) consisting of over 500 students, and finally the Men of Iron Brotherhood for men who want more!*

*Ed has dedicated his efforts to mentoring Doctors towards building massive movements, impact, and multi-6-figure businesses.*

*Ed's philosophy is: "Practice can be anything you DREAM it to BE...and SUCCESS does not have to come at the expense of your quality of life."*

After working with tens of thousands of aspiring business owners, I've discovered that when someone seems paralyzed or unable to move forward, it's due to one thing: *a fear of failure.*

Well, I have news for you.

The blunt reality is that it's very likely that you WILL fail. But you don't have to let it stop you.

In fact, there is power in the FEAR of failure...and also power in falling and failing. Because when you fall and fail, you have the opportunity to correct your missteps and try again. And in repeating your process, you'll get better and better. That improvement will eventually lead to success.

And I've found that improvement will also lead to less and less fear over time.

You see, I have less fear of failure now, a few years into my entrepreneurial journey, than I did when I started. Yes, I have more to risk.

But even if I were to lose it all, I know without a doubt I could build it all again.

So don't think of those of us in this book as all that different from you. You're just like us...a few years back. Maybe you're where I was when I had one solitary Like on my Facebook business page—and it was my mom!

As you read through this chapter, keep one thing in mind: I believe in you!

I may even have more belief in you than you do in yourself. I know you can do this, although you may still be wondering.

I want you to succeed, which is why I've distilled my process into four powerful foundations, one a week for four weeks. They are...

- *Week One: Planning*
- *Week Two: Deployment*
- *Week Three: Creation (Keep it Simple)*
- *Week Four: House Cleaning and Scaling*

Before I get started, one last word. There are two very simple secret ingredients to your "success sauce."

**One:** Create a legacy inside your business, one that will actually go on and have legs beyond the 30 days laid out in this chapter. Create something that will continue on for 5, 10, or even 15 years or more.

**Two:** As you build your successful business, commit to yourself that you'll do so without compromising your relationships, your health, or your mental and emotional well-being.

If you can figure those two elements out, you WILL be successful inside of this game we call online business.

Ready to get started? Let's dive in!

## Week One: Planning

*"If you fail to plan, you are planning to fail."*
— Benjamin Franklin

# Day 1: Personal

For any budding entrepreneur or business owner, it's critical to have a crystal-clear concept of why you want to build a business to begin with. Why does it matter? What does it mean to you?

In my experience, the answer boils down to one of two things: IMPACT and INCOME.

In the end, what matters in our lives are the substance and quality of our relationships and the depth of connection with our spouses, children, and families.

That's why on Day 1, I will prioritize what matters most to me. I'll pull out my calendar for the next 30 days and add the following:

- Daily meditation and self-care
- Twice-weekly date nights with my wife
- Weekly "dates" with my two young boys
- Regular workouts with my trainer

Once these priorities are in place, I can move through the rest of my month confident in the knowledge that I've put "first things first."

# Day 2: Radical Clarity

My life is way too short to spend it doing something that I don't love. That's why today I'm answering the question, "What do I truly desire?"

To unpack that, I will consider who is the ideal client I want to work with? What is that avatar? What relationship do I want to experience with that person? Do I want to have a group coaching relationship, consulting, a continuity group? Do I want to sell digital products or online courses?

I'll go deep into defining this ideal customer I want to relate to. Who is this person? What is their name? What are their desires and passions, their wants and their needs? Their pain and problems?

I'll write it all down, then find a picture and add it to the description. Then I'll print it out and post it on the wall, next to my workstation. This person—this avatar—will be the litmus test for my marketing and my messaging.

# Day 3: Obstacles

Today is the day I'll foresee challenges and remove obstacles that may be in the way of my success.

I'll look forward over the next month, searching out any family obligations, vacations, holidays, special occasions, appointments, or other commitments that could take time away from this project. I'll calculate the estimated hours or days necessary to fulfill these other obligations and create a plan to make up those hours in increased productivity.

Again, by planning ahead, I'm planning for success and leaving nothing to chance.

# Day 4: Avatar

Today, I'll go even deeper into my avatar.

I'll look at that ideal client and figure out what is their PAIN? What problems might they have? And going even deeper, what are the sub-problems of their main problems?

And once I have a list of their problems and pains, I can work on answering them—and speaking to them. What are the possible solutions I might have for these problems?

Once I have a solution, I can create a system.

So here's how it goes:

*PROBLEM/PAIN >> SOLUTION >> SYSTEM*

Here's an example.

- *Problem:* All health professionals have one problem in common. That is, they are the catalyzing agent in their practice (business). If the health professional is not there, money does not flow. The problem then becomes how can they separate themselves from their business?
- *Pain:* Lack of time and compromising their quality of life! Most doctors feel somewhat chained to their practice, that they are missing out on the critical years with their families.
- *Solution:* Liberation of the doctor from their practice without jeopardizing their income and impact
- *System:* Online courses, digital products, virtual consulting—

these can be highly lucrative and of massive value. The SYSTEM is the STEPS to getting the outcomes and results desired.

That's the focus for Day 4.

## Day 5: Messaging

Today, I'll take my work public by testing and refining my messaging. I'll go onto social media—Facebook and Instagram—and post a text post or live video. I'll speak to my avatar's pain and ask if the problem I've defined and the possible solution I've developed is actually what's desired by my marketplace.

I am also seeking out free (closed) social media communities that are relevant to my cause and marketplace. I would gently post and ask questions, engage, and gather momentum in these groups. (By "gently," I mean I'm not promoting my products or services in an in-your-face manner. Instead, I'm merely trying to create connections and relationships.)

Based on the responses, I'll refine my messaging as needed. (This may take a few tries, but if I do my homework up front, I should gather incredible data!)

## Day 6: Branding and Product

Based on my problem and solution, I'll create a brand for my product and for my business. I need to start that today because the turnaround for a logo can be two to three days, and I want to get it underway.

*Resources:* Youzign, Fiverr, or DesignCrowd if I want to hire a graphic designer

In either case, I'd look for someone who could return the project in 24 hours, in case I need to edit or refine the brand.

One of the biggest mistakes I see with aspiring online entrepreneurs is that they get stuck in the minutia. In this case, my target is to launch and get cash-positive ASAP. Brands and logos can be touched up later when the money is in the bank.

Okay, so how can I shortcut the logo turnaround?

1. I will tell the designer about my company and what I specialize in.
2. I'll provide any relevant website examples I may have for reference.
3. The designer will be given at least two researched competitors' logos, brands, and websites.
4. I will provide the EXACT name of my brand/logo.
5. I'll give them the preferred color palette.
6. I'll provide the tagline, if applicable.

The fastest and most effective way to create a successful and marketable brand is to research my competition. This should take no longer than 48 hours.

## Day 7: Blueprint

Today, I'll blueprint the next three weeks. I'll start with what I want to accomplish and then work backward, reverse-engineering exactly what I need to do each day to accomplish my ultimate outcome—a seven-figure funnel in just 12 months!

For instance, if my target is $1 million in one year (which is about $83,500 a month), I'll figure out what I need to do in terms of sales each of the next three weeks that can eventually be amplified to reach this target on a monthly basis.

In this first 30 days, my target is 20 customers and $20,000.

This may sound like a lot if you've never made money online before, but it is a clearly reachable outcome based on my experience. And it will give me the confirmation and knowledge that I am heading in the right direction.

My product will launch at $997 for the core offer with a $99 bump (upsell), a one-time offer of $99/month continuity, and an application high(er)-ticket offer for $4,000.

## Week Two: Deploy

*"Imperfect action is better than perfect inaction."*
— *Harry Truman*

# Day 8: Facebook

Today, I'll start marketing.

I'll create social media business pages for my product or brand and expand my personal page by requesting to join or adding myself to relevant free Facebook communities (related to my product or service) where I can add value and engage.

Assuming that I am starting from scratch, Day 8 will be foundational to building a legacy project and will set me up for my future marketing efforts for rapid success.

Here are a couple tips I'll keep in mind for adding value to relevant private social media communities.

1. Review the rules and guidelines of the community and comment that I understand them.
2. Ask for permission from the moderators to post value (not pitch) inside the group.
3. Comment on others' posts and provide feedback.
4. Add FREE unsolicited value to the community.
5. Don't be self-serving.

I'll also conduct a POWERFUL and compelling five-minute video post to be distributed on all social media channels (Facebook, Instagram, LinkedIn, YouTube). I will ask viewers to interact, share, engage, and follow me. This is where I'll share my best stuff, holding nothing back, to demonstrate my expertise and to provide amazing value.

In fact, this is so powerful, I will do this for the next 10 days.

I can search for POWERFUL and trending titles and topics on BuzzSumo.

# Day 9: Facebook Challenge Group

Today, I begin to control my traffic and maintain their attention!

Day 9, I'll create a closed Facebook community for a FREE 7-Day Challenge solving a subproblem of the MAIN problem I have identified (e.g., 7-Day Free Beach Fit Challenge, where this is a subsolution of the main problem in the weight-loss and fitness niche).

The purpose of the FREE 7-Day Challenge is to gain authority, build trust, gain case studies (to demonstrate results), and solidify the solution to the problem I've identified and confirmed with my avatar.

Inside the closed group, I'll post the rules and define the PURPOSE and desired OUTCOME of the challenge. These will be pinned to the top of the page.

For this challenge to be a success, it's critical that there's a lot of movement and action around it. And at the same time, I need to create a strong culture. It will be vital that my members inside the FREE Challenge see my daily posts and videos. I want to get them excited! Here's how:

1. Post the rules of the community.
2. Discuss the outcomes they will receive in such a short time.
3. Name the members/community with a catchy moniker (e.g., Beach Fit Crew).
4. Address new members by tagging and thanking them for joining the movement.

Another five-minute video post on all social media channels asking viewers to interact, share, engage, and follow me on my business pages.

## Day 10: Build Tension

Beginning today, I'll build tension inside the challenge by creating daily posts inside the group, showing what I'm creating and how I am going to deliver massive value. I'll also post a day-by-day countdown, in anticipation of the launch of the actual challenge within the community.

In the free groups I belong to and on my business page and personal page, I'll record a Facebook Live with a call to action to join the challenge, driving traffic to the FREE Challenge group.

To further promote it, I'll ask the people currently in the group to share and add their friends to the challenge.

But I won't stop there. Here are some RULES for adding and sharing.

1. The 7-Day Challenge members who add people must tag them in their posts.
2. Within each tagged post, state WHY they have been added to the group.
3. WHY? This sets the new member up to SEE the posts within the challenge...and get them engaging in the group. No one likes to be added to a closed social media group without their permission.

My target is to have 200 people engaged in the FREE 7-Day Challenge.

# Day 11: Blueprint The Challenge

Today's task is to lay out Days 1 through 7 of the challenge.

*Note:* All 7-Day Challenge trainings will be conducted LIVE inside the private Facebook community.

*Length:* 90 minutes

Assignments: In addition to providing resources and guides, I'll give actionable assignments that must be completed within 24 hours. I suggest a live-stream video response from the member on the private FREE 7-Day Challenge timeline. This keeps other members engaged and accountable and builds community, while making micro-agreements with my crew.

Let's face it—RESULTS are the ultimate outcome I want for these members. If I can get results for them, they'll reciprocate and invest in ME!

- Day 1: Logistics: This first training will be a "How To Get The BEST Out Of Your 7-Day Challenge...And How It Will Unfold."
- Day 2: Resources and preparation: What my members need to know to achieve their outcomes...and NO MORE
- Day 3: Value and the System: Keep it high-level and challenge current beliefs while affirming that they CAN do it!
- Day 4: Review: Days 1–3 review and a check-in to see if they're on track

- Day 5: Value training and webinar including transition into a webinar sell (Perfect Webinar by Russell Brunson)
- Day 6: Urgency, promotion, and live Q&A
- Day 7: Urgency and closing of the cart

I know that I cannot deliver too much value—ever.

All roads will lead to my MAIN solution/system to be presented in Day 5 of the FREE 7-Day Challenge webinar. I will keep this foremost in my mind at all times.

## Day 12: Opening Dialogue

On Day 12, I'll private message at least 10 of the people engaging in the Challenge Facebook Group. (Yes, you read that right—I will message individual Challenge members!)

I'll ask them to share and add friends, and ask them what outcome and value they hope to achieve. This will build deeper connection with my community members—and help me gather data on how I am doing in my messaging and marketing.

This process will take some time, and it's not very scalable in the long term, BUT the payoff will be substantial. Foreseeing possible missteps and course correcting before I make my final offer can save a ton of heartburn and stress!

In addition, I'll do an Ask Campaign and poll inside the FREE 7-Day Challenge to gather more information on how I can best serve these members.

I'll create seven daily EVENTS using the events feature on the FREE 7-Day Challenge Community page in Facebook. This will both create the events and announce the days, times, and topics of each training. Then I'll invite ALL members to join the live trainings.

## Day 13: Group Focus

Today, I'll focus on sharing inside the FREE 7-Day Challenge Community as well as sharing it inside relevant Facebook Groups and social media channels.

I will consider my targets (i.e., 200 FREE Challenge members) and what I need to do to achieve this outcome. What adjustments need to be made? I will shamelessly market to hit my target.

I'll also begin to create the content for the actual 7-Day Challenge.

I'll work on Day 1's slide training, which I'll hold as a live training (via Zoom).

> *Day 1: Logistics: "How To Get The BEST Out Of Your 7-Day Challenge...And How It Will Unfold"*

Tips on slide-deck creation to remember:

1. Create slides in PowerPoint or Keynote.
2. Hire a designer on Fiverr to create a professional slide template with appropriate branding.
3. All slide presentations should flow like this:
   a. Share or story that challenges the viewers' current paradigm
   b. Review of past trainings
   c. Overview of training
   d. Training (at a high level)
   e. Assignment
4. Approximately one or two minutes per slide (60 slides = 90 minutes)
5. Slides each contain ONE IMAGE and ONE or TWO words only

I'll be hosting that within Zoom. I'll set it up for each of the challenge trainings to be recorded automatically—going live inside the Facebook Challenge group for each one.

These will be repurposed as a stack ("bonus value") on my Perfect Webinar on Day 5, and later converted into an actual digital course to be marketed and sold!

# Day 14: Traffic Control

I'll want to start controlling some of this traffic (people inside the FREE 7-Day Challenge).

To do so, I'll need a landing page for email opt-in, so today I'll log in to my ClickFunnels account to create a simple landing page for email opt-in. There are multiple easy templates that can be customized utilizing my branding and messaging. The goal is to capture as many challenge member emails as possible so I can later connect, nurture, and offer my opportunity directly.

I'll encourage them to sign up for the email list by telling them that if they do, I can email them directly about the daily training so they can stay up-to-date, even if they should miss something I added inside the Facebook Challenge group.

Today, I will create a legacy indoctrination series of emails that will be sent automatically over the next week to those who subscribe to the email list. I'll use the Nuance speech-to-text app on my mobile to create and edit those emails and line them up to be sent out.

Finally, I'll create the content—the slides and training—for Day 2 of the challenge.

## Week Three: Creation (Keep it Simple)

> *"Knowledge is a process of piling up facts; wisdom lies in their simplification."*
> — Martin H. Fischer

## Day 15: Training

Today will be Day 1 of the FREE 7-Day Challenge.

Inside of the closed Facebook FREE Challenge Community, I will conduct the Day 1's LIVE training.

This will cover the introduction to the challenge and will last one hour, with 30 minutes dedicated to pure value. I'll challenge participants' current beliefs surrounding the PAIN and problem I have defined, and then reaffirm that they can create success or overcome problems they have. I believe in them.

I'll also create and build the slide deck and training for Day 3 of the FREE Challenge.

I'll never stop promoting and growing the FREE 7-Day Challenge...

# Day 16: Training and Value Creation

Day 2 of the FREE 7-Day Challenge!

The training, which is on resources and preparation, will be one hour in duration and will be live inside the Facebook Challenge Community.

Deliver on these Day 2:

· Websites, downloads, guides, and references that will support potential customers' success
· Stories and humor to keep people engaged

Each of these challenges must be long enough so it's virtually impossible for participants to access and consume all the content of all trainings. This way, I could actually create two or three trainings on each day, so I'm creating a massive amount of value in the group.

If my FREE Challenge members are unable to consume ALL trainings, guides, and resources, this will create the value of offering the 7-Day Challenge recordings as a STACK on Days 5–7 (Real Bonus Value!).

Today, I'll create the slide deck and training for Day 4 of the challenge.

If you've noticed, I haven't actually created the product I'm selling. So today, I'll blueprint that product, how it will actually be laid out.

# Day 17: Training and Value Creation

Day 3 of the FREE 7-Day Challenge!

I'll do the Day 3 training inside the Facebook Challenge Community.

This will be a value build, so it will include the high-level solution to part of their initial problem or challenge. In other words, it will include high-level guidance.

In addition, I'll challenge their current beliefs and reaffirm their ability to succeed.

I'll also create the slide deck and training for Day 5 of the challenge and my Perfect Webinar for Day 5, including the formulation of the offer and opportunity.

In addition, I'll create a simple landing-page order form within ClickFunnels, where someone can land and pay to purchase my program (SYSTEM) when the opportunity goes live on Day 5.

The program will be offered at a "special" reduced pre-launch pricing of $997, with a three-pay of $399.

There will be a stack (bonus offer) that includes the five days of training from the FREE Challenge. This offer stack will be valuable because, during the challenge, each day's training will be removed after 48 hours. The only way to get access to ALL of the trainings, resources, and materials will be through this Perfect Webinar offer.

I'll let participants know up front that this is how the challenge will be organized. (It will be included in the pinned "rules" post on the Facebook page.) I'll explain that the reason we're removing trainings after 48 hours in the challenge is for accountability, so people will actually do the work!

So here's the offer:

A. Core Offer: $997 SYSTEM plus the trainings for the stack (7-Day Free Challenge trainings)
B. BUMP (upsell): 30-minute coaching call with me for $99 (I consider this as a paid and qualified sales call, to upgrade my customer to my high-ticket opportunity).
C. OTO #1 (one-time offer): $99/month continuity group with a FREE seven-day trial
D. OTO #2 (high[er]-ticket item): $4,000 application to join my group coaching pod for accelerated results

I'm looking for an average cart value of $1,200 and 20 sales.

I will REFINE the blueprint for my CORE product offer (weekly trainings, specific and measurable outcomes). I will have a designer at Fiverr create digital product graphics for the Day 5 Perfect Webinar.

# Day 18: Training and Review

Day 4 of the FREE Challenge!

I'll do the scheduled training inside of the free Facebook community, careful to answer all questions and address all concerns.

I will review content from Days 1 and 2 while foreshadowing the upcoming opportunity on Day 5.

It is absolutely vital to check in with people and see whether they are on or off track for completing the challenge and getting results. I'll find out what they may need to make the challenge successful for them.

Day 4 is all about follow-up and support, engaging and building tension for the upcoming opportunity.

For example, I'll discuss how there is SO much content to cover that for lasting results and guidance, they need to stay in the challenge— at the next (paid) level.

I'll announce that the Day 5 training will have an opportunity for only the first 20 people...and encourage members to show up live!

I'll challenge their current beliefs and reaffirm their abilities to create the outcomes they desire.

Today, I'll review Russell Brunson's Perfect Webinar training and review and refine Day 5 training and my Perfect Webinar (at least three times) in preparation for presentation.

## Day 19: Webinar

Day 5 of the FREE 7-Day Challenge!

Today, I'll host the Day 5 training, transitioning to my Perfect Webinar.

I will include 30 minutes of solid value, leading into the Perfect Webinar opportunity and my SYSTEM. I'll also have urgency and the bonuses, or stack—only 20 available!

As I've done each day, I'll challenge participants' beliefs and reaffirm their abilities.

## Day 20: Urgency

Day 6 of the challenge!

Today will be about creating urgency.

I'll go inside the free Facebook community, congratulating members who have purchased and doing urgency posts, letting people know the bonuses are going away soon. I'll let people know how many have been sold, how many are left (if there's any scarcity), when bonuses will be removed, and when the cart will close.

I will announce a 30-minute live stream inside the FREE 7-Day Challenge, where I will be answering any lingering questions or challenges.

The goal is to move those who have not yet purchased to action.

## Day 21: Urgency

Day 7 of the challenge!

Today, I'll continue posting about urgency, encouraging those on the fence and procrastinators to purchase. I'll post about the cart closing and remind people that this is their last chance to get prelaunch pricing.

I'll also begin building out the CORE product and service for delivery, for seven days post-Day 21.

This will be delivered via ClickFunnels, utilizing the secure members' site feature.

Week 4: House Cleaning And Scaling

"Greatness is not a function of circumstance. Greatness, it turns out, is largely a matter of conscious choice and discipline." — Jim Collins

## Day 22: Download and Refine

Today, I am going to compile content and feedback from the FREE 7-Day Challenge Community.

1. Download all video trainings (Days 1 to 5).
2. Compile all resources and guides created for the FREE experience.
3. Capture all direct messages, member wins, and positive feedback.

I will place all this content in a folder.

I'll begin to refine and upload the new course content from the free Facebook Challenge group. I'll edit and customize the videos/trainings, and once that's done, I'll upload them to YouTube (setting them as unlisted). I'll also create a members area within ClickFunnels.

This is my value stack!

## Day 23: Core Funnel

Day 23 is fun!

I get to build a proper sales page for the SYSTEM I have created. It will include a refined sales landing page with proper copy, leading to an order form, leading to the bump offer and the two OTOs.

Now that I have made sales and have some money coming in, I have a choice of hiring an integrator (I use Integrator and Co.) to build the sales page and the new funnel on my behalf, or I can build it myself. I always prefer to scale and outsource this as much as possible—that includes my sales copy. (Lain Ehmann is excellent!)

If I were not so ClickFunnels savvy, it could take a few weeks to get a GREAT funnel designed and converting on a learning curve, and I have lots to do, so I need to make the best use of my valuable time.

## Day 24: Continuity Group

On Day 24, I will create my continuity and support group for the CORE offer buyers who selected the FREE seven-day trial (and then $99/month).

I will add those who took advantage of OTO #1 to a CORE offer continuity group. I'll start adding value to that group. (See Day 9, rinse and repeat!) I'll create a schedule and logistics for the group to drive the consistent helpful content, such as...

- Live trainings on Mondays
- Office hours on Wednesdays
- Group Q&A on Fridays

I must get to know my people—their names and personalities, too!

## Day 25: Challenge Relaunch

Today, I'll repeat the challenge launch.

Isn't it too soon?

Nope!

Here's where the innovation and scale play out. The relaunch will be completely via Facebook Messenger (resource alert: ManyChat). For the people who did not take advantage of my CORE offer and those who missed some of the FREE 7-Day Challenge trainings and resources, they'll have the opportunity to go through the challenge one more time. This time, though, it will be offered via Facebook Messenger and ManyChat software.

I'll set a date for the launch, and I'll have seven days of pre-launch marketing (see Days 4 through 14), doing the same marketing as the initial launch (Facebook Live and driving traffic), but with a twist.

This time, I'll market mainly from my branded business page and grow my bot list. Comments on the Facebook Live will initiate the Messenger bot and send them a ManyChat notification that they're in for the challenge. The challenge itself will be dripped out over the course of seven days. Kaboom!

WHY will I scale through Messenger bots?

1. I can communicate at an entirely different level through Messenger. It is both personal and automated at the same time.
2. The open rates on Messenger are UNREAL!

I'll take all the content and recordings I've created for the original challenge, and I'll load those up in ManyChat to be dripped out to the subscribers over the course of the 7-Day Challenge.

This FREE 7-Day Challenge via Messenger will lead to my Perfect Webinar on Day 5, and my CORE offer.

## Day 26: Review Results Reflection

On Day 26, I'll compile and evaluate the results and statistics from the previous launch inside the FREE 7-Day Challenge. This will give me a benchmark of performance, and I'll aim to improve those conversions and increase my cart value.

I will step back from this project and reflect. I will ask myself, "If I want to achieve a 2 Comma funnel, what needs to happen? What can I improve? What is not working?"

I'll also be marketing for the next ManyChat free challenge, so I'll do a Facebook Live to drive traffic (see Day 9).

## Day 27: Case Studies

Case studies are a powerful marketing tool.

On Day 27, I'll collect a minimum of two case studies from the first free challenge. I'll reach out for two video testimonials or two video case studies.

I'll collect screen captures of results, and I'll do a Facebook Live and continue to drive traffic to the ManyChat free challenge.

## Day 28: Dream 100

To truly grow and scale, I must expand my reach.

How can I possibly expand quickly and efficiently without expending massive dollars on traffic or marketing?

SOLUTION: I'll use Dana Derrick's book Dream 100 as a guide and create my list of Dream 100 contacts for affiliates.

I'll take the sales statistics and case studies and create two introductory emails to send to potential affiliates—one that introduces myself and one that makes the affiliate offer.

## Day 29: Outreach

Using Dana Derrick's system as a guide, I'll research and reach out to the first 10 of my Dream 100. I'll send them the case studies, the sales statistics, and the results in an email for affiliate recruiting.

I'll ask them to email for my CORE offer, and reward them generously.

## Day 30: Rinse and Repeat

I'll move on to the next 10 of my Dream 100, sending them the same outreach email.

I will celebrate all the hard work and massive impact I have created over the past 30 days!

# FINAL THOUGHTS

So there you have it—30 days to start rebuilding. Hopefully, you can see that not only have I created a substantial amount of revenue—$20,000—but I'm well on my way to expanding that number through the use of affiliates. It's not just a one-time infusion of cash. It's a system that can be grown and scaled over time.

Now you can see why I was so insistent that you create not just a business but a SYSTEM—one that you can use over and over again.

There is literally no cap on what you can do with a system like this. You can recruit more affiliates, you can run paid advertising to your free challenge, you can add more products and services to your offer, you can continue to scale and grow. And you can eventually remove yourself from much of the everyday operations because you will have already done all the hard work!

Thirty days ago, you probably thought that creating a million-dollar-a-year business within that time was impossible. But that mindset is exactly what I want to challenge, over and over again, with my audience. I want to blast it apart until nothing is left but the unshakable belief that YOU CAN DO THIS.

Remember, it's not one-and-done. It's a process of learning, revisions, and improvement. Each time you offer a webinar, each time you send an email, each time you do a Facebook Live, review what you've done and ask yourself what you can do to make next time even better.

Constant improvement combined with a proven system WILL give you the success you want. It worked for me, and it will work for you, too.

I believe in you.

# RESOURCES

- DesignCrowd (designcrowd.com)
- Dream 100 Book by Dana Derricks
- Fiverr (fiverr.com)
- Integrator and Co. (integratorandco.com)
- Keynote
- Lain Ehmann (lainehmann.com)
- ManyChat (manychat.com)
- Messenger bots
- Nuance (nuance.com)
- PowerPoint
- Youzign (youzign.com)
- Zoom (zoom.us)

# Chapter 10

# FUNDRAISING FOR NONPROFITS

*by Tyler Shaule*

# TYLER SHAULE

## *Executive Director*

Non Profit Children's Summer Camp
*www.SummerCampCoach.com*

*Tyler is the Executive Director of Forest Cliff Camp, the premier Christian children's camp in Southwestern Ontario Canada. His background in education, experience in Nonprofit Leadership and recent industry awards in digital marketing and online fundraising have made him an in demand speaker and sought after consultant for Nonprofit organizations across North America.*

# 30 Days To Bootstrap A Profitable Online Fundraising Campaign For A Nonprofit That Is Changing The World

My name is Tyler Shaule, and I'm the executive director of a Christian children's summer camp in Ontario, Canada. I was awarded a 2 Comma Club award for a successful funnel I built to reach more parents and enroll more kids in our camp programs. Over the past four years, we have doubled the number of campers, tripled our annual revenue, and 10x'd our monthly donor giving. As a leader in the nonprofit industry, I believe that we have an obligation to be as profitable as possible, because we have the BEST place to use all that money—a cause that we know will make the world a better place.

My mission is simple: I want to help nonprofit organizations launch hyper-profitable online fundraising funnels so they can get noticed and get the resources they need to change the world!

This is my 30-day plan for how I would bootstrap a profitable online fundraising campaign for a nonprofit that is making a big impact—even if they don't have a website, an email list, or any money in their fundraising budget.

I know that the best way to bootstrap a nonprofit is to be mission-driven and donor-centric. I'm going to take these 30 days to build a raving online audience of like-minded individuals who feel my same burden about the cause, and offer them a way to be involved by giving money and then sharing the experience with their friends.

I'm NOT going to spend all my time writing grant applications to foundations or looking for corporate sponsors.

For this 30-day blueprint, I'm going to choose the mission my nonprofit will address. In my experience, there are three types of causes, each with their own challenges when it comes to marketing and fundraising.

## 3 Types of Nonprofit Causes

- *Compassionate:* CARE for the vulnerable is the main focus of these organizations. Often children- or animal-focused, they serve those who can't help themselves.

- *Change:* These causes work to create justice in the world. They address an inequality or strive to protect what is not being valued by others.
- *Culture:* These nonprofits are IDENTITY-based. Basically, if you finish the sentence "I am a(n)...," you have specified this type of cause. You might say "Christian," "art lover," "accountant," or "hiker." Each of these segments of someone's identity may form the cause a nonprofit is founded around.

I will only combine two of the types of causes so that I can be specific in my mission and messaging.

I'm going to pick a compassionate cause, because I know they are easier to create a donor-centered fundraising campaign for. Specifically, I want to focus on a cause that is child-based and local, so that I can easily get access to the programs and collect video and photos.

I'm going to assume I have buy-in from the nonprofit's board or staff and they want me to lead this effort for the next 30 days to create a profitable online fundraising campaign for them.

## Day 1

I will spend the morning writing down everything I know about the cause and why I care about it. (This may seem silly, but I need to see it on paper so that I can begin to think about how to share my thoughts.) I'll jump onto Google and study the top 10 search results then write down any questions I have.

In the afternoon, I will schedule interviews with the board, staff, key volunteers, and any current donors. I would ask them the following three questions (plus any I got from my Google search).

1. What is unique about your nonprofit?
2. What would go undone if your nonprofit closed tomorrow?
3. Why do you give your money, time, or energy to this nonprofit's mission?

Then record the answers in a Google Doc.

I'll look for common themes and repeated words or phrases and capture any stories they share with me (so I can share with others). My job is to start distilling all the good work they are doing into just one message they can use to build an audience online.

Many nonprofits want to educate the world on every aspect of their mission, but as a marketer, I know that what is needed is ONE clear, easy-to-understand message. My first step to is find that message.

# Day 2

Hold a morning meeting with the key staff member I'll be working with. Outline the plan and answer all their questions.

### The 30-Day Bootstrapped Profitable
### Online Fundraising Campaign Plan

1. Set goals for how much to raise in the first 30 days.
2. Pick a social platform and build an audience.
3. Test the messages and see what resonates with the audience.
4. Create a fundraising offer (one-time gift + monthly gift).
5. Launch the TEST campaign and raise "seed" money for future campaigns.
6. Build an evergreen campaign with the assets we've made and audience we've attracted.

Take the afternoon off. Rest, relax, and get ready for the craziness that will happen in the next part of the week.

# Day 3

Goal time! Today, I'm going to work with the nonprofit to stretch their expectations for the first month of fundraising but still remain realistic. We'll make sure to reflect back on these goals DAILY to measure our success.

### Goals For First 30 Days Of Online Fundraising
- 10 monthly donors ($50/month)

- 100 individual donors (average gift of $50)
- 30 day total = $5,500
- Monthly recurring revenue of $500/month (This is where the gold is!)

We are going to cap our fundraising (marketing and advertising expenses) to just $500 for the first month.

The truth is that it takes money to make money. Many nonprofits have a scarcity-based mindset (and budget). The rest of the day will be spent talking to staff members about the goals and discussing how they feel about the fundraising targets.

## Day 4

Time to lay the foundation for building an online audience.

I'm going to use social posting and Live videos on Facebook to get the attention of people who care about the mission of the nonprofit organization. Facebook is the ideal platform for this type of attention-based audience building.

Spend time brainstorming with the nonprofit staff member about four categories of messages we can create on Facebook. On the same Google Doc as before, list the categories and all the ideas. We won't finish until we have at least five ideas under each category that relate to the solution the nonprofit provides or the problems faced by the people they serve.

*Myths:* These are ideas that are misunderstood or wrong or might be barriers for people to give to the mission. As we receive feedback from our audience, we will keep this category updated (especially with reasons they may have to not be involved or to give a gift).

*Aha Moments:* Create a list of moments when the staff members or people they know had epiphanies about why the cause is so important. Make sure to record as much detail with these stories as possible. Details make the story richer and will lead our audience to feel all the same emotions as the person who originally had the epiphany, increasing the likelihood that they will have the same belief-changing moment.

**"Kinda Like" Bridges:** Some nonprofits' missions are about curing serious diseases or addressing complex social issues, or they involve very technical explanation. We need to be able to communicate the mission quickly and be understood, so coming up with a bunch of "kinda like" analogies for the problem we solve is a must. We will be creative and resist the urge to go too deep.

**Distinctives:** List the special or unique benefits or focuses of the nonprofit's mission. It's okay for us to throw rocks here. We'll think of all the benefits that wouldn't happen anymore if the nonprofit disappeared overnight, and we'll call them out in these posts.

Phewww! That is tons of work, but now we've got all the content ideas for next week's social posts and live videos.

# Day 5

Although Facebook changes in early 2018 somewhat decreased organic reach on pages, they still represent a great place to build an audience. I'm planning to use Live videos with really engaging content to get attention and spread the nonprofit's messages and to find like-minded people.

Another amazing way to build a qualified audience for future fundraising is through Video View audiences, which we can create in Facebook's Ads Manager.

We are going to spend today setting up a Facebook page for the nonprofit.

I'm going to take the rest of the day to write a welcome message on the new page as well as to install a Messenger chatbot on the page. (ManyChat gives me FREE access) with a welcome message. I'll add a chatbot opt-in so we can send broadcast messages to users about upcoming Live videos. It is also important to ask new chatbot subscribers for their email addresses. I'll set up a new list in Actionetics and

**198**

integrate the chatbot so we can add the subscriber's email address into ClickFunnels' email autoresponder.

## Days 6–7

It's "Dadurday" and church for me and my family on the weekend.

## Day 8

Today, I'm going to train two of the nonprofit staff members on how to post socially on their personal Facebook profiles.

We are going to start with personal posting, because this nonprofit has no presence online. Leveraging the personal social network of staff is a way to accelerate the online audience building for the nonprofit.

We are going to take eight of the content ideas (two from each category) and create an outline for each post in the shared Google Doc. Each post will have a strong call to action to join the nonprofit's NEW Facebook page. They will share two posts a day each for the rest of the week, with the purpose of growing the new page's reach.

I'm also going to work with them to create a private message (PM) they can send to their full Friend list to ask them to visit the new page and give it a Like.

It's totally reasonable to expect about 100 page Likes after the leveraged PMs and profile posts.

Most nonprofits get caught up in vanity metrics on Facebook and obsess over Likes. For the online audience building, I'm going to focus on getting page Likes from people who really care about the mission (or people who work there) or have engaged with the page content by watching a video, sharing content, or commenting on a post. With this high-quality list of Likes, we can use the Boost Post feature to expand our reach to people we actually want to get our message in front of.

## Days 9–14 (Yes, Even the Weekend)

Each day, a nonprofit staff member will do a Facebook Live from the page. It will be a 10- to 15-minute broadcast about one of the most engaging content types we brainstormed on Day 4.

*Online Fundraising Rule #1: People give to people.* I'm going to coach the staff member who has the best rapport and most senior position to do all the Live videos. They need to be the Attractive Character that Russell talks about in all his trainings and books. They need to connect with the audience and be an advocate that establishes trust and leads people to take action.

Each video will be based on unique content—from one of the four categories, or perhaps an interview or interactive theme—but will have a similar format. Here are some other things I will keep in mind.

1. Schedule at least four Live video reminders on the page before I do the video.
2. I will start the video right away and not wait around for people to join. Facebook will promote the video for about 24 hours, and most people will watch the replay.
3. I'll ask for engagement and feedback often.
4. Every five minutes, I'll ask the viewers to SHARE the video so their Facebook friends can watch, too.
5. At the end of the video, I'll take a minute to tease the next day's video and remind viewers to Like the page and turn on notifications so they don't miss any future videos.
6. Finally, I'll tell viewers to make contact in Messenger if they have questions or want more information about anything that is being shared.

I'm going to regularly analyze the videos for a few key metrics.

- Views (after 24 hours)
- Engagement (Likes, Comments, Shares)
- Minutes of video watched)

If a video gets very little response, then that could mean its message didn't resonate with the audience. If a video BLOWS UP, then I'll make sure to record more videos like it and take note of the topic, because it will help me next week when I work to create a fundraising offer that people will respond to.

Every time someone engages with a video, I'm going to manually invite them to Like the nonprofit's page.

The goal is to get 200–300 views for each video and, by the end of the six days of live video, to have about 300 page Likes.

## Day 15

I'm going to start the day by opening the Facebook Ads Manager for the nonprofit's page and building a custom audience based on 50% video views. (I can make an audience of people who viewed certain videos on a page for a certain amount of time.)

The target is to see an audience size of at least 400. If we aren't there yet, then they need to do a few more days of videos OR boost the post with the Connections feature (friends of people who Like this page) and spend only $10 to get about 200–400 views.

Once I have 400 in the custom Video View audience, I will create a Lookalike Audience (1% with geographic boundaries set to either state or country) of at least 100,000.

Wow—imagine the impact of being able to reach an audience of 100,000 like-minded people with this nonprofit's message in just 14 days of effort. Crazy!

With this in place, I'm almost ready to roll out the first campaign. But first I need...

- Money for advertising
- A fundraising offer
- A way for donors to give online

The afternoon will be spent studying the people who engaged with the videos and cross-referencing that list with prior donors.

The goal is to find past donors (at least five) who have actively engaged with the online videos and to share with them our goal of raising $5,000 in the next two weeks with an online campaign. If I couldn't find any overlap with these two groups, I would ask five of the nonprofit's offline donors who are most likely to give.

The script is simple.

Share with them the 30-day goal of $5,500 in online donations and finish with: "Can you help us get started toward that goal today with a gift of $100 or a monthly commitment of $50?" At the conclusion of the call, I will THANK THEM and ask them if they would consider being a guest on a Facebook Live video this week. I will get at least two donor interviews. Asking in person is best, but over the phone can work as well.

A 20% conversion rate on the initial ask would be considered successful. I now have at least $100 to use for launching the initial fundraising campaign.

## Days 16–18

I would start scheduling the donor interview Facebook Live videos ASAP. It is important for the donors to share the emotional reasons why they gave money as well as the practical outcomes that happened because of the gift.

These videos are amazing social proof, so I'll make sure I save them, because I'll definitely be using them lots in the future.

During the live video interviews, I will make sure to promote the upcoming fundraising campaign.

The remainder of the three days will be for crafting the fundraising offer, the ask or appeal that we will use to raise the money for our goal.

I know that the offer is the key to effectively fundraising, and it is even more important when raising money online. It can't be rushed and often needs to be tested extensively and tuned regularly. However, once it is perfected for the audience it is presented to, it can EXPLODE and make a nonprofit a lot of money. That's my goal, so I'm going to spend the rest of the week on it.

### 4 Keys To A Compelling Fundraising Offer

1. A donor-sized problem (EX: we can't solve world hunger, BUT we can feed one child today)
2. A price point that makes sense to solve that problem
3. A reason to give NOW (natural urgency is best)

4. A thank-you that gives them a CAPE (I got this concept from Kaelin Poulin's presentation "The Identity Shift" at Funnel Hacking LIVE 2018. Superheroes wear capes when they are saving the world, and fundraiser organizers need to remind donors of their new identities as heroes to the nonprofit and the cause they serve by giving their money.)

The last point to consider with the fundraising offer is the hook and story I will use to emotionally connect the audience to the offer.

I've had the nonprofit test the stories and messages with the Live videos, so now is the time to study the results and find the BEST story that will draw out emotion, create belief, and connect the audience to the solution that the nonprofit creates, then move them to join by giving a donation.

I'll make a list and write pros and cons of each story as well as the engagement metrics. Getting multiple perspectives is helpful, so I'll be sure to have an all-staff meeting to get feedback on both the offer and the story.

By the end of Day 18, we'll have an offer built, along with a story and hook.

The offer will have two parts: a one-time gift option of $100 (we need to be specific on an exact donation amount) and a monthly gift amount of $50.

# Day 19

Time to build the donation page and make sure all the tech will work for the campaign we will launch next week.

Today will be spent in ClickFunnels, so I need to do the following:

- Set up the landing page where the donors will be able to give.
- Build a thank-you page (with a prominent SHARE button linking to the donation page so donors can tell their friends that they gave).
- Write two email sequences that both last five days (one email per day).

I'll use one of the donor interview videos on the donation page along with very strong copy that clearly describes the problem, the non-profit's specific solution, and the outcomes when a gift is given AND not given. (We need to remind donors of the negative consequences of not taking action immediately.) I use radio buttons for each giving option and always include the FEWEST possible form fields. (I don't ask for a phone number.)

Email Sequence #1 is for donors who give to the one-time gift option, and its goal is to thank them, demonstrate the benefit of the gift, and present the monthly giving option as a great next step.

Email Sequence #2 is for donors who gave with the monthly option. It will thank them and report on the benefits to the cause because of their gift.

Use the other donor interview video in the emails to confirm in the mind of the donor that their gift was a great idea and is beneficial.

Donation webpages are unique in many ways and are very important to the success of the campaign. Adding the Facebook pixel to the ClickFunnels donation page is important so we can track who has visited it.

## Days 20–21

Time to get some rest and relaxation before the campaign kicks off.

## Day 22

I'm going to kick the week off with a one-hour meeting to help the staff understand the promotion plan for the campaign launch this week.

They'll spend the remainder of the day working on content for the campaign. All the content should create an emotional link between the audience and the benefit being created with the money we will raise. The call to action (CTA) will be to visit the Facebook page or the donation page.

- Personal profile posts (daily for four days for each staff member—we gotta leverage their friendships to get online donations)

- Page posts (daily for six days)
- Live videos (Time to make the BEST live videos of the month. We'll use lots of stories, be in different locations, do interviews, and give updates often about the progress toward the goal.)
- Messenger broadcasts (four)
- Email broadcasts (four)

I'll work with the staff to schedule these content items over the next six days of the campaign.

I'll make sure to do last-minute tech checkups to make the sure the donation page works, the payment processor is hooked up, and emails are ready to send.

## Days 23–25

On these days, we will work hard to organically get attention and raise money with the social posting. We'll have to make sure to keep someone ready to take phone calls or answer Facebook Messenger questions in case a prospective donor contacts us.

The first few days of the campaign are to get MOMENTUM. When we have an initial amount of money raised, I know it will be easier to create advertising that will get noticed and that people will want to be involved in.

I would expect that we have at least 25 gifts of $100 by now, for a total of $2,500.

## Day 26

The last few days of the campaign, we are going to leverage the MO-MENTUM by sharing how close we are to our goal and the amount we need over the next two days. Doing it this way means that we raise the initial amount of the campaign from the most loyal donors and then use that result to encourage the less-qualified segment of the audience to give a gift to "put us over the goal."

Today, I'm going to create a video ad (edited from the best Facebook Live videos we've done) that tells the story of the nonprofit's cause and presents the offer.

In addition to running a video ad, I'll also use the Boost Post ad feature and pick three different audiences to advertise to.

a. Facebook fans and their friends
b. Custom Video View audience
c. Lookalike audience

I created the last one on Day 15 to pay for the most popular two campaign Live videos to be shown to those audiences we created using our social video strategy.

The major advantage of my social audience strategy is that I didn't have to guess at demographic or interest targeting and waste time and money while building an audience to advertise to.

Instead, I built an attention-based audience using Facebook's social tools and, because of that, I can guarantee an advertising audience of at least 100,000 all the way to 1 million that will actually care about this small nonprofit's fundraising offer...although they don't even have a website yet.

Over the next few days, I'll spend the $100 the nonprofit dedicated to advertising from the initial gifts made on Day 15.

# Days 27–28

On these days, I'll watch the ad spend, give updates on totals, and make repeated calls to action to visit the donation page and give. I'll remind the nonprofit staff to promote WAY MORE than they think is necessary. Most nonprofits get shy and don't want to "bother" people, but the truth is that it takes many communication points to be heard among the noise of social media. Not promoting hard enough or giving up too easily are common traits among nonprofits, so I won't let that happen to us.

Instead, we will make another video, send another email, write another post, and make strong calls to action to give and make a difference so we can reach the goal.

# Day 29

Whew! The campaign is done and we exceeded the goal. Time to dance around and get excited for all the good that money will do for the nonprofit's cause!

With a social audience of 100,000, it is easy to raise money fast. The reason most nonprofits fail with online fundraising is that they don't have a large or loyal online audience, and their technology is old or not optimized for seamless online transactions. My strategy provided the opportunity for this nonprofit to get their message in front of thousands of like-minded individuals and used the cutting-edge technology of ClickFunnels, the world's premier online sales and marketing software, to make it easy to do (no coders, developers, or computer wizards needed).

Even though the campaign is done, the nonprofit's job is not over yet. I'll get them to spend the next two days sending personal emails and messages to thank donors who gave and begin to sow the seeds for the next campaign.

# Day 30

With the success of the online campaign, it's time to make this fundraising offer "evergreen" with ads that run over the next 30 days, so the automated donor funnel will continue to build trust, change beliefs, and lead people to become donors.

By knowing the key metrics of the initial campaign, it is much easier to convince the nonprofit to spend $500–$1,000/month for advertising when they've already seen the same online fundraising funnel create over $5,000 in revenue!

I'll keep a careful watch over the automated campaign and make sure it remains a donor-acquiring cash machine for months to come.

# FINAL THOUGHTS

After a nonprofit launches their first profitable online fundraising campaign, it is so much easier to show them the power of donor funnels to acquire new givers. The amazing thing is that donor funnels also help to increase the average amount given per gift and increase the frequency of giving (especially when you include a monthly giving option).

# RESOURCES

- Actionetics (clickfunnels.com/actionetics)
- Facebook Ads Manager
- Facebook Boost Post
- Facebook Live
- Facebook Messenger
- Google Docs
- ManyChat (manychat.com)
- Messenger bots
- Online Donations (onlinedonations.us)

## Chapter 11

# SERVICE PACKAGES VIA LINKEDIN

## by Rachel Pedersen

# RACHEL PEDERSEN

## *Marketing Consultant and Founder/ CEO of Social Media United*

### Digital Marketing / Social Media
*RachelPedersen.com*

*Rachel Pedersen is the founder and CEO of the so-cial media agency SocialWorks Digital, and Social Media United - teaching others how grow personal brands and retain clients. Rachel is the symbol of freedom, determination, passion for life and busi-ness; making an impact by changing lives of those around her and showing anyone and everyone that they can reach new heights they never thought pos-sible. Rachel has helped 100's of individuals world-*

*wide change the trajectory of their lives by finding freedom from a 9-5 job. In just over 2 years Rachel has gone viral reaching 11.3 million, being featured in Glamour, TODAY, Cosmopolitan and US Weekly. Rachel has taken her clients from $4k months to $7k days, with a 3-22x ROAS. She has worked with Fortune 500 influencers, celebrities and clients. She has gone from a single Minnesota mom, to one of the top social media marketers worldwide.*

## Day 1

Day 1. Ground zero. Ready for what I'm going to do today?

It's going to shock you...it might be a little unconventional.

I'm going to bawl my frickin' face off, write in my journal, and drown my sorrows in chocolate ice cream.

What? You thought I was going to conquer the world today? I just lost everything! I'm a human, not a robot.

Having painstakingly built businesses, a reputation, a following, and financial security—all the while sacrificing sleep and convenience and giving it 110% for YEARS—only to have it all ripped away in a moment for reasons unexplained to me?

I'm absolutely devastated and need a moment to process the overwhelm AND to mourn the loss of what could have been.

But I better get a good night's sleep. World domination begins tomorrow.

## Day 2

Silence the noise and pressure. No one thrives when the weight of the world (such as debt) is on their shoulders. It's essential right now to silence my phone, ignore emails from debt collectors, and focus on the next 30 days.

What happens in the next 30 days will remove the noise and pressure long-term, but first I need to put on my oxygen mask and help myself.

In order to have some capital, I would go on a selling platform (such as Facebook Marketplace or Craigslist) and sell random items from around my house. This entire day is dedicated to generating capital. If I can make $1,000 today, I can breathe.

## Day 3

Since I'm starting from scratch, I get to decide what industry/niche/focus I'm going to go into. My expertise and skill lie in being a social media manager and Facebook ads manager, so I'm going to focus on the skills I know I can get the fastest results with.

Hands-down: lead generation for coaches, courses, and email list growth.

Make it rain leads—and fast!

## Day 4

Time to create my social media profiles, all created around my name (as a personal brand) since it's the quickest way to build an Attractive Character and magnetize people.

The easiest way to set up a website is through ClickFunnels, so I'm going to create a simple website that I'll add to later on. To determine my branding, I'm going to use Pinterest wedding palettes and stick with that branding throughout my social media profiles and new ClickFunnels website.

## Day 5

The main social media platforms I'm going to focus on for the 30-day build are Facebook and LinkedIn. The rest are great, but I'm going to focus on where I know I'll get the best bang for my buck...err...time.

If you don't have the money, you'd better have the time!

Making sure to Facebook pixel my new website so I can remarket to any visitors, I'm plastering the link everywhere—on my LinkedIn bio, on the bios and link spots on Facebook (both my profile and my page)—I want everyone to visit it.

While I don't have huge wins on my website yet, I can share what expertise I do have and tell a story.

## Day 6

Heading over to LinkedIn, I need to optimize my bio. I want every visitor to have NO question what my focus is—I generate leads—and they need to know how that can benefit them.

After optimizing my bio, I'd connect with hundreds of CEOs, founders, owners, presidents, and partners of companies in industries that want to generate leads for their business.

Connect, connect, connect until my fingers are absolutely numb.

## Day 7

Once hundreds of connections accept the request, it's time for outreach. I'm going to send a message to each of the new connections with intention, sharing how I can generate leads for them and set up a strategy that brings leads to their business every single day.

I want to help them with a strategy call for FREE—they'll walk away with a strategy customized for their business. And I'm not going to charge a single dollar.

## Day 8

Awesome! I got several bites overnight while I slept. (Although, let's be real—I didn't sleep. I kept connecting and sending messages on LinkedIn.)

I've gotta get them on a call, and I'm going to give them one hour of valuable strategy. It's going to intentionally be my BEST strategies, because I know that after that call, they'll need support.

Days 6–8 will be a small investment of time that I'll repeat every single day AT LEAST until Day 22.

## Day 9

Send over the full strategy report, in exchange for a testimonial and reduced monthly fee for support in implementing the proposed strategies.

The power is in the testimonials; the reduced monthly fee is just to get some cash flow and momentum happening.

## Day 10

Today, I need to add the testimonials into my ClickFunnels website. A photo-and-text-based testimonial is helpful—video testimonials are even better.

## Day 11

On the ClickFunnels website I'm building (which by the way is just a one-pager to get started), I'm going to add a scheduler.

After evaluating my current cash-flow situation, I have to decide between Calendly (which is free and sufficient but not amazing for advanced options) and ScheduleOnce or Acuity. (Acuity is amazing for adding in the next step, which I will add in the next few days.)

Yes, Acuity sounds perfect. I'll embed it into the pop-up page that appears when people click the button with the CTA. Easy peasy.

## Day 12

On both my Facebook page and profile, I'm committing to going live every single day, sharing value and AWESOME strategies that can be implemented to generate leads.

At the end of each Live, I'll say, "If you want to learn more about effective strategies to generate leads for your business, click the link above to set up a fifteen-minute call." Of course, the link goes to my awesome ClickFunnels one-page website, which now has a calendar they can use to set up a call.

I won't forget the CTA—value is great, but without a CTA I can't become a profitable revenue-generating machine by Day 30.

## Day 13

The Facebook Live videos on my page aren't getting any views, which means they aren't doing anything. (This is pretty normal for a new Facebook page, or any new social profile.)

Using Facebook Ads, I set up Video View ads to get my ideal prospective clients to watch my Lives.

I'm targeting CEOs, founders, presidents, and small business owners for these videos.

## Day 14

Today is all about community. I'm going to go into large existing communities (on Facebook) and share long-form value posts with instantly implementable steps.

After this happens, people will engage with the posts, which allows me to Friend them and send them a message.

This is NOT a pitch. It's just networking. A pitch on a platform that is highly personal will instantly repel people.

Also, more people will see my future Lives on my personal profile when my friend base on Facebook is larger. Score!

## Day 15

Using Facebook Ads, I'm going to retarget the video views from all my live videos. The goal is to send them to my ClickFunnels one-page website.

It's hard to spend money, but I have to remember that I generated $1,000 on Day 2 for this purpose.

If I can get one client within the first $1,000 in ad spend, I'll break even by month one. "The business that can spend the most to acquire a customer wins." (This is an awesome quote by Dan Kennedy that was a favorite of Russell Brunson's.)

## Day 16

Continuing to secure calls for strategy, I reorganize my website with the best testimonials I've gotten so far. However, the "free" game ends now. It's time to charge for strategy calls. I will update my Acuity scheduler to reflect this and add two options:

- Qualification Call (note the flip in confidence): 15 minutes, FREE

- Full Business Strategy Call: 60 minutes, $500

## Day 17

Now the goal is to either get people to get on a qualification call or a full strategy call.

The leads who set up a full strategy call will be upsold into a full package for between $1,000 and $2,000 per month.

The irresistible offer is that they get 50% off their first month.

## Day 18

Today, I'm going to repeat this process. I'll be at $5,000 per month with at least five clients in the next few days. Once I hit five clients @ $1,000+ per month, time to raise the prices for my first few clients.

## Day 19

Hitting a $5,000 month is something that most people only DREAM of being able to do in less than 30 days. It's powerful enough to replace a 9–5, give freedom, and pay off debt.

I am going to pivot today and start to build my own platform. I'd use a Facebook Group and invite people I've Friended over the last 19 days via a personal message.

## Day 20

Keep repeating the steps from Days 6–8 but begin sharing with people how I secured five clients in less than a month using social media and my expert lead-generation strategies.

## Day 21

Create a 100% passive product to teach people how I achieved a $5,000 month from the leads I generated.

It can be simple and small—$19—a price that is a no-brainer for anyone who wants to get similar results.

I'm sharing it with my newly growing audiences on Facebook and LinkedIn, and in my Facebook community. If I can get ONE sale, I can get a thousand.

## Day 22

I'm going to study the value ladder provided in DotComSecrets and learn exactly what the next logical step is and how I can give people more of what they want in a bigger product/course.

## Day 23

Today, I'm gonna hit the LinkedIn lead-generation process (in my old business, it was called "10 Days to $1K") hard and turn up my ad spend on the videos I'm doing live, plus the retargeting campaigns.

I know that once I hit the $10,000 month, the world will be my oyster.

## Day 24

Based on the value ladder I've created, I'm putting together the outline for my new course and seeding my following with excitement about it.

Thankfully, I know that I can create a course overnight, and that's what today is all about—recording the content and organizing it within ClickFunnels using the membership site template.

They're gonna love it.

## Day 25

Time to put 10 beta testers through my program at a cost that's a no-brainer. It'll normally be $497 or so, but the first 10 people to sign up will get to join for just $97, or $197 with a weekly group coaching call.

This is, of course, in exchange for a testimonial video.

## Day 26

Get the initial feedback from the beta testers (while this is valuable, the testimonials of their own results are more powerful) and create a sales page for the course.

This will be created with ClickFunnels templates for sales pages, since I know it'll shortcut the time I need to spend wireframing a sales page. (I don't build the prettiest funnels, but they convert and do the job.)

## Day 27

At this point, I'm getting close to a $10K month, and it's time to bring on a part-time virtual assistant (just a few hours a week) to handle emails and schedule content on social media.

This will free up some of my time so I can work ON my business in a bigger way.

Oh, you thought that I wasn't putting in 80-hour+ weeks? Ha ha, no way. I'm working 80+ every single week because I'm still FIGHTING for survival...but the end is in sight.

## Day 28

Today is all about promotion. I need everyone to see my face, hear my voice, and know my name.

I am going to pitch every single podcast in the categories my ideal person might listen to.

My goal is to book 50+ podcasts so that I can quickly build back my influence and platform.

## Day 29

Time to create my Dream 100, people who are one or two steps ahead of me in business. I want to make them affiliates/joint venture partners of my new course. I'll share 50% of the revenue in exchange for their promotion.

## Day 30

Today is a good day. It's the day I can pay the minimum balances on all bills and double down my efforts through the leveraged systems I've built over the past 30 days. Around Day 30 is when I anticipate hitting a $10,000 month—then I'm on to $20,000 months!

# FINAL THOUGHTS

Wow. It was an intense 30 days, but I've been through it before. The biggest thing to remember is that this short-term, intentional sprint can literally save your butt and change the way you see everything in life.

If you're reading this thinking, That's not replicable, Rachel, just go ask the people I've helped to do the same thing.

It's 110% possible, so now go take action!

# RESOURCES

- Acuity (acuityscheduling.com)
- Calendly (calendly.com)
- Craigslist (craigslist.org)
- DotComSecrets by Russell Brunson
- Facebook Ads Manager
- Facebook Live
- Facebook Marketplace
- Pinterest (pinterest.com)
- ScheduleOnce (scheduleonce.com)

Chapter 12

# SELL FUNNELS ON INSTAGRAM

## by Jeremy McGilvrey

# JEREMY MCGILVREY

## *Owner*

Instagram Expert
*IGBook.com*

*Jeremy McGilvrey has completely disrupted the marketing industry with his seemingly magical ability to help entrepreneurs QUICKLY flood their websites, landing pages and offers with massive amounts of cheap and targeted prospects that easily convert into leads, sales and profit.*

*Using Jeremy's innovative techniques, startups as well as established business owners are able to generate an endless flood of warm, cheap and targeted leads ON DEMAND. McGilvrey uses what he calls,*

> *"word of mouth marketing on steroids" to make cold*
> *traffic a thing of the past. The warm traffic generated*
> *by McGilvrey's new methods and techniques are ex-*
> *ponentially easier to turn into both leads and sales.*
>
> *The Huffington Post has called McGilvrey a "bril-*
> *liant entrepreneur," but he didn't earn that type of*
> *praise over night. It took years of pain, suffering and*
> *frustration for Jeremy to get where he is today, and*
> *now it's his mission to help other entrepreneurs com-*
> *pletely bypass the struggles he endured and to help*
> *them create massive success online in record time.*

Losing it all? No big deal. I've lost it all before. In 2009, I went from a net worth of $10 million and managing half a BILLION (with a B) dollars in assets to a 40-year prison sentence due to financial improprieties that took place at my wealth management firm. (Thankfully, a miracle took place and I was given a second chance.) So I have the unique perspective of having lived this before.

The first time something horrible happens, we as humans have no idea how to handle it. The second time the same horrible thing happens, it may not hurt any less, but at least we have some idea about how to cope and move forward.

Now, while someone who has never experienced this would more than likely spend Day 1 lying on the couch, stuffing their face with Ben and Jerry's, and watching Hallmark movies or drinking Jack Daniels straight from the bottle, (and understandably so)...

I would IMMEDIATELY jump into action.

## Day 1

First, I would immediately turn off ALL notifications—email, Facebook, Instagram, you name it. I would not allow myself to get addicted to distractions. Jeff Hoffman invented the airport kiosks, and he's famous for saying: "If it doesn't have to do with airport kiosks, let's chat in a year." That would be the exact focus I'd have when turning a setback into a comeback.

Next, I'd figure out EXACTLY how much money I'd need to generate over the next 30 days. (For this example, the goal is $10,000.)

Once I had my financial goal, I would select a niche market or what I call an HCBA (hungry, capable, buying audience). Hungry means they have a big pain that needs to be solved, and capable means they have the money and WILLINGNESS to pay for a solution. Because of my vast marketing experience, I know there's a TON of fitness professionals on Instagram (IG) who struggle to get leads and clients. I also know that these individuals have the money and desire to pay for a solution that will provide them with qualified leads on autopilot.

After that, I would determine HOW I was going to make the $10,000 (including products, price points, and conversion numbers).

A product I KNOW that can easily generate $5,000 to $10,000 in one month would be a done-for-you sales funnel that I could sell to fitness professionals to help them get leads and clients for their fitness coaching businesses.

The GENIUS part of this strategy (I'm actually patting myself on the back right now and typing with one hand) is that the SALES FUNNEL I will use to generate leads for this NEW business is the SAME one I will sell to the fitness professionals. All I'll have to do is customize the marketing message and email follow-up sequence to fit their business. This means I only have to build ONE funnel from scratch, and I can use it both as a means to generate leads AND as the product I will be selling.

Finally, I would use what I've learned from Russell in DotComSecrets to determine and sketch out the EXACT funnel and email sequences I would need to pull this all off.

## Day 2

In online marketing, the easiest and fastest way to make money is by SPENDING money on ads. My problem in this scenario is that

I'm completely broke. That's why I'd focus ALL of my energy on Instagram. When done right, you can get traffic, leads, and sales 100% FREE, which is pretty much impossible to do anywhere else. But it still requires hustle and thick skin.

Here are my Day 2 steps:

1. Choose an Instagram username that lets my followers know EXACTLY WHO I am and WHAT I offer just by reading it. Something like FitnessFunnelPros (Funnels for Fitness Professionals).

   * *Pro Tip: I would also go buy a website domain name, as similar to my IG username as possible. (I literally bought the domain FitnessFunnels.com while I was writing this.)*

2. Set up an Instagram page that will resonate with my perfect prospects. This includes designing an eye-catching profile image and a bio that builds authority, creates curiosity, and makes them want to click the link at the bottom. I would also develop and deploy a highly engaging content strategy to make people feel like they are missing out by not following me to see what I post next.

Here's the 100% FREE and simple process I would use to create content for my page.

First, I'd search the three websites listed below for high-quality, eye-catching fitness images.

- FreeImages
- Pexels
- Unsplash

Next, I'd upload the images I chose to Canva. In order to make the text POP, I would create a light black overlay to place on top of images. After that, I'd google "top fitness quotes" and then add the best ones as text to the images.

Finally, I'd post 12 crystal-clear fitness quote images on my page with captions (text below the post) that expounded on the quotes and added value to my followers or potential followers.

I'd also make a checklist that details all of the daily tasks I'll need to do in order to quickly grow and monetize my page. Even though I have all of these Instagram growth hacks memorized, by writing everything down, I will make sure nothing gets left out from day to day, because things are going to be crazy. This checklist will also make a cool bonus I can add to my STACK when I start pitching my done-for-you funnels to fitness professionals.

## Day 3

Nothing—and I mean NOTHING—I do in online business will matter unless I have a crystal-clear customer avatar. Knowing exactly WHO my customer is, what makes them "tick," and the words and images that will capture their heart and captivate their mind is ultimately what will determine my success. People fail online because they think there is a magical marketing tactic that will create success for them. Truth is, the MAGIC is in the messaging.

On Day 3, I would...

1. Create detailed demographic and psychographic profiles as well as document things such as which gurus my prospect follows online and what products or services they currently use.
2. Figure out what other solutions are currently being offered in this niche, to understand what may or may not be working for the competition and also to determine how I can uniquely position myself as the "logical" choice to do business with.
3. I would take everything that I learned in previous steps and use it to decide what JUICY BAIT I could use to attract my perfect prospect.
4. Because I have ZERO time to waste creating my own BAIT, I'd go to a private-label-rights (PLR) website like Master-Resale-Rights (a site where you're able to purchase the rights to high-quality, ready-made content for less than $7 and use it however

you choose). I'd borrow $7 from a friend (because I'm broke) to buy an e-book that would be irresistible to my perfect prospect. Once I start driving traffic to my IG page, I'll use this e-book to get prospects to opt in to my funnel.

## Day 4

Just because I have the same steps as a funnel that made the 2 Comma Club doesn't mean my funnel will have that same level of success. Funnel architecture is FICTION; funnel messaging is FACT.

Poor funnel design with compelling copy will beat amazing funnel design with crappy copy every time. That's why Day 4 will be 100% dedicated to developing a laser-focused marketing message that will make attracting and converting my ideal clients easier than shooting fish in a barrel.

Here's what I'd do:

1. Craft a series of headlines and sub-headlines using psychological triggers like curiosity, urgency, scarcity, benefits, and proof.
2. Next, I would write a series of bullet points relating to the BAIT I selected on Day 3, in order to add value and create curiosity. (I will later use these things to craft a compelling argument around why people NEED to download and consume my BAIT.)
3. Look into my past and create a simple "hero's journey" story I could use in my copy to create rapport with my prospect. Also, I'd search for other true stories, so I have examples not just pertaining to me.
4. I would compile everything in steps 1–3 into a swipe file that I can use when I'm building out my funnel.

## Days 5–6

Now that the "facts" that make the funnel work are in place—customer avatar, copy, and BAIT—I'll use ClickFunnels to build the funnel (including email sequences) for getting leads and making sales, and ALSO as the product I'm selling (done-for-you funnels).

Here's what the funnel will look like:

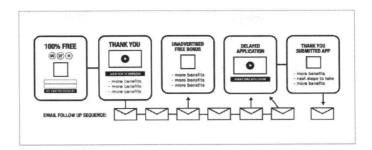

The *landing page* would have a 100% FREE (private-label-right e-book) about how to get clients and leads for online fitness professionals.

The *thank-you page* would have a short message from me acknowledging the last action they took and thanking them for downloading the e-book, and some copy designed to add perceived value and curiosity about the e-book and also to prescribe next steps.

At the same time, they would start to get emails adding more value and creating rapport on an *unadvertised bonus page.*

After a few days, they'd be sent to an *application page* to apply for a FREE strategy session with me. (This is where I'll pitch them on the done-for-you funnel.)

Next, there would be an *application submitted page* that acknowledges their past action and gives next steps.

Finally, if their application is approved, they would be sent to a free online scheduler to set up a time for their strategy session.

## Days 7–8

Even though the online marketing dream is to "make money while you sleep," sitting back and waiting for my first sale to come in would be a MASSIVE mistake. This is why my #1 focus on Days 7 and 8 is to "pound the online pavement" and go GET my first sale instead of waiting for it to come to me.

Here's how.

1. I would find 50 Instagram pages owned by low-follower-based fitness influencers (10K–20K followers) and I'd direct message (DM) them to start a conversation. People with more followers

will never see the message or won't need what I'm selling. Based on our conversation (and what I learned from creating my customer avatar), I'd determine whether they would need or be interested in my done-for-you funnel.

2. Once I had qualified them as a potential buyer, I would use the strategy I read about in DotComSecrets. I'd say, "Listen, I built this awesome sales funnel for someone who was looking to get leads and clients for their fitness business using Instagram. I charged them $1,500 and they can't make the second payment, but if you want it, I'll sell you the funnel for $750 right now."

3. It may take me throwing in some bonuses, hopping on a Skype call with them, or even making this pitch to several people if the first person doesn't take the offer, but based on my sales and marketing experience, I know I can close at least ONE person out of the 50 I messaged.

4. BOOM! I'm no longer broke, and I did it without spending a single dollar. (I do have to pay my friend back the $7 I borrowed to buy the PLR e-book). The best part is, I have $743 for paid advertising. This will allow me to drive traffic into my funnel without having to go out and interact with my prospects one by one.

# Day 9

On Day 9, I would quickly get to work on turning the $743 into $2,000.

Now that I have a little cash and proof of concept, I'm going to raise the price of my done-for-you funnels from $750 to $1,000. I'm not going to stop the DM strategy (because when you're doing something that works, you need to do MORE of it, not less) but I'd also use the $743 to buy Shoutouts from Instagram influencers.

Without going into extreme detail, an IG Shoutout is like word-of-mouth marketing on steroids. Followers of FAMOUS Instagram pages already know, like, and trust these pages (and the people behind

**228**

them). When these pages "shout you out," it's like a word-of-mouth recommendation from a trusted friend instead of interruption marketing like Facebook-sponsored ads.

I would find Instagram pages where I believe my target audience hangs out and purchase Shoutouts from them. (There is an art and a science to negotiating and crafting powerful, PROFITABLE Shoutouts, but I don't have enough room to go into detail on that here.)

While it's important for the Shoutouts to build my email list and get more people going through my funnel, the ONLY thing I really care about is earning more money to buy Shoutouts. Because of this, I'm not overly concerned with opt-in rates or other metrics just yet. If I get my $2,000 at the end, I win, no matter how few people actually opted in.

Also, because it will take a person going through my funnel a few days to get to the application and Skype call, it may take until as far as Day 14 for a lead to get to the point where they're ready to be sold.

Between the DM strategy and Shoutouts, closing at LEAST two new clients at $1,000 in the next five days is very attainable. I could probably do more.

## Days 10–11

By Day 10, the fitness funnel would be in somewhat of a "holding pattern," because it takes around three days for leads to work their way through to the application and strategy session (sales call).

Rather than taking a break, I would use this time to start a second revenue stream and to build out a similar strategy to the one I used in the fitness professional niche, in a different yet powerful niche on Instagram: motivation and goal setting.

Some people might argue that I should use this time to build out the next step in my fitness funnel value ladder. I completely disagree. I do not believe in stacking a new funnel on top of another funnel that is not fully optimized.

Because I have no choice but to wait for the data from the fitness funnel, building out something NEW and profitable is my best option.

Here's what I'd do:

1. Set up a new Instagram page in the motivation niche.
2. Go to a private-label-rights website and buy a variety of high-value e-books and video content, which I can bundle together as a free giveaway and a paid product.
3. Use ClickFunnels to build out the lead-generation funnel and offer the paid product on the thank-you page and also through email follow-ups.
4. Once the funnel and email sequences are built, I would run Shout-touts to this NEW funnel and start building my email list and getting sales in this new niche.

Yep, that's right—in just TWO days I've created a separate income stream (without creating my own products or promotional assets), which I can use to reinvest in my business.

Here's what that funnel would look like:

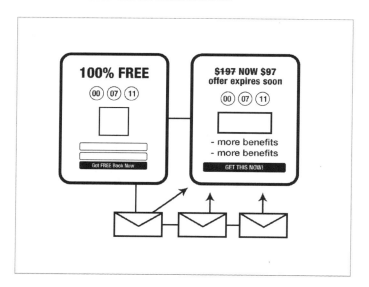

## Day 12

Now that the front end of my motivation funnel is working, I want to make sure that I nurture my list and maximize profits on the back end. To do this, I'll find great free content by googling phrases like "goal-setting tips" and "common entrepreneur mistakes." This will give me content that will add value to my list, and I will then schedule it to go out as an email broadcast two or three times each week (making sure to credit the source).

Then what I'd do is go to ClickBank and find relevant affiliate offers I could send to my list ONE time per week (after I've already sent the value emails for that week). I could set this up and schedule it out as far as I'd like (or have time for) on Day 12.

After everything is in place, all I'd have to do is drive traffic into the front of my motivation funnel with Instagram influencer Shoutouts. This strategy should easily bring in $1,000 or more every 30 days.

*Note: I skipped the in-depth customer avatar work with this because many affiliate products, including PLR, already have the copy written for you. I could have done this for the fitness niche, but because I needed it to be a home run, I went the extra mile to get it right.*

## Day 13

As strange as it sounds, no good Instagram strategy is complete without a STRONG Facebook component.

Where Instagram is more personal and great for establishing one-to-one relationships, Facebook is great for establishing a community around your BIG idea.

So on Day 13, I'd create a Facebook Group where the fitness professionals on my email list could "hang out."

I would invite everybody on my email list to join this group. Aside from creating community, I would also highlight some of the more Instagram-famous people in the group.

Not only would this inspire the newbies, it would also allow me to catch the attention of the fitness influencers who I may not have been able to reach through DM. People care MOST about themselves, so when they find out they are being featured in my group, that will be my foot in the door.

## Days 14–20

The first two weeks of my 30-day comeback was all about quickly building systems I could use to generate leads, clients, and sales (money) as QUICKLY as possible.

Days 14–20 are going to be completely dedicated to WORKING and refining the systems I put in place on Days 1–13.

My Instagram tasks would include posting, sending, and replying to DMs and reaching out to Instagram influencers to negotiate Shoutout prices.

On Facebook, I would post one value-based or conversation-starting post per day. I'd also continue to highlight other fitness pros who are on my list of potential done-for-you funnel clients.

During this seven-day period, it would also be my goal to generate enough money for Shoutouts to enable me to spend as much money as possible during Days 22–28, to ensure I hit my $10,000 in 30 days goal.

Warning: Before you seasoned marketers see my 65% opt-in rate and call "bullsh**t," you have to remember that Shoutouts are word-of-mouth marketing (warm traffic) and NOT cold traffic like Facebook-sponsored ads. Because the distrust and skepticism levels of my traffic are lower, since I am getting a personal endorsement by an Instagram influencer, my opt-in rates are MUCH higher.

Here's how the numbers work out.

### FITNESS PROFESSIONAL FUNNEL:

Total Spent on Shoutouts : **$1000**

Total Website Visits: **2000**

Optin Conversions: **1300 (65%)**

Applications Received: **19**

Strategy Sessiona Booked: **12**

Done For You Funnels Sold: **3 ($1500)**

Revenue Generated: **$4500**

Net Profit: **$3500**

**MOTIVATION FUNNEL:**

Total Spent on Shoutouts : **$500**

Total Website Visits: **1000**

Optin Conversions: **650 (65%)**

Upsell Conversions (PLR): **19 (3% @ $97)**

Revenue Generated: **$1843**

Net Profit: **$1343**

Since most of my processes are automated, it would allow me time to focus on optimizing my funnels and email sequences for both the fitness and motivation niches. Also, I would use this time to perfect the sales pitch I use during my strategy sessions. Because I'll be raising my prices, I'll have to add in more value to justify the cost. This means creating an irresistible STACK, like Russell teaches in Expert Secrets.

# Day 21

At first, making a TON of money online is really exciting. Quickly though, you come crashing back to Earth and are hit with the harsh reality that you actually have to FULFILL those orders.

Because of this, the FIRST half of Day 21 would be dedicated to making sure that my new done-for-you funnel clients had everything they'd need to be successful and my motivation customers received everything they'd paid for.

At this point, the NEED to hire somebody would become apparent, but because I don't have time to look for or train anybody right now—I'm stuck doing EVERYTHING, even if it's "below my pay grade."

The second half of the day would be focused on perfecting the scripts and presentation that I would use to close two new done-for-you funnel clients at $2,500 each over the next 10 days.

In order to do this, I would use a modified version of the Perfect Webinar that Russell teaches in Expert Secrets, as well as create an even more valuable and an irresistible STACK (also taught in his book), which would be essential to me closing sales at this higher price point.

## Days 22–28

"I fear not the man who has practiced 10,000 kicks once, but I fear the man who has practiced one kick 10,000 times." — Bruce Lee

Once you have a funnel that is "kinda" working, there is an irresistible temptation to move on to something new, or to build out the next stage of your value ladder and just let the funnel run, but in my experience you can lose out on insights and optimizations that can put your profits through the roof.

That's why in the last full week, I would repeat what I did in Days 14–20, but this time all of the funnels, systems, and processes would be much better optimized.

This would allow me to either increase my Instagram influencer Shoutout spend even more because I would KNOW that the funnels work, or to spend the same amount of money but know that the return will be greater than before.

In addition to continuing the Instagram and Facebook tasks that I listed on Days 14–20 (and have done every day since then), on Days 22–28, I would run the next round of Shoutouts to drive MASSIVE traffic into my funnels.

Keep in mind, at this point I would have roughly $4,800 to work with. Because my funnels and sales scripts are optimized, I'm going to invest $1,500 in Shoutouts, leaving me with $3,300. This means that this round of promotions needs to NET $6,700 to reach my goal of $10,000.

Here are the numbers.

**FITNESS PROFESSIONAL FUNNEL:**

Total Spent on Shoutouts : **$1000**

Total Website Visits: **2000**

Optin Conversions: **1300 (65%)**

Applications Received: **19**

Strategy Sessiona Booked: **12**

Done For You Funnels Sold: **2 ($2500)**

Revenue Generated: **$5000**

Net Profit: **$4000**

**MOTIVATION FUNNEL:**

Total Spent on Shoutouts : **$500**

Total Website Visits: **1000**

Optin Conversions: **650 (65%)**

Upsell Conversions (PLR): **26 (4% @ $97)**

Revenue Generated: **$2522**

Net Profit: **$2022**

Between the $3,300 I had before, the $4,000 I netted from the last two done-for-you funnels I sold, and the $2,022 I netted from selling the motivation/goal-setting upsell, I would have a total of $9,322.

Now you may be thinking, That's not $10,000. And you're right. BUT I've also been selling motivation and goal-setting affiliate products to my motivation email list, AND I still have two DAYS left to sell ONE more done-for-you funnel!

*My Secret Weapon:* Inexperienced marketers are so focused on front-end sales conversions and creating a positive return on investment right away, they forget about the long-term value of an email lead. After all of my Shoutouts, I quickly built a 4,000-person+ email list.

Russell taught me that email leads should be worth a MINIMUM of $1 per person per month. That's another reason why being $675 short of my goal on Day 29 doesn't matter. Earning $675 in two days from a 4,000-person email list is easy. I could definitely earn that much from ONE subscriber, but if you do the math, it breaks down to just $.17 per person.

## Day 29

The second-to-last day of my 30-day scramble would be 100% dedicated to making that LAST done-for-you funnel sale that would push me over the top to reaching my $10,000 goal. I would go HARD on DMs, sending email blasts with heavy urgency and scarcity to my list, as well as leveraging my Facebook Group.

To make sure that I was using REAL urgency and scarcity, I would let everybody know that after MIDNIGHT, the price for my done-for-you funnels would be going up to $10,000 each, and they would have the rest of that day to get in at $2,500 before that offer went away forever.

In my experience, this kind of REAL scarcity and urgency ALWAYS generates sales (sometimes MASSIVE AMOUNTS), so on Day 29, selling my last done-for-you funnel is inevitable.

## Day 30

On Day 30, I would begin work on the next step in my value ladder.

On Day 29, when I told my online community I was raising my done-for-you sales funnel price to $10,000 each, it wasn't because I want to build $10,000 funnels for clients. Instead, it's because the next rung on my value ladder would be a *done-WITH-you funnel coaching program* for which I'd charge $2,500. I would do this for two reasons.

1. As an entrepreneur, it's always my goal to stay as close to the VISIONARY side of the business as possible. And as much as I love building funnels, I can't focus on building my own business if I'm busy building someone else's. At first, I would run the coaching

program, which would help to leverage my time. But after that, I would hire and train a team member to do it and only make small "cameos" on the coaching calls.

2. In order to properly position the value of the done-with-you program, the done-for-you funnel needs to be significantly more expensive. Nobody would join the done-with-you program for $2,500 if they could get a done-FOR-you funnel for the same price.

This next rung would allow me to generate (at least) another $10,000 over the NEXT 30 days but will require much less of my time.

## FINAL THOUGHTS

I feel like it's really important for me to point out that NOTHING I did to go from ZERO to $10K in 30 days was anything I invented or some shiny-object "ninja hack." All I did was apply what I learned from the people who came before me and combined it with the natural laws of successful business—clear customer avatar, hungry buying audience, and fixing a painful need in the marketplace.

Remember, there is no magical funnel structure in ClickFunnels or "easy button" inside of the Facebook Ads Manager that will suddenly cause millions of dollars to flood into your bank account. All you really need to do is find a teacher, follow the plan, don't give up when things get tough, and realize that success can feel a lot like failure until that day when you pick your head up, look around, and realize you're somewhere more amazing than you could ever have imagined.

# RESOURCES

- Canva (canva.com)
- ClickBank
  (clickbank.com)
- DotComSecrets by
  Russell Brunson
- Expert Secrets by
  Russell Brunson
- FreeImages
  (freeimages.com)
- Instagram Shoutouts
- Master-Resale-
  Rights.com
- Pexels (pexels.com)
- Skype (skype.com)
- Unsplash
  (unsplash.com)

# Chapter 13

# LIVE EVENTS

*by Peng Joon*

# PENG JOON

## CEO

Marketing
*PengJoon.com*

*After Peng Joon made his first million online through selling products in the computer game niche, he decided to teach others how to monetize their knowledge, passion and life experience, both online and offline. Over the past few years, he has built a following of over a million entrepreneurs, spoken in over 20 countries around the world and has shared the stage with leaders like Richard Branson, Tony Robbins, and Robert Kiyosaki.*

# Day 1

It's a brand new day. Time to strategize and get to work. Objective today is to get clarity on my goals and what's needed to happen to get there.

*Goal:* $150,000 in sales by Day 30

## Assumptions
- $500 cash for instant noodles and ramen
- Credit card limit of $5,000
- Ability to work eight hours a day

*Strategy:* Build up webinar + product-launch funnel to sell offer + live event on Day 28 to fulfill.

*Day 1 Action Plan.* Begin with the end in mind and list necessary numbers to hit in order to achieve goals. In order to hit $150,000 in sales by Day 30, I will have to...

- Sell 50 tickets to live event @ $1,000 each for a total of $50,000.
- Give one ticket free for guests to have 100 people in the room, and make sure at least 80% show up.
- Achieve a 12.5% closing rate at event for $10,000 offer, for an additional $100,000 in back-end sales.

In order to sell 50 live-event tickets, I will do it via a webinar funnel. These would be the numbers to target:

- Webinar registration rate: 50%
- Webinar show-up rate: 80%
- Close rate on webinar (including replay): 10%
- Close rate on product-launch funnel: 3%

*Note: These target numbers are not unrealistic. I've done higher numbers at a higher price point, but this is a good target.*

To sell 50 tickets, I would need 500 people showing up on my webinar. For that to happen, I would need 625 webinar registrants. That would mean 1,250 targeted website visits.

From experience, I know that a webinar registrant would be approximately $10 per show-up, which would be a problem because I only have a $5,000 limit on my card. I will have to start selling some tickets fast and do my webinars a couple of times to reinvest my profits and pay off my credit card.

Next, I need to list the necessary scope of work to make it happen.

- Webinar funnel (registration page, thank-you page, live page, replay page with bullet points)
- Webinar slide deck
- Product-launch funnel
- Live-event preparation
- Ads on social media

Establish timeline targets to know what needs to be done by when.

- Day 7 first webinar (200 registrants)
- Day 14 second webinar (250 registrants)
- Day 21 third webinar (175 registrants)
- Day 28 live event
- Day 30 $10K upsell at live event

I'll have to determine the result I can generate for my target audience and the thing they hate doing so that I can generate a "How To X In Y Without Z" where X is the result, Y is the time frame (optional), and Z is the thing they hate doing.

I know I can help entrepreneurs speak, inspire, and close through sales videos, webinars, and live events. So I would come out with something like this.

*Free Webinar Training Reveals...*
*How to Launch, Sell Out, AND Close High-Ticket Products*

- Establish the three main takeaways the audience will get by attending the webinar.
- Get webinar registration page up by importing a webinar share funnel.
- Shoot simple thank-you video for thank-you page of webinar registration.
- Get a custom domain name for the webinar funnel.
- Outsource a simple logo and image design package on Fiverr, where there are tons of people willing to do it for $5.

- Register for Zoom account for webinar delivery and connect with ClickFunnels.
- Change personal FB profile header to professional-looking image with result I generate and call to action to webinar. (This can

be easily outsourced for $5 as well.)

*Example Of FB Banner With Call To Action*

- Make a post on personal profile on what I learned losing it all and what I'm doing about it to bounce back, not to get sympathy, but as a declaration to myself and the rest of the world.
- Go to related FB Groups, search for keywords (examples: live events, webinars, closing, speaking) and comment to help as many people as I can. No lame "PM me" comments. Just genuinely helping people. This is to get people to check out my profile and get targeted free traffic to my webinar. This will be done pretty much daily.
- Do due diligence and send out email to at least 15 different hotels asking for price quotations for theater seating events for 100 people. (I will not send this email as myself, as it will be hard to negotiate later. Instead, I will use a different email so that I can use third-party authority in negotiating at a later stage.)
- Watch Netflix and chill. Kidding. No TV. No Game of Thrones. No browsing of Facebook feed for the next 30 days. NO DISTRACTIONS.

# Day 2

Today is about creating the ads to fill up my webinar funnel. Since I have no more list, no Facebook pixels, and no tracking, getting this all up is priority today.

## Day 2 Action Plan

1. Install Facebook pixel throughout my entire funnel.

**244**

2. Create custom audience on the pixel based on every possible scenario there could be in the webinar funnel.
   - Landed on page but did not register
   - Registered for webinar but did not show up
   - Showed up but did not go to checkout page
   - Went to checkout page but did not buy

   These different audiences will be used to run very specific retargeting ads to get them back into the next step of the funnel.

3. Install conversion tracking on thank-you page of webinar and on purchase page.

4. Create layered audience based on Facebook Audience Insights since there is no warm audience in my Facebook account. Most people run ads just based on interest, but I want to narrow it down rather than just targeting 32 million people who are interested in, say, "marketing." I will create a layered audience based on three levels: people who like the INTEREST, who must also at least match one of the following PROFESSIONS, who must also at least like one of the following THOUGHT LEADERS. I will have about 10 listed on each of the 3 levels.

5. Think of different hooks, stories, and offers for FB Ads. The hook is the thing that stops them in their tracks and gets their attention. I'll need to link it with a story so that the hook makes sense. And from there, have the offer, which is the call to action to the webinar. You can see an example on the next page.

   Using the Content Multiplier Formula strategy, I'll be shooting five videos today, with a slightly different approach since I do not have the luxury of time.

   I usually do value videos with no call to action and retarget my engaged audience later, but this time I'll be shooting videos that give value based on different angles—origin story, opportunity, insecurities, pain of present, and objections. Each of these videos will have a call to action to my webinar.

*Example of Hook, Story, Offer Ad*

6. Run and publish the first ads (objective: conversion) to layered audience with budget of $200/day across the different audiences.
7. Queue next four videos to go out for the next four days.
8. Take a picture of myself looking shocked.
9. Run that image ad to the custom audience "Landed on page but did not register." Something along the lines of "I noticed that you landed on my page for the webinar but did not sign up!? Did something happen? Register for our next upcoming webinar here: <LINK>."
10. Accumulate images and resources necessary for webinar coming up in five days. Social proof, images to illustrate stories, successes, struggles—anything that is pertinent to the presentation.
11. Determine what makes up the offer, and outsource graphics on Fiverr so that each component (blueprint, action plan, live tickets, etc.) has a visual representation of what they will be getting.
12. Make engaging post on personal profile giving value and talking about upcoming webinar without linking to it because FB will kill the reach. Call to action is to get them to comment, and link is sent privately.
13. Go back to FB Groups, search targeted keywords within group, check replies, help others, continue engaging with targeted groups.

# Day 3

My objective today is to monitor numbers from yesterday, kill losing campaigns, work on building new audiences, and getting a rough copy of my presentation deck up.

## Day 3 Action Plan

1. Only look at campaigns that got 1,000 reach before making any decisions.
2. Determine which campaigns can be improved.
3. Scale winners by increasing budget by 10%; pause losers (based on cost per lead, or CPL).
4. Create engagement audience: people who have engaged with my

ad or post, people who have watched 50% of my last video.

5. Create 1% Lookalike Audience: people who have visited my page, people who have registered for webinar.

6. Majority of the day will be spent creating the slide deck. With the images accumulated from yesterday, it's time to flesh it out.

7. List all of the different hooks, stories, and offers that will be part of the presentation slide deck.

8. Build the slide deck (comprises four main sections: open, content, offer stack, close). I will only work on two of them today.

9. Open: Incorporate images that generate credibility and trust and that build rapport.

10. Content: Determine what I'm actually teaching them by strategically answering objections about the opportunity, insecurities, and excuses.

11. Go back to FB Groups, search targeted keywords within group, check replies, help others, continue engaging with groups. It's easy to get sidetracked with social media, so this is limited to once daily, one hour tops.

# Day 4

Like yesterday, I start off by monitoring results on Facebook and making necessary tweaks. Then I will look at the slide deck again.

## Day 4 Action Plan

1. Monitor FB ad results (scale winners, pause losers).

2. Create custom audience of "engaged" people who watched at least 50% of my last video.

3. Run ads targeting engaged audience, excluding the people who registered for webinar.

4. Continue working on slide deck words and images.

5. Offer stack: live event + other bonuses. Because the selling price is $2K, I will need to build the value up to $20K.

6. Try to think of as many done-with-you and done-for-you items to be included as part of the offer (swipe files, cheat sheets, action plans, templates, etc.).

7. Close: Incorporate all of the different closes in the slide deck.

8. Practice flow and presentation out loud.

9. Make post on target FB Groups with engaging image. Something along the lines of "What is the #1 issue you face when it comes to <RESULT THEY WANT TO GENERATE>?" Offer to help.

# Day 5

It's two days till the live webinar. There will be a lot of rinse and repeat work from yesterday. Optimizing ads, scaling them, and practicing the webinar.

## *Day 5 Action Plan*

1. Monitor FB ad results (scale winners, pause losers).

2. Scale winning ad sets and increase 5x.

3. Increase budget of winning ad sets by 10%.

4. Create custom audience of "engaged" people who watched at least 50% of my last scheduled video.

5. Run ads targeting engaged audience, excluding the people who registered for webinar.

6. Check to see if total number of registrants for webinar is on track. I'm targeting 200 registrants for this upcoming one, so I should be getting 40 a day. If numbers are below this, then I'll be looking to scale either by increasing budget and/or targeting a slightly broader audience.

7. Graphics from Fiverr on offer stack and logo should be completed and incorporated into slide deck.

8. List every single objection that I think my audience might have about why they wouldn't get it. Example: I'm too young to do this. I'm too old to do this. I don't have the time. I'm an introvert. Will this work for me if I'm in this industry? I don't have the capital. How long before I see my returns?

9. List all these objections and position them as Q&A in my slide deck after my close. This session should be at least 20 minutes.

10. My entire slide deck should be done with open, content, offer stack, and Q&A sections.

11. Monitor social media profile and groups.

# Day 6

ONE day to the big day!

## *Day 6 Action Plan*

1. Compare the different proposals from hotels and choose which one to go with. Watch out for hidden costs like projectors, audio-visual equipment, etc. Make sure they're included.
2. Check to see that FB Ads are in order as on previous days.
3. Upload checkout page, where I will be asking webinar attendees to go when I make my offer.
4. Integrate with payment processor.
5. Recap entire offer stack to be included in offer page.
6. Go through entire slide deck and presentation, and make sure final aesthetics are in place.
7. Test the entire funnel to make sure payment goes through.
8. Shoot a video to all registered reminding them about the webinar happening the next day.
9. Reply and engage targeted FB Groups and profile.

# Day 7

This is the day everything turns around.

## *Day 7 Action Plan*

1. Check webinar registrants.
2. Customize email that goes out one hour before with a personal touch.
3. Ensure there is another email that goes out 15 minutes before webinar is configured.
4. Ensure all links work (especially checkout link).
5. Thirty minutes before webinar, play Whitney Houston's "One Moment in Time" on repeat. (Of course, I will have obtained permission first!)
6. Work my magic.

7. Celebrate win with two hours of Overwatch (a favorite video game).

8. Send broadcast email to all those who showed up but didn't buy, asking them for feedback.

9. Perform full funnel audible and see where the weakest link is. Check the stats on registration page and show-up page, and find out where most people were dropping off in the webinar.

10. Go to FB Ads to see switch on retargeting ads for audience "registered but did not show up" with copy that says, "I noticed you registered but did not show up. Did life get in the way? The next webinar is happening here. Join us? <LINK>"

11. Go to FB Ads to see switch on retargeting ads for audience "showed up and did not buy" with copy that says, "I see that you're still on the fence about getting <PRODUCT>. I get it. I used to feel the same way. What I found was..." Use the feel, felt, found method.

12. Write down every single objection they might have about NOT buying, and create a retargeting ad video for EACH objection. These videos do not need to be high-quality, just from the heart. This type of retargeting ads will have the highest ROI in the entire campaign.

13. If I have testimonials, this would also be a great addition to get the fence-sitters to take action.

14. These retargeting ads for "attended webinar but did not buy" will have a direct call to action to my checkout page with a stack summary.

15. Go to FB Groups, make a post, celebrate win, inspire others. Share lessons learned and what could and will be done differently.

# Day 8

The calm after the storm. The day to recollect, strategize, and fix weakest links. I need to get 250 webinar registrants this week. At $10 CPL, I should be spending about $2,500 this week.

## *Day 8 Action Plan*

*Example Of Retargeting Ad Answering Specific*
*Objection Using Feel, Felt, Found Method*

1. Use money from sales to clear credit card debt.
2. Perform funnel tweaks based on weakest link.
3. Personally reply to those who engaged with the email, asking for feedback about why they didn't buy. Attempt to reclose them. Incorporate those objections into slides.
4. Update webinar page for the following week.
5. Extract webinar video from Zoom.

6. Set up webinar replay page with call to action button below the video. Enable scrubbing of video.
7. Send broadcast email to all registered for replay webinar.
8. Monitor FB Ads, scale winners, drop losers.
9. Create 1% lookalike audiences on leads and buyers. Lookalike buyers list will be still too small, but leads will be a good start. Remember, gold in, gold out—crap in, crap out.
10. Scale ads targeting lookalike audiences.
11. Have a proper meal that's not fast food or ramen.

# Day 9

Today is going to be heavy. Objective today is to shoot all videos in the entire product-launch funnel (three value videos + one sales video) to stack with the webinar funnel to add value to those still on the fence and convert at least another 3% of the list.

## *Day 9 Action Plan*

1. The usual Facebook stuff. At this point, daily ad spent should be about $350. Main thing to monitor is whether there's ad fatigue since it's been a week. If there is, time to swipe out with new creatives.
2. List video #1 content + framework. This should include origin story and main content explaining the opportunity. Call to action to comment below video on the biggest takeaway from the video.
3. Write up bullet points on video #2. This should include doing a case study with the main intention of answering any objections on insecurities a person might have in their inability to execute the thing I taught them in video #1.
4. Write up video #3 bullet points. This video will answer any excuses a person might have based on external factors.
5. Draft sales video script. This can be repurposed from the webinar with a few elements from the last three videos.
6. Buy a flipchart, some colored markers, and colored paper to cover up framework for video later. (See example below.)
7. Write up flipcharts.

8. Shoot all four videos in one go.

9. Upload videos and set up product-launch funnel in ClickFunnels.

*Example of Product-Launch Funnel*

*(Note: If you've never done something like this before, I know it sounds hard, but I actually did up the sequence in the exact example above in half a day in front of my students. If shooting videos is new for you, you can split this task with one video a day for the next four days.)*

10. Promote webinar replay again and email broadcast to list with scarcity.

11. Document numbers and stats from launch + replay and report back to appropriate FB Groups on lessons learned and things to do differently.

12. Send sales video to Rev for transcription.

# Day 10

Objective today is to get the first video of my product-launch funnel out and reengage the audience in the webinar sequence who have still not bought.

## Day 10 Action Plan

1. The usual monitoring of FB Ads.

2. Write up and queue autoresponder email promoting video #1.

3. Add video #1 of product-launch funnel to autoresponder se-

**254**

quence so that people in the webinar sequence who have still not bought after the replay reminders will see this email.

4. Make sure FB Ads still doing fine at $350/day with $10 CPL.

5. Post in FB Groups and help others through the usual keyword-finder method.

6. Post thumbnail of video #1 in personal FB profile talking about that video while making it engaging (polarity, making a stand, controversial, here's why most people are doing it wrong, etc.).

## Day 11

Objective today is to get the second video in the product launch sequence out.

### Day 11 Action Plan

1. Shoot FB Live video with teaser + call to action on upcoming webinar.

2. Boost FB Live video to audience engaged with page who watched 25% of past videos.

3. Render and upload video #2 into ClickFunnels page.

4. Write up autoresponder email promoting video #2.

5. Post in FB Groups and help others through the usual keyword-finder method.

6. Post thumbnail of video #2 in personal FB profile talking about that video.

## Day 12

Main task today is to get video #3 of product-launch funnel out.

### Day 12 Action Plan

1. The usual optimization of FB Ads. I should be getting 35 new registrations a day; if not, I will scale ads appropriately.

2. Render and upload video #3 into ClickFunnels page.

3. Write up autoresponder email promoting video #3, seeding that the card opens tomorrow.

4. Post in FB Groups and help others through the usual keyword-

finder method.

5. Post on personal FB profile about what I've been working on and asking those interested in getting that result to leave a comment.

6. Check to see if numbers for webinar happening in two days makes sense.

# Day 13

Cart opens today. Sales video goes out. Extra $.

## *Day 13 Action Plan*

1. Render and upload sales video to go up.
2. Take transcription from Rev and rewrite as long-form sales copy.
3. Format sales copy with appropriate headers below sales video.
4. Write up autoresponder email promoting sales video that cart opens today.
5. Reply to all FB comments of interested people and PM link to sales video.
6. Update FB status to mention that this thing is finally up. This should be a semi-long post that will be pinned later.
7. Check stats for tomorrow's webinar.
8. Finalize hotel details. Make necessary payments.
9. Set up FB retargeting campaign. Audience who "visited sales page but did not make payment" with ad answering objections with call to action to checkout page.

# Day 14

Webinar, Round 2

## *Day 14 Action Plan*

1. Check webinar registrants, which should be at approximately 250.
2. Customize email that goes out one hour before with personal touch.
3. Ensure there is another email that goes out 15 minutes before webinar is configured.

4. Ensure all links work (especially checkout link).
5. Thirty minutes before, play Whitney Houston's "One Moment in Time" on repeat.
6. Work my magic...again.
7. Celebrate with two hours of Overwatch.
8. Go to FB Groups, make a post, celebrate win, inspire others. Share lessons learned and what could and will be done differently.
9. Update personal profile with how things can change in two weeks.

# Day 15

One more week for major push to last webinar. Two weeks to live event. Target registrants for this week is lower at 175 for the week, or 25 a day, since the event is a little close to the webinar and conversions might be a little lower.

But I've promoted live events two days before the actual date and they still converted, so I know this works.

## Day 15 Action Plan

1. Use money from sales to clear credit card debt.
2. Perform funnel tweaks based on weakest link.
3. Personally reach out to those who didn't buy to ask for feedback.
4. Update webinar page for the following week.
5. Extract webinar video from Zoom.
6. Set up webinar replay page, with call to action button below the video. Enable scrubbing of video.
7. Send broadcast email to all who registered on replay webinar.
8. Monitor FB Ads, scale winners, drop losers.
9. Shoot video to broadcast to all paid attendees on "2 Weeks To Event And How To Get The Most Out Of It." Build anticipation and resell why they want to show up for it. Remind them that they get to bring a +1 to the event.
10. Feast like a king.

# Day 16

Plan for live event. Get the logistics ready. Handouts, bonuses—make it epic!

## *Day 16 Action Plan*

1. Flesh out main framework to be used at event.
2. Work on handouts and slide decks.
3. Send broadcast email to all newly registered on replay webinar.
4. Personally reply to those who engaged with the email, asking for feedback on why they didn't buy. Attempt to reclose them. Incorporate those objections into slides.
5. Monitor stats and perform funnel audible on all pages to see where the weakest link is.

All new webinar registrants should now be going through the following process, which looks something like this in ClickFunnels:

✉ **Auto Webinar Registration**

⊙ **Webinar Confirmation**

🎤 **Webinar Broadcast Room**

↻ **Webinar Replay Room**

↻ **Webinar Replay Room (Cliff Notes)**

> 🛒 **Check Out**

$ **Confirmation**

$ **Value Video 1**

$ **Value Video 2**

$ **Value Video 3**

> $ **Sales Page**

# Day 17

Whole focus today is to finalize handouts, slide decks, and bonuses to be sent for printing tomorrow.

## Day 17 Action Plan

1. Work on handouts and slide decks.
2. Do FB Live on personal FB profile of the behind-the-scenes action and process of preparing for this event and why I'm excited about it.
3. Confirm that I've been getting 25 webinar registrants daily and make necessary adjustments if that's not the case.

# Day 18

Everything has to be finalized and sent to the printer today.

## Day 18 Action Plan

1. Finalize handouts and slide decks.
2. Send to printer to print out 100 copies inserted into files. They will usually take about five days without incurring a surcharge.
3. Do FB Live on personal FB profile of the behind-the-scenes action sending to the printers and how there are a few spots left for this event.

# Day 19

Conduct entire webinar on a FB Live today to be boosted to specific audiences.

## Day 19 Action Plan

1. Scope out entire webinar on little pieces of paper.
2. Get a friend to be the cameraperson.
3. Do the entire webinar in a casual setting on a FB Live (open, content, stack, close).
4. Boost video to all audiences that have engaged with page, watched 25% of past videos, and been to any page of the funnel, excluding buyers.

5. Insert video description and a pinned comment to checkout page of funnel.

*(Note: I did not dress up for this video. I just so happened to be speaking at an event that day and decided to do a webinar on a FB Live. As you can see, the majority of the views are paid.)*

It does not matter if I do not have a following on FB right now. I only need to boost this video to warm audiences as mentioned in Step #4 and it will convert.

6. Share this video on personal FB profile.

# Day 20

ONE day to final webinar.

## Day 20 Action Plan

1. Check stats of FB Live video and create custom audience of people who watched at least 50% of it.
2. Run an IMAGE ad that targets that audience saying, "I noticed you watched my video on <TITLE> but you haven't taken action yet." Answer objections in copy. CTA to checkout page.
3. Answer all comments, PM people interested in joining the event happening next week.
4. Ensure webinar registrants are on track.
5. Send out email broadcast on live event next week, letting them know I will be closing registrations soon.
6. Reach out to videographer to see if they can record live event.

# Day 21

Final round.

## Day 21 Action Plan

1. Check webinar registrants—should be at approximately 175.
2. Ensure all links work—especially checkout link!
3. Crush the webinar.
4. Celebrate with two hours of Overwatch.
5. Go to FB Groups, make a post, celebrate win, inspire others, and mention what a crazy last three weeks it has been.
6. Update personal profile with how things can change in three weeks.
7. Pause FB Ads promoting webinar funnel.
8. Have an epic meal.

# Day 22

One week to live event—the final preparations.

## Day 22 Action Plan

1. Use money from sales to clear credit card debt.
2. Extract webinar video from Zoom.
3. Set up webinar replay page, with call to action button below the video. Enable scrubbing of video.
4. Set up auto-webinar sequence based on last video. I won't be doing a live webinar for a while.
5. Send broadcast email to all registered on replay webinar. We close registrations TOMORROW.
6. Shoot video to broadcast to all paid attendees on "1 Week To Event—How This Could Change Everything." *Note: Just because they paid doesn't mean they will show up. I need to be constantly reselling them that they made a great decision signing up.*
7. FB Live video on how cart and registrations close tomorrow. Boost to all audiences that have visited funnel in last 21 days, excluding buyers. Final chance to join.
8. Go to Upwork to hire a VA, job scope to call up 100 people follow-

ing a very simple script: congratulate them, sell them the show-up, and remind them that they get an extra +1.

9. Feast like a king.

## Day 23

Final push, focus on urgency and scarcity, cart closes today...for real.

### Day 23 Action Plan

1. Email out subject title with good ol' "FINAL WARNING—Last Day To Register For Live Event!"
2. Announce on FB profile.
3. FB Live video on page.
4. Many people leave things to the last minute, but I know not to underestimate the amount of sales that can come in just from this. Email broadcast to all buyers adding value, building anticipation, and reselling the show-up, reminding them to register their +1.
5. Collect all printed handouts and slides from the printer.

## Day 24

Cart closes, final preparation for live event.

### Day 24 Action Plan

1. Close the cart. Change checkout page to say, "We're now SOLD OUT! Opt in to be part of the waiting list should we open up again."
2. Finalize all attendees and tally up for registration.
3. Registration list should have main attendee name + guest name.
4. Hire a VA. Scope of work will be to call up everyone and get the name of guest + email and key those into Excel spreadsheet.

## Day 25

Three days to live event.

### Day 25 Action Plan

1. Look through presentation before upsell.
2. Determine what the upsell is. It should be the next logical thing

they need, not a more advanced version of the current thing.

3. Prepare sign-up sheets and order form of upsell.
4. Email out to all buyers on three days to live event, fact sheet, details, logistics.

# Day 26

TWO days to live event. There's no to-do list today. On this day, I will spend time alone and reflect on what else I can do to serve my audience at the highest level possible.

# Day 27

ONE day to live event.

### Day 27 Action Plan

1. Drive/fly over to venue and check in.
2. Set up the room, make sure the registration table, handouts, and name tags are in place.
3. Work with hotel AV team to ensure mic and music are working. (For a successful event, I do not need the rah-rah. I don't have an MC/master of ceremonies. I don't get people jumping around. I don't get people dancing. Even the thought of that makes me really uncomfortable.)
4. Shoot video at the venue itself and send out email titled "See you tomorrow!" setting expectations such as being on time and how to get the most out of the event.

# Day 28

Day 1 Of Event

### Day 28 Action Plan

1. Set up context, expectations, what's in it for them.
2. Make it awesome.
3. Videographer to record and render everything so it becomes a digital asset that can be used either as part of a product or in marketing material in future.

# Day 29

Day 2 Of Event

## *Day 29 Action Plan*

1. Continue with awesomeness.
2. Soft close via application.

# Day 30

Final Day Of Event

## *Day 30 Action Plan*

1. Give them everything.
2. Those who want to continue working with me can do so. It's $10K. No manipulation. No hard sell. No beating them up.
3. They should feel that they got their answers, even if they didn't invest in the next level.
4. Capture testimonials, the #1 asset to be used in future ads, retargeting, sizzle reel, and marketing material. After three days of just giving pure value, a 10% conversion on a $10K offer is very realistic if I've got the right audience in the room.
5. Hide in my room, eat ice cream, watch Netflix.

And that's how I would do it if I were to start all over again. Remember...you're just one LIVE EVENT away!

# RESOURCES

- Facebook Ads
- Facebook Audience Insights
- Facebook Live
- Fiverr (fiverr.com)
- Microsoft Excel
- Rev (rev.com)
- Upwork (upwork.com)
- Zoom (zoom.us)

# Chapter 14

# BIBLE SUCCESS BLUEPRINT

*by Myron Golden*

# MYRON GOLDEN

## *Bible Success Academy*

*Personal Dev. Sales and Marketing*
*BibleSuccessAcademy.com*

*Myron Golden is a bestselling author and an in demand speaker and trainer in the areas of sales, marketing, business development and financial literacy. Despite the fact that he contracted polio as an infant Myron is a Black Belt in the martial arts and has had to overcome many obstacles to succeed in his life and career.*

*Myron has assisted his clients in building businesses that do as much as $10 million per year in revenue. Myron also teaches everyday people to become*

> *wealthy often using skills they already have. If you*
> *will open your mind and allow him to share with you,*
> *his principles can truly change your life for the better.*

## 30-Day Turnaround Blueprint

As the world's foremost Bible success coach and the founder of the "Bible Success Secrets" podcast and the Bible Success Academy, I would be remiss not to practice what I preach! So I would find a Bible answer to the question: "What would I do if I lost all of my money, my list, and my JV partners, and the only thing I had was an internet connection and a one-month free trial to ClickFunnels?" This is my Bible Success 30-Day Turnaround Blueprint.

I believe that all of the important answers to all of the important questions can be found in the pages of the best-selling "business" book of all time. And yes, the Bible is a business book and a health book and a personal finance book and a personal relationship book. The Bible has all the answers to all of the questions we could ever have—we just need to learn to look at the practical application of its principles.

Let's look at a story in the Bible about a single mom who had lost everything and was about to lose her two children.

### II Kings 4:1–7

> [1] *Now there cried a certain woman of the wives of the sons of the prophets unto Elisha, saying, Thy servant my husband is dead; and thou knowest that thy servant did fear the Lord: and the creditor is come to take unto him my two sons to be bondmen.*
> [2] *And Elisha said unto her, What shall I do for thee? Tell me, what hast thou in the house? And she said,*

*Thine handmaid hath not any thing in the house, save a pot of oil.*

*³ Then he said, Go, borrow thee vessels abroad of all thy neighbours, even empty vessels; borrow not a few.*

*⁴ And when thou art come in, thou shalt shut the door upon thee and upon thy sons, and shalt pour out into all those vessels, and thou shalt set aside that which is full.*

*⁵ So she went from him, and shut the door upon her and upon her sons, who brought the vessels to her; and she poured out.*

*⁶ And it came to pass, when the vessels were full, that she said unto her son, Bring me yet a vessel. And he said unto her, There is not a vessel more. And the oil stayed.*

*⁷ Then she came and told the man of God. And he said, Go, sell the oil, and pay thy debt, and live thou and thy children of the rest.*

To fully understand the context of this story, we must understand the times in which this woman lived. She lived in a day when a woman was dependent on her father until she got married, at which time her husband would be her provider.

Please understand that there was no such thing as life insurance, and if a woman's husband died, then her husband's family became responsible for her financial well-being. So we can guess, based on the desperation of her situation when she came to Elisha, that her husband didn't have anyone who could take care of her and her sons.

Here's the practical Bible answer on how this woman turned around her situation. I would follow this same pattern, which is laid out so clearly in the pages of the Bible.

This 30-day Turnaround Blueprint is in segments for easy digestion and application.

· Preparation

- Implementation
- Monetization
- Optimization

## Segment One: Preparation For My 30-Day Turnaround (Days 1–3)

During the preparation stage, I would want to use maximum energy so that I can come up with my best options. Then I would want it to take up the fewest days for the preparation stage. I would want to use the bulk of my time in my 30 days for the implementation. (The preparation is very important, but I must get into action as soon as possible so I can have the maximum amount of time to implement my strategies when I discern what they are.)

## Day 1: Seek A Turnaround

I would passionately and persistently start looking for answers until I found them.

*The Vertical Search* I would do a vertical search. That means I would pray and ask the LORD to open my eyes to the opportunities that already exist around me. I would ask him to open my eyes to the skills and talents that exist inside me. Lastly in my vertical search, I would ask the LORD to open my eyes to those who would be both willing and able to help me (realizing that they might be a historical or biblical character or someone in my circle of relationships).

*The Horizontal Search* After my vertical search, I would begin my horizontal search and actually tap into the human resources around me in my life as well as the historical and biblical landscape and find the ones who had what I desired and begin to tap into their wisdom.

I would look for patterns as well as insights from those people who could give me direction.

*The Internal Search* The next thing I would do is look inside myself to figure out what gifts and talents I have. I believe gifts and talents can be recognized by examining both passions (the things I love), and proclivities (the things I am good at) and noticing where they intersect. This is where I will find the "delivery" part of my business model. If I love something and am good at it, it will be easier for me to work the long hours and persevere through the challenges I will no doubt face in business.

The internal search should not be the determining factor of the direction to go. It should only be a contributing factor. Too many people allow their passion and proclivity to determine the direction of their business rather than looking to the marketplace FIRST to determine the direction business should go.

The next thing I would do on Day 1 is figure out exactly how much money I desire to make in the next 30 days to solve this problem. Am I looking for a short-term bandage or a long-term solution? The reality is that I should be looking for a long-term solution that I can also use to get some cash flow very quickly.

## Day 2: Submit To A Teacher

If I hadn't already had a level of success in the past, I would go to the most successful people I know and tell them my situation and let them know that I am not looking for a handout, I am just looking for advice. I might find that advice in a book or a home-study course. If I had the most ideal circumstance, I would look for a person I knew who could mentor me (and I would do everything they said, especially when it didn't make sense to me).

The reason I would trust the mentor's judgment more than my own is because good advice from a mentor is almost always counterintuitive to the mentee. Think about it, if the mentor's advice made sense to the mentee, they would already be doing it. Beware of mentors who only give you advice that you like and agree with. A good mentor will always challenge you!

*Stop Trembling* One of the things submitting to a teacher will do is help me stop trembling! Great teachers (mentors or coaches) are great at helping us to get our emotions in check. I would be sure to find a teacher who had the ability to snap me out of anxiety and worry, because anxiety is the thief of all our dreams. We cannot ever afford to give any energy (mental or emotional) to outcomes we don't desire.

## Day 3: See My Treasure

Yesterday, I did my three-dimensional search—vertical, horizontal, and internal. Now it's time for me to start taking inventory of all my resources. We all have resources! Unfortunately, we undervalue many of the resources we have.

I realize that if you are reading this at a time in your life where you are going through a major financial reversal, you may meet this statement with some resistance. You may even downright dismiss it as WRONG, but I would urge you to keep your mind open at least until you get to the end of this paragraph. I believe that resources are always available.

The thing that is sometimes lacking is resourcefulness. And when we are lacking resourcefulness, our misperception is that resources are limited. If we think about it, we know that can't be true because there have always been people on both sides of the "resource" equation. There were even people who made fortunes during the Great Depression while other people starved.

If two people look at the same set of circumstances and one of them is feeling resourceful and the other one is not, the resourceful person will most often see the opportunity, and the person who is not resourceful will most often only see the obstacles. Remember, we rarely see things the way they are; we usually see things the way we are.

Now it's time for me to categorize and prioritize my resources. This means all of my resources—the ones that are obviously valuable and the ones that are not. I would create this inventory in a way that looks something like this:

1. List the problems in the marketplace that I can skillfully solve.
   - Personal Skill Resources (like cooking, writing, singing)
   - Technology Resources (like Facebook, Instagram, and ClickFunnels)

- Relationship Resources (Who has access to my target audience?)
- Product Resources (What valuable products do I own or own the rights to?)
- Service Resources (Do I know how to make or fix something?)
- Media Platform Resources (TV, radio, podcast, and online media)
- Testimonial Resources (Who have I produced a result for that would be willing to give me a testimonial?)

2. List competitors who have the attention of my audience.
3. Lead Magnets (What cool thing can I give my audience in exchange for their email or social media page?)
4. Headlines
5. Sales Scripts

## Segment Two: Implementation of My 30-Day Turnaround (Days 4–12)

### Day 4: Systemize Value Creation

Create a list of topics to do Facebook (FB) Lives and other social media posts on for the next 26 days. This means I will create the title and outline for the FB Lives. I would start going live on FB to grow my audience today.

### Day 5

I would start my podcast and upload it to iTunes, Google Play, and SoundCloud. I would launch it as a weekly podcast, not a daily, so I would be able to concentrate on the other tasks for the other days.

### Day 6

I would start a daily motivational call, prayer call, or Bible study call to grow my audience. I would use FreeConferencing or one of the other free conference call services to create this. The reason I would do the call daily is so that people could invite their friends to the call.

### Day 7: Systemize Lead Generation

I would create three lead magnets: a video, an audio, and a PDF. The reason I would create three different kinds of lead magnets is because different people like to consume different kinds of content. I would shoot the video, rip the audio, then have the audio transcribed on Rev and edited to sound more like a chapter from a book.

## Day 8

I would build three different lead-capture pages in ClickFunnels. Then I would set up each page to give away a different type of lead magnet (video, audio, or PDF).

## Day 9

This is the day I would set up all of my email sequences. I would set up my Seinfeld sequence and my soap opera sequence to follow up with the people who signed up for my lead magnets. I would design these sequences to keep them engaged and looking forward to the next time they hear from me.

## Day 10: Systemize My Promotions

On Day 10, I would set up my FB personal profile and my FB business page. I would put a headline, educational message, and call to action on the cover photo of my personal profile and include the links of one of the lead capture pages. I would also have a welcome video on my personal profile pinned to the top of the feed, which would give some great value in the area of Bible Success Secrets.

## Day 11

Day 11 is time to build out my FB business page. I would fill it with posts of videos, quotes, infographics, and shared content that would be of value to my audience, and I would get it ready to start piling in Likes, Shares, Follows, and Comments.

## Day 12

On Day 12, I would join a bunch of FB Groups that had my audience and go in and share valuable content, answering questions and helping people. I would be very active and trust that the value of the answers and help I gave would create enough curiosity for people to come to my profile and begin to follow me, and also to follow the links on my cover photo.

## *Segment Three: Monetization of My 30-Day Turnaround (Days 13–21)*

### Day 13: Select My Team

On Day 13, I would begin to reach out to my content creation team. Many people think that just because they come up with a course, they also have to do all of the teaching. But you can create an entire course and only teach one small part of it. The fact is that you could create an entire course and not teach any of it. Since my area of expertise is Bible success, I would find other people and get them to teach parts of the course. I would make promoting the course a prerequisite to being a part of it. I would share the entire new list with all of the people who helped promote and create it, but I would not offer to share the money from the sales. If I do a 10-module course, I would have 9 other teachers, and if we all promote it and get 200 people to register, we would each add 2,000 people to our lists.

### Day 14

On Day 14, I would begin to reach out to Instagram influencers and offer an affiliate commission in exchange for doing a Shoutout of my upcoming webinar. I would also offer them the course for free.

This is also the day I would create my webinar funnel in ClickFunnels. I would build out all of the pages so that when my influencers begin to drive traffic, these pages can drive them straight to the webinar registration page. I will be doing the webinar on Day 21.

### Day 15

On Day 15, I would reach out to bloggers and offer them an affiliate commission in exchange for promoting my new Bible Success Secrets course. Obviously, the bloggers I would reach out to would be people who resonate with my message and my brand!

# Day 16: Schedule My Team

Day 16 will be used to create the course outline based on what the different collaborative teachers told me they would teach. I would get their topics and the outcomes they would produce for the people buying the course and use this information to create the outline of each course. I would schedule myself to do the first class. I would schedule the first three classes to start the three consecutive days after the webinar, then I would schedule one training per week via Zoom.

# Day 17

Day 17 is a day to schedule the promotions from the different teachers. I would give them the email copy, which they would send to their lists. I would also create the social media copy that they could post on their pages to promote the courses. Each teacher would be given an affiliate link so they can get affiliate commissions for their promotions.

# Day 18: Sell My Treasure

Day 18, I would give the bloggers and Instagram influencers the copy I would want them to use to promote the event. I would tell the bloggers and the influencers that the copy would convert best if I wrote it. So because I would be writing it, they would make more money from the affiliate commissions. I would write a blog post and an Instagram post.

# Day 19

On Day 19, I would create my webinar outline and the outline for my part of the training. I would create the webinar outline in MS Word and save it as a text doc. Then I would import the text doc into a PowerPoint (PPT) document. If I double space between the lines, the PPT would create the slides with only text. I would make sure not to ever have more than one sentence on a slide, because I don't want them reading my presentation, I want them feeling it.

## Day 20

Day 20, I would go online and find all of the royalty-free images I could find that matched the points in my outline. I would look for emotional pictures that match the words on the slides that were created in PPT from my text doc. I am looking for pictures that make you feel all of the emotions. I want pictures that make you laugh and make you cry, that make you happy and make you sad, that make you feel scared and then relieved. I am going to create a webinar (using the Perfect Webinar Script, of course) that makes them feel all of the emotions they possess!

## Day 21

Day 21 is webinar day. I would check the number of people registered. I would do a reminder to all of the leads we generated from our FB strategy. I would send out one last reminder one hour before the webinar. I would stand while doing the webinar and keep them as engaged as possible with enrolling questions and trial closes.

## *Segment Four: Optimization of My 30-Day Turnaround (Days 22–30)*

## Day 22: Schedule Take Two

I would send out the replay to all of the people who registered but didn't attend. I would send out the sales page to all of the people who attended but didn't buy. And I would send out a personalized video email to all of the people who made it to the sales page but didn't finish filling it out.

## Day 23

I would send out an email announcing the closing of the offer. I would let all of the people who didn't order know that the door on the offer will slam shut in 48 hours.

## Day 24

I would send out an email to all the people who still haven't bought, congratulating all of the people who did buy as well as letting them know that the offer ends in 24 hours. I would also send out a last-call email telling them there is one hour left to take advantage of the offer. Then at the end of the 24-hour period, I would shut down the offer and put up a page that lets people be notified when the offer opens back up again.

## Day 25: Sustain My Turnaround

On Day 25, I would take my webinar registration list and create a Lookalike Audience in Facebook. I would do the exact same thing with the buyers list. Then I would advertise to those two different lists for the next week's webinar. I would target people on FB and on IG for the next webinar.

## Day 26

On Day 26, I would take my FB Live videos that had the most engagement and boost them for $5 per day. Then I would create a Lookalike Audience from the people who engaged with the boosted videos and promote the webinar to all of those people.

## Day 27

On Day 27, I would set up the webinar funnel for the following Thursday and send out an email to all of the people who missed the first webinar and let them know they can register for the webinar this week. I would also let all of the affiliates know that they can start promoting again.

## Day 28: Start To Teach (And Create My Course)

On Day 28, I would build out the members area in ClickFunnels and put all the titles from the outline in their respective places. I would create a welcome video and put it in the members area with all of the important information about the course. I would send out the course schedule for the live trainings as well as let them know when the re-plays would show up in the members area.

I would do the first training that night in the private Facebook Group using Zoom and then put the replay in the members area.

## Day 29

On Day 29, I will send out an email reminder to the people who have already purchased the course letting them know that the second training will be that evening and giving the presenter's name.

## Day 30

On Day 30, I would send out the email reminder to the people who have already purchased the course that the third training would be that evening with the teacher who is slotted for that training.

I would also send an email to all of the people who registered for the second week's webinar that the webinar would be the next day. I would rinse and repeat till the course was done, then I would set up the next course that I would sell and then create.

# RESOURCES

- Google Play
- Facebook Live
- FreeConferencing
  (freeconferencing.com)
- iTunes
- Microsoft PowerPoint
- Microsoft Word
- Rev (rev.com)
- SoundCloud
  (soundcloud.com)
- Zoom (zoom.us)

# Chapter 15

# ECOMMERCE FUNNELS

## by Jaime Cross

# JAIME CROSS

## *Owner*

Organic Skincare
*MIGSoap.com*

*Unfulfilled in her corporate banking career, Jaime Cross had a desire to create legacy wealth and global impact through entrepreneurship. After earnestly seeking direction, Jaime asked God for a billion dollar idea and two weeks later saw a business plan in a dream. After seven long years of trial and error... a lot of mistakes and tears... her company is now the fastest growing organic skin care company in the world.*

*Jaime stands at the forefront of business as a force for good as she paves the way for her four young* boys, and other entrepreneurs all over the world to follow their own dreams.

## Day 1

*"The only way to be truly satisfied is to do what you believe is great work, and the only way to do great work is to love what you do. If you haven't found it yet, keep looking and don't settle. As with all matters of the heart, you'll know when you find it."*

— Steve Jobs

Wow. What an amazing opportunity to begin again. This is my chance to dig deep, to come alive in ways I hadn't been before. I'll take some time today to reflect on mistakes and be empowered by them, using the pain of loss as a weapon for my success. Reflecting on mistakes and learning from them will propel me into an becoming great.

I'm not starting over, I'm taking all I've learned from my past success and failures and using it as a foundation to grow faster and more efficiently. If there were bad decisions, I can now reflect on those and internalize the vision, seeing where those mistakes could actually work for my good. It's time to be transformed and become the entrepreneur I see myself being. The world I was born to change is waiting for me, and I won't delay.

I grew up a farm girl, so I see a lot of resemblance between building a business and farming. As long as the Earth exists, there is seedtime and harvest. If I plan and plant, my seeds will produce.

Here is my primary outline for launching my vision and making it profitable within 30 days:

- Prepare the soil + planning phase
- Plant: revenue-producing action

- Produce: harvesting and gathering funds, investing, storing and managing funds
- Tools and team

Based on what I know works absolutely is that creating my minimum viable product, hook, story, offer, and my Perfect Webinar is the fastest way to grow. So the next 30 days will be focused on that strategy.

*Prepare* I'll spend the first day of my journey getting grounded and doing some preliminary strategy.

The source of success for me has always been my spiritual connection to God and access to His wisdom. Today, I will get focused on the endgame, see myself winning at every step of my new journey, and internalize success by standing on two biblical promises that keep my peace, faith, and hope alive.

1. My God will supply all my needs according to His glorious riches in Christ Jesus.

2. The LORD will open the heavens, the storehouse of his bounty, to send rain on my land in season and to bless all the work of my hands. I will lend to many nations but will borrow from none.

As I'm working, over the next 30 days, I can move forward with confidence knowing that whatever I put my hands to will prosper. It's only a matter of seeking divine wisdom and working out the knowledge I have with practical, dedicated steps. I don't need to accept failure.

It's time to get to work!

*Office/Studio Space Preparation* Knowing how critical focus is, I will create a working space that will allow me to build momentum and avoid drag, eliminate distractions, and tune out noise. NO DRAG. Everyone's situation is different, but finding and creating a peaceful space that keeps vision and inspiration in front of me will be today's goal. If I have to rearrange my office/space, move a bookshelf, or get rid of unnecessary clutter, today's the day I make it happen.

**Mind ~ Body ~ Soul Preparation** I'll create a 30-day outline that will help me keep pace with my goals and keep my mind/body in high-function mode.

1. Get up early every morning and have a few hours of reflection, prayer, and light exercise like rebounding, walking, or yoga.
2. I'll fast once a week for focus and energy.
3. I'll stick to nutrient-rich meals, only eating between 9am and 5pm, consuming foods that contain active nourishment. Shorter eating intervals will help with high-performance thinking and greater productivity.
4. I will end my day with lots of water and some chamomile tea for relaxation, a good night's sleep, and of course my evening ritual with facial rejuvenation and journaling.

Finally...I'll call all hands on deck, like my mom to see if/when she might be available to help with my four little boys during the week so I can have some dedicated time to work. I will be working early mornings, during nap time, after bedtime, and on Saturdays to get 'er done.

I will also buy my domain if I've come up with the name of the company. I'll want to snag it as soon as possible.

I'll also set up the same name on social platforms, so when people go to find us, our name is cohesive across the board.

Finally, I'll register my business name with the Colorado Secretary of State.

# Day 2

> *"Don't ask what the world needs. Ask what makes you come alive and go do it. Because what the world needs is people who have come alive."*
>
> — Howard Thurman

Before a farmer plants, he plans. He'll envision the end result, what fields he sees harvesting, where they'll be harvested, and the tools he'll need to harvest them.

Today, I will start by writing the vision and making it plain. Vision is a powerful and tangible thing that pulls us into something greater than ourselves. You know when you've encountered someone with vision. There is a substance that attracts you to their products and who they are as people. When people ask me how I've continued on in entrepreneurship, even when it was hard and heartbreaking, I tell them that vision pulls me.

Vision is inherent in each of us—we are all given one or many. If we stop listening, it can become dim and hidden, and we forget it's there. But if we steward it faithfully, we can do whatever we put our minds to. Time to wake up to true purpose and calling. Not to get distracted with projects...but rather to become focused on purpose.

Once I've taken the time to write down everything I see, not leaving out any detail, opportunities and momentum will begin to align in my favor. The right people appear at the right times, and the ideas I need in order to create something powerful are coming alive. The supernatural takes effect.

This exercise is important for any dreamer/visionary as ideas will be nonstop and even distracting. There is never a shortage of ideas. But by taking the time to write down everything that is in my heart, I can flesh out my creativity and then channel it with focus.

*Action Creates Clarity!* Then I'll lay out all my possibilities based on a convergence quadrant (CQ) chart, which is kind of like a map for creating my dream business where I combine what I am passionate about, my skills, and my experience on paper. Convergence happens when these three things connect and unite with an industry I can be profitable in.

I will start from the end and work my way back to these four categories.

Based on my CQ, my dream business would either be an organic skincare company that completely dominates or a company where I would teach, train, and equip women to be profitable in business and successful in the home. So I will fill out the quadrants, which will help me make a decision on which direction I should go.

Here's an example:

# CONVERGENCE QUADRANTS

| | |
|---|---|
| **Skills**<br>*(formulator)* | **Knowledge**<br>*(herbal alchemy)* |
| **Passions**<br>*(herbalism)* | **Experience**<br>*(created skincare line that got results for people)* |

Once I feel I've sufficiently filled in all four categories, the goal is to find out where all these qualities converge.

I am paying close attention to these indicators and asking these questions:

- What do people want?
- What problem(s) am I uniquely able to solve?
- Is it a business/product that can solve a real problem and that people want to buy over and over again?

In order to add value to others, I will find a pain point and create a solution, then I will give it to them. The solutions we create and the problems we solve can be simple. I am a big proponent of the MVP, or minimum viable product.

The key to knowing whether I am in convergence is to recognize what makes me feel alive and excited. As I imagine myself growing and running the business, do I feel energized or drained?

Also, I'll choose from either the health, wealth, or relationship categories, as these are the hottest markets, and I will niche them down during my research phase.

By the end of the day, I will have filled out my boxes with 20 gems.

I know right away after filling out the quadrants that I will start an e-commerce business in organic skincare, as it will be the simplest and fastest route to launching profitably.

*(Note: Don't let these quadrants prevent you from taking action. They are merely a tool to help with gaining clarity. You are much closer than you think you are, and it's time to take that first step and venture out into what may feel like the unknown.)*

## Day 3

*Action Creates Clarity* I've seen many people wait for inspiration or clarity, but I know that answers will come as I move forward, so I keep going, even though I may feel there are so many ideas and fears and questions bombarding my thoughts.

Now that I know my industry, I am going to determine the product I want to create by following my simple e-comm product business map.

I find out what my market is and what people are already buying, because I want to create a product based on what I know is already in demand and selling.

Being in a saturated product space or industry is okay, because I know that I can create a blue ocean and dominate when it comes time for me determine and formulate my product and begin my marketing. I know I will be able to position my unique sales proposition (USP) when I create my five-minute Perfect Webinar. So for now, I just want to choose a product that people are buying.

I am going to choose between a facial serum and a facial mask. Both are popular and in demand, but which one is the best choice?

I reach out to a number of my friends and peers and ask them what their primary concern is regarding their skin.

I also join a number of online groups for organic and herbal skincare and observe their pain points.

### Idea Selection And Validation
I'll scour the internet for feedback and reviews. I am looking to land on the simplest product to launch with the greatest profit potential.

I'll take some time and research organic skincare on Amazon to look for products that have at least a few thousand reviews. I am looking for what people like, what they don't like, particular products, ingredients, textures, essences, and any other data that will help me determine which product I should launch. I'll also google organic skincare companies and see what products are out there and what kind of site reviews they have. Reviews are a key indicator.

After researching, I decide I am going to use a formulation that I had created and stashed for a rainy day. I'll launch a facial serum with anti-aging benefits based on a few key metrics. For one, my research in the groups and on Amazon tells me that there is never a shortage of men and women who will invest in keeping a youthful looking face. A serum has the greatest margin potential of all my product options. It's a consumable, so I will be able to create a recurring subscription for customers, and I'll be able to reach my revenue goals with that one product. It's also a product I love to create and am very passionate about. I've seen the look on women's faces, and I've seen the tears when I create a product that gives them their self-confidence and their beauty back.

I decide to gather some of my already-dried herbs—and if it's a warm season, a few more essential herbs from the mountains here in Colorado—to begin my infusion process and launch the serum. The herbs I have on hand will tighten pores, nourish the skin deeply, heal scars, soften and eliminate wrinkle lines, and give a smooth and radiant complexion.

I can create a sophisticated, warm, and classy look with a glass bottle and warm tones for my label.

Here are some things that are not critical at this stage and should not be areas of primary concern:

- A logo
- A pretty-looking website
- Branding
- Expensive design and packaging

This is all fun, peripheral stuff that people like to obsess over and spend a lot of time and money on. It's so easy to gravitate to branding because it's the simpler, fun stuff, but what's really important is having a solid MVP, functioning funnel, hook, story, offer, good imagery—and one of my favorites—a home run, five-minute Perfect Webinar that grabs people and makes them want to throw their money at me. This is where I will spend 90% of my time.

A brand is not a logo or a website or even packaging; a brand is a personification of our company that will evolve and develop over time. It's who we are at our core. As we grow and learn more about our customers, we will attract our tribe, discover what they want, and give it to them. I won't spend a lot of time trying to conjure up a pretty logo or website.

We are not the heroes; our customers are. So learning who the avatar is and learning to speak straight to her heart will be an art and science that is critical to building a dominant culture. Her story is what matters. So when we tell our story and create our Attractive Character, ultimately she will see herself in us.

A friend of mine once told me "Story first," and that has always stuck with me. We want her to say, "Wow! This brand is reading my mail. I don't care what they're selling...I want in." This is done in the way we craft our messaging that will be everywhere they look, and in our email sequences. (More on that later.)

I'll build a brand that focuses on three things: pure ingredients sourced from the purest and most enchanting places in the world, products that give unprecedented results, and a world-class experience. We want to take care of people and serve them powerfully.

In order for my Perfect Webinar to be successful, here are the things I need to think through as I create my product/offer:

- What is the ONE THING, my Big Domino? Is it an ingredient? The functionality of it? Is it the packaging? What is it that will cause my customer to leave other competing products behind and choose this one? What gives her no option?

- What is the New Opportunity? I don't want to give her an improvement offer. I want either the product, an ingredient in the product, or the way she uses it to be a New Opportunity. Where she has an aha moment and says, "No wonder all these other things didn't work...I need to do this instead."

- What are my three secrets? This is where I break and rebuild her belief patterns. What does she believe to be true about hydration, her skin, anti-aging, proper skincare?

- How will I break and rebuild those belief patterns in a way that leads her to realize she needs this product? I will customize my entire creation phase based on answering these questions. This way, when I do my Perfect Webinar, I can do it from a place of complete authenticity and truth.

# Day 4

We are still in the prepare phase—determining my tools and systems for sustainability and growth in a way that creates more growth independent of me will be my focus for the day.

*Tools For Starting* As I mentioned earlier, wisdom is what makes the difference, so right away I want to reacquaint myself with the most important business resources to get the results I desire.

- *Marketing In Your Car podcast:* Hearing Russell's stories, his triumphs and failures, and his authentic journey has helped me pick myself up when I'm down and keep going with focused effort during the moments I need to feel less alone and get/stay in the zone.

- *Expert Secrets:* I know I'll need this book in order to execute my plan. From it, I will develop my story line and Attractive Character, break down my Perfect Webinar, and develop my overall marketing strategy.

- *Trello:* This is a free project-management tool for managing big-picture and minute details. I'll take the remaining part of the day to refresh myself on Trello, then I will create cards in these categories:
  - Administrative
  - Customer Support
  - Dream 100 + Affiliates
  - Fulfillment
  - Funnels
  - Manufacturing
  - Marketing
  - Research And Development
  - Social + Content

  Then I will start assigning myself cards, with due dates and titles for each task, so I can stay on track with my deadlines and goals.

# Day 5

What looks like failure in business is really an opportunity for greater things to give way and be brought to life. Every day, I remind myself of all the people I know and the biographies I've read of "failures," and I hold on to hope that this is merely the process of becoming great.

I won't spend any time worrying or getting lost in indecision or sadness.

Today and tomorrow, I formulate the serum using the botanicals, herbs, and essential oils that are readily available to me. I am never without the basics. I also formulate my product with the Perfect Webinar in mind. I am thinking about my Domino, planting seeds of doubt, and my Epiphany Bridge. I am imagining and visualizing my marketing as I create my product.

I do some more research in the groups and on Amazon so I can formulate my Perfect Webinar, and I discover a theme in commonly held belief patterns that I can break and rebuild.

I create a Google Doc for brain-dumping any ideas that come to me for creating my Perfect Webinar.

I spend some time thinking through a woman's skincare ritual. What steps is she taking, what is she missing, what kind of products is she using...what does she need and what does she want?

A New Opportunity: I add in a unique ingredient that puts a twist on functionality and puts my product in a blue ocean. This will be the foundation for writing out my Perfect Webinar, and it also gives me a foundation for creating follow-on products that encompass her entire morning and evening ritual.

## Day 6

*"See a man who is diligent in his ways, and he will stand before kings and not mere men."*

— King Solomon

If I could sum up building a business in three words, it would be stewardship, diligence, and generosity. I live by these words. Everything I do, I do with excellence and it always comes back to me. I dedicate myself to following through on what I know is my God-given purpose, and it leads to peace and favor and generosity...in all aspects. Toward myself, toward God, and toward the people in my life.

Today, I am staying focused, enjoying the day, having fun. I'll listen to my favorite music while I formulate my serum and think through my USP.

Today, the creative process means I am refining the texture, essence, and overall blend of the serum so I can test it on my friends.

I have an epiphany while thinking through all the experience I've had in organic skincare, and I determine my Big Domino. The One

Thing that will cause my audience to determine the only way to get what they want is to buy from me.

Finally, tonight I'll start reaching out to a few of my trusted marketer friends so I can line up interviews with potential traffic specialists. Time to get my persuasion on. Even though I have no product yet, I do have a vision, and that alone is enough to engage the right person and onboard them on my grassroots mission. (More on this on Day 10.)

## Day 7

Rest. I go on a hot date with my hubs and try not to talk about business stuff, but to no avail. He graciously entertains my entrepreneurial musings, and it's all good.

## Day 8

Every situation is working together for my good...

I gather a group of my friends for testing and get live feedback. And it takes me one more day to complete the final product.

I've collected some solid data over the last week to use when I begin creating my Perfect Webinar in a few days.

I stay focused on the reason I became an entrepreneur—to impact my family and the world—and I think about the day I'll be able to write $1 million and $10 million checks to causes I believe in. It fills me up and gives greater depth and life to my vision.

I set up an employer identification number (EIN) for my business (otherwise known as a Tax ID).

Then I will set up our merchant processing account.

I'll set up my business bank account so we can connect our merchant processor account.

Then I'll invite 50 of my friends to my paid FB Group, so when we start funneling in customers, there is a welcoming party waiting.

Here's my invite: "Hi, <NAME>! I launched an awesome FB Group for our organic skincare fans, and I am inviting a small group of my friends who I think would gain a lot of value and enjoy the content I will be putting out. It will be way more fun to have some friends in there with me when the new paid customers start joining, so I am creating a warm, welcoming environment for everyone. I would love to have you in there with us. Would you like for me to add you?"

## Day 9

Excellence. Craftsmanship. I will never let this become a lost art.

Today, I will finish the formulation and consider my new product complete.

Women want a product that feels good, smells good, and does what we say it will do, and this serum does just that. Super proud of my creation, and I can't wait to get it on the market.

I will give 10 of my friends a sample of the finished product to try. This way, they can give me feedback/reviews that I can use on the two-step order form of my funnel.

### Creative

I will design my product label today and take it to a local print shop like FedEx Kinkos, print them in full color on label paper, and cut them out by hand with a giant slicer. Doing it real grassroots-like means we can get our product imagery done and ship out our first 250 orders. Now is not the time to spend a bunch of money on printing labels. These will look sharp for the camera, and I will be able to serve my first few customers with them.

## Day 10

Today, I will write out my offer and the first stage of my value ladder, including my price point. Even though I've not created a skincare "system" yet, I've laid a foundation for that to happen after we start converting.

I will keep my offer simple with the one product on the front end. (I made the mistake of trying to sell a bundle on the front end of my first funnel, and it was not effective.)

Since my mission is to create a movement and go beyond selling products, I'm thinking through my offer and how I can create a value ladder that attracts raving fans and produces lifelong customers.

As I write out my value ladder, I include a subscribe-and-save option where they will save 15% on their recurring order.

I plan for three days to write my Perfect Webinar.

I bust out a stack of 8.5" x 11" paper, gather my notes and brain-dump doc, and start writing out my Perfect Webinar Script. I take Russell's Expert Secrets book and brush up on Secrets #17 and #19, but realize that since I am selling a physical product, I will make some adjustments to the Perfect Webinar, as I successfully did in the past with my five-minute version. I won't wait for the Perfect Webinar to be perfect. Since I am doing an e-comm version, consolidated specifically for physical products, I will keep it at five minutes long, replacing the stack with urgency and scarcity. Everything else will stay the same.

The first time I ever wrote a Perfect Webinar, it took me some time to come up with the Domino. Looking back now, I was overcomplicating and overthinking it. It's very simple. What's that one thing you tell your friends or family about when describing your product that gets them to say, "Oh, wow—I need that!" Talk about your product out loud. It will help you flesh out the fluff. When I first started doing my Perfect Webinar, I changed my One Thing a few times before I landed on the one that really resonated with my audience.

## Day 11

During this writing phase, I'll take a break and work on finding my ads/traffic person. Since I don't already have a functioning knowledge base, I will definitely delegate this, so I can focus on other critical areas of the business.

Here's what I've discovered about finding a trusted ads person and what I recommend avoiding in order to prevent lost time and money: Some of the best ads people are not advertising their services, and they can only be found by referral. They are hidden behind incredible companies doing incredible things.

Marketing agencies know how to market...which, unfortunately, is part of the problem. You may find a lot of lofty promises that are not backed up with the ability or noble character to deliver. A lot of agencies know how to market to you and attract you into their funnel and make the sale, but their delivery is sorely lacking. One more reason out of the millions of reasons I appreciate and admire Russell so much. He is the real deal.

Here is how to avoid the sharks and find the gems who will help you with this initial phase of conversion and growth...and possibly beyond. Remember, the person who gets you to a million may not be the person who gets you to 10 or 100 million...and that's okay. You need someone trustworthy who can help you get started.

Ask for referrals from people who have seen the success of the marketer/ads person. Someone who has a track record of creating results for people in e-commerce. Marketing and driving traffic to e-commerce products is very different than driving traffic to and marketing digital products. Make sure you find someone who has experience in your business model. Never mind the people and agencies who tell you how much they've made as a marketer, find out how much they've made for each of their clients! Ask who they've done work for and interview those people. You can find elite business owners marketing and entrepreneurial groups where you can ask for referrals for an e-commerce ads person.

As I set out to fulfill this role, I will also ask my trusted entrepreneurial friends who can refer me to a trustworthy agency or individual. As I begin, I will hire an individual or highly recommended and vetted agency with a track record. I won't worry so much about hiring in-house at this stage unless the opportunity presents itself.

I'll negotiate a deal with an ads person who will be willing to work out performance-based terms. I'll share my vision, and I will get them excited and on board, giving them an incentive to be part of my grassroots movement.

After talking to a number of friends and trusted entrepreneurs, and interviewing a lineup of potential traffic people, I hire my traffic guy. I know there will be a seasoning period where we will begin to learn who my avatar is based on data coming back from ads.

## Day 12

As I finish writing my Perfect Webinar and contacting potential traffic people, one thing I also like to do is gather some info from potential candidates' social platforms that might indicate what it would be like to work with them. Are they positive and well-spoken in their posts? Do they seem to have followers who admire and support them?

I stay true to the course and don't get distracted by shiny objects or loud marketers making shiny promises.

*Imagery* I'll build my own light box, take pics, and send the images off to a service that will do the edits for me. Product photography is different than lifestyle shots—these images should have zoom capability, look sharp and enticing, and be high-res and professional.

I will spend the end of my day writing out the first part of my welcome email and soap opera sequence, a place where my hook, story, and offer can shine!

I want to spend a good amount of time writing these emails. They are designed to create an instant bond between me and my reader. As Russell writes in his DotComSecrets book, "If you're boring, you're done."

## Day 13

Practice the Perfect Webinar out loud. As comfortable as I may be in front of the camera, I will want to get really dialed in to the flow of my messaging. There are transition pieces in the Perfect Webinar that I will want to make sure go smoothly, but most importantly, the transition to the sales proposition. I will want to bounce and flow from each phase of the webinar and go to the sale without it being awkward. This will take some practice.

Hack Russell Brunson's DotComSecrets.com funnel and start building it.

*Two-Step Order Page* I decide to go straight for the sale rather than doing a free + shipping offer, since I want to create revenue immediately. This is a premium product and, knowing what is possible with the Perfect Webinar, I can create a deep desire in my audience for the serum without giving them samples first.

**Bump** I'll start out with $3.95 cut-the-line shipping. (Cut-the-line just means that we are putting those orders at the front of the line to be shipped before everyone else's.) I am not offering the customer an expedited shipping label, so there is no additional cost to me. This will help pay for my ad cost.

**Upsell** I will offer more of the same product.

After I've launched, I will begin to work on third and fourth upsell options and continue improving my value ladder.

I'll map out my customer experience and customer satisfaction guarantees, so that when it comes time to work on the labels, creative, and case candy, I have a plan.

## Day 14

**Rest** Take a walk with my awesome hubs and the kids, go hiking, enjoy Colorado. After the kids are in bed, I'll take some time to relax my mind. I'll sip on my favorite licorice-root tea, put some local raw honey on my face to pamper my skin, and journal for a while.

## Day 15

**Facebook Live Strategy** I will map out a live video sequence so we can use them for seasoning and ads and of course for YouTube repurposing. In addition to my email sequences, this is where I will develop and promote my hook, story, and offer. I'll also want to choose topics I can use as a call to action pointing people to my serum. One out of four FB Lives will be offering the product; otherwise they will be only give-focused. My main mission is to lay a foundation so, as we grow, there is quality information and connection happening on my page.

I'll set up the FB page and do my first FB Live, giving valuable content and information four times more than I promote my products. It's okay if it's an empty room, as I am just starting out. I will talk about my new venture and about what I created. All of my FB Lives will have a call to action. I'll tell people to pound the Share button and hit the Love button and tell me where they're tuning in from, so I can give them a shout-out and say hi. Facebook loves conversation and engagement.

My avatar is a woman between the ages of 35 and 65 who is concerned with aging and loves investing in quality skincare. This is important as my price point will be quite a bit higher than the other brands on the market. Women are more than 70% of the buying power, so we will mainly focus on marketing to them. It will set us up as a premium brand in our own blue ocean. I know that my brand will evolve over time, so right now I want to stay true to the vision I see, which is warmth, a tone that is inviting yet bold with a sprinkling of dry humor and class.

I'll keep building out the funnel with copy that models the format of Russell's book funnel, then complete my first four emails in the welcome and soap opera sequence.

I should have my images back, so I can pop them into my funnel and email sequence now.

Connect the back end of my funnel and prepare for launch by doing my Perfect Webinar in front of the camera again. When we launch the funnel, I will do the Perfect Webinar live to start.

Connect ShipStation so our shipping doc is ready.

Orders will come with a welcome email and their invoice from ShipStation.

They will also receive another email confirming the order has shipped once it goes out.

Connect my merchant processor.

Test funnel at every step. I want to make sure the order loads to ShipStation, that the emails go out, and that everything is ready for my first customer.

## Day 16

Time to plant. Today we launch!

Launch funnel with Perfect Webinar live on FB.

I won't worry about who is watching...my goal is to do my webinar and get the funnel out there.

I'll take some time to watch the replay a few times and take notes so

I can do it better the next day.

Then I start creating my Dream 100 list! This is so exciting.

I follow Russell's Secret #22 in Expert Secrets and I start with list owners, bloggers, podcasters, and social media influencers.

I will put together a low-hanging fruit Dream 100, plus a celebrity list, but I want to have a seasoned page and lots of social proof before I start reaching out to A-listers.

I'll go live and do a video on "Three Secrets To Glowing Skin" that will have some nuggets that point to my serum.

Know my numbers. At this point, I have a product and packaging and I will have chosen my shipping and supplies, so it is critical that I know my cost of goods sold so I know where we need to be with our all-commodity volume and cost per acquisition.

## Day 17

Today, I am going to record video tutorials that sell. They will be training videos that point people to the product. I'll do one on the serum itself, on proper skincare rituals, and more on the skincare industry.

*Design Case Candy* You know when you buy a package and it comes with all the fun reading material and story of the company? That's case candy! I want to create stuff that will inspire women to go for their dreams, create a beautiful life, and take care of their skin. They should feel empowered and pampered when they get their package. Every one of our orders is shipped with a handwritten note and case candy.

Take the design on a flash drive to a local print store and have 50 of them printed.

Do the Perfect Webinar again with a call to action.

Here's how our order presentation will look when they receive their product in the mail: case candy with instructions and highlighted ingredients, the brand story (which is really about them and making the customer the hero), and a handwritten note.

After 17 days, they will receive a courtesy call from me, where I will ask them if they have questions and confirm that they received their order satisfactorily. If they haven't signed up already, I will also offer them our convenient subscribe-and-save option where they can save 15% on their recurring order, never run out, and alter their order anytime they'd like. Waiting 17 days is just the right amount of time for customers to receive their product, use it, and decide they never want to run out.

In the beginning, I will do what's not scalable to serve the customer and create an experience they will want to tell all their friends about. As we grow, I will eventually be able to hire a Happiness Specialist who will handle our calls.

## Day 18

Go live with a video on "How To Do An Herbal Steam For Glowing Skin" and "How To Complete My Routine Using The Serum."

Whenever there is growth, there will inevitably be weeds. Weeds show up as anything that invade our life trying to rob us of growth and prosperity. This can be negative thoughts or people. I make it a point to watch out for weeds and protect my mind and my business from invaders. If weeds go unchecked, they can take over an entire healthy crop and eventually kill it.

I also like to think about composting in farming. Composting is when you take all the garbage and repurpose it to make the soil even healthier. We all experience garbage. I am quick to look for the learning opportunities, failures, and other junk to make me and my business stronger and healthier. I've found that the more garbage I've gone through and overcome, the healthier and stronger I become. So I am always looking for opportunities to compost.

I will finish writing my soap opera sequence today, modeling Russell's, and I may even invite some friends to get their outside perspective.

## Day 19

**Produce** Going back to farming, I like to think of producing a harvest as the process of storing, growing, and managing funds.

I will make sure that I have a reserve account set up so that after

**300**

I take the time to look at our numbers based on revenue goals, overhead, and cost of goods sold, I will look at how much I would need in the bank to have six months of reserves stored.

I decide how much I will reinvest into marketing to grow the business, and I work with my bookkeeper and accountant to establish a funds management system such as QuickBooks.

In addition, I believe that we reap what we sow, so I plan to sow 10% of the business net profit to my local church as a corporate tithe, in addition to 10% of my personal income as a personal tithe. This is part of my wealth accumulation and protection strategy, and it works.

*Go Live* Do a video on "How To Eat Right For Glowing Skin." Make a berry smoothie with Bulgarian yogurt, almond butter, cinnamon, and turmeric. People love smoothie videos. Call to action is to share with their friends, and I invite my listeners to ask their #1 skincare question. I may have to start out by sharing a story of how I struggled with my skin and my #1 burning question at the time, then use my journey to connect in a way that creates a bond and deeper levels of trust.

## Day 20

*Go Live* Talk about using the right morning ritual for gorgeous skin.

I am putting together a preliminary document that my ads person can use to report our numbers.

I also make sure that my bookkeeper and I are on the same page with coding and categories for purchases.

Confirm my shipping supplies are ready to go for my first 25 orders. I would rather be behind on orders than invest a lot of up-front capital on potential orders. When it comes to supplies, material, and inventory, I am very cautious and conservative. It's better to have to make a phone call or send some emails to thank people for their patience, telling them the story of our growth and growing pains, than it is to be capital intensive on the front end. I never overspend.

## Day 21

*Rest* Another hot date with my hubs. We'll go to Barnes & Noble, our favorite place we always go to when we want to keep it simple, get a cup of herbal tea to share, and grab a bunch of home and farm magazines so we can dream about the day we will make it big...again.

## Day 22

Our Facebook page is growing. When I do Lives, I start to see a following happening.

I write another three-day journal-entry email sequence to nurture our audience. I pull the curtain back so women can see my life, what it's like to be a mother of four boys, building a business, and being an herbalist, and I will share a testimonial of someone who has seen results from our products and watch engagement on the email so we can repurpose it for ads.

We want to create three to four new ads each week, so I will build up my repertoire of emails that will story-sell our products and invite people into our world.

## Day 23

Today, I will do the Perfect Webinar live on FB and again review it afterwards.

Stay calm, look good, smile, and enjoy myself.

I'll plan how to scale our ads. We set our goal at 10% each day on FB, and we decide how we will launch on Pinterest, YouTube, and Google Display Network.

I put a 30-day plan together to get lifestyle photos done for social and email, and begin writing blog posts for content.

Continue working on my Dream 100 list!

## Day 24

Today, I will record the Perfect Webinar on my phone and use a free phone app like InShot so I can add emojis to the video then send it to my ads person.

Continue following the Dream 100 strategy from Expert Secrets and begin creating my presentation.

I'll ship out orders and make more serum!

Then I'll go wildcrafting up in the mountains so I can gather a fresh collection of my favorite herbs for a new infusion blend. People want to see my journey, so I post it to IG Stories, take a lot of pics with my iPhone so I can use them for social, and send stories out to my email list. Having stories gathered will be critical for when I hire my writer to start doing my story-selling for me.

## Day 25

Today, when I do my live stream, I'll throw rocks at the skincare industry.

By that, I mean I would share three lies that we've heard perpetuated by the skincare industry and why they're not true. Each of the truths would point back to purchasing the serum. Every FB Live will end with a call to action to buy the serum, and I would offer everyone who's listening a guarantee that we are still in stock, but that due to the nature of our ingredients, we can't guarantee they will stay in stock much longer.

Keeping the brand in mind, I decide not to incentivize potential customers with coupons or discounts. It's easy to think that this is the only way, but I have found that a stellar sales presentation, amazing positioning that causes women to doubt their entire life before this product, and a Perfect Webinar will allow me to build a premium brand, not a discount brand. I'd also download the video later and upload it to YouTube to repurpose and capture that audience as well! If I do decide to do an exclusive discount, it would be for current customers as a thank-you for being part of the family, and it would be for select holidays such as Mother's Day, Father's Day, Christmas, and Cyber Monday. But that's it.

## Day 26

I realize that I don't have a decent backdrop or lights for my live videos, so my husband and I create a simple on-brand backdrop, and I order some ring lights and a lapel mic from Amazon.

This isn't super crucial in the beginning, but it does help to have a nice setup, good lights, and decent sound.

As I am doing the FB Lives, more people are joining and having questions, so I take some time to map out a content calendar that I can use to answer questions and repurpose my content for all social platforms. So far, I know women want to know more about my facial regimen. Since I have a morning ritual and an evening ritual, I map out both.

Then I write out the different aspects of what makes our products unique, and I continue to write out FB Lives that will allow me to cover topics I can incorporate my product into so we can leverage more Lives for ads.

I create my first three journal-style, story-selling email posts, which I know I can leverage for ads as well. My first topic will be how I make our product and source from farms and how it impacts the customers and their skin.

My second journal-style, story-selling entry will be about how I take care of my skin, my morning ritual that includes some beauty-from-the-inside-out tips such as juicing and smoothies for glowing skin.

My third email will be more about our mission, how we are making a difference in the world, and how our customers are a part of something bigger than just product.

Each email has a P.S. at the end with an invitation to join our convenient subscribe-and-save option, so they will save 15% on their recurring orders and never run out of product.

## Day 27

Today, I am mapping out phase two of our value ladder, where I will gather some of my formulations and develop two more products that complete a facial method or system.

- A facial cleanser perfect for all skin types
- A rose-and-dandelion facial toner

This system will give us the ability to upsell into a complete ritual that we can continue to add to as the demand for our products grows. For now, three products is a great way to truly care for the customer with a set of products that will take care of their basic necessities.

I reach out to my local farmers whom I've partnered with to make sure that the local supply chain is in order. Some of our ingredients are precious and not readily available all season, so this is the one area where I buy more than we need.

## Day 28

I will also establish a relationship with the nonprofit I am passionate about. There will be a number of causes I will get behind and believe in, but my primary purpose for being in business—in addition to leaving a legacy for my family and living well on this Earth—is to make a huge difference in the lives of those less fortunate. To take care of the widows and orphans. So today, I reach out to Operation Underground Railroad, and I dedicate a percentage of our funds to their mission to end child trafficking. I've even had it printed on our label that "Every purchase fuels efforts to end child trafficking." It's the entrepreneurs who will change the world, and this is one of the things that drives me to dominate.

## Day 29

Our sales are increasing, and I am in lockstep with my ads person. He's giving me daily reports, and we come up with a plan to hit our first revenue goal within the next 30 days.

We continue to get reports and some possible concerns from customers, which helps us to make adjustments to our shipping process, our packaging, and our FAQ section. By answering questions before they get asked, we will be able to lighten the load on customer service.

By now, we've started getting customer feedback. We have a doc started that we can copy and paste comments to from emails we receive. When we grow, we will implement a review system that gives customers the opportunity to review our products and earn points.

Customers are asking questions that I realize I didn't include in any of our packaging or case candy. I'm glad I didn't print a bunch, so I can easily make changes and evolve our presentation in a way that better serves our customers.

Today, I am going to start the process of finding a third-party shipper! I am looking for a company that can prove a low failure or error rate, has competitive pricing, is close to our location in Colorado, and can turn shipping around within 24 hours of our customers' orders.

## Day 30

Russell once told me, "It's easy to turn up the heat and make money; it's the systems and infrastructure that will be the greatest challenge to growth." Of course he's right.

For this reason, I have a growth strategy I can implement after my 30 days has been executed.

Here is a breakdown of what that looks like for e-comm:

From the back end, I can understand how my marketing is performing with a marketing attribution tool like Wicked Reports. (It's seriously wicked—who comes up with this stuff? The minds behind these tools...wow.)

Team communication: Slack

Project management from big-picture to minute details: Trello

I'll consider a fulfillment center after I reach more than 25 packages per day.

For customer service, I could have my own team or consider hiring a call center.

I'll create a list of categories with customer inquiries, so I can begin to address those questions in an FAQ section on my thank-you page, thereby reducing the number of calls and emails that will come in.

I manufacture all of my own products, so I have a production team in-house.

The operations manager should be someone who has mastery in Excel spreadsheets and pivot tables. This person needs to be able to project how much material we need for inventory, and how much inventory we need based on data. This is important for a few reasons. It will help us avoid overspending on material and inventory. Plus, we need this information so we can turn shipping around quickly.

Back orders are a common occurrence in e-comm, so the more dialed in I can be with operations, the better.

We'll need a systems administrator that will watch team efficiency and productivity, mainly using Trello.

These are the primary areas of focus as I first begin to grow. There are many more, but this is a good start.

An executive assistant is also important, so they can help implement our vision. This person will be key to giving me the breathing room I need to grow my company and support my team.

For a content team, I hired a chief story writer, so I can capture my stories and turn them into journal-entry-style emails. My vision for content has always been to primarily nurture and inspire people in a way that compels them to buy because they love who we are and what we do so much. Stories are such a powerful way to connect with your audience, so this will also be a key role as we grow.

I'll stay on top of my numbers, take one day at a time, and let vision pull me.

# FINAL THOUGHTS

There are always great plans, ideas, and strategies...but action is where the magic happens. Especially in the beginning, it's important to be decisive and execute even when there are so many unknowns. Things will change, shift, evolve, and grow over time. The best way to know what you are doing right is by getting your product or service out there and adjusting as your audience responds.

Have a "fail forward and fail fast" mentality. Or, as I told myself over and over, "Screw it, just do it." Mistakes will happen...better to make them sooner and learn so you can evolve than to painstakingly wait and never accomplish your dreams.

When I went from selling products at farmers markets to launching with our digital strategy, I wanted to keep my capital investment extremely low, so I built my own funnel...and it was ugly. I didn't have a pretty website or a pro designer—I did my own creative, product formulations, and production, and I shipped our products myself.

You have to start somewhere. You don't need perfect—or a lot of money or an investor—you need passion, drive, determination, focus, and execution.

I believe in you...and remember, the best is yet to come. You've got this.

# RESOURCES

- Barnes & Noble
- DotComSecrets by Russell Brunson
- Expert Secrets by Russell Brunson
- Facebook Live
- FedEx Kinkos
- Google Display Network
- Google Docs
- InShot Editor
- Instagram Stories
- Marketing in Your Car podcast
- Operation Underground Railroad (ourrescue.org)
- QuickBooks (quickbooks.com)
- ShipStation (shipstation.com)
- Slack (slack.com)
- Trello (trello.com)
- Wicked Reports (wickedreports.com)

# Chapter 16

# PRE-SELL COURSES WITH WEBINARS

## by Dan Henry

# DAN HENRY

## CEO / Online Entrepreneur

Facebook Ads
*DanHenry.org*

*Dan is the CEO and founder of GetClients.com and co-founder of LeadOwl. Dan specializes in online advertising for local business, digital products, and coaching. He was able to build a $3 million business in 1 year using 100% paid traffic.*

## Day 1

Since I had almost this EXACT thing happen to me, I'll walk you through how I did $100,000 my first month on ClickFunnels. I call this the Sold-Out Courses Blueprint. Here we go...

310

Since I only have 30 days and no money, I won't be wasting time meditating or any of that jazz. I'll get right to work immediately before my morning coffee pot has met its end.

Today is a day of decision making. I'll start by identifying a skill I have that other people would love to be good at or learn. It could be an extremely small skill or a big one, doesn't matter.

I will teach <AUDIENCE> how to get <DESIRE>.

I'd then immediately create a Facebook Group mentioning that skill/desire in the name. I'll use a free graphics program like Canva to create a snazzy cover photo.

I'd then go to my personal Facebook profile and add a link to the group on my page. Then I'd create a custom cover photo of a call to action (CTA).

It will need to be centered in the middle so people can see it on both mobile and desktop, something like: "Want to Learn <TOPIC>? Join my free Facebook Group, <GROUP NAME>."

Now I'm ready. If anyone comes to my personal profile, they'll see a huge CTA to join my group immediately.

(You can see an example by searching "Dan Henry" on Facebook.)

Next, I will go join several niche groups containing people who are my target audience. Basically, people who are discussing the skill I based my Facebook Group around.

This should all get done before lunch. If it takes me longer than that, it means I'm being too picky with the graphics or I am being lazy. So I'll deny myself lunch until it gets done.

Eat.

Now I'll record a quick video with my cell phone and post in the group. I'll make it the pin post welcoming everyone and providing an up-front tip right away.

Then I'll spend the rest of the afternoon and evening providing 100% value in the groups I joined. I'll help people, ask open-ended questions, and keep my comment threads going.

People will see the value I put out, get curious, click my profile, see the CTA on the cover photo, and go join my group. They'll probably Friend request me as well.

I'll finish the night by personally welcoming each person into the group. I'll even send them a welcome message and get to know them a little bit.

Right before bed, I'll sign up for a Stripe account so I can accept payments and get that out of the way.

This is only Day 1. I know that if I stretch this out into a week, I'll be homeless by next month. So I slap myself in the face and get it done, just like I did last time.

## Days 2–5

For the next few days, I will continue providing value in other groups and networking. I'll begin making more value threads in groups and do this until my group has a couple hundred members.

I already know that I can do this fast, because this is exactly what I did before that got me to $1 million in only five months.

## Day 6

I wake up, have my coffee, and go straight to Google Forms. I'll create a simple Google Form called Free Webinar Survey. I'll then ask several strategic questions based around what they want to learn (the subject of my group). I'll ask them what's holding them back, what obstacles are in their way, and a few other strategic questions.

I'll post in my group and personal page, telling everyone I'm thinking of doing a free e-book or training on my skill set.

I'll say, "To make sure the training is awesome, please fill out this survey! I want to cover all your questions on the webinar!"

I'll then spend the rest of the day keeping open-ended sub-threads going on this post to keep it at the top of the feed. That's the secret to engagement. I'll begin getting answers in my Google Form. This will literally give me everything I need to create all my sales copy, webinars, and even my offer.

## Days 7–8

I'll continue to promote this survey while writing bullet points of what I'm going to share on this free training.

I'll begin by identifying the end result everyone wants to achieve. Then I'll find out what obstacles are in their way that they think they need to overcome to get that result. I will then find an alternative path to the end result.

For instance, if people want to learn to be speakers and think they need to network with publicists or agents first, I'd teach them how to land paying speaking gigs even if they don't have an agent or know anyone in the industry.

As long as I can identify the desire, and I know I can teach an alternative method for the main obstacle that will get them the goal, I know I will make money without a doubt.

I'll then sketch out three basic things I will teach. The first one will be the alternative path. The second one will be why this will work for them even if something they have no control over is stopping them. Finally, I will create a secret that covers why they can still do this even if they feel they can't. This follows the middle part of Russell Brunson's Perfect Webinar formula. I'll follow it much closer later when I refine my webinar, but for now a rough one will do.

To give an example, one of my courses that has done over $3 million follows this formula...

- How to easily land digital marketing clients who pay, even if you have no results to show (Obstacle = not having existing client results to help sell their service/alternative path)
- How to bring in more customers for your clients even if you have never run an ad (Obstacle = not having enough experience/internal)
- How to scale to multiple clients even if you have no marketing budget

Obstacle = not having money for marketing/external)

I won't worry about a big story or a fancy close. I'll just throw together some super ugly slides and screenshots in Google Slides.

By Day 9, this presentation should be ready to go.

## Day 9

Now I will announce that the webinar is coming. I'll put together a super simple live webinar funnel in ClickFunnels. I'll use YouTube Live as my broadcast software, and I'll start sending the link out to my group to get registrations.

I'll make sure to start my post with "Who wants to join the webinar?" That way, people will naturally comment "I do" in the comment box, constantly driving it to the top of the feed.

I'll make sure to begin promoting three days out. On the first day, I'll do a live video in the group teaching a preview of Secret #1.

## Day 10

I'll do another live video in the group teaching a preview of Secret #2. I'll continue promoting the webinar registration.

## Day 11

I'll do another live video in the group teaching a preview of Secret #3. I'll continue promoting the webinar registration.

## Day 12

Today's the webinar. I'll continue hyping it to make sure everyone is aware of it right until the last minute. I'll get on YouTube Live, embedded into my funnel, and do a super short presentation on my three secrets. I'll stick to the meat of the presentation.

If I have time to develop a nice story at the beginning, I will...but if not, I won't worry about it. A quick two- to three-minute backstory on how I was able to use this alternative method to figure this or that out is fine.

I'll teach for about 40 to 45 minutes, and then I'll make an offer. The offer will be simple.

I'll announce that I plan to launch an online course covering in detail what I shared on the webinar. However...

"I'm going to make a special one-time offer right here, right now. If you get in now, you'll not only get the course for half price, but you'll also get to take part in a group coaching session. I will personally teach it to you and take all your questions live. I'll make SURE you understand everything!"

Because people may not know or trust me yet, I'll then say that I'm going to offer something better than a refund. I'll charge them $1 that day but they won't get charged the full price until 48 hours after the live coaching session. That way, they can try it before they buy.

If they don't like it, they can simply send me an email within 48 hours after the training and request to cancel. I'll cancel the charge and they'll never even have to pay for it.

I'll then make a secondary offer. If they are 100% in and don't care about the refund guarantee, they can pay in full right then for an extra discount.

If I get only 10 people to take the offer at $300, I now have $3,000 soon to be in my pocket.

If I don't sell a single copy, I will know that there's something fundamentally wrong with my offer or niche. I can now put a halt to it right away before I waste too much time.

If I had spent the entire time creating a program, I would've wasted all that time once I discovered no one wanted it. By identifying this potential problem early, I now have time to fix it.

## Days 13–15

Given my experience and the fact that I've already done this successfully, I know I'll make at least 10 sales ($3,000).

The coaching session is in a few days. I'll spend those few days coming up with very quick and ugly bullet-point slides to teach my people.

## Day 16

Now it's time for the group coaching session. I will do it on a private YouTube Live link where I can see questions in the chat box.

I'll begin teaching each lesson doing the best I can to make what I'm teaching clear. Then at the end of the lesson, I will ask for questions. I'll answer each question thoroughly and completely.

If I feel that people didn't totally get what I was trying to teach, I will mark that lesson as needing revision. I will redo the lesson for them 100% free on a different day after revising my work to make sure that they'll love it. I'll complete the group coaching session and ask for feedback.

If feedback is overwhelmingly positive, I'll bring them on camera and ask for an on-the-spot testimonial. They will be super hyped, so the testimonial will be good.

Boom. Now I have social proof, and it's only been two weeks.

## Days 17–18

I'll now have a five- to eight-hour video file from my group coaching day. Over the next two days, I will mark out where each lesson should begin and end, notate any mistakes to get cut.

When the day comes for everyone to get charged, I'll make sure all the charges go through. If anyone wants to cancel, I will cancel their charge and get some feedback from them.

If I do everything correctly, I should get few or no cancellation requests. I only got one the last time I did this, and it was simply because the guy didn't have any money. At this point, I will have at least $2,600 in my pocket. However, the first time I did it, I had close to $4,000.

Before bed, I'll create an account on Fivver or Upwork and hire someone to edit my lessons. I'll send them the time-based edit document I made and let them work. That should cost me no more than $500. I'll continue to promote my group.

## Day 19

I'll use the questions, pain points, and feedback from the coaching session to create a free PDF report. I'll also work on my live webinar funnel.

Once I get the videos back from the video editor, I will load them into a membership portal inside of ClickFunnels. I'll also upload the end-of-coaching-session testimonials to YouTube.

## Days 20–24

Since I now have money in my pocket, I'll run my first Facebook Ad offering to give away a free cheat sheet. I'll funnel them into my

**316**

Facebook Group on the last page and in the welcome email. I'll spend about $1,000 on ads for the cheat sheet. This should get me 800 to 1,000 people on my email list and in my group over the next week.

I'll create live videos and hype up my group over the next several days. These videos will direct them to a registration page for a new live webinar. This webinar will be more refined and have a complete offer stack with an order page at the end.

## Day 25

I'll run the webinar and make the offer. I'll tell them if they want to get into the private group, they need to post in my free group and say, "Hey, Dan, I just bought the course. Please add me to the student group."

I will screen-share the live feed of the group during the offer pitch and actually show the "I just bought" posts live!

This will cause extreme mob mentality and a buying spree.

This is exactly how I did $50,000 for my very first webinar. I created a mob mentality although I barely had a list.

## Days 26–28

I'll schedule an encore webinar and promote the heck out of it for the next several days. I'll keep my cheat sheet ad running.

## Day 29

I should be able to pull $30,000–$50,000 out of this initial webinar and another $30,000–$50,000 a week later with an encore.

This brings me to (or close to) a six-figure month, starting from nothing.

I know this is possible because this is exactly what I did when I hit $100,000 my first month on ClickFunnels.

## Day 30

Two years ago, this day would have involved adult beverages and many shenanigans not appropriate for this book.

But today, I will take my wife and newborn son out on a nice private yacht cruise and enjoy the fruits of my labor with my family.

## FINAL THOUGHTS

Since creating a multimillion-dollar online education business, I've begun coaching other entrepreneurs to achieve similar goals.

The #1 thing I tell every one of them is this...

"If there is an audience willing to learn something for free, there will always be someone willing to pay for more. You only need 1% to become a millionaire and change the world at the same time."

Dan Henry

## RESOURCES

- Canva (canva.com)
- Fiverr (fiverr.com)
- Google Form
- Google Slides
- Stripe (stripe.com)
- Upwork (upwork.com)
- YouTube Live
- Online Course ClickFunnels Template (getclients.com/ coursefunnel)

# Chapter 17

# MINDMAP

## by Joe McCall

# JOE MCCALL

*Real Estate Investor /
Podcaster / Coach*

Real Estate Investing
*WLOWebinar.com*

*Joe McCall has been investing in real estate full-time since 2009, doing many deals in the USA while traveling around Europe and in his RV. His podcasts, courses, workshops, and books help beginning investors learn how to build fully automated real estate businesses that flip deals from anywhere in the world, with only a laptop and a phone.*

Okay—so let me get this straight. I suddenly lose all my money...I have no list, no audience, nobody knows who I am...all I have is my knowledge and marketing expertise?

And I have ClickFunnels?!

Awesome! Let's get to it. This is going to be so fun!

What I am going to show you is a simple step-by-step process that takes an online mind map and turns it into a book, a podcast on iTunes, a YouTube channel with followers, an active Facebook and Instagram following, a huge Facebook pixeled audience, an email list, and testimonials of students who have amazing results doing what I teach...all starting from one simple mind map.

Serious? Yep. Are you intrigued? Let's get started...

By the way, my goal is to actually get the funnel built in one week or less. It shouldn't take me any more time than that. Remember, "Done is the new perfect!" I just need to get it out there. I can always tweak it and make it better later.

## Day 1: Plan My "Fastest Path To Cash"

First thing: create a mind map for my own brainstorming. I use http://mindmeister.com. It's free and is completely online. You can create mind maps and share them with people, using view-only links, so they can't mess them up.

I would do a massive brainstorm—map out all my ideas, prioritize everything, and come up with the beginnings of a game plan.

There are a lot of things I could do, a lot of paths to take, a lot of ways to make money. I would list all the things I am really good at and the things I really love to do. But then I would step back, look at the big picture, and ask myself one simple question, "What is the fastest path to cash?" For me, the answer is simple. There are two things I am passionate about in this business...

1. I love marketing for real estate investors.
2. I love helping people make money.

How could I combine those two things and make a business out of it, while delivering tons of value to the marketplace?

Well, I know real estate investing really well. I've done lots of deals. That's easy. I decide that I will help people learn how to invest in real estate.

But that is too broad. There are tons and tons of people teaching how to invest in real estate. That's a huge red ocean. I need to niche down...

I love marketing. One of my mantras is "We are not in the real estate business. We are in the marketing business." So what if I create a product that teaches real estate investors how to do effective marketing and get leads in the fastest, cheapest way possible?

Bingo. That's niched down enough to appeal to a wide number of people. And there are not many people teaching that.

What Kind Of Results Do My Potential Clients Want?

Now I need to figure out how I can take my knowledge on marketing for real estate investors and turn it into something that produces FAST RESULTS—for me and for my clients.

You see, it's all about getting my clients results, in the fastest and easiest way possible. So I would start mind mapping out all the results my clients might want.

What they really want is to do more deals. They want to make money fast. They want to quit their jobs and find financial freedom. Well, how can I help them do more deals in the fastest way possible?

I can help them do better marketing. That is my superpower.

I know that in order to really help them, I need to do more than just teach them how to do marketing. I need to SHOW them.

And actually...I can offer them an opportunity to PARTNER WITH THEM or DO THE MARKETING FOR them. (More on that later.)

*Five Ones* I have a great start on a simple plan. It may not be perfect, but that's okay. I know it's going to take some adjustments and refinements as the month progresses. But I know it's a great place to start. I am not going to overanalyze it.

The next thing I need to map out is how I am going to do all this.

- How am I going to build an audience?

- How am I going to spread my message out to as many real estate investors as possible?
- How am I going to attract my best customers who I can help the most?
- What kind of products am I going to create?
- How am I going to create these products in the fastest way possible?

There are a million things I could focus on. Knowing myself, I would probably be getting really overwhelmed at this point. I could easily get frozen in "analysis paralysis" and nothing would get done.

But I know that unless I keep things simple and just focus on a few things at a time, this will all be a complete failure.

So I would start mind mapping out my Five Ones. (Note: I learned this from Taki Moore.)

- One Person
- One Product
- One Conversion Tool
- One Traffic Source
- One Year (to focus only on these Five Ones)

After much brainstorming, I might come up with something like this:

- *One Person:* My best customer is someone who has a passion for real estate investing and has at least $1,000/month to spend on marketing. They also need to be coachable and fun to work with.
- *One Product:* This could be a coaching program where I would do marketing for people and partner with them on deals.
- *One Conversion Tool:* I would do a $7 mind-map funnel that leads to a coaching application.
- *One Traffic Source:* I would do daily content videos about real estate investor marketing and post them on YouTube, and then turn the videos into a podcast and Facebook Live posts. (Note: I know this is not technically "one traffic source," but it's super

easy to turn a YouTube video into a podcast and then broadcast it to Facebook Live. I would create this video once and then re-broadcast it to multiple channels.)

- *One Year To Focus:* Obviously, I only have one month, but I would be so hyperfocused during this month, I would get more done than most people get done in a year. That's the power of focus!

That's a good day's work. I have everything on a mind map. I have discovered that the fastest path to cash for me is to help real estate investors do more effective marketing. And I have narrowed my focus on five simple One Things. I know who my main customer is. I have one product, one way to spread my message, one way to sell my product, and one month to focus on only this.

But if I still had more time in the day (and I should...it's not really going to take me more than a few hours to do all this), I would reread Expert Secrets or DotComSecrets from Russell Brunson.

# Day 2: Start Creating Content and Buy A Simple Domain

Now is the time to start creating my content. And if you haven't guessed it yet, my content would all be in a mind map.

This will be the foundation of everything we're doing going forward and will be created on Mindmeister. When I share this mind map with people, I will only be giving them a link to view it. They won't be able to edit or change it.

The topic of all my content (and the title of my mind map) would be something like "Marketing Secrets For Real Estate Investors: 30 Days to 100 Motivated Seller Leads."

I would then expand the map, breaking it into 30 nodes (or modules), detailing and documenting the steps for getting 100 hot, motivated seller leads in 30 days or less.

The goal would be to keep it super simple and avoid the tech overwhelm. It all has to be seen as simple and easy to implement, where people watching my videos and reading the mind map can get quick wins if they follow along and do it themselves.

**324**

Each node in the mind map would be enough content for a 10- to 15-minute video. It would be very actionable and results-focused—easy baby steps.

My content is going to be a mix of teaching and doing. Not only would I be teaching people how to do what I am doing, I would be showing them how to do it.

In all 30 videos, I would be teaching from the online mind map. The mind map will be the foundation of everything. It will have a very high perceived value. The mind map will contain all my important spreadsheets, marketing pieces, scripts, checklists, offer calculators, follow-up tools, contracts, links, references, etc.

Do you see why this is so important? *I will be giving everything away in this online mind map* so it has to be seen as incredibly valuable.

And they can get this mind map for only $7. It's an incredible offer—a no-brainer, an easy sell.

At the beginning and end of each video, I would tell people that if they wanted to get the mind map and all the valuable content that I only share inside the mind map, they can get it for $7.

**Buy A Simple Domain** It's important to buy a good domain. This is the domain I would send people to on the video to get the mind map. It should be really simple and easy to remember. I would probably get something like MindmapJoe.com.

I'll keep it short and sweet. And I won't spend more than 15–20 minutes trying to find the perfect domain. Done is the new perfect. Just need to make sure it's easy to spell and has no more than two words.

**Logos And Banners For Social Media** Because this only takes a few minutes but can take a few days to produce, I would do this right away. I would hire someone on Fiverr to create a simple podcast logo and YouTube banner with large-text background, saying something like "Marketing Secrets For Real Estate Investors."

I would also hire someone to record podcast and video bumpers (intros and exits).

- Square podcast logo (Search Fiverr for "podcast logo")
- YouTube banner (Search Fiverr for "YouTube banner")
- Podcast audio bumpers (Search Fiverr for "podcast intro")
- Video bumpers (Search Fiverr for "video intro")

The YouTube banner and audio and video bumpers should all have my call to action to go to my website and download my mind map.

All of this should cost no more than $20 ($5 each). And I can change them later and get better designs after I start making money. I won't spend too much time on this right now, just get it done.

# Day 3: Record My Content

Next, I would start recording the actual content of me going thru the mind map step-by-step. Each video should be no more than 10–15 minutes long. I'll cut the fluff and get right to the point.

Each video should start with the Who, What, Why, How script: Here's who I am. Here's what I have. Here's why you should get this mind map and what it will do for you. Here's how to get it. (That shouldn't take more than 60–90 seconds.)

Then I would start teaching and delivering incredible value. I am showing and telling my content thru the mind map. And I would emphasize all the way through my videos how the things I am showing them are only available on the mind map that they can get today for just $7 at MindmapJoe.com.

I might even tell them that I have extra video instructions in the mind map on how to do certain things with a lot more detail.

What would I use to record my content? I use ScreenFlow by Telestream, but a less expensive option would be Screencast-O-Matic. It doesn't have as many features as ScreenFlow, but it works really well. There is also Camtasia for PC users.

When I record my content, I like to make sure my webcam is showing me in the lower right corner. I think it makes my videos more personal. I want them to get to know, like, and trust me. I should be able to get at least half of my mind map content recorded in one day. If I don't, that is okay. I can finish it over the next couple days.

# Day 4: Create Main Offer And Build Funnel Pages

*Create Main Offer: High-Ticket Coaching* On the fourth day, I would start creating my offer. The key here is simplicity. The offer and funnel don't need to be fancy or elaborate. Some of my best-converting funnels have had simple white backgrounds, minimalistic design, and clear calls to action. I'll get right to the point.

Of course, I am going to mind map all this out. It is easy to get overwhelmed with all the options and possibilities when creating an offer. So I'll brain-dump and then simplify.

This is not the offer to buy the $7 mind map. This is an offer to sign up for my high-ticket coaching that people will see after they buy my mind map.

I believe there are three critical elements to creating an irresistible offer.

1. Your offer must be compelling. It can't be another "me too" product. You need a Big Idea, something that is different, unique, powerful, awesome, special.
2. You need to have urgency. Your prospects need to feel like they have to make a decision today to work with you. If they don't make a decision today, that's okay. But your offer might not be available tomorrow. And it's probably not for them anyway.
3. You need to have scarcity. They need to know that you have a limited amount of time in the day that you are willing to share with people. Your time is scarce and incredibly valuable. You can only work with a small, select number of people. And you can only work in a few select markets.

My offer is going to be really simple. To come up with my offer, I am going to answer these basic questions (courtesy of Dean Jackson):

> *"What would I do if I got paid only IF my client gets a result?"*

In other words...

> *"If I can only get paid AFTER my clients get the results*
> *they are looking for, how would I help them?"*

Wow. What a great question, huh? It's a little scary when you first hear it. But bear with me. It is actually the ONLY question you should be asking yourself when you are first starting out.

I know that in order to get people the results they want in the fastest way possible, one option is to hire me to do the marketing for them. But I don't want to provide just another "me too" marketing service. I like doing deals, teaching, and coaching. How can I combine all that into one package?

I am going to offer a done-with-you coaching and partnering program. It's going to be super simple.

## My High-Ticket Offer

- My program will start at $10,000. The first $2,500 will go toward the marketing and systems that I will help them set up. (These are the same systems I taught in the mind-map videos.) The remaining $7,500 will be my coaching fee, which they will earn back with the first two deals they partner with me on. That way, they have some skin in the game.
- If they work the leads that I know I can give them, they will get their coaching fee back out of the profits. If they don't do the work, I am not the one left holding the bag.
- I will set up their basic systems (customer relationship management/CRM, website, phone system) and schedule out their marketing for the first two months (online marketing, direct mail, virtual assistants).
- They will work the leads as they come in. They will talk to sellers, see the house, make offers, update the CRM, etc.
- I will be available to help them thru Voxer, texting, and weekly scheduled calls. I will even allow them to schedule a day with me at my office in St. Louis if they want.

**328**

See how I have created a win-win? I am setting up their systems and doing all the techy stuff they hate. They are learning from a pro about how to do marketing and flip deals as I work closely with them one-on-one.

If they do what I teach them to do, they will get all their money back out of the profit splits. This is a very compelling offer.

So now...how do I create urgency and scarcity?

My urgency and scarcity would come from several sources.

- I am only looking to go into a couple other markets.
- I can only work with two people at a time.
- I am looking to start right now. I am going to pick someone in the next couple weeks.
- Only one person per market. Once a market is taken, it's gone forever.

*Build Funnel Pages* The four pages in my funnel will look like this:
1. $7 Mind Map Two-Step Order Form
2. Order Confirmation page: This includes a special training video that sells the high-ticket done-with-you coaching. This video will be a shortened version of the Perfect Webinar. My CTA will be to invite people to apply to work with me.
3. Coaching Application page
4. Thank-You page: This explains what's going to happen on the call and how to prepare for it.

My pages would be very simple—white backgrounds, bold headlines, clear calls to action, big buttons, etc. Remember, less is more and simpler is better.

For my coaching application page, I would use a simple Google Form. I would only have five or six questions on there.

After they fill out the Google Form application (and give me their phone number), I would immediately text them and schedule a time to talk. I would do whatever I could to get them on the phone while they're hot, within the next 12–24 hours.

If I was getting too many applications, I would do a fully refundable $100 application fee, just to remove the tire kickers and time wasters. It would only take a few minutes to build this $100 product using Stripe in ClickFunnels.

I'll need to make sure I have my Facebook and Google Analytics pixels on all my pages, so I can follow my visitors later with ads.

## Day 5: Record Perfect Webinar

On the order confirmation page, I would create a special training video to sell the high-ticket coaching. It would only be around 30–45 minutes.

I would first reread the sections in Russell's books on the Perfect Webinar Script. I would pick at least three really good epiphany stories (my own and some from people I helped).

I would do hardly any teaching in this video, and it would be at a very high level. I would get to the point as quickly as possible. I would mainly talk about the opportunity and emphasize the urgency and scarcity.

I have all day to do this webinar. I will try not to overthink it. Just need to get it done. I can modify it and tweak it later as I go.

If I had more time at the end of the day, I would record more content for the main mind map.

## Day 6: Create Social Media Pages And Podcast Feed

There are several pages and profiles I would need to build. Again, I wouldn't worry about spending too much time on this. I would use the logos and banners from Fiverr that I ordered earlier.

- Facebook Group
- Facebook page
- Instagram profile
- Libsyn podcast profile
- YouTube page

My main title: "Marketing Secrets For Real Estate Investors"

For the podcast itself, I would just use Libsyn's self-hosting service.

When it comes to my podcast page, I don't need a WordPress website yet. I can hire someone on Upwork to do that later, after I start making money. For now, I'll just use the feed that Libsyn gives me.

(By the way, if you want to hire someone to edit your podcasts and videos, you guessed it—find someone on Fiverr. Search for "edit video podcasts.")

## Day 7: Write Copy

This is the day I would write some copy for my sales pages and follow-up emails. I would definitely use Funnel Scripts (if I had access to it). If I didn't, I would just follow the Who, What, Why, How script. I would try to interject as many stories into my emails as possible.

Here are some of the things I need to write copy for:

- Main sales page for buying the $7 mind map

- The thank-you page with the special training video that sells the coaching

- Physical letter to send in the mail, probably three or four pages. I will mail this one week after they buy the mind map if they don't fill out an application. This letter would just tell my epiphany story for how I got started in real estate, and how I am able to do what I do full-time.
    - I would model well-written email sequences that I have encountered.

- Follow-up emails (all done in Actionetics)
    - If they fill out an application, they will get a thank-you email. This would also include some prep work and an explanation of what to expect on the call.
    - If they filled out Step 1 but not Step 2 of the $7 mind map, they will get an additional email every day for three days.
        - These emails would send them back to buy the mind map.

- If they didn't fill out an application, they will get a series of three emails, one sent every two to three days.
  - This email will be sent every 30 days, starting one week after they opt in. "Are you not interested in learning how to get more seller leads in your real estate business? Joe"
  - "Do you still need some help with your marketing? Joe"
  - No links. Just simple one-sentence questions.
- FAQ and content emails sent to everyone who didn't fill out an application
  - These would be simple, one-page emails, answering common questions and objections to real estate investing and marketing.
  - Some of the emails would also include simple content from the mind map and videos.
  - I would try to do at least 30 of these and send them every day.
  - Each email would have a simple call to action at the end.

## Days 8–30

Wow! I've done a lot of work. It was a little overwhelming, but it was so worth it. I've just built a cash-flowing ASSET! I've done work that's going to be evergreen and last for a really, really long time. I am going to be building my list every single day—all on autopilot. This is exciting and a good reason to celebrate!

So here is what I would be doing *every single day* after (in order of priority):

1. Publish one content video to YouTube.
2. Email and text my list about the new video.
3. Publish my video and audio as a podcast on iTunes.
4. Publish my pre-recorded video to Facebook Live, to my personal profile and business FB page.
   - How would I do this? Well, there's this little-known website called YouTube. They have a couple videos on their site. I would go there and search for "How do you publish a pre-recorded video to Facebook Live?"

**332**

5. Interact with people on Facebook. Look for questions to answer. Ask them questions. Start engaging conversations.
6. Update social media channels every day with new stuff.
7. Do a separate five-minute Facebook or Instagram live video, teaching something quick, an actionable tip or something.
   - Remember to give them a clear call to action—at the beginning and the end—to watch my other videos and download my mind map.
8. Join other FB Groups/forums and share valuable marketing tips, not asking for anything in return.
9. Text people who bought the mind map and just say hello. Ask them if they have any questions and if they need any help. I could use Google Voice for this. Here are some sample questions I would ask:
   - What did you think of the mind map and videos?
   - Any questions I can help you with?
   - Tell me more about you and your business.
   - Why are you interested in learning more about marketing for real estate investors?
   - What do you need the most help with right now?
   - I have a program that can solve that. Does it make sense for us to get on the phone and talk about it?

*Sales Call For Coaching* Once I get people on the phone, I would use the consultative close and keep it really simple. I would just ask lots of questions and listen. I would try to get them to sell me on why I should want to work with them. Here are some of the questions I would ask on these calls (in no particular order):

- Could you tell me more about you and your business?
- So why are you calling me, and why are you calling me now?
- What are you hoping to accomplish? What else?
- What's on your plate now and what are you doing currently to make money?
- What have you tried so far?

- Why do you think that's not working?
- What are you going to try next?
- What's stopping you from achieving this right now on your own?
- What do you need the most help with right now?
- Where do you want to go from here?
- On a scale of 1–10, how interested are you in learning how to get more leads and do more deals?
- Do you understand that if you want success in this business, it requires an investment of time and money?
- What do you want this thing to look like?
- Is this a NOW thing or a LATER thing for you?
- This is where you are right now, and this is where you want to be. Why aren't you there right now?
- Why do you think I can help you?
- If nothing changes, what's the impact going to be on you and your business?
- What's going to happen if you don't meet your goals?
- How fast do you want to get these results?
- What are you hoping that coaching can do for you?
- So if you knew how to build a business where you could do XYZ and only work five hours a week, would you do it?
- If we could work together, do you think you would be successful? How come?
- So what do you want to do next?
- If you think I can help you, where do you think we should go from here?
- How much do you think my coaching program should cost?

## Day 31: Create A Book From All This Content

Now my 30-day challenge is over, I am starting to do deals with students and make money from coaching. What now?

Now that I have all this incredible content in the mind map and videos, I would hire a ghostwriter and turn it all into a book.

I would start doing a ton of Facebook Ads for a Free + Shipping funnel for the book. I would be targeting my Facebook Custom and Lookalike Audiences from my earlier promotions. I would also put the book on Amazon.

My order-form bumps and one-click upsells would be for the videos and mind map.

Boom! Bada bing! I just repurposed all my content. I now have a book, a podcast, a YouTube channel, a following on Facebook and Instagram, an email list, and testimonials of students I have been helping! Time to start promoting it as evergreen content. Maybe I could start doing this with other products.

If you have any questions, shoot me an email at 30DayMindmap@joemccall.com.

(Or go to MindmapFunnel.com to see this in action.)

# RESOURCES

- Actionetics (clickfunnels.com/actionetics)
- Amazon.com
- Camtasia (techsmith.com/video-editor.html)
- Facebook Live
- Fiverr (fiverr.com)
- Google Analytics
- Google Forms
- Google Voice
- Libsyn (libsyn.com)
- MindMeister (mindmeister.com)
- ScreenFlow (telestream.net/screenflow)
- Stripe (stripe.com)
- Taki Moore's Five Ones
- Upwork (upwork.com)
- Voxer (voxer.com)
- WordPress

## Chapter 18

# AFFILIATE MARKETING

*by Spencer Mecham*

# SPENCER MECHAM

## *Affiliate Marketer*

Affiliate Marketing
*Buildapreneur.com*

*Spencer is a full-time affiliate marketer, course creator, and digital teacher. He enjoys winning cars and helping entrepreneurs automate their businesses so they can live life on their own terms.*

Cancel all distractions. Netflix, sports, etc. Social media would be used, but solely for business. Get affairs in order. Build schedule. Get credit card.

Create office/filming area.

Quick cash: Upwork, Konker, Freelancer, personal Facebook page

Join the communities on Facebook where my audiences hang out, reach out to admins.

Sign up for three to five big recurring affiliate programs, preferably ones I'm experienced in.

Sign up for a lot of smaller affiliate products in JVZoo and Click-Bank, ask around on FB Groups.

Create courses and trainings around the big recurring ones (three days).

Create additional bonuses (share funnels, etc.).

Create a profitable viral share funnel.

Sign up for email autoresponder and create high-quality and low-quality lists.

Write powerful soap opera sequence.

Write high-quality email sequence that is 50 days long.

Write low-quality email that is 50 days long.

Create traffic accounts (AdWords, Bing, YouTube, Instagram, Facebook Group, Messenger bots).

Facebook Group day: build, add good content, post to personal page. Hire VA.

Create system for VA to put onto YouTube and Instagram.

Build YouTube content calendar.

Start with AdWords and Bing, any programs that allow branded searches.

Move on and do the same for unbranded searches.

Film first batch of 30 YouTube videos.

Revisit and make edits to AdWords and Bing accounts.

Start dripped solo ads to viral share funnel.

Collaborations: leverage new relationships and start offering free stuff to their groups.

## Day 1

Day 1 is all about preparation. I struggle with distraction, so Day 1 would be all about eliminating those.

Netflix is the first to go, followed by any social media sites I don't plan on using for marketing. Apps on my phone that suck my time away go next. I would likely create a brand-new email address to avoid the dozens of distracting emails I currently get every day.

I will also apply for a credit card on the first day. This takes time, and I will need the cash to pay for software and ads over the coming weeks. Day 3 is my backup plan to a credit card, assuming I can't get approved. I may also apply for a PayPal business loan or hit up relatives for small loans. Anything to get the necessary cash fast.

## Day 2

Still in prep mode. A lot of my success will ride on the quality of the content I start putting out in a few weeks. So Day 2 consists of setting up a filming studio and office where work comes easily and I can crank out videos on autopilot. A good mic and webcam could be had for less than $100. Throw in a desk from Craigslist, and I'm sitting at right about $100.

Day 2 would also consist of creating my 30-day blueprint and setting a daily schedule. Schedule is important when I will be spending time on social media sites like Facebook, because I could spend all day getting sucked into conversations and scrolling through feeds. I will need those sites for marketing, but without strict scheduling, the day disappears fast.

For me, the niche is a no-brainer: systems for creating passive income through automation. For others, that may be a harder decision.

## Day 3

I'll probably take some heat for my plan this day, but this is how I originally got where I am, and I am a fan of the system.

I would sign up for sites like Konker, Freelancer, and Upwork. For an hour a day, I will be selling my services and expertise for what is likely a lot less than they are worth.

I have always struggled with spending my own money on ads and testing. However, I am much more comfortable losing money on experiments when it is obtained through entrepreneurial efforts.

Since in this particular scenario I am penniless, this will be a way for me to obtain an initial budget for ads, etc.

My strategy is built around creating a long-term passive income. Money will not be pouring in after 30 days, but this will help get the ball moving without running everything through credit cards. It is possible that nothing will work for the first few weeks, and I'll need to make adjustments. This ensures I have the budget to do so without piling on stress.

## Day 4

Time to start making myself known online! I'm going to need a reputation and some solid connections to make things work.

I prefer Facebook Groups, where I believe a vast majority of conversation online currently takes place.

I'll search for groups on affiliate marketing, marketing automation, passive income, marketing automation software groups (such as ClickFunnels), and other niche-relevant keywords.

I will try to post relevant, valuable, and completely free content on each of those groups three or four times a week. This will be the first hour or so of each morning.

I'll also spend some of that time answering questions and interacting in these groups.

Group owners are dying for content and engagement. They will quickly warm up to me, and I can start building relationships over Messenger chats as well. Members of their groups will also start to recognize my name as an authority figure whom they can trust.

## Day 5

Time to figure out who is going to be paying the bills for the rest of my life. I need three to five solid affiliate programs to start with. These will be what I call my high-quality programs. Typically they will be software companies with recurring affiliate programs of 30% or higher.

My perfect niche is fairly new software companies (less than a few years old) with less stringent affiliate policies and less competition for paid and organic keywords. They need to be extremely useful, if not vital, to my niche's business goals.

Think ClickFunnels, email automation software, Messenger-bot software, etc. I'll also look at the trends in my niche. For example, Bitcoin is currently taking the internet by storm, so I will look for software companies that are involved in Bitcoin and have good affiliate programs.

It doesn't necessarily matter if companies are competitors, because sometimes I will be simply doing brand-based search marketing or targeting searchers that are comparison shopping.

These will be the core companies I will be using to create a truly passive income.

## Day 6

Time to sign up for what I call "complementary product" affiliate programs. These are lower paying but much easier sells. I will use them to boost my income via email and also to break even on a lot of paid-traffic choices.

I'll find these on the most well-known affiliate sites. JVZoo, WarriorPlus, ClickBank, Rakuten, and CJ Affiliate will make a good start. This will take a good bit of scouring and searching. A lot of what is sold on these sites is spammy, useless, and outdated. But each has a few gold mines (typically software, Chrome extensions, etc.).

There will be a few courses and trainings, but they are few and far between when it comes to quality.

These will be what I call my low-quality affiliate offers. Some people simply cannot or will not purchase expensive software and courses. These will be offers for them.

## Day 7

Today is my first day of rest. I do not work Sunday, for both religious and health reasons. I will spend today revitalizing myself, enjoying time with family, worshipping, and thinking about anything but my business.

## Days 8–10

These are combined because these are content-creation days for major software. To succeed as an affiliate for these programs, I need people to actually continue with the programs and succeed with them (hence passive, recurring income). I also need to give them better incentives for signing up.

I will be creating courses focused around each of these products, but not solely focused on these products.

For example, for ClickFunnels, I will design a course on how to create high-converting sales funnels. The focus of the course will be on sales funnels, but the tool the course will use is ClickFunnels. There will be share funnels, links, and all kinds of bonuses that involve ClickFunnels.

The same thing with email automation, Messenger bots, Instagram automation, etc. Each one gets a full training on the subject but revolves around specific software.

These will be used as lead magnets from YouTube videos and uploaded as units in my Facebook Group (which must be set to social learning). Some of the videos will be used as value in email automations, etc.

So with YouTube, it would work like this. One YouTube video on how to improve email open rates. I would probably name it something sexier, like "95% Open Rates." The video will focus on how Messenger bots are drastically improving open rates.

In the beginning of the video, I will mention an offer that will be coming later. At the end of the video, I let them know there is a link down below in the video description and also in the YouTube cards I have added to the video to a completely free course that can teach them everything they need to set up Messenger bots that succeed.

Obviously there will also be an affiliate link at the bottom of the video in case they just want to run with it.

# Day 11

It is now time to create bonuses and value stacks. For many programs, this would mean making additional resources for simplifying the software for users.

The point of this is to both incentivize sign-ups and also to make the products simpler for users.

For example, with ClickFunnels I would create multiple share funnels that will make getting started easier for new users. Many email automation software programs have similar features where you can share automations, etc.

Each bonus will be unique to the platform it will come with. As I teach about or promote any particular program, I will use these resources to incentivize a quick sign-up.

For example, in a YouTube video, I might finish by letting anyone watching know that they can get all the templates they need to hit the ground running just by signing up via the link below.

Bonuses are delivered via Facebook Messenger bot, giving me access to another touchpoint.

## Day 12

Today, I am going to create another valuable resource called a viral share funnel. Essentially this is a small ready-to-go funnel that helps bring people into the world of online/affiliate marketing. It comes with email sequences, shared funnels, and marketing training.

They can then use all the training, funnels, and emails to bring others into the world of online marketing.

This funnel is going to be a great place for many people who approach me with the question "Where do I start?"

It will also be where I send a lot of initial traffic from Instagram and from solo ads. This is my low-quality traffic. The goal will be to break even on any solo ad purchases and make money in the email sequences that follow.

The funnel looks something like this.

> *Opt-in (free ready-to-go business) >> tripwire offer (email sequences, additional training, etc.) >> coaching upsell >> do-for-yourself (DFY) upsell >> thank-you page (includes all the training to set up their own viral share funnel)*

## Day 13

Time to start setting up emails. I know that a large part of my income is going to come from email sequences. There are a few autoresponders I could use, but I need one that is affiliate-marketing friendly and has the ability to do advanced automation and tagging.

I will set up two lists in the beginning. One will be what I call my high-quality list, another will be my low(er)-quality list.

As mentioned earlier, people are all at different places in life. From my experience, cold traffic that doesn't arrive with a purpose tends to be of lower quality.

Let's use Instagram as an example. If I throw a lead magnet onto Instagram and start sending followers emails once their information is captured, there is a good chance they are not actively working on building an online business. More than likely, they saw a post or an Instagram Story, were slightly intrigued, and threw in an email address.

Contrast that with someone who comes in through one of my YouTube videos, such as one about how to segment lists in email marketing. Chances are high that this person is proactively attempting to create wealth using the internet. They are the perfect audience for most of my affiliate products, because each one of them helps achieve that goal.

The Instagram follower with limited knowledge and proactiveness will need a different email sequence than the online business owner. They will likely also be more prone to buy smaller items and quick one-time sales, whereas the YouTube subscriber will respond well to additional valuable trainings and recurring software offers.

Solo ads are similar to Instagram; my Facebook Group is more similar to YouTube.

# Day 14

Today is my second day of rest. It will be spent exactly like the first.

# Day 15

Today I write my soap opera sequence. One of my favorite things to do. Everyone goes through the soap opera sequence before going the way of their separate email automations.

My soap opera sequence has a few goals. The first is to establish trust. Trust comes from feeling like you know someone and can relate to them. I will try to let my personality and my values shine in my soap opera sequence. Some people may dislike this, but most will appreciate it. I like to link to a video or two of mine as well, because I have found that people trust me much more after seeing me and hearing me instead of just "reading" me.

The second goal is to establish credibility. I want people to know that I've been exactly where they are, and I was able to get myself out of it. The stuff I sell and recommend is their best chance of getting from where they are to where they want to be.

## Day 16

Time to create my high-quality email sequences. These are the automations that YouTube, Facebook Group, and all search traffic will go through after they finish the soap opera sequence. I like to do the basic Gary Vaynerchuk formula of jab, jab, jab, right hook. I would like this to be at least 50 days long in the beginning (emailing four or five times a week) and to eventually be six months to a year long.

I also break the sequence down into sections that focus on specific affiliate products. For example, I will do a multiday sequence that teaches the importance of funnels, teaches successful funnel strategies, and has a few case studies. ClickFunnels will show up intermittently throughout that sequence.

At the end of the section, there will be an email or two that focus almost totally on ClickFunnels and offer bonuses for timely sign-ups. In between sections, I will have more personal emails that don't sell or teach but continue building that relationship of trust with me. Maybe snippets about my life, my wife and daughter, things I like to do, and more.

I will also use this sequence to strengthen my ability to connect with my subscribers. It will attempt to sign them up as Messenger subscribers, YouTube subscribers, members of my Facebook Group, etc.

People tend to need multiple touches through multiple channels before they make moves. If someone checks their email and sees an email training talking about ClickFunnels, then sees the same thing in their Messenger inbox the next day, then gets a YouTube alert and sees a video on it, all while simultaneously noticing constant chatter in a Facebook Group on the same subject, they are bound to feel the need to see what all the fuss is about.

## Day 17

Today is when I write my low-quality email sequence. As with my high-quality sequence, these emails will span for 50 days in the beginning and eventually much longer.

This list doesn't do massive trainings and multiweek focuses. Instead, it looks more like this: Value email >> email to introduce affiliate offer >> secondary push of affiliate offer >> break Then it will rinse and repeat.

The affiliate offer emails are focused solely on getting them to the affiliate page, where the page will do the rest of the selling using free or low-ticket offers to get them into a funnel. The value emails will be YouTube videos, case studies, etc.

Now the great thing about this list is that they can graduate! If they go to join the Facebook Group or if they sign up for a software like ClickFunnels, they can move to the high-quality list. Now in full disclosure, I'm still working out the kinks as to how this will work in this scenario. But the concept is sound, and time will sort out the issues.

So every single person's journey with me looks like this:

1. Come in through some sort of lead magnet.
2. Receive the lead magnet.
3. Get tagged and added to a high- or low-quality list based on landing page and source.
4. Enter soap opera sequence.
5. Enter high- or low-quality email sequence.
6. If they ever make it to the end of the sequence, they get put on the broadcast list.

## Day 18

Today should be "fun." Lots of username and password creation.

**346**

Plenty of emails coming in to verify I am the person I say I am (as if an email address verifies anything).

Today, I need to set up all my accounts I will need to drive traffic.

My favorite sources currently are AdWords, Bing, YouTube, Instagram, a Facebook Group, and Messenger bots.

AdWords and Bing give me the ability to start building up my passive income quickly. They aren't cheap, but they are quickly scalable, and money can begin flowing in within hours of turning on ads.

My Facebook Group will start as a hub where anyone that comes in can congregate and ask questions. Eventually, Facebook's algorithm will start promoting my group for me, and it will become a traffic source as well as a hub. I'll use a nifty plug-in to capture emails from everyone who joins my Facebook Group and put them through the high-quality email sequence.

My Facebook Group will be created as a "social learning" group. This gives me the exciting ability to create units and courses inside of the group. I can also tag and welcome every person who comes through the group, to add a personal touch and build engagement.

Messenger bots won't be a cold-traffic source much in the beginning (meaning I won't use them to capture leads), but I will use all kinds of offers to get current leads into my Messenger bot broadcast list, because extremely high open rates are never a bad thing.

## Day 19

Sweet! I get to spend the entire day on Facebook, one of my guilty pleasures. I'll have to make sure my wife doesn't watch me this day, because she often walks in when I'm working and thinks I'm just goofing around on Facebook.

Today, I'm building out the Facebook Group. I'll take all the trainings and courses I have created and upload them as units in the course. Anyone in the group will be able to access them for free. It's important to note that everyone in the group has given an email address in exchange for the right to be there.

I'll make a nice cover photo and add descriptions.

Now I've got a nice big group...with zero people in it. I'll start by posting an invite to the group on my personal Facebook page. I'll also do a Facebook Live where I show how much free training comes in the group. With at least a couple thousand friends, I should get a decent number signing up.

Next, I'll reach out to some influencers who I have connected with in all the Facebook Groups I have been adding value to. A little schmoozing goes a long way. A nice, long message about how I'm creating a group and would love to have someone of their prestige in there should do the trick.

A few may let me post in their groups. Guess that will depend on how much value I've added, who they are, and the quality of my schmoozing.

Now that the group is up and running, I've got to be consistent with posting. I'll do all kinds of things to keep up engagement. Posting every day will be vital.

## Day 20

Time to get someone else doing the grunt work. Today I hire a virtual assistant (VA). The VA position will grow into one with a lot of responsibilities, but in the beginning I will need them for three major ones. The first will be my YouTube channel.

I will be spitting out a video a day for the next year or more, and I don't want to be the one editing the video, optimizing rankings, creating thumbnails, and doing all the other tasks to make a YouTube video achieve best results.

The second thing the VA will be doing is reaching out to collaborators on Instagram. Essentially, they will find people with followers in my niche and negotiate paid shout-outs. Eventually, I will be able to trade shout for shout, but for now I don't have any clout.

I use OnlineJobs to get VAs. The site focuses on hiring workers in the Philippines. I have found Filipino workers tend to be highly skilled and good at communicating in English, and they have a good work ethic.

I am looking for a VA who is organized and has experience in video editing and graphic design. They will make thumbnails and Instagram posts and do all the editing to my YouTube videos.

I will post a description and ask for two important things—one will be that they put a secret phrase in the subject line of their application, and the second will be that they provide a video instead of text. This helps weed out applicants who don't read the description and those who are less proficient in English.

After I get all the applications, I will narrow the choices to three people, conduct Skype interviews, and hire the best candidate on a trial basis. Assuming they do well, this step will be complete.

## Day 21

Today is the third day of rest, spent in the same way as the other two.

## Day 22

Now that I have a VA, it is time to build the systems I will put them into. Essentially, I will be handing them workflows, so nothing gets forgotten.

I will use Asana, but any project management software will do. I'll start with YouTube.

My goal is to create a template that they can follow each time I give them a YouTube video. I can create a new project task each time I create a new video and assign it to the template. Now the only thing I have to be involved in is the actual face of the video, which is exactly what I want to be doing.

The template has a subtask for me to upload the video to Google Drive. Next, the VA will create a title, find associated keywords, tag the video, add a description, and create a thumbnail in Canva or Photoshop. They will also add it to proper playlists and put it through all of my SEO systems, to increase the probability of ranking and showing up in suggested videos. They will also add cards and CTAs as appropriate.

The same goes for Instagram. A system will be created for them to create posts, get engagement, and begin building up an Instagram following. I will have to do my own stories, but they will take care of the rest.

## Day 23

Today is research day for YouTube and eventually a blog. Even better than the Facebook Group day, today I get to watch a lot of YouTube videos.

I'll start by creating a list of all the channels I can find in the segment I want to focus on. I'll take note of how they do their thumbnails, their editing style, how they organize their playlists, and eventually a list of all the keywords they seem to be targeting.

Next, I'll look for other keywords using research tools like SEMrush and Ahrefs. I'm looking for searches where I could provide value and offer affiliate links or lead magnets.

Anything involving email marketing, Messenger marketing, funnels, website creation, making money online, or marketing automation. I look for any search...

- Starting with "How to..."
- Including "versus" or "vs." (comparison shopping)
- Ending with "review" or "demo"

The plan will be to make a list of hundreds of searches I can target. This will be my content calendar. I will organize it into playlists and produce seven videos at a time, each in the same playlist.

## Day 24

I'm a firm believer in going for the low-hanging fruit first. So today I will start setting up my paid search campaigns.

At this point, I am assuming I've been able to obtain the necessary funds to implement at least a small paid campaign.

The lowest-hanging fruit is brands that allow direct linking, meaning I run ads straight to my affiliate link. This will not require landing pages, funnels, bonuses, or anything else, so I will start there.

I'll pull up all the affiliate programs I am involved in and search out their terms and conditions. I'll look for words like "branded," "bid," "search," and "keywords." If none of these words show up, they likely have no specific policies involving AdWords.

For each product that allows branded direct linking, I will create a campaign around that idea in both AdWords and Bing. For those programs that do not allow branded keywords, I'll do research on other relevant searches where that product could be helpful.

A good example of this would be "How To Create A Sales Funnel For ClickFunnels" or "How To Create A Messenger Bot" for my Messenger-bot software.

## Day 25

Today is also an AdWords and Bing day, but the fruit is not quite so low to the ground. Today, I will be creating landing pages and bridge pages to run AdWords and Bing ads to.

These are for affiliate programs that either don't allow direct affiliate linking or for the scenario that often occurs where the program does allow direct affiliate linking, but another affiliate's direct link is already winning the auction. They will also be used when the keywords that are being targeted make more sense to use a landing page (for example reviews or comparisons).

Bridge pages with AdWords and Bing are complicated to get approved, but once approved, they can usually stay that way forever. There is a good chance I will get my website disapproved in the process. Luckily, with ClickFunnels I can swap out domains in a matter of seconds.

Items I will need for approval are some sort of home page with a menu, a privacy policy, and a disclosure statement. I'll also need to make sure these pages add a lot of value and don't give the idea that the only point of the page is to go to another page.

## Day 26

Time to start filming. This will begin a 30-day cycle that will continue for at least a year. I will be batching my YouTube videos for the next 30 days. This means that instead of filming a video a day, I will film 30 videos in a single day and upload them all to an online folder. My VA can then edit and release one a day, while I can focus on other parts of my business.

After doing all of my Facebook Group posting, etc., I will film for close to five hours straight. I'll follow the content calendar created earlier. I love calendars, because I can guarantee that when I sit down, I will not want to film half the videos for various reasons, but if I have already planned them out, it will be a lot easier.

## Day 27

Now it's time to start some of the lower-quality advertising. I'll start with solo ads. I've got a viral share funnel and an email sequence all put into place, so everything is ready to maximize the profits from my paid traffic.

If the funnel is done well, every penny I put into solo ads will be made back within 24 hours, and my email list will be steadily growing.

(For those unfamiliar, solo ads are essentially connecting with someone who has already built up a large email list and paying them to promote to their list. They can be gold mines or giant money-sucking pits.)

Before I pay a penny to solo ads, I'm going to make sure I only give minimal money to honorable vendors with quality email lists.

The best way to do this is to simply ask around. At this point, I'm an active member of dozens of Facebook Groups, and I can guarantee a significant number of them contain entrepreneurs who have purchased solo ads.

I'll want a list of 10 to 20 vendors that I can start testing. Opt-in rates need to be higher than 50%, and I will check traffic-quality scores through link-tracking software. I will also watch the open rates of the next few emails that go out after each solo run. Anything under 20% usually means I won't order again.

## Day 28

My last day of rest. I will keep this cycle for the rest of my life.

## Day 29

Today is a data day. I hate numbers and diving into data, but it is important in the beginning so I'll suck it up.

If I've set up all my affiliate linking correctly in AdWords, I will now have a pretty good idea of which ads and keywords are going to do best. These ads will get budgets increased, and ads and keywords that are not coming anywhere close to making money are going to get shut down.

A majority of keywords and ads will be somewhere in the middle. I'll make adjustments to ads and add negative-search terms to decrease the charges on relevant clicks. I'll also adjust bids on some keywords, now that I know what I can afford to spend.

## Day 30

Today and for the foreseeable future, I will be creating relationships and collaborations. I know there are thousands of entrepreneurs with medium to large audiences at their disposal.

Each of these entrepreneurs has problems and struggles. For many of them, it is creating content that continues to provide value to their audiences. Many of these entrepreneurs know who I am and appreciate the value I've already added.

Now I can reach out and negotiate deals that give me access to their followers.

I have free courses, killer lead magnets, a viral share funnel, and a good reputation. I can offer any or all of these to group owners. Some will require nothing, some may want me to do live free trainings each week, some may simply say no, and some may demand money.

I can spend my days now simply producing valuable content and pushing traffic through my various landing pages and offers.

My YouTube audience growth will start off slow, but as I continue to build up digital real estate, it will eventually start to see exponential growth. Instagram and Facebook will be similar. But as I spend my days building relationships and pushing valuable content online, all will begin to steadily grow.

Eventually, I will be big enough that I can collaborate with other influencers and simply offer audience swaps, shout-outs, email blasts, etc. in exchange for the same.

# FINAL THOUGHTS

Affiliate marketing is all about providing value. When done correctly, it is a win-win for all parties. The two most important parts of my system are to have everything in place before you start focusing on traffic and to focus on the easiest methods first, and then branch out.

The easiest methods are always brand searches. Whether they take place in YouTube, AdWords, or Bing, your conversion rate will always be the highest with these. Especially if you know and love the product and can show that in your content.

After branded searches comes action-based searches, where they don't know quite what they are looking for but know they have a problem and are willing to pay to find a solution (for example, "best software to build a sales funnel").

At that point, you can start focusing on interruption marketing like Instagram, solo ads, etc.

# RESOURCES

- Ahrefs (ahrefs.com)
- Asana (asana.com)
- Bing (bing.com)
- Canva (canva.com)
- CJ Affiliate (cj.com)
- ClickBank (clickbank.com)
- Craigslist (craigslist.org)
- Freelancer (freelancer.com)
- Google AdWords
- Google Drive
- Jab, Jab, Jab, Right Hook by Gary Vaynerchuk
- JVZoo (jvzoo.com)
- Konker (konker.io)
- Messenger bots

- OnlineJobs (onlinejobs.ph)
- Photoshop (photoshop.com)
- Rakuten (rakuten.com)
- SEMrush (semrush.com)
- Skype (skype.com)
- Upwork (upwork.com)
- WarriorPlus (warriorplus.com)

# Chapter 19

# FACEBOOK LIVE SUMMIT

*by Anissa Holmes*

# ANISSA HOLMES

## Owner / CEO

Dentistry
*DeliveringWow.com*

*Dr. Anissa Holmes, a Dentist, Business Accelera-tion Coach, Social Media Strategist, and Bestselling Author, is a leader in the dental industry. Dr. Holm-es has coached and advised coaches, million dollar practice owners, and startup practices. Based on her massive success, Dr. Holmes has been featured in top dental publications, such as Dental Economics, Den-tistry IQ, and Dental Products Report, and has been featured as one of the top 25 Women in Dentistry.*

*She has also been a featured speaker at Social*

> *Media Marketing World and her Delivering WOW*
> *Dental Podcast has listeners in over 100 countries.*
> *Dr. Holmes is the Founder of Delivering WOW U, an*
> *Online Coaching Community for Dentists, and runs*
> *10X Business Acceleration Bootcamps for Dentists to*
> *10X their team performance, profits and brand.*

## Day 1

***Build Out my Dream 100 List*** Create a complete list of all of the top influencers in my space who also serve my target market.

- Facebook Group admins
- Podcasters
- SAS providers
- Speakers

Reach out to them through FB Messenger and let them know who I am. (I could also mention other things I have like a podcast, a book I've written, my FB Group, my website, or any speaking events I have participated in.)

Let them know that I'm going to be creating a virtual summit for the industry and that I would like for them to take part. I would be interviewing them on how their product or service can benefit or help change the lives of the people they serve.

The summit would be streamed LIVE on Facebook, so they would get a TON of exposure for their product or service.

I'll let them know that this will be THE virtual event for the year, and the goal is to reach tens of thousands.

They would also be able to provide a prize or offer free services for an Instagram contest to increase their following.

I would contact the ones I think would be most interested first, and as I'm letting the others know what I am doing, I would mention each person or company who is in.

The purpose of this event is to make relationships with influencers to get my name out, to build a FB retargeting audience, and to build my Instagram following.

## Day 2

*Start a FB page and FB Group, Create a Lead Magnet, and Create an Opt-in Funnel* Create a BUSINESS Facebook page and start a FB Group.

Create a lead magnet with a 10-minute video with something I help people with, and include a template that will make it easy for them to implement and get a quick win.

Create an opt-in funnel in ClickFunnels for people to opt in to be added to my email and bot lists.

Add the FB Group link on the thank-you page.

Finalize which speakers are in for the virtual summit.

## Day 3

*Start Going Live EVERY Day From my FB Page* Start doing a FB LIVE every day, giving value to those in my target group, and run ads to my target demographic. At the end of the Live, invite them to get the FREE video training.

The purpose is to give value to my target market and to grow my video retargeting and FB engagement list and build my email and chatbot lists.

## Day 4

*Start Adding Value in FB Groups* Create a list of all of the topics that I can help serve people with and do searches for those topics. NOT promoting anything, just start engaging on the posts with these questions and start answering questions.

Start creating promotional graphics for the virtual summit with a HUGE image of each speaker for each of them to share on social or with their list. Make sure to include that it will be THE event of the year.

Send graphics to the speakers for them to start promoting.

Start promoting the live summit with FB Ads, which will run for five days.

The purpose is to add value and to let people see me as an authority on my topic. Summit graphics to go to speakers so they can promote if they choose. By giving them a graphic with their image, they will be more likely to share it.

## Day 5

*Start Recording a New Course* Map out a list of topics that would be in my course, purchase ScreenFlow, and start recording a seven-session course. Once the video is recorded and edited, upload to Vimeo so that the embed code can be placed in ClickFunnels.

Set up a Stripe or PayPal account to be able to take payments.

The purpose is to have a course ready to go to promote on webinars with the Dream 100 that I'm building out with summit participants.

## Day 6

*Create Course Templates and Bonuses* Create checklists, resources, and templates that can be used as bonuses for the course. Create whatever can make it easy for them to implement.

The purpose is that when the webinar is promoted, it will be a no-brainer that people will achieve their goal. As a result, I will have more people sign up.

## Day 7

*Create a Membership Funnel for the Online Course* Inside of ClickFunnels, create a membership funnel. Insert Vimeo links into the course.

Create a new email list, create a sales page, and create product in CF.

Place a FB targeting pixel on the course registration and completion pages.

The purpose is to have the course ready to go, so that once ads are run to the webinar, the funnel and course are set up.

# Day 8

*Host Virtual Summit* In the middle of the summit, run three commercials talking about my new program, offering the first 25 to sign up with a special pricing. Send them to a sales page for the course.

If they sign up during the broadcast, they will get all of the bonuses created for the course PLUS an extra bonus, which is the recordings of the live summit.

The purpose is to bring awareness to the course and get early sales, as well as to get traffic to the sales page to retarget them with FB Ads.

# Day 9

*Run Facebook Retargeting Ads to Video Views From Summit* Run retargeting ads to those who attended the summit but did not buy course to give them another opportunity to buy.

The purpose is to continue to build my FB retargeting audience and to get more early adopters into the course.

# Day 10

*Create Webinar for Course* Create webinar slide deck for course.

Create webinar funnel.

The purpose is to create a webinar that can be promoted to my list and through FB Ads, as well as to use for webinars set up with JV partners.

# Day 11

*Create a FB LIVE, Add to my FB Page, and Set up FB Live Retargeting Ads* Continue to engage in FB Groups.

Do a Live to my FB page driving people to sign up for the webinar.

Run FB Ads to this Live, with video retargeting audience from the live summit, excluding purchasers.

Email personal list about the webinar.

The purpose is to get those who are following me and those who watched my summit and lookalikes to sign up for my webinar.

# Day 12

*Set up Bot Campaign Targeting All Bot Subscribers* Invite

bot subscribers to sign up for the webinar.

Start sharing info about the webinar in Instagram Stories. If I have 10K subscribers, make sure to include the swipe-up link.

The purpose is to get more registrants to the webinar.

## Day 13

*Go LIVE With the First Webinar* Send an email and FB bot notification before I begin.

Offer an extra bonus if they purchase while I am live.

The purpose is to get more people to purchase the course.

## Day 14

*Run FB Retargeting Ads and Emails to Non-Purchasers* Send the replay to non-purchasers.

Run retargeting ads for three days reminding them they have three days left to sign up for the course before they lose the special bonuses.

Send emails to non-purchasers from Actionetics.

The purpose is to get more sign-ups for the course.

## Day 15

*Reach Out to JV Partners About Doing a Joint Webinar* Reach out to Dream 100, including summit speakers and FB Group admins, to offer to do a webinar for their audience. Let them know that they will get 40% of the revenue generated from that webinar.

Share FB graphics and copy for the webinar with JV partners so they can use them in promoting the webinar to their lists.

For podcasters, schedule a podcast episode to promote the webinar.

The purpose is to get the JV partners to promote the webinar to their lists. This will drive thousands to the webinar registration page, so they will be pixeled to see future ads. This also has the potential to add thousands of people to show up for the webinar, which will increase total sales.

## Day 16

*Go Live in FB Groups, With Group Owners Discussing*

***What They Can Expect on the Webinar*** Share lots of stories and share the three secrets that will be discussed in the webinar.

The purpose is to get more registrants for the webinar and to transfer social proof about me from the group admin to their audience.

## Day 17

***Reach Out to my Dream 100 to See if They Would Like me to Run the FB Ads to Their Audiences, if They Are Not Currently Using FB to Target Their Lists*** I can offer to create a client list audience for them that can be used for this webinar as well as to promote future offers to their people. This will also allow them to build a video retargeting audience for their future promotions.

An agreement would be signed that I will not use their list for any other reason than to create this audience in their account.

The purpose is to use my Dream 100 to get as much free traffic as possible into the webinar.

## Day 18

***Build New Lead Magnets*** Build new lead magnets with opt-in funnels in ClickFunnels.

Add the auto-webinar replay option to the thank-you page.

The purpose is to drive more traffic into my funnel.

## Day 19

***Set up FB Ads to Lead Magnets and Auto-Webinars*** Run FB Ads to two separate lead magnets that have the auto webinar sign-up link on the thank-you page as well as an ad directly to the auto webinar.

Target video-view audiences, engagement audiences, and pixeled-page views who did not watch the webinar.

Offer the lead magnet to my bot audience.

The purpose is to drive more traffic to the webinar.

## Day 20

***Start Writing Articles For Industry Publications*** Start writing for industry publications and submit articles for consideration for publishing. Contact my Dream 100 to see if they have websites or blogs I can guest blog on.

The purpose is to increase authority in my space.

Write an e-book that can be used as a FREE lead magnet.

Create an e-book funnel with the auto-webinar sign-up on the thank-you page.

Keep adding value in FB Groups.

The purpose is to increase authority as well as to have another traffic source.

## Day 21

*Start Promoting E-book* Use Instagram Stories and FB Live to let them know about my FREE e-book.

The purpose is to bring more people into my funnel.

## Day 22

*Start Live Webinars for JVs* Start doing webinars for JV partners.

After the webinar is complete, create a funnel for them to continue to promote the automated webinar with their affiliate code.

The purpose is to drive massive traffic into my webinars.

## Day 23

*Send Nurturing Gift to Dream 100* Send a thank-you gift to all participants of the summit, thanking them for overdelivering. The purpose is to continue to nurture relationships with my Dream 100.

## Day 24

*Reach Out to Podcasters* Offer to come on their show if I haven't already. Send over a script for a pre-roll with a link to get a free e-book with an affiliate code link (using ClickFunnels Backpack).

The purpose is to continue to nurture relationships and to bring more people into my world.

## Day 25

***Do a Podcast Review*** Continue to speak on others' podcasts, giving them a link to my free e-book (with webinar on thank-you page).

The purpose is to increase traffic to the webinar.

## Day 26

***Create Content Library For Instagram, FB, and Instagram Stories*** Create short video clips talking about my content that can be used to let people know how I can help them.

Once created, edit them into 60-second videos, and use Planoly, Buffer, or Hootsuite to schedule them out.

The purpose is to dominate social in my space and to be everywhere.

## Day 27

***Start a Video Podcast*** Use Zoom to record the podcast interviews.

Once the videos are complete, add to my FB Group and upload to YouTube.

Strip the audio to use for a podcast.

The purpose is to drive traffic to the e-book.

## Day 28

***Email List and Send Out a Chatbot Message About Podcast*** Let everyone know that I've started a podcast and send them the link to get access.

Add to Instagram Stories.

## Day 29

***Create a Simple Mobile App*** Create a simple mobile app where people can access my video and audio podcasts, log in to my course, link to my FB Group for the course, and get push notifications when I add new content to my programs or when a new podcast launches.

## Day 30

***Celebrate Success, do a 30-Day Review, Map Out Next 90 Days*** Look back at what worked well so I can focus more on the things that bring the best and fastest results.

Make a 90-day action plan and then decide what I will work on for the next 30 days!

# FINAL THOUGHTS

If you follow this process, or even pieces of it, you will have HUGE success! Good luck.

# RESOURCES

- Actionetics (clickfunnels.com/actionetics)
- Buffer (buffer.com)
- Facebook Ads
- Facebook Live
- Facebook Messenger
- Hootsuite (hootsuite.com)
- Instagram Stories
- PayPal (paypal.com)
- Planoly (planoly.com)
- ScreenFlow (telestream.net/screenflow)
- Stripe (stripe.com)
- Vimeo (vimeo.com)
- Zoom (zoom.us)

# Chapter 20

# COACHING PACKAGES VIA JV WEBINARS

*by Dean Holland*

# DEAN HOLLAND

*CEO*

*Internet Marketing*
*DeanHolland.com*

You could call him obessed, and maybe not always in the right areas. Family, fun, friendship and
food (yep, that's the one he needs to cut back on!).

With a passion for helping others in his own
unique ways Dean loves nothing more than teaching
and training entrepreneurs on his Ultimate Funnel
strategy and methods. He's shared the stage with
Russell Brunson, Jason Fladlien and Tony Robbins.
He's given a TEDx talk on the subject of marketing
and has to date helped almost 800 people start and

> *grow thier business online. He is the CEO of Internet-Profits and is here to serve in any way he can.*

## Day 1

Spend full day getting on top of my financials.
- Go through all my monthly outgoings.
- Cancel everything I can that is nonessential.
- Calculate required monthly income to cover expenses.
- Review all available funds including credit.

## Day 2

Spend full day getting clear on my initial goals.
- Income goal: amount needed to cover outgoings
- Cash reserves goal: how much do I need for 90 days
- Offer pricing strategy to reach above goals

## Day 3

Spend full day planning what options I have for the type of product I can create and on what topic.

### Product Types
- Coaching program
- E-commerce
- Software
- Video course

### Topic Ideas
- Affiliate marketing
- Affiliate programs
- Funnels
- High-ticket sales

- List building
- Product creation
- Webinars

## Day 4

Ask the following question in a few popular targeted groups on Facebook as a kind of survey for feedback:

*HELP ME TO HELP YOU AND*
*WIN MY NEXT PRODUCT FREE*

*Please tell me which of the following you would benefit from the most RIGHT NOW. (As a thank-you for commenting, I will choose one person at random who will win free access to the product.)*

*A. Learning how to get more customers for any product/service online*
*B. Learning how to sell more to the customers you already have so that you can increase your impact and profits*
*C. Learning how to craft high-converting webinars that sell premium-priced products*

*Comment below and tell me A, B, or C, and one random responder will win free access to my upcoming brand-new product that I'll be creating based on your feedback.*
*Thank you in advance!!!*

## Day 5

Review the feedback to my question asked in popular targeted Facebook Groups and see which of the three options offered got the most votes and therefore is most likely to sell when created.

Let's assume that option A got the most votes. I would therefore today make the decision that I was going to create a course on the topic "How To Get More Customers For Any Product Or Service Online." Specifically, I would opt for teaching how to use and create a free + shipping offer and funnel to convert prospects into customers online.

I also now decide that the best way for me to create and offer this initially is via a live coaching program, as it can be a higher-priced offer, between $997 and $1,997, and doesn't have to be created in advance of selling it.

## Day 6

Buy a suitable domain name and plan out a rough draft of the coaching program structure.

- Program length: I decide six weeks is ideal.
- Deliverable: This will be one live coaching call per week with an additional weekly live Q&A session for the duration.
- Plan out the topic of each of the six weekly sessions.
- Community: I decide I'll have a FB Group for participants.

## Day 7

Plan out the actual offer and decide on pricing of my offer.

I'd spend the full day working on the elements of the actual offer. I'd make this the most irresistible offer possible on the topic and solve any potential problem or objections someone may have in succeeding with my method.

Additionally, I'd plan any bonuses that further enhance the value in the most complementary way possible while again overcoming any potential objections.

I decide the offer will be priced at $997.

## Day 8

Now I need to decide how I'm going to sell the coaching program.

Considering this is $997, I decide that selling it via a webinar would be my best approach. I will use Russell Brunson's Perfect Webinar system to have a proven process to follow.

I will have to commence the live coaching program in the next 30 days, so between now and then I need to sell as many places as possible.

## Days 9–13

Create the webinar presentation and also record a version of it to practice a run-through. I expect this to take about five full days.

Following the Perfect Webinar process, I'd spend my time crafting my webinar presentation. I'd first plan my hook, then my origin story, and then work on the three secrets, with the stories that go with them to break and rebuild my audience beliefs around the subject. From here, I'd then create the rest of the webinar, knowing my main components are clear.

## Days 14–15

Plan and write email campaigns.

I need to plan out the email campaigns. I need pre-webinar emails that focus on getting registrants to show up and then a post-webinar sequence that promotes the replay. The entire campaign would be seven days.

## Day 16

Plan how I will sell the live version of the coaching program.

If my budget permits, I'd ideally like to do Facebook Ads to get registrants, but as I don't have a lot of money for paid advertising, I need to figure a way to get people registered for the webinar so I can sell places.

One idea I have is to use some resources online to find who is launching products in the days and weeks ahead that are a good match to the ideal customers for my offer. Then I could approach these people with a proposal to do my webinar on the back end of their product launches.

Yes, I'll do this. I like the idea. I'll pay a 50% commission on each $997 sale.

## Day 17

Create a joint-venture (JV) page that showcases my offer ready to contact JV partners who are launching.

I'll create a simple page using ClickFunnels (CF) with all the details a JV partner would want to know to get them interested in promoting my webinar, including:

- Product details
- Pricing information
- Commission information
- Preview of the webinar (already recorded)

## Day 18

Research and create a list of all the people I can find who are launching products in the next 30 days that are suitable for my offer.

Using websites that people list their upcoming launches on, I'll be able to find out key details: their names, products, launch dates, and contact information.

I'll add all of this to a spreadsheet.

## Days 19–20

Record personal intro videos for each person on my list and make them their own JV page about my webinar promotion.

As these people don't know me and I want the best possible chance of getting their attention, I'll record a personal intro video for each person. Then I'll duplicate my JV page and make each person their own version of the page with their own video on the top. I'll use their name in the link to further show I made an effort for them.

## Day 21

Contact each person and send them a custom message with a link to their personalized JV page.

I'll write my message with curiosity to get them to click through and see the page. I know a lot will likely ignore me, but even if one or two respond positively, it could mean a lot of sales, so I'm excited. I'll continue communication with anyone who responds with the goal of booking a webinar with their new customers.

## Day 22

Build my webinar funnel pages in CF.

I'll need to create a webinar registration page and a confirmation page. I'll add a personalized video to the thank-you page and will also include a link to a simple survey to gather details about the people registering. Things like what their biggest struggles are right now, that type of stuff. I'll also make a couple of videos to send to registrants that build curiosity about what they will discover on my webinar to help increase show-up rates.

## Day 23

Build the members area using CF and add some content plus create a Facebook Group for customers. I'll set up the members area and, as the coaching is not starting live right away, I'll include some good content that delivers value on the inside to reduce any buyer's remorse and refunds. I'll also include a link to a FB Group and direct them to join and introduce themselves. In the group, I'll have a welcome video from me asking them to post a video of themselves to say hi. I'll also have them register for the live coaching sessions from within the members area.

## Days 24–30

Do a live webinar every single day and promote it using social media and Facebook Ads using the available funds I have.

I'm going to run the webinar every day so I can keep getting people registered and do it live daily to make sales from my own traffic.

I will also do as many webinars as I can get booked in from JV partners from my communications with them. If I need to do two or three webinars live every day, then I will, even though I know I'll be exhausted and likely lose my voice (ha ha). I need as many customers as I can get, and time is of the essence.

## Day 30+

I'll continue live webinars until the start of the live coaching in the next two weeks to get as many people joining as possible.

The actual live six-week coaching doesn't commence for another two weeks, so I'll keep doing promotions until then.

Once Week 1 of the live coaching is done, I'll then start selling the program on an evergreen basis doing weekly live webinars. Only now people will access the coaching recordings and be drip-fed them one week at a time, which will be one week ahead of doing it with the live group.

Also, I will then create a front-end funnel, most likely a free + shipping offer, so that I can get qualified buyers onto my webinar to sell them my $997 program.

In the weeks that follow, I will also begin to look at the next thing my $997 customers need to create and offer them a higher-ticket back-end offer.

All in all, my goal will be to create what I call the Ultimate Funnel, which will look like this:

- Free + shipping funnel to acquire customers
- Webinar to sell them the $997 offer
- Back-end application to high-ticket program priced at least $5,000

# RESOURCES

- ClickFunnels

# Chapter 21

# TEACH A MASTERCLASS

*by John Lee Dumas*

# JOHN LEE DUMAS

## JLD

*Podcasting*
*EOFire.com*

*John Lee Dumas is the host of Entrepreneurs on Fire, an award winning podcast where he interviews inspiring Entrepreneurs every Monday and drops value bombs every Thursday. With over 2,000 episodes, 1.3 million listens every month, and seven-figures of annual revenue, JLD is just getting started. Visit EOFire.com to set YOUR Entrepreneurial journey ON FIRE!*

# Day 1: Reflection

Day 1 is a day of reflection.

I would wake up without an alarm clock and immediately embark on a 60-minute walk. During this walk, I would let my mind wander freely, while taking note of where my thoughts and energies were flowing.

Upon my return, I would meditate for 20 minutes using an app like Oak Meditation & Breathing.

Immediately after my meditation, I would use a journal to write down the thoughts and musings I'd been having throughout the morning.

I would then go on another 60-minute walk, this time focusing my thoughts on the ideas that were forming in my mind during my meditation and journaling.

At the end of the walk, I would go back to my journal and write down any other thoughts and ideas that came up during my walk.

The rest of the day would be spent kicking back with the book The One Thing by Gary Keller in preparation for the next 29 days.

# Day 2: Get Down To Business

Now it's time to get down to business.

My first action of the day would be completing the free course "3 Hours to Your Big Idea" at YourBigIdea.

This would give me my BIG IDEA and therefore my focus over the next 29 days.

Now that I have my BIG IDEA, I would spend the rest of the day having conversations with people I know, like, and trust to get their thoughts on my Big Idea.

I would not let any one person's perspective sway me from my Big Idea, but I would use all the feedback and work on improving my idea.

I would use any free time to continue reading The One Thing.

# Day 3: My Vision of My Dream Life

Now that I have my BIG IDEA in focus, it's time to create my vision of my dream life.

I would sit down and write out from wake-up till shut-eye exactly what a perfect WORKDAY would look like. Not a perfect day, which might be trekking the Himalayas, but instead a day where I am working on my craft, my Big Idea, and bringing value to the world.

Once I've completed that, I would spend the rest of the day tweaking my perfect workday and use any free time to continue reading The One Thing.

## Day 4: Mindset Of Gratitude

Now that I have my BIG IDEA and perfect workday ironed out, I would spend today creating a mindset of gratitude, abundance, and focus.

I would write down all the things I am grateful for in this world beyond my family and friends. (I already know that I'm grateful for them.)

What UNIQUE things am I grateful for that I don't think about often?

Then I would write out why it's important to have a mindset of abundance as opposed to scarcity, and finish with the importance of FOCUS: following one course until success, aka my Big Idea.

I would spend the rest of the day tweaking that and use any free time to continue reading The One Thing.

## Day 5: Studying The Competition

Now that I have my Big Idea and my head on straight, I would spend today studying my competition.

I would google my Big Idea, use Facebook search, and check out Amazon and all the other places my competition is present.

I would then list out the things they are doing that I like as well as all the things I don't like.

Where possible, I would read all the reviews from their customers and comments left by potential customers.

I would get to know the strengths and weaknesses of my competition very intimately, and by the end of the day, I would know more about my competition than they knew about themselves.

## Day 6: Niche Down

Now that I know my competition, it's time to NICHE down.

I know their strengths and I know their weaknesses.

I will take today to identify an area of the market they are serving poorly, and I will craft my Big Idea to FILL THAT VOID.

I will make sure that I am serving that niche better than anyone else out there.

I will DOMINATE that niche.

I know that it's SUPER hard to gain momentum and traction, and therefore I must do it in a small niche. THEN, once I have momentum and traction, I'll be able to broaden my scope of offerings, but not until momentum is gained.

# Day 7: Creating My Avatar

Now it's time to sit down and create my avatar.

My avatar is the PERFECT customer/client for my Big Idea.

I know the niche I'm serving from yesterday's work, so now I'll sit down and write out in detail EXACTLY who my perfect avatar is.

Once I know my avatar intimately, everything will become easier. Every fork in the road I come to, I will simply turn to my avatar and allow them to guide me in the right direction.

This is a CRITICAL step that I will NOT overlook.

# Day 8: Finding My Avatar

Now that I know my avatar intimately, I will seek them out.

I will find them on Facebook and LinkedIn, in real life, on a virtual meetup.

I will study them online and see how they interact, where they interact, what they complain about, and what they talk highly of.

I will keep meticulous notes of all this to refer to in the future.

# Day 9: Engage My Avatar

Today is the day I will engage with as many of my avatars one-on-one as possible.

With my day yesterday spent observing, today is the day to ENGAGE.

I will reach out to as many of my avatars as possible and ask if they will jump on quick five-minute calls with me.

On these calls, I will ask, "What is your biggest struggle around <MY BIG IDEA>?"

I will listen to their pain points, obstacles, challenges, and struggles, and take detailed notes. By the end of the day, I will have pages full of my avatar's biggest struggles, and my mind will be spinning.

## Day 10: Find A Common Struggle

Now that I have pages of notes from yesterday's conversations, it's time to study these notes and find the common struggles.

I will then list out the common struggles and prioritize them in order of significance and opportunity.

I know my niche and avatar well by now, so this prioritization will come straight from my intuition.

## Day 11: Creating The Solution

Today, I'll spend my time creating the solution to the #1 struggle I prioritized from my list yesterday.

This solution may be a course, a product, a community, or something else.

It's GO time!

## Day 12: Create A Masterclass

Now that I have a solution for my avatar's biggest struggle, I will spend today creating a masterclass.

This masterclass will walk my avatar through the struggle they face, why they face it, and how my solution will solve it.

I'll use Keynote to create the presentation.

## Day 13: Deliver My Masterclass

Now I am going to deliver my masterclass via Zoom.

I might be delivering it to no one, but that's okay, because I know I have to start somewhere.

I will invite all of the individuals who I had a chat with, as well as anyone else I can get to attend who I know will benefit from what I have to share.

I have to get this first masterclass under my belt, so no matter what, it's happening.

If anyone does show up, I will make sure to ask for feedback afterwards. No matter what happens during this masterclass, it is a success if I hold it.

*"A journey of a thousand miles begins with one step."*
— Lao Tzu

# Day 14: Build My Value Ladder

Now that I've delivered my masterclass and will continue to improve upon it daily, it's time to build my value ladder.

My value ladder will start with a free Facebook Group, so I'm going to create that.

Then, I will map out what happens once someone joins. In time, my free group will funnel into a paid Facebook Group, one-on-one coaching, in-person workshops, virtual summits, and so on.

# Day 15: Build My Headquarters

Now that I have the above rocking, it's time to build my headquarters. I will use a simple site builder like Squarespace and be off to the races with my HQ. There are plenty of tutorials on Squarespace I can follow to get my website up. Once my site is up, I'll have a place I can call my own for my avatar to find me.

# Day 16: 100-Day Plan Of Attack

I'm going to spend today creating my 100-day plan of attack.

I will use The Freedom Journal as my guide to accomplish my #1 goal over the next 100 days, and it all starts with setting a SMART goal: one that's specific, measurable, attainable, relevant, and time-bound.

# Day 17: My Perfect Morning Routine

How you begin your day is how you begin your life.

Knowing this, I will spend today crafting my perfect morning routine that will involve hydration, exercise, meditation, and journaling.

## Day 18: My Workday Structure

After completing my first perfect morning routine, I'll spend the day crafting my workday structure.

I will use The Mastery Journal to help me craft this structure, utilizing the Pomodoro technique as well as reminding myself of Parkinson's Law: tasks will expand to the time allotted.

## Day 19: Finding A Mentor

Now it's time to build a strong foundation that is centered around a mentor.

I need to find someone who is currently where I want to be.

It might take several swings to connect with a mentor who is willing to provide the guidance I need, but I will keep swinging till I do.

A mentor who is currently where I want to be will be able to connect me with the right people, put me on a fast track to learning the things that matter most, and help me avoid the potholes and roadblocks that will delay my progress.

I will not rest until I have a mentor who fills this role!

## Day 20: You Are The Average

*"You are the average of the five people you spend the most time with."*

—Jim Rohn

This is at my core, so today I will find two to four other people I know, like, and trust, and who are willing to join together in a weekly mastermind session.

These other members will be people who will raise my average and who are experts in areas that I am weak in.

Each week, we'll share a quick win and something we will accomplish in the week ahead that the others will hold us accountable to.

Then, one member (on a rotating basis) will be in the hot seat for the rest of the session and will discuss their biggest struggle. After, the remaining members will provide guidance and support.

## Day 21: Create A Team

Now it's time to create a team.

I am only one person, so I need to start growing my team by bringing people in who are strong where I am weak.

StrengthsFinder 2.0 is a great test to take to identify what my greatest strengths and weaknesses are.

I will use sites like Virtual Staff Finder and ZipRecruiter to find and build my team, starting with just one member.

## Day 22: Creating A Consistent Content Plan

Today, I will be focused on creating a consistent content plan to help grow my audience.

I will observe the main social media channels and identify where my avatar is most engaged. Then, I'll study what they're talking about, asking about, and complaining about.

I'll then make a list of potential content topics, making sure it's focused on providing microsolutions to the microproblems my avatar faces.

## Day 23: Building My Product Suite

Now it's time to start building out my product suite.

Given everything I've learned about my avatar's biggest struggle up to this point—and taking into consideration what content I've created or answers I've given that they've reacted best to —what are potential products, services, or communities I can create to serve them on a higher level?

## Day 24: Creating My First Funnel

Now that I have a value ladder mapped out from a few days ago, plus a list of potential products I can create for my avatar to help solve their biggest struggles, it's time to create my first funnel.

My funnel will bring my avatar on a specific journey that leads to a valuable offer.

I will start to reread DotComSecrets and Expert Secrets to establish my plan of action and start my execution!

## Day 25: Dream 100 List

I will take Russell's advice and create my Dream 100 list. This will include people in my niche who would be very valuable allies and partners. Then, I'll establish a plan that will help me be consistent with creating and nurturing these relationships on an ongoing basis.

## Day 26: Financial Check

Now that I am rockin' and rollin' with all of the above, I have to make sure my business and finances are being taken care of from a setup perspective.

I'll email Josh@CPAOnFire.com and ask for his advice on the best way to handle any current and future revenue I generate, how to set up my business structure to maximize tax benefits, and how I can best prepare for tax season.

## Day 27: Outside Passions

I will spend today thinking about the ways I'll enjoy the passions I have outside of work, too. It can't be all work and no play!

I will carve out specific time slots in my weekly schedule to make sure I'm stepping away from work and also doing the things I enjoy outside of the office.

## Day 28: Financial Freedom

Today, I will spend the day thinking about what financial freedom means to me.

What are my financial goals per month, per year, and in total? So that I know what goals I'm reaching for.

Once I have those numbers in place, I will have a benchmark to aim for and a clear picture of what financial freedom means to me.

## Day 29: Online Advertising

Now that I have the groundwork in place, I'll start to study online advertising. This is going to allow me to scale and leverage my money and reach more of my avatar.

Once I reach more of my avatar, then I can lead them into my funnels and analyze the ROI (return on investment).

Facebook Ads, Instagram ads and influencers, YouTube ads, and Google ads will be my primary focus.

If I have a physical product on Amazon, I will also study Amazon ads (or ACoS, advertising cost of sales).

## Day 30: Start A Podcast

Now it's time to start a podcast.

A podcast will give me a platform to share my mission, message, and value with the world.

I'm now well on my way to reaching—and impacting—my avatar around the globe!

# RESOURCES

- CPA On Fire (cpaonfire.com)
- DotComSecrets by Russell Brunson
- Expert Secrets by Russell Brunson
- Keynote
- Oak Meditation & Breathing app
- Pomodoro technique
- Squarespace (squarespace.com)
- StrengthsFinder 2.0 (gallupstrengths
- center.com)
- The Freedom Journal (thefreedomjournal. com) by John Lee Dumas
- The Mastery Journal (themasteryjournal. com) by John Lee Dumas
- The One Thing by Gary Keller

- Virtual Staff Finder (virtualstafffinder.com)
- Your Big Idea (yourbigidea.io)
- ZipRecruiter (ziprecruiter.com)
- Zoom (zoom.us)

# Chapter 22

# HIGH-TICKET SALES VIA WEBINARS

*by Rob Kosberg*

# ROB KOSBERG

## *CEO*

Publishing and Media
*BestsellerPublishing.org*

*Rob Kosberg is a 3x best selling author and found-er of BestSellerPublishing.org*

*Rob's Publish. Promote. Profit.™ system has been used by thousands of authors in dozens of countries. He shows entrepreneurs how to become the go-to authority in their market by writing, launching and profiting with a best selling book.*

*Rob and his signature systems have been featured on ABC, NBC, CBS, Fox and Entrepreneur magazine as well as hundreds of other shows, podcasts, maga-*

*zines and articles.*

*Since 2010, Rob has been the go-to teacher for coaches, consultants and entrepreneurs who want more authority, more exposure, and more clients. Rob works with clients who understand that the way to 7 figures and beyond is via a best selling book and authority and celebrity that comes with it.*

## Day 1

Today is a day of reflection and meditation and a focus on quiet determination. I want to consider what went wrong previously and what can I learn from both what I did right and wrong. To do this, I will journal and seek out input from friends and mentors. I will NOT allow myself to become discouraged but rather will focus on gratitude. All progress begins first with honesty but must also contain encouragement and appreciation of what I have. I still have the most important things: my skills and perseverance.

## Day 2

Every single day will start with a strong morning routine. There will be temptation to be anxious and worried, and I need to clear out negative emotions. Every day, I will spend time in prayer, meditation, and learning, typically from a video or book. Afterwards, I will write out my goals for the day and dig in.

Today, I will make contact with those I owe money to and ask that they give me several months' relief so I can focus on what needs to be done and pay them in full. I will handle this one time and then get back in touch with them when agreed. No calls from creditors will be taken during the next 30 days. I need to focus on the goal at hand.

## Days 3–4

Time to dig in and decide exactly what I want to build for myself and my family. I will remind myself daily in my morning routine and throughout the day exactly why I am doing this. My greatest motivation lies outside myself and with those I love. I must succeed for them and others who are relying on me.

Today and tomorrow, I look at three things closely.

1. What am I great at?
2. What do I enjoy doing?
3. What does the market want and need?

The intersection of these three things is where I will find something I can excel at and have longevity in.

## Day 5

I decide on the things that I am great at and enjoy and look for where the market intersects. I decide that I am best working directly with people and engaging with them in both the sales process and in delivering something awesome. I am both great at it and enjoy it, so it should be a model that I can do for an extended period and build a business around.

I also consider the skills that I have and where I have succeeded in the past, and I decide to help people get media attention and use it to grow their businesses and authority, as I have done in the past for myself and others. The market will be business owners who are hungry to grow their business revenue and their authority in the marketplace.

## Day 6

Today, I need to identify the complete model I will follow for my business. I need to outline three specific areas.

- Proposal: my offer to the market

- Platform: where I will find my clients
- Process: how I will bring them on as clients

For proposal, since I am going to directly engage with potential clients, I will be offering something higher-ticket, in the $3,000 to $10,000 price range. I also decide that I need something of value (lead magnet) to offer first to a potential client to both warm them up to me and inform them of the opportunity.

The platform will be focused on social media. LinkedIn is where I can find business owners and connect with them personally. I will also use Facebook, since it is a platform I can use to connect with my audience via posts, FB Lives, and video.

Lastly, the process will be me personally bringing on clients via a consultative sales call where I offer both value and an opportunity for people to take next steps with me.

## Day 7

Everyone needs to rest, but I am more motivated than ever at this point. Today is more a day for me to reconnect with my family, love up on them, and be reminded why I am doing everything I am doing.

## Day 8

Now that I have my proposal, platform, and process mapped out, I need to create my lead magnet to begin engagement with potential clients. I create a lead magnet that focuses on the benefits of media and PR and how a business owner can use it to grow their business.

I also more fully develop my initial offer and decide to guarantee results for my clients so as to completely reverse the risk. I decide to start a "video a day" campaign on Facebook Live where I offer some training and resources and end with offering my lead magnet for those who connect personally with me on FB Messenger.

## Days 9–13

My routine for the next five days will consist of the following:

1. *Daily FB Live and personally messaging those who reach out for*

*the lead magnet.*

2. *Daily outreach on LinkedIn to business owners who are a good fit for my offer.* Initially, I will just reach out looking to add value and connect, but when asked, I will share what I do and my value then offer the lead magnet.

3. *Daily outreach on FB Groups that focus on business and/or media and PR.* Serve first and then look for opportunities to offer my lead magnet.

## Day 14

Enjoy a day with my family and share some of the initial successes. I will also spend some time in the evening looking at my results from the week. Was my lead magnet being requested? Is the title effective and enticing? How has my outreach gone and what can I do better? Make a plan for the week and course correct where needed.

## Day 15

I will continue my routine on Facebook and LinkedIn and make changes as needed based on my results. I will make one additional post today. Since I have been giving value for the last week in groups and FB Lives, I will create a post asking about my offer with a desire for feedback and potential clients such as:

> *"If you are a business owner, I would love some feedback from you. Does this sound interesting to you? Get on TV and media for your business and ONLY pay when you are booked! I am trying to dial in my offer and was wondering if that is something business owners would be interested in? Thanks for the feedback!"*

This will stir up interest and give me feedback as well as opportunities.

By now, I have begun to take sales calls and am getting feedback on my offer. When it is completely dialed in, I will expect to close one in three calls to a high-ticket offer of between $3,000 and $10,000. For now, I will be happy with 1 in 10 while I dial my offer and language in.

## Days 16–20

My routine for the next five days will consist of the following:

1. Daily FB Live and personally messaging those who reach out for the lead magnet.
2. Daily outreach on LinkedIn to business owners who are a good fit for my offer. Initially, I will just reach out looking to add value and connect, but when asked, I will share what I do and my value, then offer the lead magnet.
3. Daily outreach on FB Groups that focus on business and/or media and PR. Serve first and then look for opportunities to offer my lead magnet.
4. Continued follow-up on FB chat and LinkedIn with prospects who have reached out for the lead magnet but have not asked for a call.
5. I have a goal of at least three consultative sales calls per day. This will enable me to close a minimum of one or two deals this week.

## Day 21

Enjoy a day with my family and share some of the initial successes. I will also spend some time in the evening looking at my results from the week. How has my outreach gone and what can I do better? How have my sales calls gone and how can I close more deals? Make a plan for the week and course correct where needed.

## Day 22

By now, I have closed one or two sales and need to both take care of my clients and get them quick, amazing results. First, I set up an initial project management call and assess what the best hook is for their media appearance. I create a segment proposal for each of them and begin pitching them.

Since I have a process that can get someone booked on media very quickly, I expect to have them scheduled within the first couple days.

Then I call and tell them the good news.

Since they are ecstatic with the fast results, I ask them for a quick video testimonial/case study on Zoom. Afterwards, I ask them who they know who would like results like this. I thank them for the referrals and ask them to contact that person to let them know I will be calling and sending them something (a lead magnet).

I also continue with my outreach and daily FB, LinkedIn, and call routine.

## Days 23–27

My routine for the next five days will consist of the following:

1. Daily FB Live and personally messaging those who reach out for the lead magnet.
2. Daily outreach on LinkedIn to business owners who are a good fit for my offer. Initially, I will just reach out looking to add value and connect, but when asked, I will share what I do and my value, then offer the lead magnet.
3. Daily outreach on FB Groups that focus on business and/or media and PR. Serve first and then look for opportunities to offer my lead magnet.
4. Continued follow-up on FB chat and LinkedIn with prospects who have reached out for the lead magnet but have not asked for a call.
5. Set up new client onboarding and focus on client results.

## Day 28

Another family day. Also, I will consider my capacity now that I have several clients and am focused on fulfillment. Make a plan for the week and course correct where needed.

## Day 29

I now have clients who are experiencing success as well as giving me referrals and testimonials. It is time to consider both raising my prices and figuring out what more I can offer them. Can I get them on continuity for my offer? Is there a product I can create that will help them to better take advantage of the media I am getting them?

Besides considering these things, I will stay the course with my FB and LinkedIn outreach and my consultative process.

## Day 30

With clients to help, income coming in, and a process that works, I am now out of the danger zone. I can take a deep breath and consider how I can scale this business without it being primarily focused on and all about me.

This is what I have done with several of my businesses—growing them to millions in revenue. I will spend some time considering where I can get some help to scale the business and make it as fun and profitable as possible.

# FINAL THOUGHTS

I want you to know that I recognize how easy it is to write something like this—much easier than actually doing it! However, I can assure you that not only would this work, but it already has worked for me in the past (though some things are obviously different). I'd say the key lies in two areas.

First, what your skills are and how they intersect with the desires of the marketplace. For example, if you are good with people and at sales, then you can massively shortcut your success, as I outlined in the previous pages. Also, your ability to deliver on something amazing for a client in exchange for their hard-earned money cannot be emphasized enough.

Secondly, none of this is easy, nor should it be. What I have outlined looks and smells like hard work because it is! Doing anything daily requires intense effort and discipline, and those who succeed deserve their rewards.

Do not search for a get-rich-quick method, as it doesn't exist. Instead, hone your skills and put in the work, and like others who toil for years to become overnight successes, you will be as well.

# RESOURCES

- Facebook Live
- Facebook Messenger
- Zoom (zoom.us)

# Chapter 23

# EBOOK LAUNCH

## by Natalie Hodson

# NATALIE HODSON

## *President / CEO*

Fitness
*NatalieHodson.com*

*Natalie Hodson is a mom of two, who is best known for her ability to connect with women and their real-life situations. Natalie's wildly popular blog gets nearly half a million monthly unique visitors where she shares stories and tips for balancing family, fitness, and a healthy lifestyle.*

*Her followers most often describe Natalie as "real, genuine, authentic, and relatable." She is an ISSA Certified Personal Trainer, GGS Pre/Post Natal Certified Trainer, content writer, and contributor for sites and publications including: Bodybuilding.com, Oxygen Magazine, Train for Her Magazine, Strong Fitness Magazine, and more.*

*Natalie also is the co-author of the Abs, Core, & Pelvic Floor program that has helped over 35,000 women improve their core and pelvic floor dysfunction after pregnancy. This program put Natalie into the 2-Comma Club just four months after the release of the ebook.*

## Day 1

I am going to write out a plan this week. If I don't write it out, it won't happen. I have learned this the hard way. It's really easy to get full of a LOT of ideas and then feel overwhelmed about where to start.

I am a very visual person, and I am a huge fan of whiteboards. I have them randomly all over my house, even when they don't fit into my decor. I have a massive whiteboard I bought at Lowes for $15 (they are near the sheetrock section) and nailed to a section of my wall.

This might seem silly or trivial, but this whiteboard will be very important over the next 30 days. The act of writing things down—physically writing them down (not just typing)—makes them real and helps my brain create a path to follow.

From here on out, each morning I will do a daily huddle with myself and write three to five things on the whiteboard I need to get done that day. EVERY DAY. If I don't write it down, it won't happen and I will get distracted by emails, family, social media, etc.

Bonus: Today, I'll try to find an accountability buddy who is at my same level or slightly above. If I have someone rooting for me, checking in on me, and pushing me when necessary, it will help a lot.

I'll remind myself that just because I failed does not mean I am a failure. The best way to see success is to show yourself grace while following a solid plan. I've got this.

## Day 2

My goal for today is to figure out the #1 thing I am good at and the #1 thing people are usually interested in when I have talked about it in the past. I'll write these ideas on my whiteboard.

Right after I went through my divorce, I felt like my back was financially against a wall and, because I didn't have a financial security net anymore, I needed to buckle down and figure out what to do with my business. So I decided to look at the Google Analytics for my blog. I figured this was the best way for me to see what my audience was already telling me that they liked. I looked at my top five blog posts and said, "Okay, here is what my audience apparently likes. I am going to make an offer (an e-book) around each topic."

And so I did. My #1 blog post was "What is Diastasis Recti?" so I wrote an e-book on diastasis recti, which went on to sell $1 million in four months! My #3 blog post was "11 Healthy And Inexpensive Crockpot Meals," so I wrote a crockpot recipe e-book, which I use as an order bump and now has a 40% take rate. I also wrote a few other e-books that didn't really sell very well. But I am telling this story because the reason the e-books were successful is that I looked at what my audience actually wanted instead of what I thought they would want.

At that time, I had the benefit of an audience and following, but if I don't have that now, I can ask my friends. Do an Ask Campaign or reflect on conversations I've had with others. What do people regularly come to me with questions for? What topics do I have a compelling story around?

So e-books are my jam. They have worked really well for me, and I have built an entire business from writing, sharing vulnerable moments, and creating e-books.

Once I have decided what I want my topic to be, I'll begin the outline for my e-book.

I don't have to write the entire thing yet, just put together the bullet points of what I want to talk about in an outline.

Then, once I have the bullet points, I'll begin to fill in what I want my book to say, starting with the easiest things first. For example, when I was writing my previous book, I wrote about my personal experience first, because that was the easiest to write. Next, I wrote about how frustrated I felt after having my babies. I saved the parts that felt the hardest to write for the end—it felt much less overwhelming that way.

If I need to, I can partner with an expert to get the quality content I need. For example, when I wrote my e-book, I partnered with a doctor who specializes in pelvic floor dysfunction/diastasis recti. (She also happened to be an old college friend of mine.) This helped me feel like I had the credibility I needed, and it helped me get the book written much faster than I would have been able to on my own.

I am going to have to share vulnerable stories if I want to quickly connect with people. Vulnerability is like a magnet and is the ultimate human connector, but it's not always easy to be vulnerable. I'll start thinking about stories I can put in my book that will help my audience relate to me. The real, raw stories. Stories that might make my stomach churn when I think about sharing ALL the real details. Stories I think I will be too embarrassed to admit or share publicly. These are the stories that will create instant connections with my audience, and I NEED them right now to create wildfire-quick audiences.

Examples: stretched skin, peeing in pants, divorce, going bankrupt, not being able to pay mortgage, depression, abuse, addiction

# Day 3

Today, I'll begin my Dream 100 campaign. (If you aren't sure what this means, geek out on the content Russell has put out about Dream 100.)

Then, begin networking like crazy.

Reach out to every influencer I genuinely follow online. Offer to help with no expectation of anything in return. When I message them, I'll make it personal, not just copy and paste the same message to 100 people. Show them that I actually follow them by talking about recent posts they've made or things they've talked about. Whatever

I am talented in, offer to help them in this area. Offer to write blog posts that their audience might connect with, create videos surrounding their content, send them my product that could help them, etc. With no expectations in return.

I will expect a lot of non-responses and rejection. When I did this before, out of the 100 people I reached out to, I only got one yes. BUT... that one yes paid off. I made a video for that one influencer that took off, went viral, and gained me 100,000 organic followers. This method can work, but I'll have to put a lot of time into connecting with the people I want to connect with at the start.

## Day 4

Start documenting exactly how I feel right now. When I am feeling like a failure, I'll write it down. When I am feeling scared, I'll write it down. When I am feeling excited, I'll write it down. When I feel proud, I'll write it down. Even if they are just shorthand notes, the raw, vulnerable, internal feelings I have right now will be very useful to me later. These moments and feelings will help me connect with my audience later, once I am in a place where I am ready to share them. I don't have to spend a lot of time on this, just keep notes on my phone or a private Google Doc.

These vulnerable moments and feelings will be gold for me later. I will be able to relate to and help so many people because I will have all my real emotions to draw on when I am writing content later on.

(For more information on this, watch some of Brené Brown's TED talks or read her books Daring Greatly and Rising Strong. She explains this much better than I do, and her work on shame and vulnerability has impacted me more personally and professionally than any other author.)

## Day 5

To avoid slipping into depression, I'll post three things I am grateful for each day on social media or in a gratitude journal I keep near my bed. Gratitude turns what you have into enough. Whenever I am in a time in my life where I am struggling, I focus on what I am grateful for—even if it's as simple as a stranger smiling at me on the sidewalk or a cool breeze hitting my face.

See, your brain is a muscle just like any other muscle in your body, and it can be trained. When you consciously focus and make the decision to be grateful every...single...day, then when you hit failure (as we all will)—when you screw up, when you fall down—your brain is already trained to see a sliver of beauty in the situation. It's the gratitude you've trained yourself to have day in and day out that will help you brush off your knees, pick yourself up, and keep trying. Learning to be grateful—even when everything else in your life seems to be falling apart—is something you have the ability to control and decide. I encourage you to try it. The feeling of gratitude can shift you from feeling negative and dark to things suddenly feeling beautiful, even when nothing else changes around you. The only thing that changes is that you decide you are going to focus on the things you are grateful for.

## Day 6

Continue reaching out to my Dream 100. I will reply QUICKLY to the ones who respond and get them exactly what they need.

## Day 7

I am going to release my program 23 days from today, so I need to act fast on my relationships with others who have big lists. Stay up late writing content for them, obsessively studying their audiences, and making videos that their audiences would relate to. This step is crucial, and I am going to need to leverage the momentum I get from this when I launch. I won't take things personally when people don't respond but continue reaching out. And I'll freaking hustle to get them good quality content.

## Day 8

Figure out where my ideal customer is. Use the tips Russell teaches in his DotComSecrets book. Literally take a notepad and go through that book page by page and write down how I would implement the concepts in his book into my offer. (FYI, this is exactly what I did when I launched my programs.)

## Days 9–11

Focus on getting my e-book finished. Literally set deadlines on my phone if I need to in order to finish a chapter. Call up my accountability buddy if I need to.

Find a designer on Upwork who can design the e-book cover and format the book for me.

Create an Amazon S3 link to deliver the program to my customers.

Triple check to make sure I have no typos. (It helps to read everything out loud and have someone else look over it.)

Purchase a couple of my competitors' programs if needed to see how they did their books.

Done is better than perfect. Even Apple had to have a 1.0 version, and look where they are now. But they never could have had their advanced versions if they were too afraid to put out the first one. It's okay if my first version isn't perfect. It just needs to be done.

## Days 12–14

Focus on the ClickFunnels side of things. I need to have a funnel to promote my new e-book.

If I can't do it myself, I can go on forums and see if I can barter with someone who has funnel-building skills and is willing to trade with a skill set I have.

Or I can see if someone would do a profit share with me to create this first funnel. (This isn't my ideal recommendation long term, but for the first one, time is of the essence and I need to act quickly.)

Wireframe (that is, draw out) my funnel on my whiteboard. (Russell has many examples of how to do this on his YouTube channel, Funnel Hacker TV.)

Make a Google Doc where I write out the sales copy for the funnel. A Funnel Scripts membership can massively help with this.

Use Funnel Scripts to create my template for my video sales letter (VSL).

Film the video for my VSL. This does not have to be fancy. I can film it on my iPhone and edit it in iMovie.

## Days 15–17

At this point, I should have a handful of people (influencers) who have responded. Hopefully, they have shared my content on their platforms. If I did a good job, there will be a good response.

So I will LEVERAGE THIS.

For each new follower I get, I will treat them like gold. Respond to every comment and every question that they send. I nurtured the relationship with the influencer, now I must nurture the relationship with my new followers.

Spend the next couple days getting the content to those influencers, following up on messages to people who haven't responded or committed yet, and make sure the content I am creating for them is GOOD.

## Day 18

Create a pre-launch FB campaign, even if I need to put it on a credit card. Create some ads that will put together a pre-launch audience.

## Day 19

Make sure I am posting good, free quality content daily on my FB page that helps position me as an authority figure. If I can get the newly developed influencer relationships to reshare my stuff, even better.

## Day 20

Give myself permission to take a day off. Go for a hike, spend quality time with my kids, go fishing, or visit a farmers market. Sometimes giving your brain time to clear can give you clarity you wouldn't have had otherwise. If I can get outdoors and shut off my phone, it's even better.

## Day 21

Send a free copy of my e-book to EVERYONE I know who could share it to their friends/audiences. Make them an affiliate inside ClickFunnels (using Backpack). Let them know the advantage they will get from sharing my product, give them the launch date, and let them know how my product can impact their audience and community. Make it about THEM, not about me.

## Days 22–24

Put a few of my friends through the program as guinea pigs so I can get testimonials. Even better if I can find someone comfortable being on camera. Video testimonials are gold.

Begin mapping out my plan for the following week. The week before I launch my program, I'll map out what emails I am going to send and how I am going to communicate with my potential customers.

Nurture my waiting-list campaign.

Tease my audience with snippets of what is coming.

Give REALLY GOOD QUALITY content to my waitlist while they are waiting. Emails, Facebook videos, blog posts, etc.

Make sure I have an order bump and at least one OTO (one-time-offer upsell) in mind. This could be a simple continuity program or it could be a course that I build out week by week.

I need to have my value funnel clear or I will be missing out on valuable real estate during launch week that I could be upselling people into.

## Day 25

Begin my pre-launch week.

Send quality emails giving interesting information and stats.

Create shareable content. Remember this important fact: people share content that improves their perceived status. I will think about this when creating my videos. If someone shares this, will it make them look better or feel better?

## Day 26

Continue to retarget people on FB who have been watching my videos. Create lookalike audiences.

Do test purchases and run-throughs to make sure my funnel works properly and my Stripe accounts are set up accurately.

# Day 27

Double check my email sequences to make sure they are set up properly in ClickFunnels and that the automations work so my purchasers get the follow-up emails I have written.

Make sure my Facebook pixel is properly set up in the funnel so I can retarget people who checked out my program but didn't buy.

# Day 28

Write out a condensed Perfect Webinar, FB-Live style, meaning that I will follow Russell's script for the Perfect Webinar but write it out so I can do it as a FB Live. This will work like gold if I can pull it off, and then I can retarget people who watched my video.

When I first did this, it was not perfect. In fact, I made a lot of mistakes! But it still made me money. I simply handwrote the bullet points I wanted to talk about on sheets of paper, taped them to the wall, set my iPhone up, and went live on Facebook.

It also really helped me when I watched other people's webinars.

# Day 29

Touch base with all my affiliates. Make sure they know tomorrow is launch day. Remember that this is a big day in my world but probably not in theirs. Give them as many assets as possible to make it easy for them to promote. Offer to do split-screen Facebook Lives through BeLive for their Facebook audiences, offer to write the emails to their email list, etc. Make it as easy for them as possible.

# Day 30

Launch day!! I will remind myself that things WILL go wrong today. For every single launch I have ever done, nothing worked perfectly. Know that my success today will be my ability to adapt and respond to problems, keep my cool, and fix things as they go wrong.

At the end of the day, I'll make an honest assessment of how things went and how I can continue with this momentum and improve or make adjustments moving forward.

Celebrate! Regardless of the results from this launch, I did something scary—I executed—and I kept the promise to myself to launch something. I learn and grow every single time I do something scary. I will be proud of myself when I go to bed tonight.

# FINAL THOUGHTS

If you ever find yourself in a situation like this...

No alcohol. Your brain gets lazy and you won't be able to work long hours if you are drinking. This isn't a long-term thing, but for these 30 days when you need to hustle and grind, you need to have all your energy on this project.

Spend a little bit of time each day on self-care. You are going to likely be sitting in front of your computer a lot each day, so make sure you are going for a morning walk or run, and try to get in at least 10,000 steps. It's easy to logically justify to yourself that you need to spend every waking moment on this project, but the truth is, my best ideas come usually when I give myself permission to move, to exercise, and to eat right. If you just sit in front of your computer all day, you will likely only move around 2,000–3,000 steps per day. Focus on taking one or two 20-minute walks per day to get some extra movement in. This will keep your brain focused and clear, I promise.

# RESOURCES

- Amazon.com
- Backpack (ClickFunnels feature)
- BeLive (belive.tv)
- Daring Greatly by Brené Brown

- DotComSecrets by Russell Brunson
- Facebook Live
- Facebook pixel
- Funnel Hacker TV (funnelhacker.tv), Russell Brunson's YouTube channel
- Funnel Scripts
- Google Analytics
- Google Docs
- iMovie
- iPhone
- Rising Strong by Brené Brown
- Stripe (stripe.com)
- Upwork (upwork.com)
- Whiteboard and markers

# Chapter 24

# COACHING 1-ON-1 AND MASTERMINDS

## by Pat Rigsby

# PAT RIGSBY

## Coach / Entrepreneur

### Fitness Business
*PatRigsby.com*

*Pat Rigsby is a business coach who has built over 25 businesses in the fitness industry, with 7 becoming million dollar or multi-million dollar ventures. Two have been multiple time winners on the Entrepreneur Franchise 500 with another being a multiple time honoree on the Inc. 5000 list of fastest growing businesses in the U.S. Pat now coaches fitness & health entrepreneurs who want to build their own Ideal Business. You can connect with him at PatRigsby.com.*

## Day 1

The first day in this journey is quite possibly the most important one. It's about making the decision to go from "I could" to "I will."

Every success starts with that decision, yet only a few choose to make it. We consider the vast array of things we could do or would like to do, but we fail to actually make the most important decision in building a successful business: the decision to start.

So Day 1 is about committing to the process and deciding that over the next 30 days, I'll discard the reasons why it won't work, let go of past failures, and focus on simply moving forward every day.

I know that it takes just as much effort to think big as it does to think small, and that I can accomplish some pretty meaningful things if I'm willing to work hard. The foundation of me getting back on my feet in just a month is the inner belief that I can do it if I simply execute my plan.

## Day 2

The first step to crafting my plan is to take inventory of what I do have.

It's my belief that the foundation of creating an ideal business is playing to your strengths, so that's the first place I'd start—identifying my strengths.

For me, that would be experience in building and operating successful health and fitness businesses and coaching others to do the same.

With that in mind, I'd document those specific strengths.

- Business Strategy
- Coaching
- Marketing
- Sales
- Team Development

Completing this first step of planning would give me confidence that I have something valuable to bring to the market.

# Day 3

Now that I'm confident I can build a solid business foundation and have something valuable to offer the market, I need to identify the target market I want to serve.

The easiest place to start here is to look at the target markets I've been a part of, currently belong to, or have successfully served.

To narrow this even further, I'd identify where my strengths match the biggest available opportunities or most pressing needs.

If I didn't know what those opportunities or needs were, I'd join a few Facebook Groups and start diving deep into research to discover what the pain points for my target market were. In this case, it would be helping health and fitness professionals with their strategy, marketing, and sales through offering coaching solutions.

# Day 4

Now that I know who I want to help—fitness-business owners, with a focus on business growth—it's time to craft my initial offer.

Since I don't have a reputation in this scenario, my irresistible offer needs to really remove the risk for the client, since I can't fall back on a well-known track record or a library of social proof to create trust.

With that in mind, I'd lead off with the offer of a free coaching call where we'd talk for an hour and I'd identify untapped opportunities in their business—no strings attached.

At the end of the call, if they wanted my help in an ongoing way to execute the suggestions I'd identified and to optimize the other growth opportunities in their business, I'd offer two options.

*Option A* We'll work together for the next six months and you'll only pay me based on the delivery of the results I promise. For every new dollar I generate for your business above what you're already making, you pay me $.25.

I'm only paid for results and only for new business.

*Option B* We work together for the next six months and I guarantee

**414**

that you add $6,000 to your recurring revenue. Your investment is just $2,000 per month...and if you don't increase your recurring revenue by $6,000 in that span, I'll refund every penny.

The logic is simple—I first deliver results in advance with the free call and then make two zero-risk, irresistible offers and let the prospective client choose between them.

## Day 5

Now it's "build day." I've got to build my funnel to get prospects to schedule the initial call, so I'd create a pretty basic video sales-letter funnel from the templates available in ClickFunnels with the focus of hitting the hot buttons that I identified on Day 3 and how I can help... at no cost to them.

## Day 6

Today is the day to set some initial goals and start executing the plan.

I'd initially want to schedule a minimum of three calls a day, with the expectation that at least two would show and that I'd close one sale on either the A or B offer.

To start toward achieving this goal without any ad spend or an email list, I'd reach out to anyone I know who fits my target market and offer to help them by providing the free call.

Through this outreach to my personal network—a network that each of us has that often goes untapped—I'd expect to be able to schedule 15–20 calls.

Where would I find those connections?

I'd start by pulling out my phone and going through all of my contacts there.

Then I'd move to my Gmail contacts and finally my Facebook and LinkedIn contacts.

While I don't expect that everyone would respond positively, with personal outreach and a truly risk-free, high-value offer, I am confident that I'd be able to schedule those 15–20 calls.

Okay, I've now crafted a plan and started the initial execution of it... in less than a week.

## Days 7–9

These days are basically dedicated to two things.

First, I would really focus on doing a great job delivering results during my calls with prospects and converting them into clients for one of my two offers.

Second, I'd begin delivering great coaching videos on Facebook Live, basically treating it as my own business-coaching TV show on a daily basis and then offering my free coaching call at the conclusion of the video.

Between that video and continued outreach to my connections, I'd expect to be able to add another one or two scheduled calls per day during those three days.

Since I'd already scheduled 15–20 calls, I'd expect 6–8 of those to have happened in that 3-day window (knowing that some wouldn't schedule that quickly and others would no-show or reschedule). From those six to eight calls, I'd expect at least three or four sales with one or two taking the flat monthly rate and one or two taking the pay-for-performance plan.

## Day 10

With $2,000 to $4,000 in cash collected from the initial sales, I would be able to start some small-scale advertising, spending $20 per day to keep driving prospects to the free coaching call and boosting any of the Facebook Live videos that got any traction.

This approach would keep a modest but steady flow of prospects signing up for calls, with roughly a call being scheduled every day and a pace of a sale every two to three days...for now.

## Day 11

Because of my past experiences, aside from generating immediate clients and cash flow, I'd also place a significant amount of energy into list building.

My goal has always been to build businesses that were stable and not dependent on any single traffic source or promotion, so beginning on Day 11, I'd start investing a couple of hours each day on build-

**416**

ing a lead magnet that would be a high-value asset.

In this scenario, I'd create a small book.

Now, before you think that this sort of thing is overwhelming, here's the plan I'd follow:

**Step 1** I'd outline the three biggest problems I help my clients solve. In this case, it would be...

- Not enough leads
- Poor conversion to clients
- No strategy to scale and still have a life

Then, I'd identify three things I do to solve each of those problems. It would look something like this:

### Problem: Not Enough Leads

Solutions:
- Identify a target market.
- Develop a predictable plan to consistently generate leads (by creating a marketing calendar).
- Grow from the inside out (i.e., referral marketing).

### Problem: Poor Conversion to Clients

Solutions:
- Develop a great offer.
- Follow up consistently and effectively.
- Deliver a great high-converting success session.

### Problem: No Strategy to Scale and Still Have a Life

Solutions:
- Hire and develop a team.
- Build your role around your strengths.
- Find leverage points within the business.

So now I'd have an outline like this:

Chapter 1: The 3 Problems Fitness Business Owners Face
Chapter 2: Identifying A Target Market
Chapter 3: Developing A Predictable Plan To Consistently Generate Leads
Chapter 3: Growing From The Inside Out
Chapter 4: Developing A Great Offer
Chapter 5: Following Up Consistently And Effectively
Chapter 6: Delivering A Great High-Converting Success Session
Chapter 7: Hiring And Developing A Team
Chapter 8: Building Your Role Around Your Strengths
Chapter 9: Finding Leverage Points Within The Business
Chapter 10: Putting It All Together

**Step 2** I'd take each chapter and list out three to five talking points about each on a slide.

**Step 3** I'd schedule time to record five chapters during each of the next two days. Each chapter would basically be me talking. At 1,250 to 1,500 words per 10 minutes, I could have a short book draft dictated in a couple of hours of recording.

By now, my days would be a mix of coaching the handful of clients already on board, doing calls with prospects, and investing a couple of hours in generating leads or building my first marketing asset.

Things are starting to feel like a "real" business!

# Day 12

I'd basically be executing on things I've already plotted out. I'll be recording the first five chapter drafts, doing a call with a prospect, and coaching my clients.

By now, I'd have converted at least one or two more prospects, and my advertising efforts would be keeping a lead or two coming in daily.

Now things are starting to take shape.

I've got a foundation of a few clients to build from.

There are enough prospects coming in to yield a few clients, some cash flow, and some additional revenue based on production.

And now I'm creating a marketing asset that will help me build a list and will serve as a positioning tool moving forward.

## Day 13

Aside from coaching the five or six clients I have at this point, I'd be focused on recording the final five chapter audios today.

Hopefully, I'd have at least one coaching call with a prospective client and I'd be sure to get another FB Live coaching video posted, too.

## Day 14

Two weeks in and I'm feeling good.

I've got five or six clients, and a couple of them are already getting great results after just a week of coaching, uncovering some previously untapped opportunities and adding enough revenue to cover the full six months of coaching with me.

My FB Live coaching videos are getting good feedback and, combined with my ads, I'm up to doing one free coaching call a day and selling one coaching program about every other day.

I've recorded 10 chapters, and now it's time to get them transcribed.

I want to conserve funds, so I pick an artificial-intelligence-based transcription service called Temi over the live transcription options. The total transcription will likely come in at under $30.

## Days 15–17

These three days are more of the same as far as coaching—doing a free coaching call each day, yielding one new client, and doing another FB Live coaching video. The rest of my time is spent editing the transcripts that I got back from Temi.It takes a while to shape spoken words into something that reads well, and I want this to make a great first impression with anyone who gets a copy, so I spend a lot of time reading and editing until it flows.

## Day 18

I submit the draft of the book to someone who does editing on Fiverr and pay to get it turned around in a day, so I can then hand it over to a designer from Fiverr tomorrow.

At the same time, I hire the designer to create a cover, so I can start promoting the book before it's finished.

While I'm waiting on the editing of the book to get finished, I log in to ClickFunnels and model Russell's book funnel so that's it's ready to go when I have the book completed.

## Day 19

I get the book back from the editor and immediately hand it over to the designer to format it, again paying for the 24-hour turnaround.

I get the cover art back and like it, so no changes are needed. It helped that I gave the designer three examples I liked that were all best-sellers on Amazon. Model what works.

To generate some buzz about the book, I do a post asking if anyone wants a free copy when it's done and telling them to just comment below if they do. It gets some traction pretty quickly, so I boost the post.

My clients are continuing to get great results, but my free coaching calls are slowing down a bit, so I'm pretty happy and relieved that I'll have the book ready soon.

## Day 20

I change my FB Live video up a bit today and interview one of my successful clients, basically sharing a case study for my coaching program. This produces some immediate interest and yields six more scheduled calls, so I boost that video.

## Day 21

The PDF version of the book is ready, so I share a copy with the fitness entrepreneurs who replied to the previous post wanting a copy. In addition to that, I create my first ad promoting a free copy of the book, with the second step in the funnel now being the same page I've been using for the free coaching call.

From the FB Live case study video I boosted, I'm up to 12 scheduled calls and I've already gotten two clients from it, so I schedule another case study video for tomorrow.

## Day 22

I send the book to a fulfillment center that does print-on-demand so I don't have to pay for a lot of books up front. The cost per book is higher, but I'm not doing enough volume for the potential loss of a couple dollars per prospect to scare me, since I'm still converting about 33% of the prospects who schedule calls into one of my two coaching offerings.

So far, I'm up to 10 clients with 4 of them paying the flat monthly rate, producing $8,000 in cash for the month.

Plus, I've got about 40 other fitness entrepreneurs who've downloaded the book, so I send them a quick personal (very informal) email asking if they'd like to jump on a quick call to see if I can help them apply some of what's in the book.

Four take me up on the offer, but I'm starting to send a daily email with a quick tip, idea, or story that educates and motivates all of them, so when they're ready, I'll already have a relationship with them.

## Day 23

By now, my days are divided between these tasks:

- Coaching my one-on-one clients
- Doing a daily FB Live coaching video as a marketing vehicle
- Writing a daily email to my small but growing list of entrepreneurs who've downloaded my book
- Connecting with one or two prospects for free coaching calls and closing about half of those I talk to with one of my two coaching offerings

While things are going well, I'm already recognizing that to keep scaling this, I need to start moving to a coaching model that isn't only one-on-one, and I need to be able to keep growing my audience without doing four times as many prospect calls.

So I decide that I'm going to launch a mastermind group, and I amend my offers to be...

***Option A*** We'll work together through my exclusive mastermind program for the next 12 months, and you'll have the option to either only pay me based on the delivery of the results I promise or pay a flat monthly fee. If you choose the pay-based-on-results approach, then for every new dollar I generate for your business above what you're already making, you pay me $.25. In this case, I'm only paid for results and only for new business.

If you prefer the flat fee option, you pay me just $1,000 per month.

Either way, we'll meet weekly as a group on a video conference, you'll have unlimited Voxer access to me, and we'll meet in person three times annually for two days per meeting.

***Option B*** If you'd rather collaborate one-on-one, we'll work together for the next six months, and I guarantee that you'll add $6,000 to your recurring revenue. We'll begin with a strategic planning session to outline your game plan for success and talk on a weekly basis, as well as using Voxer for open access.

Your investment is just $2,000 per month...and if you don't increase your recurring revenue by $6,000 in that span, I'll refund every penny.

Now I've got one option that provides me with a little more leverage, and both are still sold with me first delivering results in advance with the free call and then making two zero-risk, irresistible offers and letting the prospective client choose between them.

I'll put this amended set of offerings to the test over the next few days.

## Days 24–26

I've upped the ad spend, I'm averaging two to three free coaching calls per day, and I'm still closing about half...with about two-thirds of them going for the mastermind option.

That's good, because my schedule is getting tighter with client coaching calls, the weekly video conference, calls with prospects, and scheduled calls that are either rescheduled or result in no-shows.

## Day 27

After pushing straight through for 26 days, I'm taking today off.

I read for a while, get a decent workout in, and go the park with my family before catching an evening movie.

It's nice to celebrate the win of getting some traction with my new business in less than a month. That sort of appreciation for things that are going well professionally and personally is something I didn't do enough of when I was younger, and I'm not going to fall into that trap again.

## Day 28

After a refreshing day off, I'm back at it and energized.

I've got 3 people enrolled in the mastermind, and I'm up to 13 private clients.

The next step in the process is to craft a webinar to start pre-qualifying and pre-selling prospects before I do a call.

I log in to ClickFunnels and start reviewing Russell's Perfect Webinar format.

Between writing my daily email, delivering my quick video (another case study with a successful client), and my calls, I start scripting things out.

I get the first version of the webinar slides done and decide to sleep on it, getting up early tomorrow to tighten it up and record it while I'm fresh.

## Day 29

I start the day by reviewing the webinar slides and Russell's training.

Admittedly, I'm a bit nervous about recording the webinar, as it's not something I've been practicing...but I know it will save me a lot of time over the coming months by pre-qualifying prospects, so it's a valuable asset that I'm committed to getting done.

I start recording and stumble a few times, but I get it finished.

For the most part, I leave it as is and don't worry about the small hiccups, feeling like the informality seems more congruent with my business-coaching approach anyhow.

So between calls, my quick daily FB Live and email, I get everything done and the webinar is ready to go.

For now, I'm going to use it immediately after someone downloads the book and offer it as a free training. Once the book offer slows down, I'll start running ads directly to the webinar.

Either way, if everything goes as planned, it should improve my show rate for the prospects who schedule free coaching calls and pre-sell them on my coaching options.

## Day 30

We're here—a month into the new business.

I've got 4 mastermind members and 13 private clients, and I've collected $12,000.

In addition to that, I'll be able to start the billing for the first couple percentage-of-results-based clients later this week and will have some of that revenue coming in throughout the next few weeks as each of their first months comes to an end.

I've built an email list of over 100 additional prospects who've downloaded my book in the 10 days it's been available.

Speaking of the book, I've now got a solid lead magnet and positioning tool, and I will have print copies available within the week.

When I get these, I'll have the option to start running a free + shipping offer but will need to get something else tied in to the funnel to increase the average cart value so I don't lose money on the front end if I can avoid it.

I'll also send copies of the book to influencers along with a gift, to see if I can start to do some guest posting or be a guest on some podcasts to reach my target market in different ways.

I've got a nice rhythm with my daily FB Live and my short daily email, so I'll keep that going and—while I don't have much of an idea of how the webinar is working yet—it feels good to have version 1.0 live and working.

I'm not sure how many more one-on-one clients I want to add, so I may up the cost of that program to steer more of my prospects into the mastermind—at least while my lead flow and conversion rate stays about where it is.

## FINAL THOUGHTS

Overall, it's been a great first month, and now I can look at ways to hand off some of the administrative work to free up a little time, as I've got some recurring revenue to cover the expense.

Beyond that, I'll also create a few done-for-you funnels for my clients to share with them as an incentive to get them to join Click-Funnels, also creating an offer I can use for the prospects who don't join either of my coaching options that will still yield recurring revenue for me.

Not a bad first 30 days.

# RESOURCES

- Amazon.com
- BuzzSumo (buzzsumo.com)
- Facebook Live
- Fiverr (fiverr.com)
- Temi (temi.com)
- Voxer (voxer.com)

# Chapter 25

# ONLINE COURSES VIA AUTOWEBINARS

by Caitlin Pyle

# CAITLIN PYLE

*Owner, BCP Media, Inc.*
*d/b/a Proofread Anywhere*

Information Products /
Work At Home / Education
*ProofreadAnywhere.com*

*Caitlin Pyle is a former freelance proofreader turned multimillion-dollar mediapreneur whose on-line empire has helped thousands of people learn the skills they can use to generate income from home. Caitlin firmly believes that living the life you want is possible -- if you're willing to work for it. She's been featured in various notable media outlets such as*

## Day 1

I'd start Day 1 just like every day before it: get up, get dressed, and get moving.

I start every day with some kind of plank to wake up my body, then I do anywhere from 10 to 40 minutes of "formal" training, which is usually barre or circuit training. Then I follow up with 20 minutes of moderate-intensity jumping on my fitness trampoline while I watch a show on Netflix.

Even over the next 30 days as I rebuild my business, I will start every single day this way. It's critical to create a positive trajectory as soon as I can when I wake up—that's how I happen to my day, and my day doesn't happen to me!

Then I'd go to the grocery store and (using my credit card) buy enough healthy-ish canned and frozen food to get me through the next 30 days. I don't want to give myself any reason or excuse to not be successful as quickly as possible.

## Day 2

Today, I sit down and write a brief timeline on what I want to accomplish: building an automated webinar funnel for a general proof-reading-business-building course. Although it took me many months the first time around, I plan to launch the rebuilt course and funnel after just 30 days this time.

I begin by contacting everyone I've trained one-on-one in proofreading in the last several years—including my many years as a freelance proofreader as far back as 2007—and scheduling interviews with them on video. I use Calendly and Zoom because they are free (and I'm

**428**

broke). I'd also contact former clients from when I was freelancing and ask for testimonials for my sales page. I collect these in Google Drive.

Since I don't have my former reputation, I have to create my own credibility.

## Day 3

Using a Google Doc, I start outlining the content for my training program.

When brainstorming course content, I always write down questions potential students might ask. Many of the questions I can easily anticipate based on my one-on-one training experience. The answers to those questions become the bedrock of my course content.

## Day 4

I expand my outlines into more robust content—basically brain-dumping everything I know about my topic, dividing it logically into course units within the member area.

Using free screencast software—QuickTime Player built into my MacBook Pro—I also create basic tutorials to go along with my written content. I do this as I go along because for my minimum viable product, I don't intend to go back and add or fix things until after I get feedback from my initial students.

## Day 5

I'm finishing up my course unit drafts today and starting to create the course units and modules within a ClickFunnels member area. I use a template because I can always go back and make it pretty later.

## Day 6

I film a few short (10–15 minute) interviews with people I've trained one-on-one in the past.

I ask each person four questions.

1. What did your life look like before you worked with me?
2. What actions did you take as a result of working with me?

3. How has your life improved since taking those actions?
4. Would you recommend working with me to your friends, family, and colleagues?

Then I use the exact language they used to answer these questions as I begin outlining my sales letter.

## Day 7

Using my outline, I draft my sales letter in full. I make sure to include where I'll put my testimonial videos, and because I've started receiving testimonials from my former freelance clients, I make sure I include those in the sales page, too.

## Day 8

I build my sales page copy into ClickFunnels using a free template.

## Day 9

I draft an outline for a webinar based on the Perfect Webinar Formula. My webinar is a free workshop on how to monetize your proofreading skills.

## Day 10

I expand my outline into a webinar script, carefully following the Perfect Webinar Formula.

My main focus for the workshop—and for pretty much anything I create—is to make it a no-brainer offer. That means I do things like open the workshop with an incentive to stay to the very end, include tons of juicy bonuses in the value stack, and top it off with a generous fast-action discount for people who invest in the program quickly after viewing the webinar.

## Day 11

Using Google Slides, I paste my finished webinar script into the notes section of a slide deck and begin developing slides to match. I read my script out loud and ensure that every word sounds like it came straight out of my mouth. I even add in "uh" and "you know" in a few places to make it seem more natural and unscripted.

## Day 12

I write the copy and create the webinar registration page at the same time. I pull copy directly from my sales letter and webinar script to make this easier. There is no need to reinvent the wheel, and because I used the verbiage from my interviews, I already know what my target customer struggles with, what actions they need to take, and what results they want—more money, higher status, more freedom and flexibility in their lives, etc.

## Day 13

Using a template, I create the webinar countdown page and the webinar watch page.

I outline a six-email follow-up sequence for attendees who do not buy during the webinar and for the folks who register but miss the webinar.

## Day 14

I flesh out my email sequence outline into full-blown emails. I go ahead and input them into Actionetics and test to ensure that opting in on the registration page properly triggers the first email in the sequence.

## Day 15

I create the order forms (one for the fast-action/webinar-only price and one for the regular price) and the confirmation page for people who invest in my program.

I finish setting up the members area funnel, including customizing the automated email that buyers will receive.

I test everything to make sure it all works.

## Day 16

I revisit my slide deck and read my entire script aloud several more times, making tweaks to it as necessary.

I ask a friend to proofread my webinar slides in exchange for half of my frozen pizza.

## Day 17

Recording day! I convert my slides with notes into a PDF, which I load onto my iPad. Using free screencasting software and my Apple earbuds, I record my webinar using my Perfect Webinar Script. I edit the recording myself, upload it to Vimeo, and plug it into my watch page in ClickFunnels.

## Day 18

I set up the affiliate center in ClickFunnels, and script, record, edit, and upload a short video introducing people to the program.

## Day 19

I research and make a list of 10–15 potential affiliates for my program. I send a personalized email to each of them, making sure that it's a no-brainer to work with me. My offer includes a generous commission and an offer to create unique content for their blog, with very little work from them.

## Day 20

I write three swipe emails for my new affiliates. They are simple invitations they can easily customize for their audience. Each email invites the reader to attend the free "Monetize Your Proofreading Skills" 60-minute workshop.

## Day 21

I create advertising banners for affiliates to use on their websites using Canva and PicMonkey.

## Day 22

I type out answers to questions from several bloggers I reached out to who want to create a Q&A piece with me on their blogs. I make sure the answers to every question are unique, even if the questions are similar.

## Day 23

I contact 10 proofreaders on Fiverr and offer them free access to my course for life in exchange for proofreading services, feedback, and a video testimonial to use on social media and my sales page/funnel. Even though these folks are already making money proofreading, my training program would teach them how to make even more money by using proactive marketing strategy versus the passive sit-and-wait method they use on the Fiverr platform.

## Day 24

I set up a Facebook Group for my students. I draft a welcome post, create a few snazzy graphics, and invite my past one-on-one trainees into the group (especially if they're one of my video interviews) and start a few relevant threads to get things going. That way, when the new students join, it's not just crickets chirping in there!

## Day 25

Write an automated email sequence for paying students to help them through the content. I make sure to ask for their feedback along the way, knowing that it will help me improve the course and their results.

## Day 26

Sign up for Help A Reporter Out (HARO) and start watching queries like a hawk. Reporters of all kinds (blogs, TV, magazines, etc.) are always looking for sources to quote or to contribute to their articles, and HARO is a great way to make contact with these reporters. You almost always get a link back to your website!

## Day 27

I get on a Zoom call to get feedback from my Fiverr proofreaders. I record the whole thing and take copious notes because I can't afford a transcriptionist.

## Day 28

I take all the Fiverr proofreaders' feedback and apply it to my course content. That may include rerecording some videos and adding or rearranging content.

## Day 29

I follow up with the four or five affiliates who responded to my initial email, confirm the publish dates for their posts, and ensure they have everything they need from me.

## Day 30

I test everything one last time in preparation for turning on the funnel tomorrow. This includes a final proofread of my landing and sales pages. ALWAYS PROOFREAD!!!

# FINAL THOUGHTS

My original automated webinar funnel for the Proofread Anywhere general proofreading course launched on April 25, 2017, and generated $1 million in eight months.

*I never did the webinar live.*

Even though Russell recommends doing webinars live many, many times before ever automating them, this is one rule I personally don't mind breaking.

I say "personally" because it won't work for everyone.

Who would it work for? Well, if you have a knack for writing scripts and speaking through them naturally—and you follow the Perfect Webinar Formula—it IS possible to crush it with an automated webinar right out of the gate. I'm not an anomaly!

Obviously, it's important that you deliver over-the-top value during your webinar and that your product actually works. If you try to automate a webinar up front just because you're lazy and are looking for a shortcut, it will bite you in the tush.

If you don't have a knack for speaking scripts naturally—meaning you listen to the recording and it sounds choppy, flat, and/or robotic—doing webinars live will give you a lot of practice.

Oh, and regarding affiliates—I'd work with the four or five who responded to my initial email, pour a ton of effort into building those relationships, and get them excellent results. Then, I'd reach out to the bloggers who didn't respond and drop the names of the bloggers who did—including their excellent results. Social proof is critical not just for customers but also for affiliates!

Lastly, some encouragement! In 2014, I was earning $45,000 annually and knew nothing about digital marketing, course creation, or sales funnels. I've since acquired skills I can use to easily generate that much revenue in a day with a single email if I wanted to. Something just short of magic happens when you learn new skills and apply them. My life transformed because I learned marketing and funnels. Yours can transform, too. You already have everything you need to succeed—now you've just got to use it!

# RESOURCES

- Actionetics (clickfunnels.com/ actionetics)
- Apple earbuds
- Calendly (calendly.com)
- Canva (canva.com)
- Fiverr (fiverr.com)
- Google Docs
- Google Drive
- Google Slides
- Help A Reporter Out/HARO (helpareporter.com)
- PicMonkey (picmonkey.com)
- QuickTime Player
- Vimeo (vimeo.com)
- Zoom (zoom.us)

## Chapter 26

# COACHING CLIENTS VIA FACEBOOK

*by Akbar Sheikh*

# AKBAR SHEIKH

*CEO*

Ethical Principles of Persuasion
*AkbarSheikh.com*

*Akbar Sheikh is a #1 international bestselling author, speaker, master of the 7 Ethical Principles of Persuasion, has helped 7 funnels hit 7 figures, father, and philanthropist with a concentration on orphans and giving the gift of vision to blind children. Prior, he was homeless, overweight, in a terrible relationship, and suffered from a crippling anxiety disorder. He does what he does because he believes that entrepreneurs are inherently good people that want to make more revenue so they can give to their families,*

> *communities, and favorite charities, hence making the world a better place.*
>
> *Akbar is on a mission to use persuasion for good, helping people break through, the ethical way.*

So I have no money, huh? All I've got is my knowledge and my Click-Funnels account? Here's the good news: that's all I need. I don't need anything else to rebuild. I really don't even need a roof over my head. Let's do this.

## Day 1

Here's the thing...as an entrepreneur, I am an artist, and as an artist, my mind is my canvas. My canvas needs to be clean, and my tools are the knowledge I have. But if I'm in debt and I have lost everything, my mind is going to be pretty cloudy. My canvas is going to be pretty filthy. I need to declutter and have a talk with myself, inspire myself, and tell myself, "Hey, all that stuff...it doesn't matter. This happens to everyone at some point, but this is what builds character. Am I going to just curl up and accept failure, or am I going to go make it happen?"

So I will go on a walk. Pray. Journal. Know that everything I need is within. Know that I will crush it in the upcoming weeks. Know it is scientifically impossible to fail if I don't give up and I keep going in the right direction.

## Day 2

Now that my mind is clear and the canvas is clear, I will read some inspirational stories of top leaders who've all been at the bottom—who failed but overcame it. I know that this is my litmus test to prove that I'm worthy, that I can make a difference in the world and can rebuild. I will not let this define me.

Next up, I will make a list of my skills, spend some time reviewing materials, and read some books. Just sharpen my tools a little bit. Just spend a day or two doing that.

My skill set: funnels, mindset, ethical principles of persuasion, psychology, and business strategy

*To Do:* Read inspirational stories. Write down my skills. Sharpen skills if necessary. Start documenting this journey.

## Day 3

Now I'm going to identify who can benefit immensely from these skills. In the past, I've helped coach seven funnels to seven figures. I can do it again. No problem. I started with zero before, and I can do it again.

Realize that this whole game is nothing but problem and solution. I have the solution in my skill set. Now I just need to go find the people who have that problem I can provide the solution for. These are the people who might say things like this:

*"Oh, I don't know...*
   *...how to make a good funnel."*
   *...how to write good copy."*
   *...what kind of emails I should be using."*
   *...what strategies I should use to scale to seven figures."*
   *...what kind of mindset I should have to be happy."*

Those people are typically marketers and entrepreneurs.

I will identify which audience will benefit the most from my skills... it doesn't matter what level I am on...there is always someone a level lower who can benefit.

*To Do:* Continue sharpening the tools. Identify who can benefit immensely from my skills.

## Day 4

So I know my skills. I've got the problem I'm going to solve figured out. And my mind is clean. Now, I can't go out there and just put a bunch of Facebook Ads up. I don't have the money for that. So I've got to do it organically.

No matter what industry you're in, people have problems. Now there's something called Facebook Groups. These are very profitable. Here's what's gonna happen.

People ask questions. I go answer them, and give them real, seriously valuable responses.

"Aww, man, my funnel's not converting."

"Oh, hey, my funnels convert! Here's how..."

So I'll search for entrepreneurs on Facebook and find the best groups for that particular niche.

Questions to ask include:

- How many people are in the group? It should be over 1,000 people.
- Look at the engagement. Are people engaging in the posts? Are people giving each other value? Or is it just kind of like anything goes and there's a bunch of spam?
- Are the kinds of expert positioning posts you want to do allowed?

So I go in these groups and see that 99% of people are asking questions. Let's say I'm in the health niche.

- "Hey, how do I get a six-pack?"
- "What kind of supplements should I take if I'm tired all the time?"

Let's just say I'm awesome at getting people in the best shape of their lives in the health industry. Then there's a question for the group: "Who can get me in the best shape of my life?"

Now this is a very powerful question for several reasons.

1. The person asking the question is a red-hot lead. They are looking for that solution, that result.
2. There's a ton of other people following the question who also want to get in the best shape of their lives, so they're keeping an eye on the answers.

Now this is where I get lucky. Most people in there say, "Me, me, me, me, me!"

Useless.

So I've got to remember that most people are lazy. Would a FB page owner go in there and investigate every single person who commented? No, of course not. They're going to pick the person who gave the best response.

So if I type something like "Hey, man, I can help you get in the best shape of your life. Actually, I've helped several people get in the best shape of their lives," or "I've been helping people get in the best shape of their lives since 1991," that is more likely to catch their attention.

There's a little authority in there, too. If I don't have a lot of proof, I won't say how I did it or that I've done it for a long time (though if I've been doing it for that long, I should have proof). But I start giving value.

I could respond: "Oh, by the way, one thing you should know is that in my group we drink a lot of water because that hydrates us, which depletes our fat cells, and then we take a special mushroom because that kills the veins that nourish our fat. And we don't exercise too much. I hope you don't mind. We just do some light stretching." (Obviously I'm not a health coach.)

A good prospect will respond with something like: "I want to lose the weight. I don't want to exercise. And you can make that happen??" Winner!

Not only will I get that dude as a client, but I can get several others at the same time. I won't get scared by my competition. My competition is honestly irrelevant.

*To Do:* Participate in groups. Sharpen the tools. Post in at least three relevant groups a day and answer questions in different groups for one or two hours a day.

# Day 5

I find that most groups really aren't very good. So once I identify those diamonds, I would hire a virtual assistant (VA) for $10 an hour for an hour or two a day. That's like $100 a week.

The goal is to get the VA to do a lot of these research tasks, and that's going to empower me not to burn out. I don't want to burn out on the little detail tasks or the tasks that someone else is better suited for than me, because I have to keep my eyes on the big picture.

Every day, my VA or I will scour these groups by typing in particular key words. We're just gonna stick with the health theme. So I'd type in "six-pack" for example. And then the people asking about that topic are going to need an opinion, a solution.

So my VA should be scouring these groups looking for those posts and answering the questions. We will spend like two hours a day just answering questions in detail.

Since I'm giving so much good advice, reciprocity kicks in, and people just get magnetized toward me, the leader, the person who is giving valuable content. So people are going to send me Friend requests. I can accept them and then start a conversation.

*To Do:* Respond to questions and post valuable comments. Make some new friends and talk to them. Hire a VA from Upwork to help with certain tasks

## Day 6

So now I've been answering all those questions. This will probably happen at Day 4 or Day 5, because it's really just how human nature works.

So I accept their Friend requests and say, "Hey, how can I help you get into the best shape of your life?"

I'll just get right to it. Don't do any small talk like:

"Hi, how are you? Where are you from?"

"Dallas."

"I used to live in Dallas."

It's nonsense. I hate that stuff. I never do any of that. No one's interested in that. It's just a formality. Cut right to the chase. Nobody will mind, because everybody wants results. Nobody cares where you're from or where your aunt lives, nobody cares where you went to high school. Nobody cares.

*To Do:* Have conversations where I get straight to the point to start helping people with their problems. (I am getting very close to making some wonderful sales.) Continue documenting this journey.

## Day 7

So what's really happening now is that more traffic is coming to my Facebook profile page. That's what organic marketing is. Now I need to optimize my Facebook banner. I might say something like "Helping people get six-packs since 1991" or whatever the case is. I'll make sure it's a picture with authority that explains exactly what I do. If I'm teaching people about six-packs, I should probably have a six-pack myself and show that.

Next up, my bio. A lot of people put these useless things like "world traveler" or "serial entrepreneur" or "I like cats." Nobody cares. I will inject more authority and credibility here, with something like:

- Certified health coach
- Olympic qualifier
- healthcoachasdf.com

These are just some examples. So now people come to my profile and see credibility and authority. Now right below that in Facebook, I can link to my website. Or I can just put it in the bio.

I will then add authority pictures to my main profile—not me with my cat or eating a cake. I'll show pictures that say, "YES, I know what I'm talking about." Pictures of me with someone famous from my niche or getting an award or helping people out.

Now they're going to go to my website and want to talk to me. They know what I'm about and that I'm an authority. I will keep accepting the Friend requests and starting these conversations.

*To Do:* Set up my Facebook profile for success. (I could also open a separate FB account if I want, because this is going to be purely for business.) Keep answering questions.

## Day 8

So up until now, I've just been answering questions, which is good... but there's another way I can draw even more attention to myself, especially now that I've had these conversations: I can see the commonalities and comment publicly on them. This kind of post is called a value post. Now I'm gonna have to identify which groups allow me to give others value. Every day, I should do at least two value posts. I won't sell anything, just give pure value.

"Here's a little golden nugget. Water is good for you, but it's very hard to drink a gallon of water a day. Here's an awesome little trick to get it done..."

People get a little bit of benefit from me. Now what's going to end up happening is I'm actually building a team of salespeople, because I'm just giving all this value. The best part is that this team of salespeople who will be working for me 24/7 is completely free.

Then the cycle begins again. People start asking questions. "Hey, who's the best person to get me in shape?" People I've never even met are going to start tagging me and saying, "This guy knows what he's talking about!" That third-party social proof is highly valuable, and with that kind of credibility, I'll get a ton of business.

This is the plan to get a ton of organic business. It's through these conversations that I can make those first sales.

*To Do:* Figure out which groups allow value posts. Do two value posts a day. Await upcoming massive success.

# Day 9

Now it's up to me. I can either coach people (which doesn't really cost anything for setup), or I can sell people a digital course. This is made so much easier with a ClickFunnels (CF) account. If I have a computer or even an iPhone, I can record my screens and show slides. Some of the best courses I've taken in my life are just slide shows. Making an online course is really no big deal at all.

I decide to start off with coaching because it requires the least amount of setup and is very lucrative, and I can start making sales today.

*To Do:* Post value in groups. Decide whether I'm doing an online course or coaching. Create slides or devise my coaching system. The coaching system is a simple opt-in page with an authority pic and a one-liner that resonates perfectly with my audience, like "I'll help you

**444**

get a six-pack with no exercise. See how we have helped others do this 10 times recently!"

That goes to a simple virtual software library page, where I create a short video talking about who I am, what life used to be like for me, what life is like now, and the method I used to get where I am today. That method is what I will be selling. I'll highlight what's unique about me, be friendly, and be myself...people buy from those they like and trust. This makes my competition irrelevant.

That page can go to a simple scheduling page (Wufoo) where they can book a call with me and I can close them as a client!

## Day 10

So I'll continue building conversations and remember to start off by getting straight to the point. People in the community are gonna know what I do now and send me Friend requests. Here is the structure for a conversation I'll need to have with people to close them as clients. Let's say I'm working in funnels.

"How can I help your business grow?"

"Why don't you show me your funnel?"

(They send me a link.)

"Oh my God, the checkout page is missing X. This testimony is useless. The copy is terrible."

Truth is, they're going to know all this, but I'm going to agitate their pain.

"You're spending all this money on Facebook. This is why you're not converting. You see that, right?"

"Yes, of course I see that."

Then, I'm going to paint them a picture of what their success can be by asking, "What do you want to be earning?"

Predictably, they're gonna say a million dollars.

"Why?"

I am tapping deeply into their emotions now.

"Okay, well what would life be like if you were to get there?"

I'm still painting the picture here. I'm getting them to imagine life that way.

Next up, I just tell them how I can help them with that EXACT problem. Close them. Put them on a coaching deal. Work with them one-on-one to help them scale their business. Then they're going to ask about pricing.

I remember that right now I have no fame. I've got no list. I've got nothing. So I gotta start a little small and that's okay. So here's the offer I'm going to give them:

"Hey, man, I wanna work with you, and I want to give you this amazing deal. I'm actually in the process of building case studies. I'm gonna give you something called case-study-based pricing. The everyday price for all this is $6,000. Okay? But I'm in the process of collecting case studies, so if you're ready to make a deal right now and promise to give me a complete case study when you're getting the kind of results you're looking for, then I'm going to knock off half of the investment, and it's only going to be $3,000."

Boom shakalaka. That line alone has closed me a TON of sales. Top 1% kind of money. That will be my magic line. Following this structure WILL close deals 25% and up.

Whether I close them or not, I'll stop there for the day. That's a lot. And I'll be doing a lot of these calls. I might fail for a while until I make my first sale, but I will NOT give up. I WILL make sales.

*To Do:* Write out my sales script integrating those qualifying questions. Get on some sales calls. Remember how blessed I am that I am paying nothing for hot leads to get on the phone with me. Life is good.

## Day 11

Time to troubleshoot the sales script a little bit now.

If I'm not closing deals, that means I need to show more social proof. I need to show more testimonies. How am I going to get testimony?

Well, I've got all these friends now on my Facebook profile and all these people know I'm in the funnel game. They know I'm in the online entrepreneur space. So now I'm going to say, "Hey, everyone, guess what? This is insane. My services are very expensive, but I'm actually building a brand. I want to get some brand-new case studies. The next three people who comment, "Yes, give it to me baby," I'm actually going to critique their funnels for free!

I'm painting a picture of my ideal client in this post. Like someone I know who I can really help. Like if I'm in the health niche, I might say, "I need someone who hates eating leafy greens."

I don't want someone who already loves eating healthy food. How am I going to help them?

What happens next? People comment. "Yes, yes, yes."

Now there's one more qualification for these people. They need to act fast on this stuff, so I'll make sure that's in the post.

So the beautiful part about any of this stuff is that things work relatively quickly. So right away, I'll get two or three people and can get to work immediately.

So I get on a screen-share call and say, "Okay, show me your stuff. Let's change this, change this, this... The checkout page is no good. Your strategy is good. Do you have a VA? Get a VA. Let's tweak this copy. Let's tweak your mindset, up this price..."

Whatever field they're in, I'm just telling them what to do. Then they're going to get results almost immediately—they're going to be floored. They're going to be so grateful because they didn't pay anything.

Now I'll ask if they can record a quick testimony for me, and they'll absolutely do it!

"I just went over everything with Akbar, and oh my God, I am floored. I feel like I have a seven-figure blueprint. We changed my entire business. I now have clarity. I now have direction."

These are the buzzwords. What do people lack? What do they want? They want clarity. They want a plan for growth, and I want those buzzwords in the testimony. People will automatically want to leave me good testimony because of reciprocity, because I gave them value and coached them well. And I will also coach the testimonies a little bit. If they give me something really bland, I'll let them know they should structure their testimonies as how life was before, during, and after meeting me.

"Before...I was here. During...service was amazing. After...I had clarity."

Simple, right?

*To Do:* If I'm having trouble closing calls, I'll help some people for free and collect testimonies. Share these newfound testimonies on my profile and scheduling page. By now, my opt-in page should be collecting email addresses, so I will email my list these new testimonies and ask them to jump on a call with me.

## Day 12

Now I've got all these testimonies for free, and it just cost a little bit of time.

I will get in the mind frame that I am in the case-study-collecting business. Simple math.

More testimonies = more revenue.

If someone sets up a call but is totally not qualified, I will kindly cancel with them. I don't have time to fool around.

*To Do:* Respect my time and only talk to people who are ready to help themselves.

## Day 13

So my next post on my Facebook profile should be something like a little video of myself talking about the niche, giving a little bit of value within the industry—how I help people grow and how it helps people give to charity. Then I will have these testimonies there to back it up and cement that even further.

Now I've got more people asking for my help. I'm having more conversations. I'm closing a call or two. I will not give up.

Maybe I started at $500, but now I'm closing $3,500 coaching clients. Now I need to just rinse and repeat. I started off charging people $3,500—now I have packages that can go up to $25K. I gotta build my way up. The more testimonies I get = the more I can charge.

*To Do:* Make a video or do a Facebook Live for my personal page sharing some value and giving results.

An example would be a live funnel critique or live health critique. I should also start doing a daily FB Live on my page, giving nothing but value—a daily vlog. People will fall in love with me and will be begging to work with me, because they work with people who they like and trust.

## Day 14

These strategies are universal. I can do this strategy on Facebook Groups. I can do this strategy on LinkedIn. I can do this strategy on Instagram. I'll do it where my target market is. I need to just rinse and repeat in order to keep growing my organic reach.

The truth is, I can make seven figures organically. It takes a little longer, but it's easy to start with coaching. That's really the whole strategy, and it's not going to take me that long at all.

In fact, I probably don't need the whole 30 days. It's really more like two to two and a half weeks. I could probably pick up an easy $10,000. It's actually possible do a lot more, because I'm going to charge $3,500 per client, and I can easily get three clients without a dime on advertising.

*To Do:* Rinse and repeat.

## Days 15–18

Things are going to snowball. They'll pick up. The word is going to get out there about me.

Now it's going to happen. I have to do a little bit of outreach, maybe even pay someone, but I'm going to get invited to podcasts. And here's the thing—podcasts are FREE.

Now that I've been giving value in these groups for a little while, my next step is to reach out to some of the group admins and see if I can do a Facebook Live with them. These guys are dying for content and, because my stuff is relevant and valuable, they will likely take me up on the offer.

Now I get to do this Facebook Live in someone else's group for free. I'm just giving out value. Then I can actually take it a step further and offer to guest write value posts and give them to people to send to their lists or put on their blogs. I can take this down so many roads.

Once I get enough notoriety, I might be invited to a speaking engagement.

Over the past few weeks, I've been positioning myself as one of the few people out there who gives value. And because I do that, I'm going to attract those clients, those interviews, those speaking engagements.

*To Do:* Rinse and repeat. Do outreach to grow within new marketing avenues—podcasts, guest posts, guest Lives, and speaking engagements. Pick one for each of the next four days.

# Day 19

Now I need to refine my brand angle. I've got some success, so I just need to put the word out there about it. For my brand, I want to help entrepreneurs grow and scale, because I know they're inherently good people and they're going to give a portion of that newfound wealth to their families, communities, and favorite charities to make the world a better place. My brand angle is really a statement about what I believe in. I'll say it in every single appearance I make like a broken record—emails, FB Lives, posts, podcasts, interviews, etc.

*To Do:* Spend time refining my brand angle. Do a Live about it once I figure it out.

# Day 20

Now that I have some success and I've created time by getting that VA, every night I will practice gratitude. And gratitude and patience are really the same thing. When I have a rough day, I will still be patient and grateful. When I'm having a good day, I will be patient and grateful. Every night, I will reflect, What did I do right today? What did I do wrong today? What can I do better tomorrow? Constant daily reflection makes every day better. I will start this from Day 1.

I don't have a lot of time, but frankly it's more than enough time to make this really work, to make an impact in this life. I will constantly reflect in order to get my mind right, and continue to sharpen my tools. One way to do this is just to read a half an hour a day, to keep up my knowledge. It's essential to keep myself an expert at the cutting edge of my niche because when I do that, I can answer more questions and create even more valuable posts. If I don't feel like reading, I could watch something or listen to a podcast—no excuses!

## Day 21

Now I can actually scale up. I should have enough money to start testing some Facebook Ads. I can pay off some of my bills now. I might promote my VA to work a regular part-time schedule instead of just two hours a day. If I get them to work part-time with me, I'll be creating more time for myself. And I can be sure to take care of those coaching clients.

## Day 22

Now that I've got my clients in a proven system (because I got testimonies, so my stuff must work), I could start to automate and spend a little time creating a webinar. If I'm just saying the same thing over and over and over, I might go with a course.

I would launch a course on how to crush it with funnels. Making a course on whatever my niche is—that's really the blueprint.

It's amazing how things can turn around quickly if I have goals, and every single day I do at least three things to move my business forward. Give value in different places and answer questions. Talk to people. That was my mantra. I just talked to people and had conversations and worked to close deals.

## Day 23

Time to build a course in a few days. This day is easy. I'll just write down what eight things people need to crush it in my niche. My niche is funnels, so my modules would look like this:

1. Mindset
2. Funnels (webinar/visual/opt-in/book/e-comm)
3. Copy
4. Emails
5. Strategy
6. Team building
7. Scaling

8. Organic traffic

These are all the things someone needs to crush it in the funnel game. Then I'll sleep on it.

## Day 24

Now I'll take a recording app on my phone and start recording. Start talking through each and every one of the eight modules. (I only want to record the first three.) Just teach step-by-step how to master that step. Give the blueprint. Just talk freely and enjoy that. This will take me all day to do, so I'll take breaks and have fun. If I get a little stuck, I'll read up on the topic to sharpen my skills. This will give me the boost of confidence I need. And I will take breaks and stay hydrated. This is a loaded day!

## Day 25

Now I'll go to Upwork and hire someone to transcribe all my voice notes and turn them into slide shows—one slide show per module. Doing just the first three will be more affordable and quicker. I can do something called "dripping out" the content where I start with one module and release a new one every week.

## Day 26

While they are making my slides, I need to go into my CF account and build a quick webinar funnel with a members area. From the template in CF, I will tweak the following:

1. *Opt-in Page:* I will make the headline "We do X by doing Y. Watch our free masterclass showing you how to <RESULT>." I will also have a main picture on this opt-in page that shows the optimal result my audience wants. For example, if I were in the dental niche, I could show beautiful people smiling, showing their pearly whites.

2. When they opt in, they should go directly into a webinar replay

room. I'll just use the standard template for that.

That's all I have to do today.

## Day 27

Watch my top competitors' webinars. Write down what they are doing. Create an outline based on what they are doing. It will look something like this:

1. Introduce myself and show the success I have today.
2. Talk about how life wasn't always like this. "I used to have all these hardships..."
3. "Then I discovered this formula that changed everything. And that's what I'm going to show you on today's webinar."
4. Housekeeping rules
5. Disclaimers
6. Teaching
7. Stack
8. Close

Now I have it written out. I would do this with my top three competitors. Take what I like, leave what I don't. I don't copy words, I copy structure.

## Day 28

Now I have my webinar outline. I'll create my own slides and record it. When recording, I'll be confident and relaxed. As far as tech goes, I'll keep it simple and just use Zoom to record my screens, putting the slide show in full presentation view. Doesn't matter what slide-show app I use—Keynote, Google Slides, whatever I feel like. I don't even need a professional mic, but if I have the budget, I'll use a Yeti.

## Day 29

Add my webinar to my funnel template and let it go live! Now I'll start driving all my organic traffic to it and watch the sales come rolling in. Test. Tweak. Scale.

## Day 30

Rest, and then...

Take the documentation I have done, the journal I just created while documenting the last 30 days, and turn that into a PDF. This will be my new freebie. How I went from X to Z in 30 days!! The BLUEPRINT! Zero to hero!!

Then I'll do a Facebook Live, breaking down everything I have done over the past 30 days. And at the end of that, I'll ask, "Do you want to do the same? I can coach you on how to do the exact same thing. Sign up here. Okay? We're going to go from zero to hero. All right? God bless you guys. Love you guys. The only person in the world who's stopping you from doing this is you. Absolutely anything is possible."

*To Do:* Go on vacation. Do a Facebook Live and tell people how I got there. Invite them to my program!

Okay, guys, that's it!

Remember, I went from broke, fat, alone, and homeless to...

- Being a top 1% earner and a #1 international best-selling author
- Being featured on top podcasts and invited to speak all over the world
- Having a complete team, including a right-hand man
- Being named a top social entrepreneur
- Having a solid email list, group, and following
- Sponsoring a lot of orphans
- Giving the gift of vision to blind kids
- Supporting my family and giving them whatever they needed
- Vacationing whenever I want
- Hosting live events
- Being in top inner circles
- Impacting this world and making it a better place
- Helping seven funnels hit seven figures

Plus a lot of other cool stuff.

And guess what?

It all started from the EXACT strategy I just gave you! Implement and reap rewards. Always do things ethically, and always give back.

Love you...peace!

# RESOURCES

- Facebook Groups
- Facebook Live
- Google Slides
- Keynote
- Upwork (upwork.com)
- Wufoo (wufoo.com)
- Yeti (microphone)
- Zoom (zoom.us)

# Chapter 27

# 3 WEEKS TO WEBINAR LAUNCH

*by Rhonda Swan*

# RHONDA SWAN

## *CEO*

Personal Branding/Business Development
*Freedom-preneurs.net/thrive*

*Like you, world traveler, online brand strategist, social media expert and bestselling author, Rhonda Swan has experienced the online world and the digital economy defined numerous ways over the last 13 years.*

*Rhonda's work has been featured in Forbes, Business Insider and The Huffington Post. She retired herself and her husband from corporate 13 years ago and has now traveled the world full-time for the last 10+ years with her "Unstoppable Family". Their*

> *message is living your perfect day, everyday all while inspiring the world to connect, live free and to build a brand that leaves a legacy they are proud of.*

## Plan From $0 To $30K In 30 Days

Hi, I'm Rhonda Swan. The Unstoppable Momma of the Unstoppable Family!

I have been working online for 13 years (since 2004), and I quit my "cushy" corporate job to work online because I didn't want to ever put my child in daycare.

In my first 90 days, I generated $36K, and I retired myself and my husband in the first year from both of our multiple six-figure positions. I was a pharmaceutical executive, and my husband was a robotics engineer. The skills I used to build MULTIPLE seven-figure businesses from the ground up with NO marketing dollars, before social media existed, are the same strategies I use today...only now with an updated social flare!

This question rings true to my heart: "What would you do if you had to start over?"

Because three years after starting our business and quitting our former jobs, we lost everything in a bad real estate investment. *I mean EVERYTHING!* We went from making $50K+ per month to nothing. Lost over HALF A MILLION in cash, three cars, a $1.7 million home, and much more.

We couldn't even afford Skype credits! To top it all off, my brand-new baby girl, Hanalei, had just been born.

So what I am going to share with you in this chapter are the exact steps I took to go from $0 to $30K in 30 days after losing everything we had, and becoming UNSTOPPABLE!

## 458

# Day 1: Get Real

After losing it all, I will have to get clever...

The first thing I would do is start looking around the house for any valuables I don't need. That includes TVs, video games, cell phones, furniture, and jewelry. ANY excess, anything that would throw me off my game.

I need to come up with $5,000 for marketing in the next seven days, so I can have a solid foundation, clear my head, and build a business!

First, I am going to contact any BIG debtors about payments that will need to be made in the next 45 days and request a deferment of two months. I will not be able to make payments for 60 full days, so this way they will stay off my back.

Next, I'm going to come up with three quick and easy plans.

1. The Mind Game
2. The Online Game
3. The Ground Game

*Mind Game* I will write down in a calendar a countdown to the exact day I will launch my product or business. Also for these next 30 days, I'll set a reminder on the calendar or in my phone to NOT hang out with friends excessively or go out to dinner, unless it's with my immediate family or people who add VALUE to my day and/or life.

No frivolous partying, no binging on Netflix, only calculated action. This is going to help take my mental game to the next level!

Next, I'm an early riser. This means waking up at 3am EVERY MORNING and going to bed at 9pm every night! This gives me a complete 18 hours in my day to focus on myself, what I want, and how I'm going to launch my business.

I'm breaking those 18 hours into 3 parts of 6 hours each. The first 6 are going to be dedicated to my personal development and mindset.

*Hour 1: Mental Mapping* I get up at 3am and say my mantra.

I look at myself in the mirror and tell myself exactly who I am, what it is that I do, why I'm doing it, and the results that I'm going to get for myself. I'm basically reminding myself that I'm awesome.

My Actual Mantra:

> *You are a powerful leader and business woman. You care, you give, and you provide value to those who need it and want to take action. You live up to the vow you gave to your daughter to never put her in daycare and to show her the world. Today, you will be better than you were yesterday. You are UNSTOPPABLE!*

**Goals And Objectives** I am going to write down my exact goals and objectives for the next 30 days.

*Monetary Goal:* $30K in 30 days

*Why:* I made a vow to my daughter to never put her in daycare and to show her the world, even when I lost everything, I still keep that vow. I want to be a guiding light to other women to take a stand for what they want and MAKE THEIR OWN MONEY so their children want to be like them when they grow up. They should be confident and passionate about their gifts and not be afraid to sell them to someone who can use them. It takes focus and determination to get the prize, and I'm a winner—and I will win over my fears!

*How:* I am going to create a massive amount of value for a new audience and solve their main problem. In 30 days, I will make an offer and sell a $997 product (one that hasn't been built yet). I call this "building the plane while I fly it." Then I will make an upsell offer of $4,997 to work directly with me for eight weeks.

*What:* I will sell from a webinar after the 21-day plan. With my experience, I am confident that if I provide enough value during these three weeks for those who register and join LIVE, I will close 18%–28% of those live attendees. So my goal is to get them LIVE.

Here are conservative yet strong numbers:

- 150 high-quality registrants
- 70 show-ups
- 18% close: 12.6 buyers x $997 = $13,000

- 3% additional before-cart closes = $2,000
- $15K generated from webinar
- Upsell 3 buyers to high-ticket product at $5K = $15K

*Total in 30 days:* $30K
Rinse and repeat!

*Hour 1: Mental Mapping Continued* Then I'd write down in my journal the TOP THREE things I'm going to accomplish for the day. When I'm done with my morning mantra and journaling, it's time to read one chapter of Think and Grow Rich by Napoleon Hill. It's important to do this BEFORE starting any work in my business.

Now it's time to exercise. For one hour while working out, I'd listen to an audiobook. The books I choose to listen to will be related to my niche and add value to my mindset. Books like Crushing It! by Gary Vaynerchuk and Super Brain by Deepak Chopra. I'll basically listen to any book that aids in shifting my mindset.

Before I actually start my mind and body workout session, I'd put my phone on airplane mode so I can focus on the information I'm taking in.

After the workout, I'd come inside and eat a SUPER FOOD, such as a juice called Jamu we have here in Bali, which contains turmeric, and of course a Bulletproof coffee. This coffee is my absolute favorite because it's good for maintaining mental focus and stamina during intermittent fasting. I can also be the most productive at my peak-performance state during the first three hours of "me" time.

(If you don't know anything about Bulletproof coffee, I suggest you read The Bulletproof Diet by David Asprey.)

For the next three hours, I'll plan my online and ground game.

*Online Game* I'm going to map out and write down the EXACT person I can either transform with my work, create a result for with my product, or solve a problem for. I'd write out:

- Who they are: age, what they read, what they do, their fears, problems, etc.

- The ONE THING I can solve for them with my product, service, or program
- A list of 21 problems this person has or could potentially be looking to solve

*YouTube And Video Research* I will use Google Keyword Planner to look for keywords to create videos that people are searching for on YouTube. This will help build my organic online game. For example, if I owned a car repair shop, I'd write down things like engine repair, dry-rotted tires, dent removal, dent repair for cars in Daytona, Florida, (which is geotargeting), etc. These are just a few examples.

Again, I'm thinking about the exact problems they have, so I can be specific with my marketing and message. Thinking market to message MATCH!

*Relevant Facebook Groups And LinkedIn* Now it's time to find Facebook Groups that are relevant to my product or service. Groups where I can help people by adding value and begin posting once I start my 21-day plan. After I've selected a few groups, I'm also going to create a LinkedIn account, to provide content and to reach out to potential joint venture partners.

The goal is to get $5K for a marketing budget, then create an organic online plan, then a strategic paid marketing plan. Then, map out my mind game, my ground game, and my online game. These are the things I'm going to do on a daily basis, and the online/ground game is the plan to execute.

The #1 thing for the online game is going to be creating my 21-day plan. So the first week will be preparing for that, and after Day 7 is when I'll execute this plan.

*9pm:* Go to bed...NOW.

# Day 2

Yesterday, I got my structure set up and organized. Today—and every day this month—I will wake up at 3am, repeat my mantra, and read one chapter of Think and Grow Rich.

Then I'll plan and write out the top three things I want to accomplish that day and journal what my goals are and what I will reach by the thirtieth day of this plan.

Day 2 is the setup for the 21-day plan.

(Download a copy of this PDF using the link in the Resources section of this chapter.)

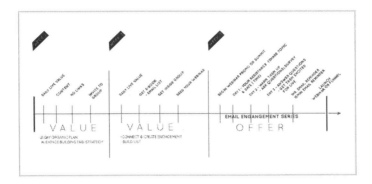

This plan is an ORGANIC structure for Facebook Live and YouTube videos. I already mapped out and planned a YouTube strategy, now I'm creating a Facebook Live schedule. The live videos will be similar to using the keywords for YouTube, but these will be set up specifically to create a following.

This has a Pied-Piper effect by adding daily value to my Facebook page and attracting my perfect "sexy" client/customer, because I'm going to solve their problems!

For this 21-day execution, I'll need to brainstorm for 15 minutes per day EXACT problems this customer has that I can solve with bite-sized bits of info.

Using the PDF guide (see Resources at end of chapter for link), I'm going to plot out a topic for each day.

This is how the Live structure works. Each live stream needs to be set up exactly like this:

1. *The Setup:* What's the topic being covered today? I must state what I'm going to talk about within the first six seconds. This

will help me grab the attention of my audience. I won't worry if people aren't on the Live yet, because each of these videos will be used for marketing later.

2. *The Payoff:* The payoff is the content. It's the exact one to three points I'm going to discuss or solve for my audience. I'll give them something actionable they can do that day or that can at least create an aha moment for them. This action will take no more than 10–15 minutes!

3. *The Call to Action:* In the first week, I will not use a "hard" call to action. And no links! I'll only give them "soft" calls to action. Example: "See you tomorrow. I'll be here every day at this exact same time, educating you on X topic/niche."

4. *The Open Loop:* This is where I keep them "cliffhanging" to make sure they show up to my Live the next day. Example: "Join me tomorrow at 6pm. I'm going to talk about X." I'm creating an "open loop" statement that makes people want (or not want) to be affected by whatever my content is. This has to be something that makes them say, "OMG, I have to be at this Live tomorrow for that!"

Now that I've got a structure for my Facebook Live 21-day plan, it's time to map it all out!

(Download the Launch Plan Outline using the link in Resources section of this chapter.)

The first week of the 21-day plan is going to be topics that are engaging and solve problems but are targeted more toward the negative side of my industry/niche. These are more fear-based or fear-versus-logic topics. As much as I may want to be happy-go-lucky, not everyone wants to hear positivity. They want to see the "train crash" and be challenged with topics that no one else is talking about.

**Week 1: Value (V)** Remember, in the first week, I won't have any links, just soft CTAs, invitations to the next Live, and a request for them to leave comments on the post. The second week will be based more on logic. I'm going to use the exact same structure, but the topics will be more logical, with more logic statements. This brings people to the realization that I can help them, and it's a simple way to make adjustments and changes.

Examples:

- *"How To Lose Weight In 30 Days: Follow These 3 Simple Steps!"*
- *"Earn $30K In 30 Days: A Step-By-Step Guide To Injecting Revenue Into Your Business"*

I'm breaking down old belief patterns about what the audience thinks is real versus how easily they can get what they want or avoid what they don't want.

The 21-day plan IS the V-V-O Plan (value, value, offer), or if you're Gary Vaynerchuk, it's "jab, jab, jab, right hook!"

**Week 2: Value (V)** In Week 2, I provide links. This is the time where I can offer them a lead magnet, like an e-book, a quiz, or access to a Facebook Group. The reason I leave these out of Week 1 is because I'm creating know, like, and trust in a new audience that doesn't know me.

Note: Since I'm still in planning mode, I don't have an e-book yet. But I'll have one done and ready to go before launch.

**Week 3: Offer (O)** Week 3 is when I'm going to lead up to bring people to a live webinar or masterclass where I offer them my product, service, or a chance to work directly with me.

Day 2 of this plan is vital because I'm going to execute starting on Day 8! The first seven days are devoted to planning, setup, and figuring out how I'm going to execute this thing. Now that I've got my 21-day plan mapped out, I'm going to start on the second half of the day.

## Day 2.5: Who You Know

My next move is to write out whether I've ever known or know of anyone RIGHT NOW who can benefit from or use my product or service. NOT friends and family, but what businesses or individuals could use me? (This is where I get creative again.) This is the start of my ground game.

Once that's done, I'm going to research events I can attend that are either in my niche or related to my industry. In the next 30 days, how many networking events are in my area? This is also part of the ground game.

Now, who do I know close enough that could be an affiliate of my product or service? Whose business can I add VALUE to? Who could invite me to be a live guest on their webinar? Who could I allow to promote my offer to their audience? I'll write down at least 10 people.

This is part of my online game.

At 9pm, I'm going to reward myself with good food and a glass of wine before bed. This helps me unwind and feel good about my plan. (Only one glass...and make it Italian. LOL)

Before lying down, I say my mantra and visualize my goal of selling $30K in 30 days with this plan.

I listen to rain sounds to put me in a state of peace as I drift into a deep sleep. I use the app Relax Melodies.

## Day 3: Lead Magnet

Day 3 is all about setting up the structure of my offer. Today, I'm going to put together a map of what my lead magnet can be. Either an e-book, a quiz, a giveaway, or access to a Facebook Group.

I could record a video series that brings people forward to learn more about what my product or service is going to be. This video, or series of videos, would solve a problem that my customer/client has.

I'm also trying to get them to know, like, and trust me by becoming the expert on video, which will be seen as high-value training. These videos should be just 12 to 15 minutes long. On the same page, there needs to be a tripwire offer. This offer should pop up around minute 12 on the funnel I create.

So what am I going to offer? Within these 30 days, I have to break down EXACTLY what it is that I'm selling. What does my product offer to people? Also, what are three bonuses I could offer that have HIGH perceived value and are easy and low-cost for me to give away or sell as low-ticket items. This is where I figure out what my business is going to be!

Since I'm relaunching my business, I've got to ask myself a few questions. I'd take out some paper and write out: "What skills do I have right now that I could package up, productize, and use to solve someone's problems?"

After that, I'd start by drawing a big "T" on my paper. On the left side, I will write "What I Want My Day To Look Like." On the right side, "What I Don't Want My Day To Look Like."

I do this because I can organize exactly how I want to structure my day. For example, if my offer was to coach, but I don't want to work with people every day, then coaching won't be a good offer for ME.

Next, I draw one last "T." On the left, "Who I Want To Work With." On the right, "Who I Don't Want To Work With." (Download sample templates of these charts using the link in Resources section of this chapter.)

This helps me figure out the ideal person to target and work with in my business. It also helps me avoid wasting time and energy on people who aren't the right fit for me and vice versa.

Once I'm done brainstorming and figuring out what I'm going to do and offer, it's time to plan my funnel.

Here's everything I'll need:

- Lead magnet
- Main "SEXY" offer
- Sales funnel
- Thank-you video
- Tripwire offer ($7–$47; this is how I monetize this process)
- Webinar

At this stage, all I'm doing is planning. I'm not actually going to make a product until I sell it! It's called the build-the-plane-while-you-fly-it method. Tomorrow, I will start recording videos. And on Day 5, I'm going to build my sales system with ClickFunnels.

## Day 4: Execution Day

Things are starting to come together! The early stages are the most important...I've got to keep going.

Today's tasks are to...

- Film YouTube videos (record all video topics).
- Reach out to people and businesses (ground game).
- Reach out to potential affiliates through email/messenger (online game).

For YouTube videos for this project, I'd like to keep them between three and five minutes. I'll make sure to open each video with the EXACT keyword I'm targeting. Then, I'll give a bit of content and invite the viewer to learn more by clicking the link in the description.

The objective of these videos is for the people searching for the problems I'm solving to be moved AWAY from YouTube as fast as possible! This is to eliminate distractions. Each video will either link directly to an e-book, a Facebook Group, or a webinar registration.

After I've recorded all my videos, I'll construct my emails/messages to people I feel I can help right now with my product. (Downloadable examples available via link in Resources section of this chapter.) With these, I'm basically inviting them to take me up on my offer.

"Call me" or "Click here to claim this offer."

***Affiliates and JVs*** Now it's time to reach out to affiliates. These are people who can put me on a webinar for their community where we can share revenue between 30%–50% per sale. Or I'll reach out to someone to become my affiliate by promoting my webinar through email or other platforms.

If I didn't have an "identity" yet, I could look at people in my niche, reach out to them, and ask if they'd be willing to invite their community to my offer, AFTER I explain what I do, show them my product, and win them over on what I'm all about!

Day 4 is the execution of the setup for Days 1–3. I'll use the templates to send emails or messages to potential affiliates for my product.

# Day 5

Today is all about setting up my sales systems and building out funnels for the launch. This may seem like a lot of work—because it is. But the process is A LOT quicker and much easier than it looks on paper.

## Part 1

1. Get autoresponder.
2. Set up basic account.
3. Create lists.

This is pretty straightforward. I need an autoresponder and a list to add people to when they download my lead magnet. Then I'll create a buyers list to add people to when they purchase my product/service at launch. I will create these two lists then select them during Part 2 of this setup.

## Part 2

1. Get ClickFunnels.
2. Set up basic account.
3. Integrate PayPal.
4. Integrate autoresponder and lists.

Again, it's straightforward. Get a ClickFunnels account and configure it. None of what I'm doing will work without this system in place. So it's very important to do this right the FIRST TIME around. This way, I don't have to go back and fix things later in the middle of my launch.

## Part 3

1. Build a lead magnet funnel.
2. Create an order form for my product(s).
3. Build a webinar funnel.

First, I'll download a lead magnet template from the ClickFunnels marketplace. Either an e-book or a video series template. Once I'm done customizing this simple funnel and adding my list to the back end, I'll set up my order form.

I could always just send people to a PayPal checkout, which is perfectly fine, but the built-in forms from ClickFunnels look great, are proven to convert at higher rates, and allow me to increase the average order value (AOV) of each customer on the FRONT END by enabling "order bumps."

Now it's time to build my webinar funnel. The webinar will be the EXACT topic I'm going to teach in order to create a result for participants and sell them my product/service. At this point, I'm almost done building my sales systems. When completed, they'll make money for me on autopilot, as long as I drive traffic to them and continue giving value at each step of the 21-day plan.

The last thing to do here is integrate my webinar software. After everything I've done so far, I'll save this task for tomorrow and give myself a mental break for the evening. Time to pour myself a glass of wine and take a warm bath.

## Day 6

Today's tasks are very simple.

1. Get a WebinarJam account.
2. Set up basic account.
3. Integrate with ClickFunnels.
4. Get ready for the event.

That's it! I already created the webinar funnel yesterday, so all I have to do now is make sure the two programs are "talking" to each other properly.

## Day 7

I will enjoy today and take a break from the computer.

## Days 8–14

Day 8 is the day I finally launch the 21-day plan! This first week will be SEVEN DAYS OF PURE CONTENT. No links, no offers...just quick

**470**

LIVE videos of me solving people's problems.

Again, the structure of each Facebook Live will be:

- *Setup:* Present topic within first 60 seconds
- *Payoff:* Content, 15–20 minutes max
- *CTA:* What to do next
- *Open Loop/Cliffhanger:* What's coming

At the end of each video, I will seed the next "episode" using an open loop. This basically tells viewers to show up to tomorrow's Live to learn more about the next topic or see a continuation of the current video's content.

This is why I spent so much time planning at the beginning of this chapter, so when it's time to go live, everything is in place, and I know what the topic of each video is going to be every single day for each week of the first cycle.

Note: For the first run of this plan, I will release a video each day leading up to the webinar/mastermind/event. However, if something comes up, or if I need a day or two for rest, I could release content for five days instead of seven. At the VERY LEAST, Mondays, Wednesdays, and Fridays. But for this demonstration, and for the BEST results, I should be posting every day for 21 days.

And speaking of cycles...

Ideally, I want to repeat this plan three or four times. This will ensure I'm building a following, creating content that I can repurpose and syndicate to other platforms, and of course making money—assuming my offer is any good, meaning that it is something people are actually willing to pay me for.

It also takes 21 days to form a habit and 62 days to create a ritual, which creates a new neural pathway in my brain, anchoring in my success habits and rituals. This way, the 21-day plan becomes part of my DNA!

## Days 15–21: Organic And Paid Traffic

Now it's time for the second week of videos. I'm following the exact same formula from the previous week—ALL VALUE.

The only difference is that I now start introducing links. I'm still giving value and still NOT asking my audience to buy anything yet.

Starting Day 15, I'm offering my viewers to download a free e-book or video series, or to join my group, in exchange for their email address. This is the "ethical bribe" I'm using to build my list and prepare for the upcoming launch!

I'm using soft calls to action instead of begging for people to click my link. Just mentioning the free offer and telling them to "Click the link below to get access."

I must ALWAYS REMEMBER to open the loop for the next video, because people need a reason to keep tuning in.

On Day 18, I'll switch gears a bit. I will still be giving value and solving problems in each video and using open loops. But now it's time to start "seeding" the live event. Nothing fancy or complicated about it, just tell people there will be a live event soon and that they should keep watching for more details to be revealed in the next video, each day telling a bit more about what the event will cover.

This will continue up to Day 21.

Note: Week 2 is when I start to "syndicate" my content. Starting with my YouTube videos, I will post one per day to a different platform. One to my fan page, then boost it. Another video will be sent out to my email list, etc. On the flip side, the first week's videos from the 21-day plan will be uploaded to YouTube at one per day. This is my organic plan in action.

It's not necessarily a requirement, but it definitely helps build authority and organic traffic when repeated for a few cycles.

**Paid Traffic/Boosting** After the first week of Lives and organic syndication, it's time to do some paid marketing to stay in front of my audience using Facebook Audience Insights, boosting each video to capture a Video View and creating an audience that Likes and engages with my content.

**Facebook Audience Insights** Now that I have organic syndication, I need to work some magic with that $5K I raised in Week 1. I start with Audience Insights and FB Ads. The greatest thing about Facebook advertising is the ability to reach super-specific audiences. I can narrow them down not just by location, age, and gender, but also by education level, relationship status, life events, and of course, thousands of unique interests and behaviors.

Many advertisers select audiences that are way too generic and end up wasting a lot of their advertising money—and that's exactly what Audience Insights solves.

Instead of promoting my videos for, let's say, running shoes to people who are interested in "running" (which includes more than 46 million users in just the United States), I can use the tool to discover laser-specific interests that will include only the most passionate runners.

Even if I've already found an audience that converts well, I can use Audience Insights to find dozens of other related interests to scale my campaigns and get more eyeballs watching my videos, more registrants on my webinar, and ultimately more sales. Understanding how to target will get me the most value from my marketing dollars for my 21-day plan. I'll do $10–$20 per day per video for the first two weeks, or about $100–$150 a week.

## Days 22–27

- Shoot a promo video about upcoming webinar, inviting them to register.
- Use webinar registration links in all videos.
- Market each video and promo video to webinar registration $300–$500 ad spend.
- Create offer.
- Create slide deck.

## Day 22

The day has finally come! It's all about registering for the event/webinar.

I'll do a quick recap of the last few episodes, cover the actual topic of the webinar, reveal the exact date and time, and explain why it's so important for them to sign up NOW. I want as many people to attend my event as possible. That means getting my audience to sign up early so I have a rough idea of how the launch might perform.

And of course...I will always remember to open the loop for the next day.

Place video ad for my webinar with a $300–$500 spend, targeting my specific audience.

## Day 23

Today's video is about my struggles with the webinar topic and how I overcame them with the info I will share when they show up. I'll mention two or three quick points on how things were before my breakthrough and how much better my life was once I was able to rise above them.

*CTA:* Register for webinar.

Creating Offer Content: This outline will help me organize my content and offer that I will be presenting in my webinar. It's the best way to hash it out and write it out like a story. My mentor Lisa always says, "Sell the destination, not the plane." This is how I want to make my offers irresistible.

(Download copies of webinar planning and offer creation resources using the link in Resources section of this chapter.)

## Day 24

Today's Live video will be all about engagement. Throughout this process, I should have enough comments and questions from previous videos that have helped generate ideas for content. I can talk about one of the most common questions I've gotten and tie it to the upcoming event. I will then invite viewers to ask questions in the comments below, which I will answer in tomorrow's show.

Also in these final videos, my calls to action are hard and straightforward. I'm very deliberate and focused on getting the final people to sign up before it's "too late." I've got to get my audience EXCITED about the webinar!

*CTA:* Register for webinar!

Syndicate my video.

Prepare slide deck following the formula provided in the webinar planning resources (which can be downloaded using the link in Resources section of this chapter).

## Day 25

In today's video, I will answer the next most common question and tie it to the event. Then I'll give a hard CTA to sign up.

*CTA:* Register for webinar.

Organize offers and decide which offer will be targeted on the webinar.

## Day 26

Today's video: answer any question from my previous videos, tie it to the event, and give a hard CTA to sign up.

"There are just 48 hours left to secure your spot, and seats are almost full! This means that if you wait, you might not be able to attend, because there will be no more room!"

*VALUE VIDEO:* I'll send an email to the registrants, a "value video" preparing them for the upcoming webinar. I'll shoot a 15- to 20-minute warm-up video with a download to prep them and place this on a CF page with the PDF to download.

## Day 27

In today's video, I will answer any questions from my previous videos, tie them to the event, and give a hard CTA to sign up. Here is also where things get real. It's time to "close the doors."

"You've got less than 24 hours until the event starts! This is your LAST CHANCE to sign up before tomorrow! Click the link below this video to grab your seat, if there's still an opening!"

There will always be people who wait until the last minute. For some reason, some people don't take action until there's a threat of losing something or missing out. This is why I make it "real" by always having a time AND attendee limit on the event.

Each of these last videos are all about continuing to solve problems and getting people FIRED UP for the webinar. If I did my job right, I should have a list of 200–500 people who are ready to be sold on my product tomorrow!

## Day 28

And so it begins. Today, at a pre-determined time, I will be doing a live webinar with the intention of giving value, solving problems, building my brand, and—most importantly—making money!

Before I actually launch, I'll do a final check of my systems. I want to make sure that...

- ClickFunnels is up and running and integrated with my payment processor, Stripe.
- The following are functioning properly:
  - My order form is able to accept payments.
  - My autoresponder and WebinarJam are integrated with ClickFunnels.

When doing this launch, I fully expect to make money. However before I go live with my offer and start raking in cash, I'm going to hop on the phone with PayPal. I need to let them know that I'm promoting my product and that a certain number of payments will be hitting my account. Hopefully in large quantities.

Why do this? Because if my account doesn't usually have large numbers of payments come through at once, PayPal might LOCK it until they can investigate possible fraud. If this happens, I won't be able to access any of my funds!

ONE hour before I go live, the first automated email goes out letting people know it's almost time to start.

FIFTEEN MINUTES before launch, the final warning email is sent. This is the moment I've been building up to from the beginning of this chapter. Everything I've been working toward falls on this very moment!

All I have to do now is stick to my script; be engaging, informative, and entertaining; present my BUY NOW link; close the event with a hard call to action; and let the universe take care of the rest. I'll close out this day with a warm bath, a well-deserved glass of red wine, and (if all went as planned) a new list of buyers and a bank account full of cash!

## Day 29

*Execute the 21-day promotional plan.* Yesterday's webinar was a success!

I reached my goal of $30K!

- 150 high-quality registrants
- 70 show-ups
- 18% close: 12.6 buyers x $997 = $13,000
- 3% additional before-cart closes = $2,000
- $15K generated from webinar
- Upsold three buyers to high-ticket product at $5K > $15K

Total in 30 days: $30K

Now it's time to "build the plane while I fly it," which I mentioned at the beginning of this chapter. In a nutshell, I'm going to structure and package the training program that I pre-sold on the webinar, as well as the higher-ticket upsell to work with me directly.

I'll also send out an email to my list with a link to the replay of yesterday's event. This is done just in case the people who wanted to attend live couldn't make it for whatever reason. It gives them a chance to see what they missed, learn some new information, and purchase a seat in my $997 training before I close access!

For this first run, I am going to do an eight-week program with a 21/7 (3 week/1 week) promotional cycle.

## Day 30

1. Wake up at 3am, repeat my mantra.
2. Plan and write out the top three things I want to accomplish today.
3. Start program with clients.

Again, I am building the plane while I fly it, meaning that I will create the program as I work with clients each week. The first week of material will be prepared inside a membership site so that the clients will have onboarding and what-to-expect modules to work through before our first group sessions. Each week, I will prepare the lessons and recordings and drip-feed the content to the clients before the weekly call.

By the eighth week, the complete course will be ready, and I will have already started to promote it using the two-day plan.

This is my plan. I am excited to see you execute it!

Rhonda Swan

# RESOURCES

- Rhonda's Downloadable Chapter Resources (30days.com/rhonda-resources)
- Bulletproof coffee
- The Bulletproof Diet by David Asprey
- Crushing It! by Gary Vaynerchuk
- Facebook Ads Manager
- Facebook Audience Insights
- Facebook Live
- Google Keyword Planner
- Jamu Juice
- PayPal (paypal.com)
- Relax Melodies app
- Stripe (stripe.com)
- Super Brain by Deepak Chopra
- Think and Grow Rich by Napoleon Hill
- WebinarJam (webinarjam.com)

# Chapter 28

# FACEBOOK MARKETING SERVICES

*by David Asarnow*

# DAVID ASARNOW

## *Chief Monetization Officer*

Funnel Marketing Agency
*BusinessNitrogen.com*

David Asarnow is a visionary entrepreneur, digital marketing leader and author of the book "The Competition." David is passionate about helping entrepreneurs create massive value, leverage and profits through his proprietary monetization strategies. So much so that several of his clients call him "The Monetizer!"

David has an MBA in business results! In his 20's David built a $45 million new division for a 50-year-old $60 million company over five years. In his 30's

*David launched a National Franchise company that was ranked in Entrepreneur Magazine's Franchise 500 in less than three years and was rated a TOP 15 HOT Franchise in less than five years.*

*After this success, David wanted to help more businesses than he could within his franchise and decided to conquer his fear of stage fright and become a business speaker.*

*In less than two years David was speaking for business icons Tony Robbins and Chet Holmes. From there he combined his passions and formed the digital marketing agency Business Nitrogen, where he has become the go-to expert for entrepreneurs, executives and small business owners looking to monetize and accelerate their business results through Funnel Marketing.*

*David is a four time Click Funnels Two Comma Club 2018 8-Figure Award Winner.*

*David loves to laugh and create connections wherever he is. According to David, "I feel blessed to start every day with my wife Jen, and torment my two kids Maddie and Josh with dad jokes."*

## I Took The 30-Day Challenge Myself

What you're about to read is real. It's not just some theory on what I might do to make 6 figures in 30 days—it's what I did do. Even though I have four 2 Comma Club awards and one 8 Figure Club award, I decided I could not tell you what I would do without trying it out myself. So the steps I'm sharing below are the same exact ones I used myself to create an additional multiple six figures in revenue in less than 30 days, while simplifying my business. At the end of this chapter, I will share with you a way to get more insight into my day-to-day activities. Enjoy!

### From Corporate To Crushed I'm about to tell you something I don't really talk about.

The scenario this book is based on isn't new to me. Ten years ago, this WAS me. I'd lost pretty much everything. My back was against the wall, and I had nothing left but the knowledge inside my head. And when I say "lost everything," I mean like the shirt off my back, my wife's gonna leave with the kids, and the late notices are addressed "urgent."

At that point, I had no choice but to start over...and it HAD to work.

I had built a very successful career in corporate America. But I always had a desire to be self-employed, to be an entrepreneur, so one day, I just resigned.

I spent the next year and a half finding myself, going on a perpetual journey of self-sabotage. I didn't know what to focus on and burned through A LOT of money in the process.

### The Reality Check You know the story of "I was down to my last dollar..."? Well, that was me. I had nothing, zilch, nada, zero in my bank account, NOTHING left in my savings. Oh, and my credit cards? Yeah, those bills were in the hundreds of thousands.

You'd think I would have figured this out before burning through cash like a summer wildfire, but here I was, sitting in the ashes of my dreams when I suddenly said to myself, "Holy cow!" (I may have used stronger language.) "What am I going to do? I've got car payments. I've got mortgage payments. I've got a family to take care of!"

Then it clicked. I already knew what to do. I had already grown a division of a previous business to $45 million annually and built another to a Top 15 Hot Franchise as its CEO. How? By helping solve a need. I liked my job in corporate America, but I felt constrained by all the rules and limitations. I wasn't passionate about building someone else's empire. But helping people? That part I loved.

That epiphany helped me begin to redesign my life. I vowed to only

**482**

help businesses I felt aligned with. I vowed to stop feeling sorry for myself. I vowed to be grateful every day for the opportunity to help others. And not only did my bank account grow, so did my happiness.

Over the next 30 days, I laid the groundwork for a six-figure business of my own, and I've replicated those practices over and over since then for multiple six- and seven-figure businesses.

The things I did in those 30 days are things you can do, too, right now. And you're already way ahead of me—ten years ago, ClickFunnels didn't even exist.

All right, you ready to dive in? Here's what I would do now.

## Day 1

*Get Clear* The first thing is to forget about the phone ringing. Forget about the creditors. Forget about whatever setbacks or failures I've experienced.

Now is the time to get clear and FOCUS. When I KNOW I can help someone else, all of a sudden—BOOM! I can turn my whole life around very quickly.

I will make the commitment to spend at least five minutes every day getting clear with a walk, yoga, or just deep breathing. When my mind is clear, amazing things just flow into it. I also believe that things can drastically change within the next 30 days.

And when I change my life, I'll have an opportunity to change the world.

*Focus Exercise* These questions will help shape my next 30 days. I know if I get this part right, the rest will come more easily. So I dig really deep and write it all down on paper.

- What am I passionate about?
- What am I good at? What do other people say I'm amazing at?
- Where have I had the greatest successes in my life?
- What do I want to do?
- What's most important to me?
- If I could wave a magic wand right now to get anything, be any-

thing, or do anything, what would that be?
- How can I use all of that to help others?
- Who do I want to serve?
- What is my end goal?

# Day 2

*Set My Goal* I'm going to think about what I want to achieve in the next 30 days then set a purposeful goal. I will write it out so it's clear and staring me in the face. I can't just make a mental note of it. I know all too well that if I don't write it down, it will be too easy to dive in to self-sabotaging behavior when the going gets tough.

In fact, I will write it out by hand, in cursive, every morning and every night over the next 30 days. That simple act of writing will help me focus and remind me to be open and grateful for all I have in my life. It will also help me be more aware of those around me who I might be able to help.

The Goal-Setting Formula

Here's my goal-setting formula:

By <DATE> or sooner, I will achieve <GOAL> or greater.

This is what I believe I want; however, I am open to receiving something greater.

# Day 3

*Pick My Niche* Today, I will determine WHO I can best help using ClickFunnels, my unique set of skills, and my knowledge. Currently, I have no money and no list, so I'll need to go out and find an individual or business that needs my help.

Identifying a profitable niche is simple—and free! All I need are a few free tools and what is in my brain. Here's the process I'll use:

1. Brainstorm a few different niches where I know I can provide a client with a 2x–10x return on investment (ROI) in 45 days or less.
2. Use Google Keyword Planner to identify some high-value keywords for those niches. This will show me what the pain points and needs are, making it easy for me to provide solutions for cli-

**484**

ents in this niche.

3. Create an ROI calculator that will show my prospective clients how their investment in my knowledge and skills will pay off.

4. Qualify my niche by asking myself the following questions:
   a. Do they need what I have to offer?
   b. Do they want what I have to offer?
   c. Can they afford what I have to offer?
   d. Are they willing to invest in what I have to offer?

If I can't answer yes to those four questions, then I'll choose another niche. I can get a few good clients within 30 days to start generating income and then reevaluate my niche later on if I need to.

*ROI Calculator* Here's an example of what I would use to help clients see the value of my services.

| The form fields in Yellow can be changed | | | | |
|---|---|---|---|---|
| Enter your pricing info | | | | |
| Your Price | $7,000.00 | Advertising Budget | | $3,000.00 |
| % profit margin | 73% | Cost per click | | $5.00 |
| Profit | $5,110.00 | | | |
| Sales Conversion Rate | 2.00% | | | |
| ----- This takes into account the Advertising Spend ----- | | | | |
| Revenue | $84,000.00 | | | |
| Pre adspend profit | $61,320.00 | People to your site | | 600.00 |
| ad spend | $3,000.00 | | | |
| Marketing + Marketing Overhead | $6,000.00 | | | |
| Profit | $52,320.00 | New Customers | | 12.00 |

# Day 4

*Qualify, Qualify, Qualify* I recently walked into a med spa while on vacation. When I arrived, the owner's wife and I exchanged the usual small talk.

"So, what do you do for a living?" she asked.

"Well, actually, I help doctors grow their practices," I replied.

She looked me straight in the eye and said, "We need to talk."

It soon became clear that her and her husband's interest in what I do was genuine. I told them stories about my business and asked them questions about theirs. It didn't take long to see that I could help them fix their business struggles.

I can qualify my connections on the spot in four easy steps:

1. Be open. I never know when I'll come across someone I can help.
2. Be prepared to share information about my skills.
3. Be willing to ask questions about their needs.
4. Be ready with how I can offer a solution.

I will use this process today and every time I have the opportunity.

**Qualification Questions** How do I know if someone would be a good fit as a client? It's all in the questions I ask. Here are some of my favorites:

- What are you doing in your business to achieve success?
- What are the pains, problems, and struggles your business is facing?
- How did you start your business? How long has it been since you started?
- What have you done to market your business?
- What are your goals for your practice?
- If you could wave a magic wand right now, what is the one thing you would want?
- How close are you to getting it?
- What one thing would you most like to improve in your business right now?

# Day 5

**Remove The Resistance** Today is the day I've been waiting for— time to build a funnel! I take all the research I've done on my niche and everything I know about what I can do and build a funnel that will show ANY prospective client in my niche what I can do to help them.

Having a sample funnel that shows the basic concepts I use to help my clients gives prospects something concrete to look at. It goes a long way toward breaking down the internal objections people naturally have when it comes to parting with their money and changing up the way they do things.

**Search And Rescue** Time to go find some more people to help— and I don't even have to leave my house to do it. I just go to Facebook and find a group full of people in my niche. In the ClickFunnels group alone, hundreds of people a day are coming in asking for help.

They are asking for help... and I can help them.

# Day 6

*Plan My Proposals* After hearing me talk about using funnels to drive traffic and converting people into paying clients, and after seeing my sample funnel, my prospective client is blown away. I've hit on their pain points by asking the questions from Day 4. They know they need my help, and I can tell they're a good fit.

It's time to plan out a proposal. Here's how I plan to write one that will land that first (and next) client:

1. *Personalize it.* I'm not afraid to put myself into my proposals. I talk a bit about what I do and why.
2. *Customize it.* This is no time for a one-size-fits-all proposal. Personalized proposals leave a memorable impression.
3. *Be detailed.* I lay it all out for them, step-by-step and day-by-day, so they know what to expect.
4. *Ask for a down payment.* If I require a payment up front, they're a heck of a lot more committed to the project. I figure out the investment they will have to make for the project and break it up into three parts: a down payment plus two equal payments for the remainder.

*Putting Myself Into My Proposals* When crafting my proposals, I'm not afraid to talk about why I do what I do, what makes me stand out from others, and why I'm there to serve them. In fact, that's what sells me best.

Today, I'll take a few minutes to write it out. This is something I can have ready in advance and then add in to proposals as I create them.

## Day 7

***Design My Ultimate Life*** It's time for a check-in. I've been at this for a week now, so I'll take a step back and evaluate how things are going. I ask myself these questions:

- Why am I doing what I'm doing?
- Am I on the right path?
- What positive, happy, healthy, and wealthy steps am I taking today to make me the best version of myself?
- Is the business I'm building now aligned with my vision, mission, and goals, or is it just a means to an end?

Does that last question strike a nerve? Building a business aligned with my vision, mission, and goals is better for long-term sustainability. Anything else is just another roller coaster that will land me back at Day 1 in short order.

Over the next 21 days, I'll be building this business to be the vessel or vehicle that can take me where I want to go over the next decade. I'm not just talking about getting to six figures. I'm talking about setting myself up for wild success, whatever that means to me. And to do that, I have to take moments like this to assess and reflect where I am and where I want to be over the next week and the next and the next.

I will take a few minutes and write down my answers to these two questions:

- What does my ultimate life look like?
- What does achieving my ultimate life mean to me?

## Day 8

***Make First Contact*** It's time to make first contact with the people I found in Facebook Groups on Day 5 who need my help. I remember to choose people in my specific niche, and I send them a private message (PM). I let them know that I read their post and have a few ideas

**488**

that could help them. Then I invite them to join me on a call.

I always try to use video calls because they give me the opportunity to meet with people face-to-face, see their reactions, and bond on a more personal level. Face-to-face nurturing moves them to a place of decision so they take action faster.

Today, I draft an intro message to use as a template when I make first contact. Having the basic framework for the message ready not only saves time but also saves me from those "What do I say? How do I say it?" moments. I type it up, save it in a file, and pull it out when I need it.

The template intro message is just a guide. It's VERY IMPORTANT to make sure I personalize each message for the person I'm contacting and the need they face.

# Day 9

*Remove Pricing Objections* So I'm getting calls scheduled and it's going great. Then it happens...I get the standard price objection.

"That sounds great, but I cannot afford that right now."

Now what? Well, business strategist Roy Cammarano says, "You can always have your way if you have more than one way." I modify this slightly and tell people, "You can always win when there is more than one way to win!"

While I still have them on the call, I ask them a couple of key questions. These questions will give me more information to work with so I can still make this a win—for both me and the prospective client.

- If money were not an object, would you want to work with me?
- If I can come up with a way for us to work together and make it so that you could move forward, would you do so right away?

If they say yes, I schedule another video chat in a few days. Then I get to work finding a way to make it a win. Whether I incentivize the offer with more value bonuses or provide payment-plan options, I can still turn this around while showing my dedication to helping them succeed.

*Sell Small, Win Big* Another effective strategy is to provide service on a lesser scale for a set amount of time. If the prospective client believes they can't afford to have me build out a full-on launch, what if I just offer to build a funnel for the lead magnet for now? Once the leads start pouring in, they can reevaluate and move on to the next level of service.

I think about creative ways I can divide up my proposal into more financially manageable chunks. I want them to see results and feel comfortable bringing me on for more.

## Day 10

*Sign And Onboard My First Client* Today's task is to follow up on my first round of proposals. When I have that signature on the dotted line, I celebrate. I'm on my way! I use ClickFunnels to set up a funnel to automate the client payment process and send my new client the link.

Woo-hoo! I just got paid. Now I repeat the same process for the next client and the next.

*Create A Client Intake Form* In order to get started doing the client work, I need access to their platforms, ad accounts, Google and Bing accounts—all the platforms I need in order to serve them well. To keep this process streamlined, I sit down and create a client intake form that explains what I need from them and how they can give me access. I keep a template version and save it in a file with the first contact message template for later use.

## Day 11

*Set Up For Long-Term Success* Up to this point, my sole focus has been on selling and getting clients. Now that I have a client (or two or three), I have to be careful. The temptation lurks to let up on the gas and turn my focus to the client's project. I can't wait around to start looking for more clients until the project is done.

I must keep pushing on the gas to set myself up for long-term success. Yes, this makes for long days in the beginning. But when I start to get worn down and tired, I think about a turbo jet. They need full throttle to take off, and then once airborne, the pilot can let up on the power. I'm in takeoff mode right now, so I need full acceleration.

*Stage My Day For Success* In order to keep momentum going, I have to devote time to all areas of my business each day. The only way to accomplish this is to be purposeful about my time. My challenge today is to sit down with a planner or calendar and break my days into stages. Here's an example:

- Getting clear and focused; setting my happy, healthy, and wealthy goals > 1 hour
- Process and strategy > 2 hours
- New client gathering/lead generation > 4 hours
- New potential client presentations > 3+ hours
- Current client calls > up to 1.5 hours
- Building funnels and assets > 4+ hours
- Happy and healthy goals >.5+ hours

# Day 12

*Map Out The Campaigns* Things are going to get hectic, especially when I start running projects for multiple clients. I need a good system to keep all the parts in order. I start by mapping out each campaign with the following:

- A funnel (of course)
- A follow-up process, including a remarketing plan for buyers and non-buyers
- Email nurturing sequences
- Facebook and Google pixels installed in funnel
- Facebook and Google ads and ad assets, including images, video content, and copy

As I create this campaign map, I make sure I have a very clear understanding of the client's target market and a plan for which kinds of Facebook Ads will be most effective.

*Take A Break For Fun* I've been working hard, so today I'm going to get out there and have some fun. I'm going to do something just because I enjoy it, to give my brain a break for an hour or two.

# Day 13
*Check In With The Client* While I'm building funnels and designing the ad campaigns, there's one thing I don't want to forget: my client.

I make sure to keep the client updated on their project. It doesn't have to be an elaborate report, just a simple email giving them an update and letting them know how excited I am to be working with them. Now is a great time to ask them for anything else I need, like graphics or video.

*Get Those Referrals* I keep my foot on the gas and pop back into Facebook Groups to look for people who need my help. I also want to ask for referrals.

# Day 14
*Keep Building The Base* The base of my business is my clients. During this first 30 days, I must be committed to building my client base. By now, I've talked to a number of people about how I can help them. So I follow up on all the proposals I've sent.

I find out if they have any questions or concerns. If they've verbally agreed to work with me but I haven't received a signed agreement and payment yet, I ask when I might expect to receive it. I continue to get them excited about working with me by setting up a follow-up launch call the next day.

*Talk It Up* I commit to having conversations with three new prospective clients today. I make it a goal to book at least one video call. Then I do it!

# Day 15

***Push Warm And Lookalike Traffic*** I ask my client for a .csv file with an email list of their best 1,000–5,000 customers. Why? Because warm traffic converts faster and cheaper than cold traffic. I use their email list to create a custom audience for Facebook.

Once I create the custom audience, I can also tell Facebook to create a Lookalike Audience based on the email list. Facebook's algorithm is powerful! It has an amazing engine that will help me identify other potential customers for my clients.

***Check Myself*** I'm halfway there. How's it going? I take a few moments to ask myself:

- Where am I today compared to where I was 15 days ago?
- Where do I want to be 15 days from now?
- Am I doing everything I can to make that happen?
- If not, what can I start doing today in order to get there?

# Day 16

***Teamwork Makes The Dream Work*** Today, I think ahead to the future of my business. If I'm building a business with real revenue, I will eventually need a team. I evaluate what I do well and what I might need help with. Then I ask people who they know with skills in areas where I'm weak or may want additional support.

- Automation
- Copywriting
- Design and graphics
- Facebook
- Google/Bing/Yahoo
- Video
- Webinars

When I create strategic alliances or partnerships with people I can help and vice versa, it's a win-win for everyone.

*Find A Tribe* I am not alone. There are other entrepreneurs out there who will walk beside me as I build this business. Facebook Groups are a great place to connect with others like me, grow my knowledge base, and share ideas and strategies. Today, I find one that resonates with me.

## Day 17

*Plan For My Team* When someone is a good referral source, I provide an ongoing monthly recurring revenue for anything that they bring to us. For example, other funnel consultants often bring us business because it's easier for them to bring us the clients and have us do all the work. Today, I brainstorm a referral system that is win-win-win all the way around.

I think about who might make good referral partners, make a list, and reach out to them.

*Stack My Successes* I take stock of what I've accomplished thus far and stack those successes. I write my accomplishments down so I can use them to create a win stack that will attract more prospective clients.

A win stack is a social media post that celebrates the things I've accomplished for my clients and invites others to learn how I can help their businesses get similar results. I include things like:

- Created a new business.
- Created new clients who will become raving fans.
- Helped many people by providing advice on the Facebook forum.
- Set up payment processing and received payment.
- Launched a funnel for a new client.
- Set up ad campaigns.
- Set up automation.
- Reviewed progress and started optimizing for success.

## Day 18

*Check In Daily* My clients are essentially trusting me with the growth of their businesses. I can show appreciation for that by sending short daily updates on their projects. They will feel important and included, and that will lead to them being more involved in the process. They'll be more excited about what I'm doing, which means they're more likely to respond quickly if I need something from them.

Sending short daily updates also builds in an extra layer of accountability—for them and for me. One of the biggest regrets I have from my earlier days in business is not giving clients a daily update on what we were doing for them. The client felt isolated and it was easier for things to fall through the cracks. So I build 30 minutes into my (or my team's) day to reach out with an email or message.

***Practice Gratitude*** Sometimes when my nose is to the grindstone, it's easy to forget to look up and be grateful for the people and things around me. Today, I challenge myself to do two things to help nurture a sense of gratitude in my life:

1. Make a list of 18 things I'm grateful for.
2. Call three people out of the blue and let them know why I'm grateful for them.

# Day 19

***Stay Visible*** By now, things are really shaping up for the projects I'm working on. It's time to share that with my audience. After all, no one will know what I do and how awesome my results are if I don't tell them. So I hop in to Facebook and get ready to share.

Here are my two favorite methods for communicating wins:

- Do a funnel review via Facebook Live. I walk through what I've set up and why. I remember to share the results the client is having.
- Type up a text post with my client's success so far. I make it about them—celebrating their progress publicly with them.

***Remember My Morning Clarity Session!*** If I've forgotten to take five minutes every morning to get clear on my goals, I reset that practice today. I remind myself who I'm serving and why. I also set one big goal to accomplish each day along with my daily happy, healthy, and wealthy goals.

## Day 20

*Multiply My Progress* I've been working hard, and I'm starting to see results for my clients. If I've helped one business owner to be successful, there's no telling how many lives I'm touching through them. And that's just one business. How many lives do I want to change?

I keep making connections with people who need my help. I stick with the process of sending the initial contact message, booking video calls, and following up. Not every prospect will bite immediately, so I follow up every week or so with those who don't book at first.

*End My Day Well* Ending my day well makes a big difference in moving forward with my goals. I take a few minutes at the end of each day to debrief and set focus for the next day.

- What went well today? What didn't?
- What should I do more of tomorrow? What should I avoid?
- What is one big thing I can do tomorrow to keep moving the needle forward in my business?

## Days 21–29: The Final Stretch

I'm in the home stretch now! It's important I continue to stay focused in order to keep making progress and getting great results for my new clients and my own business. The #1 way I've found to continue producing steady, continuous growth is to block schedule my days.

By blocking out my day for specific activities at specific times, I can really dial in on that ONE THING. Many times, if something is not scheduled, it will never happen. The phone will ring or I'll get sidetracked by emails. I can't fall for that trap. I'm amazed at how efficient I become when I do this consistently.

**496**

Here's an example:

| | |
|---|---|
| > 1 hour | **Work On My Business**<br>Turn off my phone and work only on my own business development. |
| > 2 hours | **Process And Strategy**<br>Turn off my phone and work only on my clients' processes and strategy. |
| > 4 hours | **New Client Gathering And Lead Generation**<br>This doesn't have to take place in one huge four-hour chunk, but it's most effective if I do at least 30 minutes at a time. |
| > 3+ hours | **Revenue-Generating Activities**<br>I set aside time for new potential client presentations and short 20-minute video call meetings. |
| > 1.5 hours | **Current Client Calls And Follow-Up** |
| > 2-6 hours | **Tactical Tasks And Testing**<br>This is the time I spend building the funnels and the assets. I align with or hire those who can help me. Then I set up a process to test everything and make sure all the elements are operating smoothly. |
| > 1+ hours | **Me Time And Family Time** |

***Keep It Simple*** In the past, I have created some pretty complex funnels, but the ones that have converted the best were simple. They were very focused and targeted, and they had a plan to build value and created a message-to-market match. When in doubt, it's best to keep it simple.

Today, I review my schedule. If something seems jumbled or complicated, I consider ways I can simplify.

## Day 30
### *The Finish Line...Or The Starting Line?* Congratulations to me! I've arrived! I am well on my way to having the six-figure business I desire.

However, this is really only the first step on the journey. Building a successful business takes time, planning, and perseverance. It takes saying yes to success and forgetting excuses. If I've learned one thing in the past 30 years in business, it's this:

Those who achieve the highest of highs focus on how and why they can SUCCEED and waste little time complaining or discussing the reasons for lack of success.

# FINAL THOUGHTS

No matter where you are, no matter what your goals, I wish you massive success. Building a business may not be easy, but it is certainly rewarding.

If you follow me through the course of this 30-day journey, you will dig deep—and not just in terms of the time and energy it takes to create a 6-figure business in 30 days. You will delve deep into your purpose and your plan and begin designing your ultimate life. Being aligned internally with what you want to achieve is key to not only your well-being but also to the external success of your business. This makes your business sustainable in the long term. And I want you to know something...

The sky's the limit, seriously.

So many people remain in jobs, careers, and even relationships that aren't working for them. The status quo is more comfortable than the fear of the unknown. Remember, excitement and fear are the same

**498**

emotions with a shift in perspective.

You can be, you can do, and you can have all that life has to offer. You are worth it.

Take little steps (or big), one at a time, and surround yourself with a tribe of like-minded people who are rising together. Believe amazing things will happen and, when obstacles appear, realize they are just challenges testing your commitment to the future and the life you want to create.

I wish you all the success in the world.

David

# RESOURCES

- ClickFunnels

# Chapter 29

# CONNECT ON INSTAGRAM

*by Raoul Plickat*

# RAOUL PLICKAT

## *Owner*

Sales and Marketing
*www.IBuildBrands.com*

*New York Times bestselling Author Neil Patel called Raoul Plickat 'the Kingmaker' for his abilities to massively leverage the success of influencers. He is the strategic mind behind the biggest sales and personal development trainers in the German speaking market with more than 100.000 live attendees p.a. He is also e-commerce advisor for the biggest brands in sport and nutrition market.*

What would I do if I had 30 days to start over again?

## Days 1–3

I will define my strengths.
What am I good at? What can I do better than others?
Where can I help others to solve their problems with my strengths?
First, I would define five categories where I could help others.

- Building funnels
- Making Facebook Ads
- Building e-campaigns
- Writing copy
- Growing an Instagram channel

Next, I would go to Amazon and, for each topic, order a couple of books to help me train the unique selling points and provide potential clients with a lot of value up-front when I meet with them so they have the feeling that I'm exactly the person they are looking for.

My focus is on getting my product ready to sell. Nothing more. Later, I can optimize it and make it look nicer.

I would focus on one industry, because focus is key. For example, local restaurants, hotels, lawyers, or doctors.

*"The man who catches two rabbits catches neither."*
— Confucius

Before I continue with the acquisition process, I need to define my purpose. I have the skills, but without a purpose, I can't excel! Money is the easy part. But money motivation takes you only so far. A real purpose with a meaning brings you further than everything else.

So where can I help others with my skills to make a positive impact?
I need to define the purpose really clearly. Otherwise it's useless.
So for example, it could look like this:

*I want to help people in <INDUSTRY> with my extraor-*

*dinary skills in copywriting so they can sell more of their amazing products to the people who really need it and help them end their suffering.*

## Days 4–6

Time for goals.

First, I'll define the long-term goals. Before I can do that, I'll list three role models and write down what I admire them for.

Here are some of my role models:

- *Dwayne "The Rock" Johnson:* I admire him for his work ethic. For waking up at 4am, hitting the gym twice a day, and making successful movies.
- *Elon Musk:* I admire him for traveling the unpaved road. He must have all the same doubts and fears as many of us, yet he still keeps going and achieving.
- *Cristiano Ronaldo:* I admire him for working so hard on his skills to becoming the best footballer in the world. He's the best example of mastering one skill in a lifetime with a laser focus. Training almost every day for more than two decades while others were partying.

Now I need to put these into context with my long-term goals. I will set long-term goals for four years, eight years, and twelve years from now.

It's all about the person I want to become. In order to transform, I need to have the habits of this future person.

The size of the goals makes a big impact. Whether I want to lead 10, 100, or 1,000 people may seem in the beginning like a small decision. But it's like a one- or two-degree difference when we aim a rocket at the moon. In reality, it makes a big difference whether we hit or miss the target.

So I need to go big or go home.

What do I want achieve in eight years?

- Company with 100 people
- Habit of going to the gym four times a week
- Vegetarian/vegan diet
- Car
- Ten apartments

Then I will cut the time frame in half. Four years is enough for those goals. After I have achieved this, I will ask myself what I want to have achieved eight years later. And cut that timeframe in half also. I'll follow the same process until I have goals set for the next twelve years.

Short-term goals should be set for these time periods:

- Each quarter
- Every six months
- One year
- Two years
- Three years

Short-term goals are milestones to compare what I have achieved and also hold myself accountable to push forward.

Let's start with the money.

I want to earn $10,000 per month.

For that to happen, I need one of these results:

- 5 clients per month x $2,000
- 2 clients per month x $5,000
- 1 client per month x $10,000

Then I would move on to calculating how many appointments I would need with an estimated closing rate of 40%–50%.

In order to have clear goals, I also need to link my long-term goals with the numbers. So how much money do I need to earn until year X to buy this car, these apartments, and so on for the whole twelve years.

For the eight-year goal, these numbers might seem crazy right now.

## Days 7–9

Now it's all about the vision. I have the purpose. I have the long-term goals. But the numbers might seem a little bit high. A little bit uncomfortable. Maybe even unrealistic. But what's real and what's not? My mind decides.

So I need a vision. I need to get creative. To dream a little bit.

Key questions here are:

1. What can I do differently to achieve this goal?
2. Did anybody else achieve something similar in another industry? If yes, what did they do?
3. What should the structure look like to achieve this?

When these questions are answered, I have the mindset part done. Vision, purpose, and goals are clear.

I know why I want to wake up every morning and work my a$$ off. Great feeling.

Now it's about client acquisition. About 80% of the time should be spent on selling. Not on logos, offices, etc.

So I focus on one industry I can help with their pain points. I start in the local market.

I first find all the business meetings, lunches, and dinners I can on LinkedIn and plan to attend in the following months.

Because contacts are everything. And the people I surround myself with are key for my success.

As a second step, I will review a few bigger local potential clients' websites, ads, or emails and send my notes to them with an offer to optimize these for free in return for a testimonial. My goal is to get three to five testimonials.

I will make a template for short case studies, which I will use the testimonials for.

## Days 10–17

On LinkedIn, I will look for the owners or CEOs of my target local businesses. When I find them, I will also try to find them on Instagram. A lot of important, wealthy people are on Instagram with a small number of followers. So to engage with them in a non-salesy way after finding some similar interests is way easier there than on LinkedIn, and doubles my chances of landing a deal. I would not offer them my services in the messages there but simply engage with a picture or a story.

If they follow me back, this will be a key success. Because now I can show the work I do on Instagram Stories and share the testimonials I got for free, without addressing it directly. And these people will feel that I might be able to help them without feeling like I need them as a client.

So I automatically position myself as an authority. This, in addition to the testimonials from the big names, will allow me to charge higher prices. Because my prospects will want the same results.

I will also turn my personal Facebook profile into a business profile so I can leverage my success with Facebook Ads.

I will set up a basic lead-gen funnel with ClickFunnels. At the beginning, I will take the basic account for $97 per month. I will connect it with Active Campaign and take their basic lead account as well, for $49 per month. Then I will fill the pipeline with prospects to call and qualify, and also build in some basic automation.

I will then do some basic Facebook Ads. I plan to spend no more than $100–$150 per week. I will send these people all to my website, where they can request a custom review of their website or their services for free.

- Campaign #1 will only be for the local market within a few miles and only for my chosen industry and some additional interests.
- Campaign #2 will be a retargeting campaign for people who interacted with me on Instagram. Since I'm using this site daily for non-pitchy prospect engagement, these people will see my offer from my ads, which will boost my authority and help me to automatically close them.
- Campaign #3 will be a repeat of the second campaign but for website visitors and Facebook page engagers.

I will now focus on delivering the reviews. For that, I will do Zoom calls with each prospect, making a voice-over as I review their content and mixing in a presentation filled with case studies where I show how I changed similar things for others and brought them X% more clients.

Some people prefer to meet in person, so I will also offer that, showing up with a notebook and giving a live presentation. At the end, I will hand out a service contract with a zero-risk guarantee and present an offer stack like Russell explains in his books.

## Days 18–20

Time to get the unique selling proposition (UPS) clear, which will give me an advantage in the market.

Three aspects of a rock-solid USP include:

1. It needs to appear unique.
2. It has to be useful. It's always better to promote something (a feature) that is useful and make it look unique, instead of having a unique feature with no use in the market (yet).
3. It must be simple enough to be understood by a ten-year-old.

Here is an example:

> *We help lawyers in <CITY> find more clients with Facebook Ads while you spend not one minute in the ad account! Get your FREE review now, and find out if this is applicable to your business. Click here to RSVP now!*

I would now refine all my ads with the new USP. I would also make a video with the case studies including the hero's journey and the Epiphany Bridge concepts mentioned in Russell's book Expert Secrets. I'll put these on Facebook and YouTube and advertise them for $20 per day.

With my brand, I will be known for...

- One amazing story (backstory)

- One carefully mastered competency (my skill)
- One great characteristic that others admire (such as integrity, discipline, or humbleness)

For this, I would pay the income of one client for a short professional movie. I see it as in investment, because people buy from people.

To create an experience with my business, now I would ask myself the following questions:

- How can I help my clients feel like they are members of something special?
  - What do they like? What do they do in their free time?
  - Everything I can collect will be put into the content relationship manager so I have all the details for each customer in one place.
- What is my specific message for my target market? Not the USP, but what words do THEY use? What is their language?
- What is my business really about?
- Can I offer a faster service?
- Can I offer a more personal experience? (Not every industry needs a "personal" touch, but this could also mean providing reports delivered on time with a little bit of personalization.)
- What can I further automate?

# Days 20–30

The last 10 days of the month will be spent on scaling and automation.

I've got customers. Now I need more customers. And maybe I need upsells. And at the same time, I'm still alone and need to make time for new clients, so I need to automate some things, which will save me time that I can then invest in money-earning activities.

*First automation: Facebook Ads* Facebook has a feature called Rules. With Rules, I can define actions. For example, when a lead gets too expensive, I can reduce the ad set budget by 15%. Or scale the ad set when the lead is very cheap. All automatically. Now I can set a couple of rules and the Facebook Ads for all my clients will be automated.

Another tool I will choose to use is Companion Labs, which give performance updates of my ad campaigns within five minutes, saving me around an hour a day and helping me with the budget settings and scaling of single assets.

**Reports** For reports, I will use the tool called AgencyAnalytics. It will make beautiful reports for my customers and save me a couple of hours every week. It will also help to improve my customers' happiness. A big plus factor for my services.

**Bookkeeping** For invoices and expenses, I will switch from Excel to Fiskl. This tool helps me to write and send invoices within just a few minutes and gives me a clear picture of my actual cash situation right now. It also reminds me about the expenses and outstanding invoices with a beautiful dashboard.

**Automated Webinar** I will use ClickFunnels' automated webinar feature for this with some Funnel Hacker CF pro tools like the chat box and some check-box features. Over the next 10 days, I will try to generate leads for the webinar via Facebook and LinkedIn and send them directly to an offer page. For the payments, I will use CopeCart, which will automatically send perfectly taxed invoices to customers and can transfer the money straight to my bank account without me having to set up a Stripe, PayPal, or any merchant account.

**Second Scaling** During the last five days, I will spend my time on radical scaling. I need to grow now and also need money to hire people.

So everything now is about asking the right questions and extreme implementation.

1. *What do I have to do to increase the average spend of new and existing customers?*

   Answer: I need to bring in upsells. For example, extremely fast setup in the next 48 to 72 hours instead of 3 weeks. I can argue that in the saved 21 days, the customer will get an instant return on their investment, after the second customer gets their money back.

For existing customers, I need to bring in a value ladder. So when something is working, I'll expand the services further. For example to Google AdWords or LinkedIn advertising. About 20% of customers buy the premium option. I'll offer consultation for high-ticket prices, bundle products, and have a sales campaign every six weeks.

2. *How can I increase my own daily revenue?*

Answer: Check to see whether my numbers are correct. Do I get more income than I spend on my own advertising? If yes, I can set a rule to increase the ad budget every day by 5% as long as I'm profitable. Are the people buying? How is the follow-up looking with prospects who don't buy? Is anybody complaining yet? Increase the follow-up and automate it.

Also, I need to hire salespeople.

3. *What else do I need to do to get more customers?*

Answer: Ask for referrals from existing clients. Go to the next nearby town. Test different target groups in the ads. Do A/B tests of my lead-gen page. Test every single step.

4. *What is the most radical action that will make the absolute biggest impact?*

Answer: A very good offer. Maybe newspaper ads. Maybe an event. Maybe a charity event. Maybe a launch. Social proof.

5. *What is the fastest way I can double my new customer rate?*

Answer: For whatever works well right now, increase the input. Is it ads? Double the ad spend and pay close attention. Is it referrals? Ask for more referrals. Is it follow-up? Send more follow-up emails. Is it a Facebook Group? Invite more people, do more live streams, pitch more. In essence, DO MORE OF WHAT WORKS NOW!

## 510

What I would do after the 30 days:

1. Hire salespeople.
2. Hire people for daily tasks, one for each department: one for emails, automation, and copy; one for landing pages and design; and one for Facebook Ads.
3. Outsource bookkeeping and taxes.
4. When I break the $60K per year mark, hire a chef.
5. When I break the $100K per year mark, hire a driver.
6. When I break the $15K per month mark, I'll buy in to a high-end mastermind to surround myself with the right people.

I would focus on three things.

1. Buying more time.
2. Cutting the learning curve. Avoiding mistakes others made already.
3. Working ON the business instead of IN it.

That's it. I wish you a lot of success.

Raoul Plickat

# RESOURCES

- Active Campaign (ontraport.com)
- AgencyAnalytics (agencyanalytics.com)
- Amazon.com
- Companion Labs (companionlabs.com)
- CopeCart (copecart.com)
- Expert Secrets by Russell Brunson
- Facebook Ads
- Fiskl (fiskl.com)
- Google AdWords
- Instagram Stories
- Zoom (zoom.us)

# Chapter 30

# HIGH-TICKET CONSULTING

## by James P. Friel

# JAMES P. FRIEL

## *CEO*

### B2B Consulting
*JamesPFriel.com*

*James P. Friel is an author, entrepreneur and consultant who helps entrepreneurs systemize, grow and scale their businesses by getting them out of the day to day operations of running their companies so they can make more money and have more time and freedom.*

*Prior to running his own companies, James was the Global Head of Digital Strategy for HSBC Bank, where he led teams across three continents and five countries to double online sales for the bank.*

*Since leaving the corporate world in 2011, James has simultaneously run multiple 7 figure companies and has consulted with CEOs, entrepreneurs and executive level staff at companies ranging from Fortune 50 corporations to smaller, more entrepreneurial ventures helping them systematically increase efficiency while also growing their sales.*

*James holds a Bachelor of Science from Embry-Riddle Aeronautical University and lives in Boise, Idaho where, in addition to being a student of the game of business, he enjoys working out, drumming and skiing.*

## How To Start A Successful High-Ticket Consulting Business In 30 Days Or Less

Being asked to write this chapter was actually a pretty exciting proposition. Not because I have a strong need for recognition among the other giants who have written chapters in here (though I am grateful for that opportunity), but more because in the entirety of my career, I don't think I've ever been challenged so much with the question posed in this book.

If you had lost everything and needed to start over in 30 days, what would you do?

What an incredible question and thank you, Russell, for asking it. Thankfully, it's been a very long time since I found myself in a situation like that.

At the beginning of my journey, there was so much trial and error, one chapter certainly wouldn't be able to contain it. But having experienced this situation in real life nearly 20 years ago and turning my raw hunger and desire for success into actual success, I'm eager to share with you what I would do now if given only 30 days to get myself back on stable and successful footing.

My 30-day plan that follows is not wizardry, and there is honestly nothing very fancy about what I'm going to share. I am focused on doing a few simple things right and not worrying about all the rest. These are the steps I have taken to go from a broke kid who desperately wanted success to the businessman who is now writing this chapter from a rooftop terrace in Venice, Italy, while enjoying a glass of beautiful Italian wine without a care in the world.

I'm not interested in hustling. I'm not interested in grinding. What I am incredibly interested in doing though are those few simple things that make the biggest difference in allowing me to have the space and time to create exactly the life that I want.

For you, that may be buying the home of your dreams, giving your children more than you had when you were growing up, taking a dream vacation, or as crazy as buying a professional sports team. It doesn't matter what the specifics of your goals and ambitions are, it all starts with the fundamentals. And the better you get at the fundamentals, the more often you will win at whatever you choose to do.

This chapter is about mastering three things: prioritizing what you should focus on, understanding the people you are selling to, and selling them something that solves a problem. That's it. Nothing fancy.

But don't let the simplicity of these things fool you...when done following the steps I'm about to share, you can literally control your destiny—even if you are starting from scratch, just like I once did.

I am grateful for the honor to share with you, and I know that if you implement the steps I'm about to outline, you WILL be successful.

So with that said, let's get started on my 30-day plan!

## Day 1: Set My 30-Day Goal

It's vital to know what I am shooting for. For some people, it might be creating $10,000 per month in income; for others, it will be more or less but by only working a certain number of hours per week; for some, it will be to lay the foundation for a multiple seven-figure business.

There is no right or wrong answer here. It is my goal. The important thing is to identify what I'm shooting for. I believe that we're all like heat-seeking missiles—if we give the missile a target, we're much more likely to hit it than if we just fire away without any specific goal in mind.

If I don't know what I want, the chances of me getting it are slim to none. I can always modify or adjust my goal later on, but I absolutely need to be clear on what my first target is.

For a long time, I heard that we should all "shoot for the moon" and have big, hairy, audacious goals—goals that make people laugh at us. I subscribed to this train of thought for a long time...until I heard about research that clearly states that in timeframes of less than three years, if your goal feels scary or possibly unattainable, it will actually be counterproductive.

So with this science-based research in mind, I will set a goal that feels like a bit of a stretch but doesn't terrify me. This means I will pick a target that I think I can reasonably achieve in the next 30 days. I would definitely prefer to hit my first goal and keep going over choosing a goal that scares the living sh*t out of me and then throwing in the towel four days in.

With that said, I'll pick a goal that is aggressive yet reasonable for me to hit in the next 30 days. This could be anywhere from bringing on my first paying client, making an extra $10K per month, or something beyond either one of those.

I'll spend as much of my time today as possible reflecting and thinking about this because this will be my ABSOLUTE target for the next 30 days. In fact, I don't need to get anything else done today. Right now, this is what matters most.

## Day 2: Take a Deep Breath And Set up a Daily Routine

Some people like to rush into things, but I really don't think that's the right move. In fact, Abraham Lincoln once said, "Give me six hours to chop down a tree and I will spend the first four sharpening the axe."

Considering he was one of the most influential men in the last several hundred years, I would pay close attention to those words.

Preparation is the key to victory. If I rush into something without contemplating my strategy and how I'm going to move forward, I might be super excited, but it will possibly be in the wrong direction. Understanding that progress is not measured simply by activity but by the ground I've gained toward achieving my goal, it's imperative to take a few moments to center myself and make sure I am clear on how to move forward.

That's what Day 2 is all about.

Today, I want to set up a daily routine.

Have you ever seen a professional NBA player like Lebron James take a free-throw shot? He does the EXACT same thing each and every time. This is the routine he uses to get himself in the right state to be able to consistently deliver when it counts. And it's not just NBA players. Professional athletes in all sports use routines to get their minds into the games they play. From golfers to soccer players, athletes who are competing at the highest levels imaginable use routines to perform at their best.

Now, I'm not talking about getting myself psyched up for a physically intense battle, but rather about the routine I'll use to get myself ready for my day so that I get the most out of it and make all of my effort and energy count toward my goal.

There are a few important parts of my routine that I want to build today.

1. *Pick a time I will wake up.* This might sound silly, but if I can't control what time I get out of bed, I'll have a much lower chance of controlling the way the rest of the things in my life play out each day.

2. *Visualize my goal after I wake up.* This could be picturing it in my mind, writing my goal down five times, or displaying a vision board in my office. I just need to find a consistent way each day of reinforcing my goal to myself so that I am clear about what I am shooting for.

3. *Create a time block on my calendar for "deep work."* Deep work

is the stuff that actually creates the results once I strip away the busywork. The remaining steps in this 30-day plan will be the deep work that I need to do, and it's super important that I have dedicated time for it; otherwise, all I'll be left with are good intentions.

Just to elaborate on why Step 4 is so important, I want to share the following.

See, most of us fall prey to sacrificing our attention to the urgent things flying at us from all different directions—Facebook, email, text messages, phone calls. And while some of these things may be important from time to time, the MOST important thing you will ever do during your day is understanding what you truly need to do that day that will give you the biggest bang for your buck.

Cal Newport wrote an incredible book called Deep Work. While I think you should absolutely pick up a copy and read it, I will summarize it for you in a sentence. Anyone in history who has ever accomplished ANYTHING substantial and lasting has carved out the time to make that thing a priority.

So today, I want to build out my "pre-game" routine. Much like a professional athlete has a pre-game or pre-shot routine, I want to have a clear plan on what I will do each and every day to set myself up for success.

1. What time will I wake up?
2. How will I visualize my goal (writing, visualization, looking at pictures)?
3. What time during the day will I be focused on my deep work? This can change each day if needed, but I will make sure I have at least one hour blocked out for this every day.

# Day 3: Talk With Everyone I Know and Find Out Where People Are Struggling

So for the first two days, you might possibly be thinking this 30-day plan is going to be all about me climbing high on a mountain in Tibet

**518**

somewhere and strategizing my way to success. It's not. But setting the stage for being as effective as possible is important if I actually want to get results.

That said, Day 3 is where the action begins. Now it's time to roll!

So I'll begin the shift into starting to sell something and make some money.

As a precursor to Day 3, I think it's important to remind myself of something that, once heard, is blindingly obvious but not always remembered.

Success in business comes down to one main thing—finding a problem someone has and then getting them to pay you to solve it for them. That's it.

So today is about finding that problem.

I will be reaching out to everyone I've ever met (in person and on social media) letting them know I'm starting a new business and then asking them this question: "What is the single biggest challenge you're currently facing in your life or business right now?"

I'll let them talk with me. Write down everything they say and listen like my future depends on it, because it just might. This is an intentionally open-ended question. I want people to spill their guts to me.

Some of them might say that their spouse is holding them back from pursuing their dreams, others might say they feel like they have no energy to get things done and "crash" during the middle of the day, and some might tell me they just can't find qualified leads to buy their widget.

Regardless of the responses, I'll keep track of them and won't try to force people to say what I hope they will.

One last thing for Day 3. How many people will I need to talk with in order for this to work? I will simply talk with everyone I possibly can—5, 10, 20, or better yet, 100 people. I will go for broke here and make sure that I am sprinting on this day and getting as many responses as possible. If I only have a few people to talk with, so be it. But I bet I have more people than I expect. And I'm not trying to sell these people anything right now—I'm just doing market research to help chart my course.

## Day 4: Sort Responses Into Three Categories

Whatever responses I received from all of the people I talked with on Day 3, now I need to categorize them into one of three buckets. I love the way Russell Brunson simplified this in his book Expert Secrets. He said there are three main niches that you can make money in: health, wealth, and relationships. So almost any problem people have that they want to solve will fall into one of those three categories.

So today's assignment is pretty easy...take all of the responses I got yesterday and make three lists by sorting them into one of those three categories. I don't need to worry about anything else right now. I just need to categorize ALL responses to the question "What is the single biggest challenge you're currently facing in your life or business right now?" into one of those three buckets.

## Day 5: Evaluate My Strengths and Market Opportunities to Look For a Match

Today, it's time to be brutally honest with myself. I'll need to accurately self-evaluate what I am great at doing and what I'm not so great at.

Every single person on planet Earth has only a small group of things that they are really, really good at and also has a whole bunch of things that really aren't in their wheelhouse.

Some people have the patience of a saint and can be a first-grade teacher dealing all day with children who have runny noses and can't sound out their words, while many of us (including me) would want to run straight out of that classroom and make a beeline for the nearest bar. And then there are some people who adore spreadsheets like it's their love language and others who break out in hives if they think there's even a remote chance they'll need to open Microsoft Excel.

I won't judge myself for not being good at everything, because nobody actually is. It's way better to find the few things where I really shine and focus on those.

The good news is that I'll make far more money by focusing on my strengths, and chances are really good that I'll be much happier as well.

And I can make really good money doing almost anything. As long as there are people who have a problem that I can solve, I'll be able to make money. So during this exercise, I won't censor myself to try and figure out what the "right" answer is.

I will just focus on today's activity with as much objectivity as possible.

So going back to the three main categories from yesterday, now it's time to rank my strengths and passions from 1 to 3. Which one of those things do I have the most experience in, knowledge of, and passion for?

For example, I might rank them like this:

1. *Wealth:* helping people make money
2. *Health:* helping people get fit and healthy
3. *Relationships:* helping people have satisfying and fulfilling relationships with others or themselves

There are no right or wrong answers.

Once I'm done with this initial ranking, I'll take my top area and create a list expanding on all of the things that I'm good at within that category.

For example, if my top category is health, what exactly am I really good at regarding this topic? It might be bodybuilding or it could be running in obstacle course races like the Tough Mudder. For others, it might be dialing in on a specific diet revolving around macronutrients or an advanced understanding of supplements or biohacking.

So under my TOP category, I'll create subcategories that expand on all of the things I am good at and enjoy.

## Day 6: Cross-Reference Market Opportunities and Look for a Match

Today, I will take all of the answers I had for my strengths for each category and subcategory and match them up against the responses I got from my market research. I only need to worry about the responses I got that are in my top-strength category. So if my top category is wealth, then I only need to examine the answers people gave me that fit under the wealth umbrella.

What I'm looking for in people's answers are patterns. Patterns of what areas they are struggling with, where they are feeling pain, and challenges that are preventing them from having the lives that they want.

For example, this entire chapter is written for people who are challenged in getting their financial life back together or starting out in the first place. It's clearly under the wealth umbrella.

Contrast that with someone who is awesome at helping people get fit and in shape. Their strength falls under the health category, and they would be writing a chapter along the lines of "How To Melt 10 Lbs. Of Fat And Become A Living Example Of Vibrant Health And Energy In The Next 30 Days."

Generally speaking, even when I ask, most people are not going to be able to tell me EXACTLY what they want, but their answers should serve as the basis for helping me get in the ballpark.

Henry Ford is widely attributed as saying that if he had given people what they wanted, he would have simply built a faster horse. As we all know, he built a car instead, which more effectively served his market, even though they didn't know how to ask for it.

So I'll have to use a little deductive reasoning here, but based on responses, I should get a decent idea where the pain in my market is.

Fortunately, my job here is not going to require an intense amount of innovation. I'm not going to spend hours in research and development to come up with some new technological innovation. Instead, I'm focusing my energy much more on something short term—finding a set of specific problems in my market that aligns with my expertise and then consulting people to help them get specific results.

## Day 7: Identify and Write Out my Avatar

Okay, with the exercises from Day 6 complete, I'm now getting clearer on what problems exist within my market that I have the background, experience, and ability to solve for people. Now it's time to sharpen up my focus on exactly who I will be selling to and doing

**522**

this service for.

Although every single exercise in this chapter is important, I don't think the importance of defining my avatar can be overstated. The reason is this: the clearer I get on who I am selling to, what their pains and struggles are, and what is keeping them up at night, the easier it will be for me to identify them and for them to know I'm the right person to help them.

Put another way, I'm going for the sniper approach here. A sniper knows his target, finds his target, gets them in the crosshairs, and takes careful aim. This is in contrast with someone who is using a shotgun and sprays a general area.

Snipers go after high-value targets, and when you're looking for a specific person with a specific problem, that's what you're doing as well. I must be precise. EVERYTHING else will fall into place much faster and easier if I spend time to wrestle with these questions.

For something as important as this step, I'm going to include a real example I created a long time ago for one of my businesses, AutoPilot Entrepreneur.

I learned these simple questions and this approach from the legendary copywriter, John Carlton, who I had the privilege of studying with directly. Not so surprisingly, he has used these exact same questions to help him get started on many, many successful copywriting engagements.

As you read the example below, what I want you to notice is how this isn't just some demographic nonsense. It paints a clear picture of who this person is and what problems and challenges they have.

I encourage you not to dismiss the simplicity of these questions, and I'm extremely confident when I say that your ability to zero in on your avatar is one of the greatest determining factors of success in your future.

## Example Avatar

Who am I selling to?

- Entrepreneur
- Ambitious and growth-oriented

- Male
- Age range is 25–45
- Has been successful at getting traction with his own business and has gotten things "off the ground"; in many cases, he is even to a point where sales are performing reasonably well
- Has at least a two or three people working for him, but in some cases already has a larger team of 10, 15, or 20+
- Is comfortable with technology
- Is seen as the "creator" or "visionary" of the business

What are his needs? Where does it hurt?
- He is a bottleneck in his business—too many things still depend on him, and this has him feeling stretched thin and sometimes overwhelmed.
- He doesn't always know what the people working for him are doing. Suspects that they could be more productive, but doesn't know how to make that happen.
- He would like to spend more time working ON his business, but still spends too much time working IN the day-to-day operations.
- He doesn't necessarily like having to manage people, but does so because he knows getting the right people doing the right things will give him leverage.
- His team is not on the same page as him about what needs to be done. This leads to lots of wasted time and effort and also pulls him in when it shouldn't really be necessary.
- He wants to be able to have more "free" time to do with as he pleases, whether that is spending more time having fun with family or friends, pursuing a hobby, working more strategically on his own business, or any combination of those things.
- He wants to step away for a trip or a vacation, but knows he will be stressed the whole time thinking of all the things that could go wrong.
- He keeps track of way too many things in his own head or on scraps of paper, on sticky notes, or in an online system that has been poorly adopted. This results in many things falling through

the cracks.

- He wants to grow his business, but knows that things aren't systemized and that too much growth would cause things to fall apart.
- He feels scattered, disorganized, and far less productive than he would like. This is true for him and his team.
- He always feels there's too much to do and too little time.
- He feels stuck inside his business.

What does he need to hear from me to feel good about buying?
- His problems are normal and he is not the only one facing these challenges.
- Because of the success he's already had, systemizing his approach to operating his business won't take a huge time commitment or an agonizing system implementation project.
- It is not as hard as he thinks it will be. This proven method has worked for many other entrepreneurs.
- This new system will not require him to do yet another job, rather it will empower his team to do things with greater clarity and efficiency and put him in a position to see everything all in one place.
- My training comes with a 100% money-back, risk-free guarantee.
- With my approach, I can systemize most businesses in three hours or less.
- I will include video training for any new hires he brings on in the future so he won't have to waste time getting new people up to speed. They will be productive from Day 1 because there will be a system for them to plug into.

## Day 8: Build an Offer

Now that I've gotten a clear picture of who I'm selling to, it's time to actually start doing some marketing! A lot of people think that marketing is just about spending money on advertising. That's not true at all and really short-changes the true art and science of marketing.

Marketing is creating a message targeted to your ideal client with the goal of getting them to raise their hand.

Paid advertising may or may not be a part of that. People who just run out and start spending money on ads without considering their avatars, hooks, and offers will undoubtedly flush money down the toilet. So it's imperative to understand that I need to get a hook and an offer in place to start getting people to raise their hands.

My offer needs to showcase the result that people can expect to get when they work with me. It doesn't have to list out every detail that I'm going to do for them, but it needs to help them understand what to expect.

It is literally what I am OFFERING to do for them.

It should be able to be summarized in a headline, but it doesn't need to be (nor should it be) all hype, which will either go over most people's heads or just turn them off.

Here are a few examples of offers expressed as headlines for each of the main categories discussed earlier.

- *Wealth:* "How To Get 5 New Seller Leads A Day For Your Real Estate Business Without Paid Ads"
- *Health:* "How To Easily Lose 10 Lbs. Of Fat Even If You've Already Tried Keto, Paleo, Intermittent Fasting, And Every Other Diet Fad Out There"
- *Relationships:* "Restore Your Marriage To Honeymoon Status In 14 Days Even If You Are Currently Headed To Divorce Court"

Clearly, these offers will appeal to different people, which is why once again it's so important to know who I'm talking to and what challenges they're facing.

For the right people, these offers will be appealing. For the wrong person, they will barely even notice, which is exactly the point.

If your relationship is rock solid, you'll never even pay attention to the third headline above, but if your marriage is crumbling before your eyes and you'd love to save it, the third headline is going to call out to you.

This is the essence of marketing—target and offer.

# Day 9: Find My Keystone Client and Build My Initial List in the Process

Today, I'll take my newly minted offer and knowledge of my avatar and go looking for a very important person in this whole process: the Keystone Client.

Because I want to be able to charge top dollar for my consulting, in a really counterintuitive move, I'm going to find my first client and deliver massive value to them for free.

You see, many people actually slow down their sales growth by trying to go in for the kill too soon.

Here's what I mean: If you're new in business or just starting something new, you're an unproven entity, and most people will have a hard time paying you if they feel like they are your guinea pig. And if they do pay you, it's not going to be top dollar.

So today, I'm going to make my offer to the market totally irresistible by giving it away for FREE.

Everybody likes free, but they will also be a little suspicious of WHY it's free. There's got to be a catch, right?

Of course, I'm in business to make money, not to just get people to like me, so there is a catch. It's pretty straightforward though. If I deliver the result that is important to my target client, I simply want them to create a testimonial video for me to use to help me find more people like them.

So I'll go back to the people I already talked with, post on social media, pick up the phone, and call the ones I know might be interested. I'll also ask my friends and family for people they know who might want what I have.

I'll let everyone know there is no charge, I am simply starting a pilot program, am looking for people I can help with my new approach, and would like to create an amazing case study.

Basically, I'll share the offer that I wrote yesterday and then ask people to raise their hands if they would like to find out how to be part of this pilot program.

A few awesome things will happen when I take this approach.

First, even though I only need one person to be my Keystone Client, chances are really good that way more people than that will raise their hands. This is my initial list. Later on, after I've created great results for my Keystone Clients, I can go back to these same people and make the same offer, but at that point I will be charging for it.

Second, if I have any level of "sales jitters," this will help me get into the game and start interacting with my ideal client without having to get all bashful about charging for it.

Lastly, this will give me an opportunity to refine the way I communicate my offer to my target client based on the feedback I get from my market.

## Day 10: Develop and Document My Strategy and Process

Back in the day, I studied aerospace engineering in college, and some of my classes like physics and chemistry required labs. In those labs, we had to follow the scientific method very carefully to make sure that were documenting our experiments in such a way that they could be repeated again and again and still yield the same results.

Now, while I don't need to get all super nerdy, I do need to create at minimum a high-level outline with the steps and sub-steps that I will take my client through to help them achieve the result.

I don't need to overthink this. Because this is my area of expertise, I will be able to just write down how I'll approach getting my new client the result I promised as part of my offer.

Writing this down will help in a few ways.

First, it will be a good roadmap for me to follow so that I stay on track. Also, if something goes wrong, I'll be able to more quickly isolate where the trouble might have occurred so I can fix it for the next time. And lastly, I'll be setting myself up for future success, so that as I start onboarding a number of new clients in the near future, I'll have a systematic way of serving those clients.

## Days 11–13: Implement Strategy for my Keystone Client

Today is a really exciting day and a key milestone, because I am now working with my ideal client and helping them in the way my offer suggests. Because I've followed the steps above for each day before this, I am in good shape to deliver an outstanding result for my new client and get a great case study!

If I'm going to be a great consultant, I must learn to master managing expectations.

One of my earliest mentors was an exceptionally successful businessman. His name is Keith Cunningham, and one of my favorite quotes of his is: "All upset comes from unmet expectations."

Think about the last time you got annoyed or upset by something. Got a memory in your mind? If so, I bet you expected something different than what actually happened.

No matter how hard you try, you're never going to be able to control every part of a consulting engagement, so it's important to have realistic expectations going into it. And it's equally important that you clearly communicate your expectations with your client.

The last thing in the world I want is for my client to expect that they will be getting fresh, hot leads within 24 hours when it actually might take 5 days. There's a lot of relationship capital put on the line during any consulting engagement, so it's best not to waste it trying to calm someone down after they're already fired up.

Put another way is one of my favorite quotes from Einstein: "Intellectuals solve problems; geniuses prevent them."

Setting the proper expectations up front and all along the way will make me look like a consulting genius.

(If you ever want some excellent reading on the topic of managing client expectations as a consultant, pick up a copy of Peter Block's book Flawless Consulting.

Now it's time for me to get down to business and start delivering the value I promised in my offer.

For various projects, this can literally be anything from running Facebook, Google, or Pinterest ads to creating a custom workout plan for people who are looking to get chiseled, to get over a bad breakup, or needing a sales funnel or new branding.

The point is that I can make money consulting on almost any topic imaginable. I just do my thing and get my client over that hump of whatever is holding them back. That's my biggest job over these next few days.

## Days 14–20

There are three main things I need to do over the next week.

1. *Continue working to create a KILLER result for my Keystone Client.* This is the time to go all in on making this client engagement an overwhelming success. Even though I'm not getting paid cash on this engagement, I will be getting paid in credible social proof that will yield dividends for months and years to come. So I'll work on getting my client a KILLER result like that is my only job...because it is. That is the only thing that matters right now. If there's a snag, I'll fix it. If I sense that expectations are out of alignment, I'll recalibrate them. Continue to maintain clarity on the result I am trying to help my client achieve, but it must be real, tangible, and specific, because the more I can quantify the results I got for my Keystone Client, the easier it will be to sell similar engagements to similar clients in the upcoming week. I should already have a clear idea on what results I expect to get for my client, so now I'll just do everything within my power to make sure things are on the right track.

2. *Share the journey and progress of my Keystone Client on social media and with others who expressed interest.* There's tremendous value in taking other people along for the ride. It makes you feel more real, believable, and authentic when others see you while you're in the process of creating something versus just after you have a finished product.

   Here's what I mean: I was sitting in the train station one day waiting to go from Rome to Florence, and there was a small restaurant where through the window I could see a lady making the dough that would soon become the fresh handmade pasta the restaurant was known for. Now imagine another restaurant

**530**

where I can't see the lady making the dough, yet they also claim the pasta is handmade. Which one feels more believable and real? The first one, right? Of course. And it's because they are taking me on the journey with them.

As long as I'm not divulging anything confidential, I should feel comfortable revealing how I'm taking my Keystone Client from Point A to Point B. It's also okay to reveal any snags or issues that arise along the way. People already know that I'm not perfect, and it will also help future clients have properly calibrated expectations when they sign up to work with me.

Most importantly though, if I'm creating a killer result for someone, other people will begin to want that same result and want to hire me to do it for them. Think of it like planting and watering seeds that will soon sprout and yield a harvest when the time is right.

3. *Sharpen up my sales training.* A good entrepreneur should always be sharpening their salesmanship. In my opinion, it's the most useful tool in your toolkit regardless of your area of expertise. As the saying goes, the salesperson who can't close deals is the one who has hungry children.

I'd like to recommend a few really good books that you can blast through in a week.
- Pitch Anything by Oren Klaff
- Influence: The Psychology of Persuasion by Robert Cialdini
- The Ultimate Sales Machine by Chet Holmes
- Secrets of Power Persuasion for Salespeople by Roger Dawson
    Read these, listen to them on Audible, or whatever you need to do. These will be huge assets for you.

# Day 21: Gather Results From Initial Engagement With My Keystone Client. Identify the Specific Results I Created for Them

I've been focused, on fire, and fully committed to getting my Keystone Client the results they needed. Now it's time to start reaping the benefits of all my energy and hard work.

What I need to do now is gather up the most specific wins that I and my clients agree we've created during our work together. It could be a certain dollar figure in new business, a number of leads, time or money saved, etc. I need to be as specific as possible because this is going to feed into our next step tomorrow, which is turning all of this into a killer testimonial video. And while my client is likely to say nice things about me, people aren't going to pay me because I'm nice—they are going to pay me because I'm the person they've seen create specific results for someone like them.

## Day 22: Get a Killer Video Testimonial and Referrals

Now that I've held up my end of the bargain and gotten my Keystone Client the result they really needed for FREE, it's time for them to pay me back in the way we originally agreed: through a testimonial video. Because we've agreed to this up front, this shouldn't come as any surprise to the client, and if I got them a killer result, they will almost always be thrilled to return the favor.

There is one issue. Most people aren't very good at knowing what to say once they get on the camera, so if my Keystone Client is one of those people, I may need to coach them through the process a little bit.

Here are the highlights I'll need to make sure they include in their video:

- Their name and what they do
  - People need to know they're real and whether they have anything in common.
- Why they originally wanted to work with me
  - This is where they will describe the challenge they were facing before they started working with me and what it was costing them financially or emotionally to not have that problem solved.
- What result I created for them
  - This is where they will need to use the specifics that I gathered

yesterday.
- An endorsement
  - This is where they need to give their open recommendation to others like them who want a similar result, telling them they should get in contact with me.

Testimonial videos can be more elaborate, but the basics here should do just fine. There's a few logistics things to consider. If I'm working virtually with a client, I can simply record a Zoom meeting and capture the video that way; if they're local, I can just use my iPhone to record it, making sure the lighting and sound quality are good. It doesn't have to be studio perfect, but I don't want my Keystone Client sitting in the shadows like he's in the Witness Protection Program or sounding like a kidnapper demanding ransom.

This is the end of my free engagement with my Keystone Client. Consequently, it also represents my first sales opportunity if there is room for ongoing work of some kind. If that's not likely, I won't sweat it, but if I can find a way to keep working together, it should be a lay-up sale.

Lastly, I will do my best to enjoy this experience. I've earned it, and not only have I created a great result and a happy client, I'm about to leverage this experience to get my first PAYING clients. Cash is right around the corner.

# Day 23: Conduct a Wrap-up Session

About 10 years ago, I had the chance to spend a couple of days with the British gold-medal rowing team. I honestly don't even remember the guys' names without googling them, but I do remember what they said helped them make it to the top of the podium.

It's called the wrap-up session. Anytime they were done with a row—whether it was long or short, in the sun or in the pouring rain—they wouldn't go back inside until they had their wrap-up session.

They asked themselves two simple questions:

1. What went well?

2. What could we do better?

Today, I will do a quick wrap-up session and figure out where things went remarkably well during my initial engagement and where there is room for improvement.

Also, I'll see if there's any area where I feel like I can tighten up my offer, either based on the specific results I created or where I noticed there was more pain and challenge on the part of my clients. This will help make sure things are even tighter as I go.

## Day 24: Build a High-Ticket Funnel

This is literally going to be the simplest online sales funnel I can imagine building. I'll create a single-page funnel inside of ClickFunnels with the following structure:

*Headline: "Attention: <IDEAL CLIENT>"*
*Sub-headline: "<OFFER>"*
*Video testimonial of my Keystone Client*
*Button: "Click here to become my next case study."*

To help illustrate, here's a headline and sub-headline I've used before that worked really well.

*Attention: 6- And 7-Figure Entrepreneurs*
*How To Turn Your Executive*
*Assistant Into An Operations Rockstar*
*To Help You Scale Your Business*

When a person clicks on the button, it will send them to a Wufoo form (yes, I'll need a paid account for this, but it's not too expensive). I'll create a form with key questions for them to fill out to apply for a call with me to see if they're a good fit for my program.

Here is some of the info I will collect:

· Name

- Email
- Phone Number

But I'll also ask a few qualifying questions, such as:

- What is the biggest challenge you're facing in <TOPIC> right now?
- Why is now the time to do something about it?
- There are limited spots in this program, so if you are a good fit, are you in a position to invest in yourself (or your business)?

People who give me weak answers on these questions don't need to get on the phone with me. I'm looking for someone who connects with my message and knows they have the problem I can help them solve. There are many ways to warm people up over time, but right now I only want to get on the phone with people who have a high chance of becoming my next raving fan.

## Day 25: Create an Email for Keystone Client to Send Out to Their Network

Depending on my Keystone Client, this may or may not work, but if they go along with it, it would be ridiculous not to ask them for a little extra help.

I'll simply write a very short email that they can send to some people in their network who they think might benefit from my program.

Basically, just a simple message they can cut and paste and link to my new high-ticket sales funnel. It should very briefly hit the highlights that they shared in their testimonial video for me. The goal is simply to get people to click through to the landing page with the full video. I'll let the video do the work—the email is just to get them there.

Finally, in the subject line, I'll ask them to put something friendly but also curiosity-inducing, such as "Check out what I just did!"

If they can simply copy and paste this email and send it to some of the people in their network, that will be a killer introduction for me, and it will take very little of my Keystone Client's time or energy.

# Day 26: Close the Loop and go Back to my Original List

Reach back out to those people on my newly formed list that I created on Day 9 and anyone who expressed interest before. Tell them that I am considering taking on more clients to help people like them get results just like I did for my Keystone Client.

Also, to generate more buzz, I'll keep posting all over social media that I am now considering taking on more clients and will continue to share the specific results that I got for my Keystone Client. This should also yield some considerable interest since I was posting my progress with my Keystone Client along the way during Days 14–20.

For anyone who expresses interest, as soon as they reply, I'll just send them the testimonial video. I won't send them to the landing page if they are already engaged in a conversation with me. Then I will book strategy sessions for those who are interested and qualified.

# Day 27: Write my Sales Script

Today, I'm going to write my sales script, because tomorrow—if all is going according to plan—I'm going to start having some live sales calls.

Here's the key with sales scripts—I could overthink them and make them really robotic if I'm not careful. So I will try to keep things simple. Hit the basics and get my mind right.

After all, they are the ones who raised their hands to talk with me. They are the ones who have a challenge that I've proven I can help with. I'll never make the mistake of believing that money is a scarce resource. Money is literally everywhere. Everyone has it, some more than others, but it's way easier to find money than it is to find an expert who genuinely knows how to solve a thorny problem. My prospect will need to prove themselves worthy of working with ME just as much as I need to demonstrate to them that I know what I'm doing.

Here are the highlights of a good sales call:

- Ask them why they wanted to have the call with you. Make them give you specifics.

- Ask them what not solving their problem is costing them. Again, ask clarifying questions and make them give you specifics. Find out where they are really in pain. Is it money, time, relationships? They will give you surface reasons until you start to dig.
- Ask them when they would like to do something to make their problem go away.
- Ask them if they'd like your help with making their problem go away.
- Assuming they say yes and you think they are a good fit, explain the RESULT that you will help them achieve. DO NOT get lost in the weeds of how you'll do it. That's largely irrelevant and will only cause them to have more questions.
- Ask them if they'd like you to help them get that result now.
- Make your offer.

Most people screw up sales calls in a few very common places.
- They don't take control of the call. The person asking questions in any conversation is the one in control. Maintain control of the call at all times. You are the expert.
- They don't get to the root of the prospect's problem. Dig, dig, dig and listen, listen, listen until you find out what is really driving this person. Most people think salespeople are talkative and pushy—those are the rookies. Great salespeople listen and allow people to be heard so they then buy.
- Choose a price that you feel confident offering. A lot of people get nervous when it comes to asking for the money. My solution to that is to pick a price that you feel so confident in that you think people would be crazy to say no. Then the longer you stay in the game, the more your confidence will rise and then you can raise your prices along with your confidence. The goal here is to start getting paid and create a snowball of success, not to try and wait until you harpoon Moby Dick.

## Days 28–29: Conduct Sales Calls

Put my sales script and training to good use by taking sales calls.

Remember the call should end with a yes or no. There is no maybe.

Make sure my prospect understands why it is in their best interest to work with me. What is it costing them to not work with me now? Make sure I show up in a way that will hold space for them.

If my offer and results are in line with what my people need, I should be able to close at least one out of five.

## Day 30: Onboard at Least Two or Three New Clients

I've done it! I've started from scratch and built the framework for a successful consulting business that will pay me handsomely for as long as I choose to do it!

If you ever find yourself in a similar situation, make sure that when you onboard your new clients, you are getting agreements in writing so everyone's expectations are aligned.

Don't bite off more than you can chew. Scaling a consulting business is an entirely different conversation, but in the beginning, just make it a rule of thumb that you will only have the number of clients for which you feel confident in your ability to get them great results.

One last thought that will make this either the greatest thing in the world or the reason you want to poke out your eyes with a spoon— only work with people you genuinely can help AND those who you like. You could not pay me enough money to work with someone I don't like, because I wouldn't want to spend my precious time with them.

I truly hope this has been helpful for you, but I've got to go now. I've got a speed boat picking me up in 10 minutes for an evening tour of the canals while on my trip here in Venice. I promise you that almost nothing in my life would be possible today if it wasn't for using the information I've shared with you here. Please put it to good use, and if I can ever be of any help to you on your journey, please reach out.

All the best,

James

# RESOURCES

- Audible (audible.com)
- Deep Work by Cal Newport
- Expert Secrets by Russell Brunson
- Flawless Consulting by Peter Block
- iPhone
- Influence: The Psychology of Persuasion by Robert Cialdini
- Pitch Anything by Oren Klaff
- Secrets of Power Persuasion for Salespeople by Roger Dawson
- The Ultimate Sales Machine by Chet Holmes
- Wufoo (wufoo.com)
- Zoom (zoom.us)

# References

Asprey, David. *The Bulletproof Diet: Lose Up to a Pound a Day, Reclaim Energy and Focus, Upgrade Your Life.* Random House LLC, 2014.

Block, Peter. *Flawless Consulting: A Guide to Getting Your Expertise Used.* Pfeiffer, 2011.

Brown, Brené. *Daring Greatly: How the Courage to be Vulnerable Transforms the Way We Live, Love, Parent, and Lead.* Avery, 2015.

Brown, Brené. *Rising Strong: How the Ability to Reset Transforms the Way We Live, Love, Parent, and Lead.* Random House, 2017.

Brunson, Russell. *DotComSecrets: The Underground Playbook for Growing Your Company Online.* Morgan James Publishing, 2015.

Brunson, Russell. *Expert Secrets: The Underground Playbook for Creating a Mass Movement of People Who Will Pay for Your Advice.* Morgan James Publishing, 2017.

Brunson, Russell. *Marketing in Your Car* podcast. http://blog.dotcomsecrets.com/category/marketing-in-your-car/.

Chopra, Deepak and Rudolph E. Tanzi, PhD. *Super Brain: Unleashing the Explosive Power of Your Mind to Maximize Health, Happiness, and Spiritual Well-Being.* Harmony, 2013.

Cialdini, Robert. *Influence: The Psychology of Persuasion.* Harper Business, 2006.

Dawson, Roger. *Secrets of Power Negotiating: Inside Secrets from a Master Negotiator.* Career Press, 2010.

Dawson, Roger. *Secrets of Power Persuasion for Salespeople.* Career Press, 2008.

Derricks, Dana. *Dream 100 Book.*

Dumas, John Lee. *The Freedom Journal: Accomplish Your Goal in 100 Days.*

Dumas, John Lee. *The Mastery Journal: Master Productivity, Discipline, and Focus in 100 Days.*

Dumas, John Lee. *"Your Big Idea."* Online course. https://courses.yourbigidea.io/courses/3-hours-to-your-big-idea.

Ferriss, Timothy. *The 4-Hour Workweek: Escape 9–5, Live Anywhere, and Join the New Rich.* Harmony, 2009.

Friel, James P. *"3 Productivity Hacks."* Jamespfriel.com. Blog article. January 6, 2016. http://jamespfriel.com/3-productivity-hacks/.

Hill, Napoleon. *Think and Grow Rich.* Sound Wisdom, 2016 (Original 1937).

Hoffer, Eric. *The True Believer: Thoughts on the Nature of Mass Movements.* Harper Perennial Modern Classics, 2010.

Holmes, Chet. *The Ultimate Sales Machine: Turbocharge Your Business With Relentless Focus on 12 Key Strategies.* Portfolio, 2008.

Keller, Gary. *The One Thing: The Surprisingly Simple*

*Truth Behind Extraordinary Results.* John Murray Press Learning, 2001.

Klaff, Oren. *Pitch Anything: An Innovative Method for Presenting, Persuading, and Winning the Deal.* McGraw Hill India, 2011.

Marshall, Perry. *80/20 Sales and Marketing: The Definitive Guide to Working Less and Making More.* Entrepreneur Press, 2013.

Newport, Cal. *Deep Work: Rules for Focused Success in a Distracted World.* Grand Central Publishing, 2018.

Parkinson, C. Northcote. *Parkinson's Law of The Pursuit of Progress.* J. Murray, 1961 (reprint edition).

*"Pomodoro Technique."* Wikipedia, last modified July 10, 2018. https://en.wikipedia.org/wiki/Pomodoro_Technique.

Poulin, Kaelin. *"The Identity Shift."* Presentation at Funnel Hacking LIVE 2018.

Robbins, Anthony. *"Guided: Tony Robbins—10 Minutes Morning Routine."* YouTube video (from TonyRobbins.com). https://www.youtube.com/watch?v=hBP-YBX597s.

Robbins, Anthony. *MONEY Master the Game: 7 Simple Steps to Financial Freedom.* Simon & Schuster, 2016.

Robbins, Anthony. *"Personal Power II: The Driving Force."* CD set, 30-day program.

Vaynerchuk, Gary. *Crush It!: Why Now is the Time to Cash in on Your Passion.* Harper Studio, 2009.

Vaynerchuk, Gary. *Crushing It!: How Great Entrepreneurs Build Their Business and Influence—and How You Can, Too*. Harper Business, 2018.

Vaynerchuk, Gary. *Jab, Jab, Jab, Right Hook: How to Tell Your Story in a Noisy Social World*. Harper Business, 2013.